Economic Problems of Latin America

This book is produced in full compliance with the government's regulations for conserving paper and other essential materials.

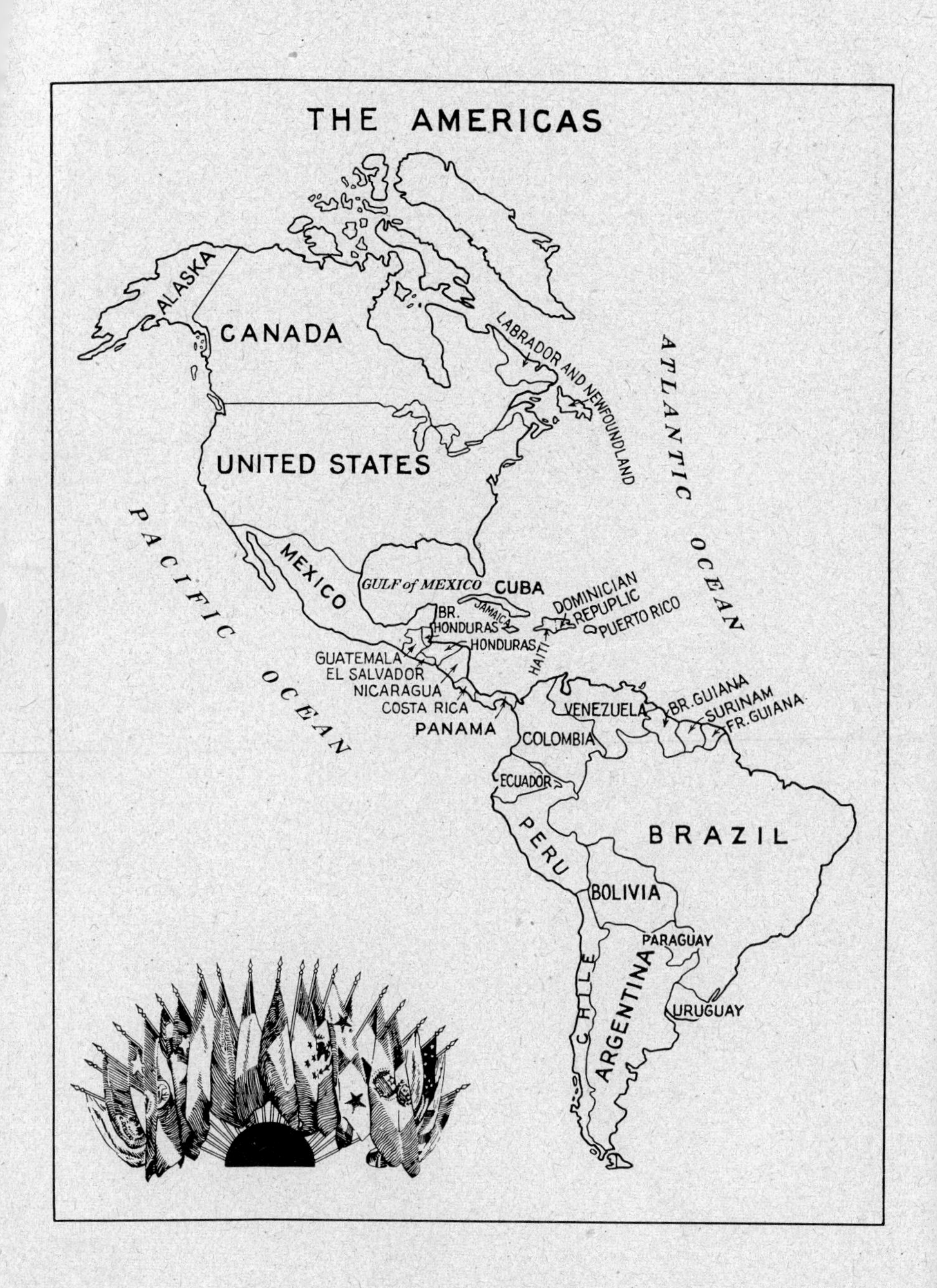

(*Frontispiece.*)

Economic Problems of Latin America

EDITED BY

SEYMOUR E. HARRIS

ASSOCIATE PROFESSOR OF ECONOMICS, HARVARD UNIVERSITY; FORMERLY DIRECTOR, OFFICE OF EXPORT-IMPORT PRICE CONTROL

FIRST EDITION

McGRAW-HILL
BOOK COMPANY, INC.
New York . . . . . London
1944

ECONOMIC PROBLEMS OF
LATIN AMERICA

PRINTED IN THE UNITED STATES OF AMERICA

THE MAPLE PRESS COMPANY, YORK, PA.

This volume is dedicated to
the continuance and expansion
of the Good Neighbor policy

Preface

THIS volume is a cooperative undertaking in which each of 17 economists, most of them in government service or formerly so, has written a chapter on some aspect of Latin American economics. Each writes as an expert in the field or area he covers, having devoted considerable time to the study of the particular problem or country of his chapter. It would be regrettable if the results of their studies were interred in government archives. As all who have searched know, economic information on Latin America is not easily obtained. That is the case even in Latin America, as I learned in the course of a trip there about a year ago. Few books are available that might aid the investigator or lighten his task; much searching—often unsuccessful—is required to obtain but a modicum of essential materials. This volume, then, is in a small way an attempt to correct that situation. I wish to thank each contributor who in spare time from heavy official or business duties took the trouble to write the results of his study for publication here.

The book is divided into three parts. Part I consists of an introduction, which treats of several general economic issues of outstanding importance and common to all countries of Latin America. Part II is devoted to the more important special aspects of Latin American economics. Part III contains studies of 10 countries, covering 80 per cent of the population and 90 per cent of the area of Latin America. We may reasonably assume that the economic problems of the remaining countries differ only to a minor degree, if at all.

I acknowledge the aid of the Seminar on International Economic Relations of the Graduate School of Public Administration of Harvard

University. This aid provided funds for research and made possible visits by many of the contributors to my Seminar on International Economic Relations, in which many points were thrashed out in vigorous discussion from which both students and contributors profited. One of the contributors, Dr. Frank Waring, Director of Research of the Office of Inter-American Affairs, kindly provided many of the charts and the appendix in the book and made many helpful suggestions. Mrs. Margarita Willfort is responsible for the index, and she also helped with the manuscript; my secretary, Miss Lillian Buller, helped in innumerable ways.

My greatest debt is to my wife, Ruth B. Harris. As "editor's editor" she assisted greatly. She went over the entire manuscript with care and is responsible for a large part of the editorial work and the reading of proofs.

I wish to emphasize that all statements of the contributors are their personal views. They do not speak for any government agency, department, or business firm.

SEYMOUR E. HARRIS, EDITOR.

FOUR WINDS FARM,
WEST ACTON, MASS.,
October, 1944.

Contents

Contributors

Henry Beitscher. Chief, Latin American Section, Foreign Information Branch, Office of Price Administration; formerly Assistant to Economic Adviser on Latin American Affairs, OPA; Assistant to Economic Adviser on Latin American Affairs, Office of Coordinator of Inter-American Affairs; Author of *Brazil, Price Control, Etc.* (January, 1943), *Price Control and Rationing in Republic of Colombia* (March, 1943), *Venezuela, Price Control and Rationing* (May, 1943) (mimeographed).

E. G. Bennion. Staff Economist, Standard Oil Company (New Jersey); formerly Instructor and Tutor, Department of Economics, Harvard University; author of articles in economic journals.

Miron Burgin. Principal Economist, Research Division, Office of Co-ordinator of Inter-American Affairs; Editor in Chief, *Handbook of Latin American Studies;* formerly Economist, War Trade Staff, Office of Economic Warfare.

Henry Chalmers. Consultant on Commercial Policy, U.S. Department of Commerce; formerly Chief, Division of Foreign Tariffs, Department of Commerce; served on United States delegations to many international conferences, including Mexican-American Conference for the Suppression of Smuggling, 1926, Pan-American Conference on Consular Procedure (Secretary-General) 1927, 4th Pan-American Commercial Conference, 1931, London Monetary and Economic Conference, 1933; author of *Japanese Cotton Goods Industry and Trade* (1921), *European Tariff Policies since the War* (1924), *Preparing Shipments to Latin America* (1928), *Impact of the War upon the Trade Policies of Foreign Countries* (1941), annual reviews of the Department of Commerce on trends in foreign commercial policy (since 1926), *Wartime Controls and Stimuli upon the Foreign Trade of Latin America* (1943).

Corwin D. Edwards. Consultant on Cartels, Department of State (on loan from the Department of Justice); formerly Chief of Staff, American Technical Mission to Brazil; co-author of *Economic Behavior* (1931); *Economic and Political Aspects of International Cartels* (Monograph 1, 78th Congress, 2d Session, Subcommittee on War Mobilization of Committee on Military Affairs, re S. Res. 107, 1944), and numerous articles in scientific journals.

P. T. Ellsworth. Adviser, Division of Financial and Monetary Affairs, State Department (on leave from the University of Wisconsin); formerly Chief Economist, Board of Economic Warfare, Guggenheim Fellow; author of *International Economics* (1938), *Chile: An Economy in Transition* (1944).

Seymour E. Harris. Associate Professor of Economics, Harvard University; formerly Director, Office of Export-Import Price Control, member of the Policy Committee of the Board of Economic Warfare; Adviser on Price Control to several Latin American governments; author of *The Assignats* (1930), *Twenty Years of Federal Reserve Policy* (1933), *Exchange Depreciation* (1936), *Economics of Social Security* (1941), *Economics of America at War* (1943); Editor, *Postwar Economic Problems* (1943), and others; Managing Editor, *Review of Economic Statistics.*

Don D. Humphrey. Chief, Price Analysis and Review Branch, Division of Research, Office of Price Administration (on leave from George Washington University); formerly Economic Adviser to the Haitian Government; author of *Family Unemployment: An Analysis of Unemployment in Terms of Family Units* (Government Printing Office), "Price Control in Outline," *American Economic Review*, December, 1942, and other articles.

Ben W. Lewis. Chief, Advisory Staff on Economic Organization, Office of Economic Programs, Foreign Economic Administration (on leave from Oberlin College); formerly Chief Economist, Consumer Division, National Defence Advisory Commission; Chief, Rubber Price Section, and Special Adviser to the Deputy Administrator for Price, Office of Price Administration; Chief, U.S. Price Control Mission to Colombia; author of *Price and Production Control in Great Britain* (1937), *Public Utility Regulation* (1940).

William A. Neiswanger. Special Assistant to the Deputy Administrator for Price, Office of Price Administration (on leave from the University of Illinois); formerly Price Executive, Machinery Branch, OPA; Consultant on Price Control to the Bolivian Government; author of *Elementary Statistical Methods as Applied to Business and Economic Data* (1943) and numerous articles.

James R. Nelson. Economic Analyst, Office of Price Administration; formerly member of the Price Control Mission to Colombia, 1943; member of the Price Control Mission to Bolivia, 1943–1944.

Norman T. Ness. Assistant Director, Division of Monetary Research, U. S. Treasury; formerly Research Economist, National Planning Association.

George R. Taylor. Professor of Economics, Amherst College; formerly special representative of the OPA to advise the Paraguayan government on price control, 1943; Price Executive and more recently Chief, Field Operations Office, Price Division, OPA; co-author of *The United States: A Graphic History* (1937), *Barriers to Internal Trade in Farm Products* (U.S. Department of Agriculture, 1938).

Robert Triffin. Associate Economist, Board of Governors of the Federal Reserve System; formerly member of the U.S. Technical Mission to Honduras, 1943, U.S. Monetary and Banking Mission to Paraguay, 1943–1944, and of missions to various Latin American central banks, 1943 and 1944; author of *Monopolistic Competition and General Equilibrium Theory* (1940) and numerous articles in scientific journals.

Henry C. Wallich. Business analyst in Argentina and Chile; expert on Latin America for a New York banking institution; author of "The Future of Latin American Dollar Bonds," *American Economic Review*, June, 1943.

Frank A. Waring. Director, Research Division, Office of Coordinator of Inter-American Affairs; formerly Special Adviser on Latin American Affairs, U.S. Tariff Commission; co-author of *United States–Philippine Trade* (U.S. Tariff Commission, 1937), *Report*, Joint Committee on Philippine Affairs (1938), and *Silverware* (U.S. Tariff Commission, 1940); co-author of *Analysis of Trade Agreement between the United States and United Kingdom* (U.S. Tariff Commission, 1938) and *Foreign Trade of Latin America* (U.S. Tariff Commission, 1940); author of *Latin America as a Source of Strategic and Other Essential Materials* (U.S. Tariff Commission, 1941) and *Report of the American Technical Mission to India* (1942).

L. A. Wheeler. Director, Office of Foreign Agricultural Relations, U.S. Department of Agriculture; formerly employed in research and investigational work in the Bureau of Foreign and Domestic Commerce, U.S. Department of Commerce; Associate, Senior, and Principal Agricultural Economist and Chief, Foreign Agricultural Service, Bureau of Agricultural Economics, U.S. Department of Agriculture; Adviser, Secretary of State Hull, 2d Meeting of Ministers of Foreign Affairs of the American Republics, Havana, July, 1940; Adviser, Undersecretary of State Welles, 3d Meeting of Ministers of Foreign Affairs of the American Republics, Rio de Janeiro, January, 1942; Member, American Delegation to the 2d Inter-American Conference on Agriculture, Mexico City, Mexico, July, 1942; author of numerous bulletins, articles, and speeches in the field of international trade in agricultural products.

Part I

INTRODUCTION

Chapter I

Some Major Issues

by SEYMOUR E. HARRIS

THIS introduction deals with a few problems not treated in the body of the volume, but mainly it emphasizes a few major aspects of Latin American economics. There are two broad economic issues common in varying degree to all Latin American countries. They are (1) international equilibrium—a matter of transcendent importance to Latin American countries—and (2) inflation and savings. These two problems are of course related, and they touch other economic matters of significance: fiscal policy, monetary policy, and the standard of living of the masses. The problems discussed in this chapter generally relate closely to these subjects. It is hoped that this chapter will serve to integrate the material in this volume.

Almost every chapter in this volume brings out the facts that our neighbors to the south are the victims of international forces, and that inflation looms large in each country. The reader will ask whether these countries can isolate themselves from these external influences or whether they can control them; whether inflation has been a force for good or evil and whether or not its rate has been the appropriate one. Let us try to answer these questions.

I. THE STANDARD OF LIVING

The 20 Latin American republics have a population of less than 130 millions and include approximately 7⅛₁₀ million square miles as compared with a population of 136 millions in the United States and 3 million square miles. In other words, whereas the populations are roughly equal, the area of Latin America is roughly 2½ times as great. In Brazil the population is one-third that of the United States and the area is larger.[1] This gives some indication of the relatively sparse settlements and perhaps suggests that, in view of the large and diversified national resources, Latin America, under favorable conditions, might support a much larger population and at a higher standard of living than at present.

Income figures are not in general available. Chile has published an estimate of national income for 1942 of approximately $600 million for a population of about 5 millions, or roughly a per capita income of $120 per year; and Mexico one of $1.6 billion, or $80 per capita, for its population of 20 millions. In Brazil the product per capita has been estimated at $14 for over two-thirds the area, $13 over the northeast, and $51 over the south. From other evidence—though fragmentary—one may conclude that in general the average per capita income in Latin America cannot be much more than $100 per year and is probably less. The national income of all Latin America might then run to about $10 to $15 billion as compared with a current (1944) income of $155 billion in the United States.[2]

These figures should, however, be accepted with many reservations. It is important to note that a considerable part of their economies is carried on without the use of money: *i.e.*, a very large part of the population has very little use for money—particularly the agricultural part, especially so in the areas where Negroes and Indians live in large numbers. Perhaps three-quarters of the population of Bolivia and Mexico, for example, do not participate in the money economy. In other words, national income expressed in terms of dollars has much less meaning in Latin America than in the United States. In Latin

[1] An appendix, kindly contributed by the Research Division of the Office of Coordinator of Inter-American Affairs, gives population and areas in detail.

[2] Colin Clark (*The Conditions of Economic Progress*, pp. 35–37, 42) presents a few rough estimates of income in Latin American countries. Income for Argentina is given as $2550 million for 1916. His per capita figures do not check with the total, however. At any rate, per capita income in Argentina is undoubtedly substantially more than for the average of Latin America. Possibly the figure may be as high as $200. Approximately one-half the working population seems to be in industry and commerce. *Cf.* Ch. IX. Net product of agriculture and industry (this is less than total income) approximates $125 per capita in a recent year.

This figure of $10 to $15 billion of national income for Latin America may be checked with total exports of $2.4 billion in 1943. At the mean figure for income, the export trade comes to one-sixth the national income. This may be a low proportion. If the correct percentage is higher, the national income would be less than $12.5 billion (*cf.* next note). Government budgets of the 20 republics are around $1 to $1.5 billion. If budgets run only at 10 per cent of national income, the corresponding income would be $10 to $15 billion (*cf. Senate Document* 132, discussed later in this volume, pp. 30–33).

America, income to a considerable degree is real, and output is not sold on the market for money.

The point is that the total national income expressed in money terms is not so significant as in more economically advanced countries. Nevertheless, the average per capita income when expressed in monetary terms is very low. We know, for example, that even as a result of recent increases in the minimum wage in Brazil the minimum wage level is set at between $6 and $12 per month. We are also aware of the fact that a relatively small part of the total Latin American population works in commercial and industrial enterprise, though the number varies from country to country; and the ratio of industrial workers to *total working* force is large for several countries. It is much larger, for example, in Argentina than it is in Bolivia. It will be noted from the chart on page 374 that, whereas in 1930 but 15 per cent of the working population of Mexico was employed in manufacturing, the contribution of manufacturing to total production in 1939 was 38 per cent.[1]

In comparing the relative well-being of countries of Latin America and, for example, the United States, relative prices should not be left out of account. Although the average per capita income in the United States might very well be twelve times as high as it is in Latin American countries, one must remember that, in general, a dollar will buy more in Latin America than it will in the United States. Comparisons are not easy, however, because identical commodities and services are neither available nor desired. Here again it is necessary to allow for differences as between countries. Undoubtedly prices are lower in Brazil than they are in Colombia or Argentina. Concrete statistical evidence is lacking. Any traveler—and he need not be especially discerning—will attest that prices are much lower in Rio de Janeiro than in Bogotá. That the American who lives in Rio can obtain excellent hotel accommodations and three superb meals a day plus tea for $4 a day and that similar food and service—even if they were obtainable, which they are not—cost twice as much in Bogotá, Colombia, does not, however, mean that prices are twice as high in Colombia as in Rio. These differences may reflect, rather, the greater facilities for visitors in Brazil than in Colombia.

[1] *Cf.* Chs. IX–XII, on Argentina, Bolivia, Brazil, and Chile.

Mr. La Varre estimates exports to national production or income in a recent prewar year as follows: Chile = 4.0; Argentina = 37; Colombia = 22; Brazil = 18. Quoted in P. R. Olsen and C. A. Hickman, *Pan-American Economics* (1943), pp. 5–6.

Nevertheless, few will dispute the fact that a dollar will generally buy more in Latin America than in the United States. The dollar will buy more, especially of services and labor. Since labor is the largest element of cost and since labor is cheap in Latin America, domestic commodities are low in price. Yet the comparatively low price of labor does not necessarily mean it is cheap. A Latin American worker is paid 50 cents to $1 a day as compared with $3 to $10 a day in the United States. Unfortunately, the Latin American laborer is not so well educated or trained or so healthy as our laborer; he does not have expert supervision, nor is capital so plentiful and available as in the United States. In purely domestic commodities which do not require high skills or much capital (*e.g.*, servants) the low wages paid are reflected in low prices. Where high skills and much capital are required, prices may be higher than in the United States. Manufactured commodities, for example, will be high priced because they are imported or because they are frequently produced domestically owing to restrictions on importation. In relation to these commodities —which, of course, are available to a very small part of the population—the value of the dollar is less than in the United States.

We need scarcely be reminded of the elementary fact that, in general, prices of international commodities are equal the world over, abstracting transportation costs and other obstacles to free movements. When the distance of Latin America from its main markets is considered, and the high tariffs and other restrictions, we may conclude that the dollar buys less rather than more of international commodities in Latin America than in the United States.

In summary, per capita incomes are much higher in the United States than in Latin America. Even when allowance is made for the larger relative importance of commodities consumed on the farm in Latin America and for the lower prices of domestic commodities (inclusive of grains and meats in most countries), a vast difference still remains. Even a cursory examination of nutritional standards, clothing, housing conditions, transportation, and medical services will convince any observer of the reality of this difference. Incomes are very low, but prices are high in comparison with income. These high prices reflect inefficiency, lack of education, lack of power, poor transportation, and inadequate capital.[1]

[1] *Cf.* Chs. IX–XI and XVII on Argentina, Bolivia, Brazil, and especially Paraguay.

Standards of living would be higher if better use were made of the land. In many countries a system of no taxation or preferential taxation of land, and in some cases a system of costless labor, result in idle land and wasted resources. Increased taxation of land and a breaking up of the semifeudal system in some countries would increase agricultural production.[1]

II. DEPENDENCE ON FOREIGN ECONOMIES

Latin American countries are dependent upon foreign economies to a considerable degree. Their imports or their exports are a large part of their national income as a rule; therefore, any variations in exports will play a very important part in the total economic situation. The significance of international trade for most of these economies is of the same order of importance as for Canada or the United Kingdom. Exports of $2.4 billion for all Latin American countries in 1943 may well be 20 per cent of the national income or even somewhat more. Exports are especially important because they fluctuate greatly and because, compared with the situation in more industrialized nations, they are much more important than savings and investments. Savings in Chile, for example, were recently estimated by the Minister of Finance at but 5 per cent of the national income. Not only are domestic factors of less importance for these countries, but the amount of investments is in no small part dependent on foreign contributions; and these in turn are dependent on the state of the foreign exchange. In economies which are not greatly disturbed by independent domestic factors (*i.e.*, investments), export trade, which accounts for a large part of national income and fluctuates greatly—both absolutely and in relation to imports—becomes the most significant determinant of economic activity. In the United States, Germany, or the United Kingdom, on the other hand, the level and fluctuations in investment will largely determine whether the country is prosperous or not.

For these reasons, the export trade of Latin America is of decisive importance. When export trade suffers a reverse in Great Britain, there is no doubt as to what happens to the British economy. But export trade in Great Britain shares with investment the role of *the* important independent variables. In the Latin economies, investment plays a much smaller role than exports as a determinant of economic activity. These economies are therefore most vulnerable to

[1] See Chs. IX, X, and XII on Argentina, Bolivia, and Chile.

international forces since they are so dependent upon the exports and export prices of primary products. Cuba depends upon her exports of sugar, Chile on nitrate and copper, Brazil and Colombia on coffee, Argentina on wheat and wool, Bolivia on tin, Guatemala on bananas, Venezuela on oil, etc. When the export demand for these commodities falls and prices tumble, the depression in these industries is quickly translated into general depression. Even in the case of Argentina and Brazil, the economies of which are diversified both in manufacturing and agriculture, foreign markets are of great importance. And again, I repeat, they are dependent on foreign capital for investment.

Cycle theorists used to hold that agricultural countries do not suffer such large fluctuations as industrial countries and that an aftermath of industrialization is large fluctuations. The economic history of Latin America does not support this theory. Undoubtedly in a country like France—which had a very diversified agricultural output and also a substantial amount of industry—economic fluctuations have not been so severe as in Germany, England, and the United States. France did not, however, suffer from the large variations in export trade; nor was she so dependent upon the exports of a few products as most of the Latin American countries are. The latter are not so fortunate in the degree of diversification as was France.

One may also underestimate fluctuations in Latin America. For example, fluctuations in employment are not of large proportions. Then again, as already noted, the total fluctuations in national income will not be given in a satisfactory manner by any calculations of what has happened to national money income or even to other monetary variables, the explanation being again that a large part of many of these economies does not deal with money. Monetary changes strike the monetary part of the economy with sledge-hammer effect because, although their direct incidence is related to a comparatively small part of the economy, the blows are concentrated. Nonmonetary parts feel the effects indirectly. When depression strikes a Latin American country, the result is unlikely to be an increase of unemployment of the proportions which the United States and Great Britain can expect. Rather, the effect will be a small reduction of employment. The major losses are taken in the form of transfers of workers to less productive enterprise, where they become what Mrs. Robinson has called "members of the disguised unemployment group." In other words, workers operate at a lower efficiency and a lower productivity than they customarily do. In periods of prosperity there will be some rise of money income and a small rise in employment, and there will be a transfer of workers from low-productivity industries to high-productivity industries: from the farms to the mines, from the mines to the factories, from the sale of lottery tickets, peddling, and bootblacking to commercial and manufacturing jobs. Many workers may well increase their wages by 100 per cent through a change of occupation. The amount of unemployment or amount of employment changes relatively little, however, except in a fairly industrialized country like Argentina.

III. SECONDARY EFFECTS OF INCREASED INVESTMENTS OR EXPORTS

Lord Keynes has argued that an initial impulse through an increase of investment or exports will have a larger effect on the total national income and employment than the initial impulse might lead one to expect. In other words, if, in response to improved economic conditions abroad, Latin American export trade rises by $1 billion, then, according to numerous authorities, the national income of the Latin American countries might well be expected to rise by $2 billion or more. This follows because, when the export industries profit as a result of higher prices or larger exports, they tend to buy more domestic goods, with the result that still others profit and obtain more income, which they in turn spend. In each successive cycle of expenditure, however, there are certain leakages, with the result that, whereas the gains (say) are $1 billion in the first cycle, they may be only $½ billion in the next and $¼ billion in the next, etc., the total gain being approximately $2 billion.

Dr. Wallich, in his chapter on fiscal policy in this volume,[1] has pointed out, however, that the secondary gains are not likely to be large when a Latin American country starts an expansionist program (*e.g.*, public investment), even if it is favored by a rise of exports. In technical jargon, the multiplier (in this case the ratio of the rise of income associated with an initial impulse of a rise of dollars of exports) is low for Latin America. Of every dollar spent by a Latin American, a relatively large proportion is for goods purchased from abroad. The stimulative effect, therefore, is felt by the foreign seller, rather than by the domestic seller, and therefore there is a leakage of part of the original expenditures. Second, the elasticity of supply, *i.e.*, the

[1] Ch. V.

response of additional output to the offer of increased demand, is not great. A given rise of demand will have a relatively large effect on prices and a relatively small effect on additional output in the Latin American economy. This follows in part because of the manner of business organization and technical organization and in part from the fact that at any one time employment is relatively full and mobility of the factors of production—*i.e.*, the movement of capital and labor in response to higher rewards—is rather small. Insofar as the secondary spending results in a rise of prices rather than in an increase in output, the total beneficial effects of any expansionist program, whether brought on by government deficit spending or by an increase of exports, are not likely to be so great as in the United States or even in the United Kingdom.

Here again we must note the fact that most Latin American economies are not free to attune their economic policies to their own needs to the same extent as the United States or the United Kingdom. They cannot pursue independent economic policies, except to a very limited degree, without being confronted with rising prices, adverse balance of payments, depreciated exchanges, etc.—all of these contributing toward a reversal of the original expansionist program.

We can put the issue in a somewhat different way. We may say that, if the United States and the United Kingdom and Germany embark on an expansionist program, then the beneficial effects will be felt by Latin American countries and the latters' export markets will grow and will be able to expand, insofar as their limited economic resources allow, without significant rise of prices. In other words, their economic activities are in no small degree related to what is happening in these countries. If they, however, take the initiative, then they do not in any important sense contribute toward the prosperity of the other countries. Each Latin American country is too small, and its income relative to world income too insignificant, to set the pace. Colin Clark estimated that the United States in recent years (1925–1934) accounted for 25 per cent of the world's income and the United States, Great Britain, Germany, Austria, and France for almost 45 per cent. Wealthy debtor countries (inclusive of four South American countries) accounted for 4 per cent, and the rest of Latin America plus 11 other countries had 3 per cent of the world's income.[1] Confronted with inelastic supply conditions (a small rise in output brings

[1] Clark, *op. cit.*, p. 56.

a relatively large rise of unit costs) and being dependent on foreign countries for a significant proportion of the supplies needed to make possible a continued expansion, the Latin American countries will soon discover that their imports will rise and (since domestic commodities will also be more in demand at home) their exports will be reduced. Pressure on the exchanges will be felt and will soon put an end to a nascent boom, for the monetary resources required as a condition of expansion will not be available.

IV. MEASURES DIRECTED TOWARD STABILIZATION

It has already been noted that possibilities of obtaining more stable conditions through domestic investment policies are distinctly limited. The obstacle of rising prices and unfavorable balance of payments is reached at an early point. Perhaps more direct attacks in the international field are possible, however. Would it be possible, for example, in a period of domestic expansion, for a Latin American country to take direct measures aimed at improving the balance of payments? Or else would it be possible for that country to take measures in the international field, so as to prevent an adverse effect from international disequilibrating influences?

Let us first consider the problem of unfavorable balance of payments arising from, say, a reduction of demand for Latin American export products. This may well happen in the postwar period.[1]

The first corrective step in that case might be to use up excess reserves. This would be a temporary expedient, it is true, but it may be of some importance since reserves of gold and foreign currencies are more than three times the prewar level and may very well attain a level of $3 to $4 billion before the war is over.[2] This figure of $3 billion is twice the annual average of imports in the prewar years. This may therefore be a rather significant cushion to prevent adverse effects resulting from the decline of export trade. Any program for an international clearing fund might also help. At best, however, these are temporary expedients. It would be more important to increase exports

[1] In Ch. III on agriculture, Dr. Wheeler makes clear the possibility of an excess of supply over demand at remunerative levels; similarly, Chs. X and XII on Bolivia and Chile include discussions of inadequate markets for minerals in the postwar period.

[2] An estimate by the National City Bank of New York puts the foreign exchange and reserves of Latin America at $2.7 billion at the end of 1943 and by April, 1944, at least at $3 billion (*New York Times*, Apr. 6, 1944). Our Department of Commerce put the figure at "over $2 billion" at the end of 1943 (*New York Times*, Apr. 7, 1944).

or to reduce imports or to put off the day of payment through large capital imports, anticipating that these, through favorable effects on productivity, will increase the export potential in later years. Any measures that are effective in stabilizing prices of primary products might also be helpful in maintaining trade. This explains the large interest of Latin America in production control and international agreements to limit production and sales. In general, the difficulties in the export area may be reduced to some extent through rationalization, through better financing, and through more efficient labor and improved technical education.[1]

Exports may also be stimulated through exchange depreciation. A reduction in foreign exchange value tends to make products cheaper for the foreign purchaser since he can buy the Latin American currency with a smaller number of units of dollars or pounds, and yet the domestic prices of Latin American products do not usually rise in proportion to the increased cheapness of the Latin American currency.

Dr. Triffin notes in Chapter IV that this technique is not likely to be very effective. If country *A* introduces exchange depreciation, country *B* could do likewise and therefore the advantage to *A* would be reduced because *B* would obtain similar advantages in a lower price for the export product. Where, however, the production of a particular country for a particular product or for a particular market is a small part of the total, exchange depreciation may in some cases be helpful. For example, in the prewar picture, exchange depreciation could help Brazilian cotton producers a great deal, whereas it might not help Brazilian coffee producers nearly so much. The point is that in the case of Brazilian cotton any gains at the expense of competitors were relatively small since Brazilian cotton was a relatively small part of the total market for cotton and therefore competitors were not forced to take similar action to meet the increased Brazilian competition.

But even in the case of coffee the gains might be substantial, not because Brazilian coffee is a small part of total export sales of coffee of all countries, but rather because there may be a considerable elasticity of demand for coffee and if, through exchange depreciation, the price of coffee should be reduced by 25 per cent, it is conceivable that the total number of dollars expended on Brazilian coffee might rise. Here one should take into account the fact that the elasticity

[1] Many of these issues are discussed in the chapters on Argentina, Brazil and Bolivia.

must be high enough for the particular product so that if prices, for example, on world markets fall by 50 per cent, total purchases would increase by more than 100 per cent—therefore an increase in the total number of dollars would result. Even here an allowance must be made for the additional cost involved in producing any additional coffee or for storing more supplies.

It is necessary also to take into account the fact that, even though exchange depreciation might be helpful in the case of commodity *A*, commodity *B*, and commodity *C*, it may not be quite so helpful for all the exports of the countries depreciating their exchanges. This follows because in this case one has to take into account the total income, the total spending potentialities, and the total exchanges available of the countries that are purchasing these supplies. They may spend more dollars for Brazilian coffee and even for Brazilian cotton, but can they spend more dollars for all coffee and all cotton and all nitrate, all tin, etc.?

As has already been noted, the circumstances are not always so favorable as for prewar Brazilian cotton or even coffee. Depreciation, for example, would probably not be very helpful for Argentine wheat growers because the Argentine contribution is large and the demand for wheat is highly inelastic. In other words, if Argentina depreciated her exchanges in order to capture a larger part of the world market, other wheat-exporting nations would follow with depreciations or subsidies and, furthermore, total consumption would not increase greatly as a result of the reduction of the world price of wheat.

Yet all the gains even here are not to be put in terms of increased markets, the ousting of competitors, etc. That Latin America has had a long history of depreciation is explained *only in part* by its capacity as a small contributor to world markets to capture a larger part of world markets. The fuller explanation lies in the fact that export interests are powerful. They have been disposed to press for inflation and depreciation because they thus obtain more *pesos* but less *dollars* for each unit of product. When demand is elastic in response to lower world prices, they may even get more dollars for *total* sales. But the main gain has been a rise of receipts in domestic currencies. This is a method of redistributing income within a country. Exporters obtain more pesos; consumers and especially purchasers of imports pay more.

In order to increase exports, other methods are available. Some of these techniques have received wartime publicity. Dr. Waring in his chapter discusses, for example, the Brazilian techniques for increasing the prices of export products through government or semigovernmental control of production and allocation of export markets. The government or the semipublic agencies determine how much will be produced, how much will be diverted to the export market, and at what prices domestic and export buyers will purchase. This technique aims at charging what the traffic will bear on the foreign market and to some extent subsidizes the domestic market. In the present war Latin American countries have been very successful in pushing this kind of export price control in favor of the domestic seller or producer. In more normal world competitive conditions this particular method of raising export prices may not be quite so successful.

Another technique aims at reducing import trade in such a period by the use of tariffs or exchange control and various other forms of trade restrictions. Exchange control is applied, *inter alia*, in order to assure a country that whatever exchange is available will be used for the most essential purposes. In other words, imports of essential raw materials are allowed—and even at favorable foreign exchange prices —and imports of luxuries are either prohibited or the importers forced to pay a very high price for the foreign currency. Under an effective administration of exchange control the government may make certain that all who receive foreign currencies turn these currencies over to the central authority at prices determined according to national interests. To express this in another way, exchange control may be used not only to discourage unnecessary imports but also as a form of selective encouragement of exports. Whereas exchange depreciation more or less gives a lift to all export industries whether or not they need the additional lift of a higher number of local currency units for a given dollar price on world markets, exchange control provides a lift only insofar as a particular industry requires the stimulus of a higher price at home.

Restrictions on imports, whatever the technique used, may not yield so large a net gain, even from the viewpoint of international equilibrium, as may appear on the surface. When supplies are not very elastic (*i.e.*, easily increased in response to price rises), the issue arises as to whether the imports to be excluded are dispensable. If they are not, exports may suffer more than imports through a substitution of high-cost domestic components for less costly foreign supplies.

A final technique for dealing with the problem of the balance of payments, the use of higher tariffs or other kinds of trade restrictions, will be discussed below.

V. STABILIZATION ON THE UPSWING

I now turn to the problem of stabilization in a period of prosperity. At present we have a good opportunity for a case study of attempts to stabilize economic conditions—even though the rising tempo of economic activity in foreign nations is unusually rapid. Is it possible, under these conditions, for Latin American countries to isolate themselves from the inflationary expansionist forces at work all over the world? Wartime experience does not seem to indicate the likelihood of any great success along these lines, granted the desire to do so. As prices and incomes rise abroad and as the tempo of the war increases, the demand for Latin American products rises rapidly. This rise is primarily brought about by the intense demand for war products and would have occurred even if prices had not first increased in the United States. Actually, even when the domestic rise of prices has begun to outdistance that in the nations actively waging war—or at least in the countries that are experiencing the largest amount of armament activity—the demand for Latin American products continues to grow. In this case, the shift of demand and the rise of income in the United States and in the United Kingdom play a larger part than relative price movements in determining the volume of Latin American exports. As noted in several instances in this volume, the effects of this intense wartime demand for Latin American products are (1) increased purchases of Latin American goods; (2) an inflow of capital from the United States to Latin American countries; and (3) a restriction of shipments to Latin America—also as a result of the insistent demand for products of the United States and the United Kingdom. This limitation of imports to Latin America is of course made imperative by lack of shipping space. The net effect is then a large favorable balance of payments for the Latin American countries;[1] and this is followed by an accumulation of dollars, pounds sterling, and gold and an increase of central bank reserves and credit of domestic banks. We, therefore, have a strong inflationary pressure, which is explained in part by the increase in the supply of money and the reduced availability of supplies of goods.

[1] See Ch. II by Dr. Waring.

Latin American countries may try to stop this flood through various controls at home, many of which are discussed in Chapter VI on Price Stabilization Programs in Latin America.[1] In addition, these countries may resort to exchange appreciation, *i.e.*, a rise in the value of their local currencies in terms of dollars. Dollars then become cheaper; pesos become more expensive. A survey of exchange rates in the present war indicates, however, that Latin America has had recourse to appreciation only to a limited degree. Appreciation may consist in a general increase in the official rate of the local currency in terms of dollars or in a rise in the free rate of the currency and sometimes in a reclassification of the differential rates which are applicable to sales of particular groups of commodities.[2]

VI. IS APPRECIATION A SOLUTION?

Appreciation brings about a reduction in the price of imports from abroad and should also in general bring about a reduction in the prices of commodities that are exported from Latin America to other countries. Actually, of course, in many cases a rise in the value of the domestic currency which brings about a reduction in the supply of local currency obtained for a given value of exports may very well be a signal for an increase in the dollar price of the commodity and therefore may not really be deflationary. This has happened in many instances; frequently countries have allowed an appreciation of their exchanges only in such cases where a rise in the dollar price may follow or accompany the increased value of the domestic currency, thus ensuring Latin American exporters an unchanging number of units of the domestic currency per unit of their export products.

In this manner the foreign purchaser is forced to pay more. Countries thereby improve the terms of trade, *i.e.*, give less exported nitrate, beef, etc., for foreign chemicals, machinery, etc. The Latin American exporter is thus protected: he gets less pesos per dollar but obtains more dollars per unit of output. Nevertheless, exchange appreciation has not been a popular solution.[3] Authorities have been more disposed to allow the inflation and expansion abroad to be translated into inflow of cash and monetary expansion at home. A third way out,

[1] See also Chs. XII, XIII, XVI, and XVIII on Chile, Colombia, Mexico, and Venezuela.

[2] See Ch. VII on Exchanges and Prices.

[3] *Ibid.*

viz., exchange stability accompanied by sterilization of dollars and pesos, has been used to some extent.

Dr. Triffin has well shown[1] that in the expansion of the twenties the banking system of Colombia did not operate in such a way as to stop the inflation of the United States from being translated into an expansion in that country. In a similar way it can be shown that in the present war the rise of monetary resources and national incomes and output in the United States and United kingdom has not been accompanied by a monetary policy that has tended to stop the expansion in Latin American countries.

Latin America has thus experienced a large rise of reserves and a significant increase in central bank deposits and also in the total volume of deposits of commercial banks.

Appreciation of limited proportions is, however, only one aspect of the problem. Not only are dollars somewhat cheaper—at least since 1941—but more are made available. Prices are of limited significance in controlled markets. What may be of more importance than the dollar price is how many dollars are available for purchase. In other words, in addition to the gains which result from the fact that the price of the dollar, etc., is cheaper for the Latin American purchaser, the buyer of foreign currency is much more free to buy as many units as he desires and at lower prices than previously. This has to some extent resulted in encouraging the exportation of capital, which tends to reduce the value of the Latin American currencies. In some markets, however, against the apparent gain of a rise in the dollar price of the peso is to be put the unavailability of dollars at cheap prices. Cheap dollars are made increasingly scarce if they are to be used, for example, to purchase products of protected industries.

Even if appreciation had gone significantly further, it is dubious whether the effect on prices would have been very serious. In other words, under present wartime conditions the exporter who is confronted with a reduction in the number of pesos he can obtain for his dollars will charge a higher price in dollars for his export commodity. Appreciation frequently is applied in markets when higher dollar prices can be exacted. Market conditions will allow him to get by with this. Export prices are therefore not depressed. The importer, however, if he is confronted with a cheaper price for foreign commodities, will be inclined to buy more, but unfortunately he may not

[1] See Ch. IV.

be able to obtain the additional supplies. His imports are cheaper, but purchases may not increase substantially. In fact, exporters from the United States (say) could easily increase their dollar prices as the peso becomes more valuable. Only export price control in the United States prevents this. In other words, how much is imported depends upon shipping and the allocation of scarce resources in the exporting country. Trade is determined much more by war and political considerations than by the price that is charged. Insofar as commodities are allowed to go out of a country, prices, under current demand conditions, are a secondary consideration.

In general, Latin American governments have not been disposed to accept appreciation in any significant amounts, for (1) there was fear of harm that might be done to export industries that were still fearful of competition from abroad; and (2) finance ministers, dependent upon export industries for revenue, were fearful that a reduction in the local currency yield of exports might have an adverse effect upon their budgets. Furthermore, it was felt that even though the local currency might be too cheap at the present time, it was better to hold it at its present undervalued rate and thus avoid the necessity of depreciating later on, when competition was really to be feared and when the availability of low-priced pesos might be a material factor in the export market.

VII. MODERATION OF EXPANSION

In the light of the large influx of dollars, sterling and gold, the expansion of money in Latin America has not been large. The commercial banks have been able to repay their loans at the central banks and have not expanded so much as might have been expected. Yet prices as a rule have risen more than in the United States. The explanation of this fact lies in the reduction of imports, the limited elasticity of domestic supplies, the less efficient price control in these countries, and the rather limited use of rationing as a means of holding down demand. Only in the import area has there been any serious attempt to restrict demand through allocation.[1]

It is impossible to estimate the rise of national income since 1939 in Latin American countries as compared with the United States. In the light of numerous production indices which cover but limited

[1] Virtually all the chapters on special countries respectively deal with these problems. See especially Chs. XII–XIV, XVI–XVIII. Also *cf.* Ch. IV.

areas and which, in any case, cover only part of the economies (since the economies are to a great extent on a nonmonetary basis), one might perhaps estimate very roughly that the expansion of output in Latin America at the very most has been of the order of about 20 per cent, as compared with an expansion of 75 per cent in the United States. The rise of *money* income (restricted to the money part of the economy) might very well be 60 per cent, as compared with a rise of more than 100 per cent in the United States. Accepting these estimates for Latin America, which are of the crudest kind, however, and should not be taken without the most serious reservation, we may conclude that money national incomes have risen about one-half as much as in the United States and prices about twice as much. For a *given amount* of expansion of output, their price rise has been four times as great. It must be emphasized that these are very rough averages and that many countries have done much better than the average (*e.g.*, Colombia and Argentina), and some (*e.g.*, Bolivia) have probably done worse.

In short, the Latin American countries have had a significant amount of inflation, and their exchange policies have not contributed greatly to moderating the degree of the rise in prices. They have, moreover, been handicapped by breakdowns in transportation, the relative immobility of labor, and other factors of production and also by rather inflexible tax systems, which are ably discussed by Drs. Wallich and Bennion in this volume.[1] The inflow of currencies and gold has been large and the manufacture of new money substantial. The excess of demand over supply at prewar prices has been large, and therefore prices have continued to rise. Attempts to deal with this situation through price control, rationing, and allocation have had varying success in different countries, but on the whole the success has not been great.[2] The rapid rise of prices has had rather serious economic effects on the distribution of the available supply of goods and has certainly had unfortunate political results, as one might very well suspect from the Bolivian situation. A given excess of monetary supplies or income over the supply of available consumption goods is likely to have a greater inflationary effect in Latin America than in the United States, both because of the difficulty of absorbing excess purchasing power and because of inelastic supply conditions;

[1] Chs. V and XVIII.
[2] *Cf.*, however, Ch. XIII on Colombia.

on the other hand, the significance of inflation is reduced for Latin American economies because they are partly nonmonetary.

VIII. SAVINGS AND INFLATION

Provision of adequate capital is one of the most pressing problems of Latin America. As has been observed repeatedly in this volume,[1] the rate of interest in Latin American countries is very high according to Anglo-Saxon standards. Payment of rates of 8 to 16 per cent is not at all uncommon, and even governments may have to borrow at rates as high as 8 per cent. (In Brazil, Federal bonds pay 5 to 8 per cent and real estate mortgages 9 to 10 per cent, and banks pay 7 to 12 per cent interest on deposits.) There are exceptions, as, for example, Argentina, where rates are much lower.

The rate of interest is high because the volume of savings is small as compared with the demand. Generation after generation of lenders in Latin American countries have lost their savings by inflation. Borrowers pay back in currency which is worth considerably less in terms of purchasing power than what they borrowed. Cognizant of the rising trend of prices, the lender in Latin America demands a higher rate of return than he would have done had prices remained stable. In other words, as Prof. Irving Fisher observed many years ago, the lender will demand compensation in a higher rate of interest when he becomes aware of the fact that the money in which he is paid back will be money of a smaller purchasing power than that he had advanced.

Moreover, inflation is brought about because the government is frequently unable to borrow on the capital market and therefore has to have recourse to the banks and to the issue of paper money. For purposes of expansion, industry also will borrow from the banks directly or through governmental corporations because the supply of capital available on capital markets is distinctly limited. The net effect of this borrowing from the banks and the issue of paper money is a rise of prices.

That the government and industry will also borrow from abroad does not help matters. Foreigners lending money to Latin America are aware that financial risks there are greater than at home: there is hostility toward foreign control; taxes on foreign capital are likely to be high; and in recent years the difficulties of obtaining foreign

[1] *Cf.* Chs. IV by Dr. Triffin and XI by Dr. Edwards.

exchange to finance foreign loans has aggravated the problem of transfer. Foreign lenders therefore demand a higher rate of return in order to compensate them for the additional risks they incur. The transfer problem in many cases is aggravated by continued depreciation. Brazilian public utilities, for example, are unable to finance their foreign loans because they are unable to increase their net revenues in proportion to the depreciation of the cruzeiro.

It is unlikely that in the future foreign loans, other than direct investments by corporations already operating in Latin America, will be forthcoming, unless these loans are guaranteed by the United States government. In 1940, the United States had $3.7 billion invested in Latin America. Additional loans (inclusive of direct investments) made since this period have been large.[1] These investments in 1940 were almost 40 per cent of all foreign investments of the United States (see accompanying Chart 1). It will be noted that about three quarters are direct investments and one quarter is indirect investments. The distribution by countries is also given, the largest borrowers being Chile, Cuba, Argentina, Brazil, and Mexico, in that order. A second chart (page 380) further breaks down direct investments in Mexico and compares the amount loaned by the United States and other countries.

In the future these loans will necessarily be made under the control of the governments involved. (An example of this technique is given in Chapter X on Bolivia.) In general, the respective governments should make agreements concerning the respective contributions of capital by the two countries involved, the use of the capital, the provision of revenue to meet the financing charges, and the provision of foreign exchange to cover payments (inclusive of agreements concerning domestic policies which might jeopardize transfers abroad and yet should not infringe upon the sovereign rights of the borrowing country). Private capital may then be forthcoming under a full or partial guarantee by the United States government. If, despite these safeguards, losses are incurred, they should be paid by the American people, since the main economic and political gains are shared by them. These economic gains are the improved demand and employment resulting from the stimulus of additional exports in periods of less than full employment. Investors, on the other hand, should not expect 6 to 15 per cent return on their investments under these conditions.

[1] *Cf. Expenditures and Commitments by the United States Government in or for Latin America* (Senate Document 132, 1943), p. 97.

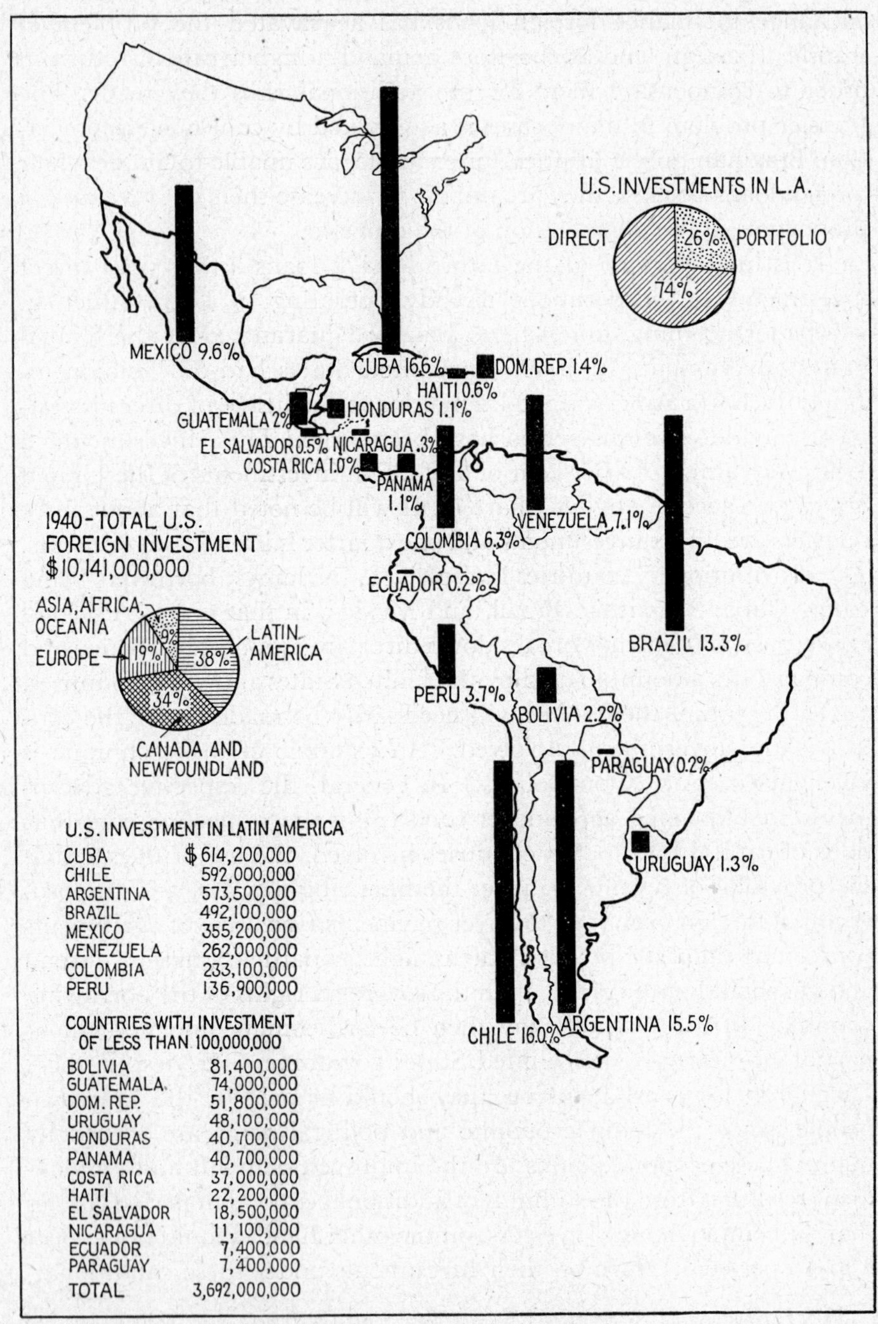

U.S. INVESTMENT IN LATIN AMERICA

CUBA	$ 614,200,000
CHILE	592,000,000
ARGENTINA	573,500,000
BRAZIL	492,100,000
MEXICO	355,200,000
VENEZUELA	262,000,000
COLOMBIA	233,100,000
PERU	136,900,000
COUNTRIES WITH INVESTMENT OF LESS THAN 100,000,000	
BOLIVIA	81,400,000
GUATEMALA	74,000,000
DOM. REP.	51,800,000
URUGUAY	48,100,000
HONDURAS	40,700,000
PANAMA	40,700,000
COSTA RICA	37,000,000
HAITI	22,200,000
EL SALVADOR	18,500,000
NICARAGUA	11,100,000
ECUADOR	7,400,000
PARAGUAY	7,400,000
TOTAL	3,692,000,000

CHART 1.—United States investments in Latin America and in the rest of the world, 1940. (*Source: Coordinator of Inter-American Affairs.*)

Latin America thus moves in a vicious circle. In order to obtain required supplies of capital when savings are inadequate, government and business enterprise have to borrow from the banks and thus obtain additional supplies of money. As the money is created, prices rise and the rate of interest increases. This further accentuates the financing problem of the government and private enterprise. Confronted with inadequate supplies of capital at home, the relevant interests borrow abroad. Here again they are confronted with high rates of interest. It is unnecessary to add that these high rates of interest and the scarcity of capital retard the economic development of Latin American countries.

It should also be observed that the expansion of money is likely to result in a rise of prices at a much earlier period than in more industrialized countries, because the expansion of money is not directed to putting unemployed resources to work. Monetary expansion and deficit financing have been justified on these grounds in the United States, England, and Germany by Keynesian economists in the 1930's. Monetary expansion in Latin America is directed rather to increase prices, raise *forced* savings, and ultimately make the employed factors more productive. Expansion of money for purposes of putting unemployed resources to work plays a minor role. Unemployment is at a relatively low level, and therefore any increased competition for the limited factors of production, given the rather inadequate mobilization of economic resources, will result in rapidly rising prices. These rises in prices cause further increases in the rate of interest.

It has long ago been noted by D. H. Robertson that the process of raising capital through the expansion of monetary supplies might very well increase investment. When voluntary savings are inadequate to meet the increased demands for investment in periods of upswing it becomes necessary to rely on monetary expansion, which accounts for forced savings. This is a chronic condition in Latin America. Newly created supplies of money compete with existing supplies of money, with the result that existing holders of purchasing power are squeezed out of markets for the available supplies of labor and goods. New borrowers are thus enabled to purchase labor and other economic factors and produce real capital. More resources are then made available for capital purposes, and less for consumption; or, to be more exact, insofar as more resources are made available for purposes of consumption, this consumption is had by certain wage earners at the expense of those who had existing rights to consumption goods—those "certain wage earners" being those who are now enabled to add to the country's productive machinery. In other words, a redistribution of consumption goods in favor of the new productive laborers has taken place. This is what Lord Keynes has called a transfer of consumption from unproductive to productive consumption. It is anticipated, furthermore, that, although during this period of capital accumulation consumption per capita might well decline, in the long run average consumption will rise consequent to the increased productivity resulting from the creation of new capital resources.

Although as a general principle controlled creation of capital through the use of monetary resources is to be approved, in Latin America this process is fraught with danger. Where the standard of living is so low as it currently is in most Latin American countries, it is a serious mistake to cut that standard substantially in order to provide capital resources which may improve living standards in the far-distant future. To state it another way, the sacrifices of the present generation to the future must be restricted where standards of living are very low, and particularly where most of the pressure is put upon the low-income groups. In Latin American economies, given the current systems of indirect taxation and the rather weak organization of labor, the rate of inflation must be carefully controlled if the present burden on the masses is not to be excessive.

Again, authorities must be certain that the investments being made out of these forced savings will in fact contribute toward a future higher standard of living. Frequently the resources are used, not to improve water power or technical education or build new and modern machinery, but rather to build hotels, apartment houses, etc. Current speculative building in Rio de Janeiro is an example of unwise investment policy or rather absence of any policy. It should be made certain that private investors, government, and *Fomentos* use capital in the most productive manner possible according to future needs of the country and pattern of consumption demand. It is particularly important, when the low-income groups are being asked to make sacrifices in order to provide additional capital resources that these resources be of the most effective kind and type possible. The future reward for these hard pressed groups should be a higher standard of living[1] for them, not fashionable hotels and the like.

[1] *Cf.* Ch. X on Bolivia.

Finally, the rate of expansion of prices and the diversion of resources to capital must be adjusted to the requirements of international equilibrium. This means that if the Latin American countries are not in step with other countries of the world they will soon be confronted with exchange depreciation. If, however, they are receiving a substantial proportion of their capital from abroad, then they may continue to expand and yet not suffer from an adverse balance of payments. In this case, the adverse balance which might follow from the more rapid expansion of income in Latin American countries would be offset by the inflow of capital. Despite the rise of income, moreover, prices may not rise greatly if large inflows of capital bring significant inflows of goods. Authorities should, however, be certain that they are developing the industries which will make it possible to reduce their imports in the future or, preferably, to expand their exports. Otherwise, the problem of adverse balance of payments will plague them in the future.

In summary, the process of inflation and forced savings which has gone on for a long time in Latin American countries is not by any means to be condemned on all grounds. It is, in my opinion, a *sine qua non* for the economic development of countries that are short of capital. This is not to deny that at times the rate of inflation and the rate of diversion of resources to capital have been too rapid. When large proportions of the population are at a starvation or almost starvation level, it is not sound economic policy to deprive low-income groups of, say, 25 per cent of their real income (*i.e.*, command over goods) over a period of a few years in order to provide capital resources for the future. To express this in another way, in such circumstances the degree of rise of prices should be moderate, and therefore the diversion of resources to capital purposes should also be moderate.

On this score, the inflation since 1939 in most Latin American countries may be considered excessive. I agree with Dr. Ellsworth, for example, that the rate of expansion in Chile has been too great, although it is quite certain that to some extent inflation is almost the inevitable result of expansion abroad.[1] Latin American countries cannot be expected to isolate themselves from the expansion that is world-wide. Nevertheless, with all extenuating circumstances considered, my conclusion is that the rise of Latin American prices, which

[1] *Cf.* Ch. XII; see also Ch. XVII on Paraguay and the interesting defense of inflation in Ch. XV on Haiti.

perhaps has recently averaged about 15 per cent per annum (variations for individual countries are great), has been too high. This has tended, given the rather weak bargaining position of labor and the current tax systems, to effect an undesirable redistribution of income and consumption. Undoubtedly many of the political difficulties of Latin America may be associated with the relatively excessive rates of expansion and inflation that have gone on in the last few years. It is not, however, easy to prescribe practical remedies to slow down the rate of expansion although an attempt has been made to do just that.[1] It is certain, finally, that in the next generation or two this process of raising capital through a continued rise of prices will be not only necessary but desirable. Throughout this period, however, a delicate balance must be drawn between the needs of capital and the necessity of not cutting substantially the standard of living of low-income groups whose incomes do not rise or respond to rising prices.

A rapid inflation, moreover, is undesirable for many other reasons which are well known to all of us: hoarding increases, productivity declines, international disequilibrium is introduced, etc. In this chapter, I have emphasized the adverse effects on low-income groups because that seems to be the most important aspect of the problem in Latin America. Any adverse effects on total supplies merely aggravate the position of these groups.

IX. THE POSITION OF LABOR[2]

The foregoing discussion of inflation has touched upon the position of labor. Clearly those laborers who participate in the money economy are generally affected adversely, in the short run at least, by large doses of inflation. Real wages are low both because labor is not highly productive and because wages generally do not rise so rapidly as prices. Lack of strong labor organization in most Latin American countries further contributes toward a low standard of living for workers. In order to contend with these conditions governments have taken numerous measures to improve the status of labor.

Many of these countries have introduced social security programs. Uruguay began as far back as 1919. Mexico introduced a compre-

[1] *Cf.* my Ch. VI on Price Stabilization Programs in Latin America.

[2] Since there is no chapter in this volume devoted exclusively to the subject of labor conditions in Latin America, the main outlines of the picture have been summarized here. The data from which this summary is drawn are available in my files.

hensive program in 1942 calling for 6 per cent contributions by employers, 3 per cent by employees, and 3 per cent by the government. Chile apparently has an even more ambitious program. Other countries have introduced modest programs, among them Argentina, Brazil, and Colombia.

Too much should not be expected of these programs. An adequate social security program requires, as Sir William Beveridge has noted, a redistribution of income and a guarantee of a decent minimum standard of living. When 90 per cent or more of the population live at close to starvation levels, a social security program cannot be very effective. In fact, some of the programs can be condemned on the grounds that excessive collections are made by the government at the expense of workers (through pay-roll deductions or wage reductions imposed by employers) and these funds are put into hospitals and other real property. Receipts are much in excess of disbursements: workers accept cuts now which they cannot afford with a promise of reimbursement later. Here again we have investment stimulated at the expense of low-income groups.

Help has also been forthcoming in other areas of legislation. Labor legislation is popular. Legislation has been directed in particular against foreign capital operating mines and public utilities. Improved labor conditions in foreign enterprise operating in some Latin American countries have had a favorable effect on labor conditions in other industries. Governments have set minimum wages and limited hours of work. Almost all Latin American countries have enacted minimum wage laws. They are not always enforced too well, however, and frequently do not cover important groups of workers. In the last few years, the large inflation has been responsible for significant rises in the minimum wage levels. In some cases (*e.g.*, Mexico) the increase in the minimum has been as much as 50 per cent. Hours have frequently been restricted to 48 hours or less though temporary wartime exceptions have been made.

Here again too much must not be expected. Improved labor legislation and enforcement await increases in productivity which in turn rest upon progress in technology, transportation, and education.

An examination of statistics for Latin American countries (admittedly spotty) yields the following conclusions. Total wages and salaries have tended to rise. This is to be expected in view of the development of industries, the rise of hours, and the increase of employment in industry. Yet the rises in all cases have been surprisingly small (Chile seems to be a notable exception) in view of the great rise of prices and, in some cases, the significant increase in employment. In general, real wage rates have declined since 1939 though total real (goods value) wage payments for all workers have frequently risen. Of this much we may be certain: Labor in Latin America has not done so well as it has in the United States in respect to (1) the rise of employment, (2) money or real wage rates, and (3) total money or real wage payments.

Perhaps the failure to improve labor conditions more may be associated with the weakness of trade unions in many of these countries. Chile and Mexico, however, seem to have made much progress in recent years.

Employment has of course not risen to the extent that it has in the United States, where the total working population and those in military service are up more than one-third. The increase in hours of work in the United States of about 15 per cent is additional. Once more, relevant recent figures are unavailable in most Latin American countries. By 1943, *industrial* employment seems to have risen about 15 per cent in Argentina and 20 per cent in Chile, two countries with substantial developments of new industries. The percentage rise of employment is, however, a much smaller part of the total working population.[1]

X. TARIFFS AND THE REALLOCATION OF ECONOMIC FACTORS

In his chapter on agriculture Dr. Wheeler[2] has shown clearly the danger of market gluts that may confront Latin America in the post-war period. Demand is likely to be short of supply at remunerative prices. This danger period will come a few years after the end of the Asiatic war: old areas of production will be reopened and additional restrictions on imports may be introduced in potential markets. Countries producing cotton, rubber, rice, vegetable oils, coffee, grains, etc., may well be confronted with a deficiency of demand. Additional difficulties will confront those that produce important mineral products: coal, copper, nitrate, manganese, etc.[3] How serious these problems will be will depend in part upon the protection that is introduced

[1] See Ch. X on Bolivia, pp. 256–258.
[2] See Ch. III.
[3] *Cf.* Chs. on Bolivia and Chile.

against agricultural and mineral products sold by Latin America in the postwar period, and also upon the economic conditions in the major industrial countries. The more favorable the economic conditions in these countries, the less Latin America will have to fear; for industrial countries will buy more and they will be less disposed to shut out imports, the higher the level of employment and income.

Protectionist measures are on the increase in Latin America. This fact is evident from a study of several of the chapters in this volume. The protectionist measures are not only higher tariffs, but various forms of bilateral agreement and also exchange control. Through the latter a government can easily prevent the importation of commodities. It is interesting that in 1943–1944 when the shipping situation had eased somewhat, several countries attempted to increase their restrictions on commodities which once more were to be had in larger quantities. The war has in itself imposed certain tariff barriers or at least certain restrictions on the movement of goods with the result that numerous domestic industries have developed. These industries provide supplies that were previously available from other sources.[1]

During the present war the proportion of Latin American exports taken by other Latin American countries has increased by about 100 per cent. This, of course, has been made necessary by the unavailability of other and generally cheaper sources of supply. Dr. Chalmers has well shown[2] the long history of attempts on the part of Latin American countries to increase trade among themselves. They have frequently attempted to introduce special tariff concessions in favor of one another. These agreements, however, may cause much harm since they raise certain issues in relation to the most-favored-nation clause. Insofar as special concessions are made among the various Latin American countries, the net result is discrimination against the rest of the world. The effect, therefore, is likely to be resentment on the part of countries so discriminated against; and since they provide the major markets for Latin American products, it is rather unwise for Latin America to carry this technique too far. There are many who will doubt the effectiveness of British imperial preference. A similar technique applied to Latin American countries is even less likely to be successful because of the greater dependence upon outside sources

[1] Effects of the protection offered by shipping restrictions are ably revealed in Ch. IX on Argentina.

[2] See Ch. VIII.

by these countries, and also because the ties among them are not so strong as the ties between the British dominions and the mother country. These bilateral agreements, moreover, are not to be confused with the bilateral agreements that were imposed upon Latin America before the war by various European countries that had purchased more from Latin America than they had sold there. In these cases Latin American countries had no alternative but to accede.

The war years have witnessed a significant rise in domestic industry and particularly of manufacturing in Latin America.[1] In general, the industries that have tended to grow have been rather elementary manufacturing industries, *e.g.*, paper, beer, pharmaceutical, and especially textile. Trade figures reveal to some extent the tendencies along these lines. It will be noted not only that countries nurturing these new industries now may very well import less manufactured goods but also that they may well import more raw materials and in some cases even export manufactured goods.

The percentage of total exports of Brazil is as follows:[2]

	Raw materials	Foodstuffs	Manufactured goods
1940	43.2	54.2	2.6
1942	40.6	44.2	14.9
Part of 1943	32.5	46.5	21.0

One might raise some questions concerning the possibility of significant developments in manufacturing in Latin American countries. There clearly are some areas where significant advances might occur. Wages, for example, are not likely to be more per hour than 10 to 20 per cent of wages in the United States in manufacturing. It does not follow that the costs of labor are therefore lower; but it does follow that if the labor is not highly skilled important reductions in labor costs as compared with corresponding United States costs might follow. Latin American countries might also obtain a comparative advantage, *i.e.*, utilize their economic factors effectively as compared

[1] See Ch. IX on Argentina, XI on Brazil, XII on Chile, and XIII on Colombia.

[2] *Departmento de imprensa e propaganda*, Nov. 6, 1943, and *Foreign Commerce Weekly*, Nov. 11, 1943.

with other alternative uses in industries where the amount of capital required is not large and where, in general, advance techniques are not required. They may also profit greatly in the production of commodities where savings on transportation costs are large, because the manufacturing industries either are near the sources of raw materials or are close to the markets, and where at the same time transportation costs for the raw materials and the finished products are substantial. It may furthermore be necessary that the industry operate on a large enough scale so that the maximum economies of large-scale production might be obtained. In such industries as the beer or textile, the level of output need not be high in order to attain this objective.

It follows that there are numerous industries where the progress may well be justified on economic grounds and where present backwardness may well be explained by the failure to take the initiative. It is probable that in some, perhaps in many, cases these industries will survive after the tariffs are removed. Nor does it follow from this that the development of these industries will be detrimental to the interests of the United States. Trade *may* still increase as it did between England and Germany while the latter was rapidly developing her manufacturing industries. In trade between Latin America and the United States, it is still probable that the United States will concentrate on the more highly skilled manufacturing industries and agriculture and Latin America on agriculture, minerals, and the more primary manufacturing industries. As incomes rise in Latin America following industrial development, these countries, despite their rise in manufacturing, will be able to buy more products from the United States.

Many arguments may, of course, be adduced in favor of the protectionist policy in Latin America. One has already been adumbrated above, *viz.*, the more than century-old infant-industry argument.

A second argument has also received attention, *viz.*, the need of reallocation of economic factors that might arise as a result of the postwar reduction of demand for primary products, inclusive of minerals. A domestic investment policy inclusive of public works and new industries may not be approved when labor and capital can be productively used in export industries. Yet if the alternative is unemployment or ruinously low prices for exports (*e.g.*, 5 cents a pound for Argentine beef because the United States will buy only over a high tariff wall), then protection may well justify itself. Resources may be diverted to industries which will yield more to labor and capital than is obtainable in the production of meat salable at 5 cents per pound. The British justified their protection and domestic investment on similar grounds in the thirties. If foreign nations insist upon protecting their agriculture against Latin American grain, beef, and raw materials, then Latin America has no alternative but to reciprocate through increased protection against foreign manufactured products. If, again, various countries insist on bilateral agreements, then Latin American countries must also have recourse to bilateral agreements in order to ensure themselves a fair share of the shrinking volume of foreign trade. In other words, the possibilities of a liberal trade policy in Latin America depend in no small part on the leadership of such countries as the United States and the United Kingdom.

A third point is that of stability. That issue was discussed in an earlier part of this introductory chapter. Here it need merely be said that Latin American countries might tend toward diversification to be induced through tariff and restrictionist policies. Their preference may be based largely on the desirability of relatively stable conditions, even if the total costs are greater and the standard of living is lower over the whole period as a result of the reduction of international specialization. That is, these countries may prefer stable conditions, at a lower standard of living, to unstable conditions. In the former case, the economic conditions will depend less on world-wide forces—*i.e.*, on whether prosperity or depression prevails in the major industrial and buying countries.

XI. ALTERNATIVE APPROACHES

Are there any alternative solutions? Numerous attempts have been made in Latin American countries to control supplies and the allocation of supplies as between domestic and export markets. Such policies are directed toward keeping export prices up. These countries have also attempted in many cases to reduce import prices through the introduction of various trade-restriction policies. In this manner they attempt to achieve more favorable terms of trade, *i.e.*, a larger number of units of manufacturing (say) products for a given number of units of wheat, beef, or copper. In this manner also, Latin American countries may help solve their problems of balance of payments, and at present when wartime competition is not very strong they may have had a moderate success.

This particular tack is not likely, however, to be successful in the long run. Larger and more powerful industrial countries will probably be in a better bargaining position; and since they are larger, they can put up a stronger monopoly front. Furthermore, the Latin American countries would generally have to face competition in most of their primary products and therefore may not be able to exact more favorable terms from their purchasers.[1] It is clear from history that the exaction of more favorable terms of trade by countries producing primary products will depend upon collaboration between the various countries producing these products. One-sided arrangements, or one-country arrangements, are not likely to be successful. In this connection one need only recall the failure of Brazil's coffee program and the sugar program of Cuba. In the present world situation there is considerable discussion as to whether there should be restrictionist production policies which are more or less favored by Latin American countries—or whether there should be merely provisions for buffer stocks, a program which has been favored by the United Kingdom in particular. So far the buffer-stock program has not been very successful in preventing overproduction.

Another alternative which may be considered a temporary solution is the increase of capital importation into Latin American countries. In this manner the Latin American countries may be able to improve their competitive position in certain elementary manufacturing industries because in some of these industries the greatest lack is adequate capital. These importations of capital may be a long-run solution if they are carefully scrutinized and if they have the effect of making Latin American industry more productive, thus putting some of their manufacturing industries on a competitive basis with foreign industries. The state of the capital market and the conditions under which foreign loans should be made have already been discussed.

We have already mentioned the alternative of exchange control and exchange depreciation. Fundamentally the price paid for exchange control is regimentation and control of the allocation of economic factors. It is a high price to pay in order to ensure, if it does, the best possible utilization of dollars and pounds that are made available. Furthermore, exchange control is of course not really an alternative because it is a form of restriction of imports and is frequently protectionist in its intention. Exchange control is also a means

[1] Consult Chs. II, III, and XI by Drs. Waring, Wheeler, and Edwards on these issues.

of improving a country's terms of trade, the exporter of highly competitive commodities being ensured a high local price for his dollars, and the exporter who has more or less a monopoly position abroad getting relatively few pesos for his dollar. The net gains through exchange control, moreover, are limited by similar activities on the part of other countries. In other words, the net result may well be bilateral monopoly rather than unilateral monopoly. Where the balance of payments is very seriously affected by marked depressions or reversals of economic conditions, it may nevertheless be absolutely essential for the government to determine what shall be imported and at what price, and what shall be exported and at what price in terms of domestic currency. This technique should, however, be reserved for periods of great crises.

All economists will agree that the best possible solution is prosperity in the buying countries and liberal trade policies by them. Free trade or a relaxation of present tariff barriers and other restrictionist policies will have the effect of bringing about similar liberalization in Latin American countries. If the advanced industrial countries can maintain a high level of employment and a high national income, then they will also be more disposed to introduce and push free-trade policies. As a result of these conditions and measures, the likelihood is that Latin American countries, too, will not resort to exchange control, exchange depreciation, excessive tariff barriers, etc. Even in this case some tariffs, introduced in order to put an infant industry on its feet, may well be justified. Each case, however, should be considered with great care to make certain that the industry can stand on its own feet once it has grown up. Both British and American experience do not promise too much on this score.

XII. THE ECONOMICS OF OUR GOOD NEIGHBOR POLICY

Numerous statements have been made concerning our present policy of buying our way into better political relations with Latin America. In particular, we have estimates of Senator Butler that our friendship policy in Latin America has involved the government in loans and disbursements of almost $6 billion in 3 years.[1] Senator Butler emphasizes especially the large gifts made and the folly of

[1] See *Expenditures and Commitments by the United States Government in or for Latin America* (Senate Document 132, December 1943, 170 pp.). Report by Hon. Hugh Butler and reply by Hon. Kenneth McKellar.

setting up plants in these countries that will compete with American industry. "Our total South and Central American program calls for an investment by American taxpayers of about $6,000,000,000 by the end of 1944."[1]

Is Senator Butler's position sound? First, on the sums involved, the government has shown that only $324 million has been spent by the government, excepting the purchase of strategic materials and ships. Second, can his position be defended?[2] The answer is no. We have gained much more from the vast majority of outlays involved than have our neighbors to the south. We have obtained indispensable commodities for winning the war we could not have obtained so readily elsewhere.

Most economists would agree that the generation that carries on a war is the generation that pays most of the bill. They work harder or do without various consumption goods, and many of them have given their lives. This does not mean that the later generations may not suffer as a result of distortions, political instabilities, etc., that arise as a consequence of the war. Nevertheless, the conclusion substantially holds that the generation living during the war pays the bill for it. In this respect, Latin Americans have also contributed greatly toward the winning of the war. It is true that large advances were made to Latin American countries in order to enable them to produce the goods that we require for the winning of the war. But it is also undoubtedly true that the requisite supplies of goods would not have been forthcoming without this help. What could the United Nations have done without the Latin American tin, copper, nitrate, beef, wool, cinchona, manganese, vegetable oils, etc.? It is certain that without this help the war would be a much longer and a much costlier one. The Latin American contribution is well revealed by the table shown on page 36, submitted by the Foreign Economic Administration as part of the evidence in reply to Senator Butler's charges.[3]

What have we paid for this help? We have, of course, purchased these commodities and sometimes at very favorable prices to Latin American economies, and in order to sustain the relevant economy we have at times agreed to take commodities that we did not need greatly in the course of the present war. Yet one should not lose sight

[1] *Ibid.*, pp. 36, 46–48.
[2] *Ibid.*, p. 99.
[3] *Ibid.*, p. 135.

of the fact that the Latin Americans in general have not received in payment for these goods, for which they have worked harder, more products from the United Nations or from the United States or from Great Britain, and it is products that they need. In fact, they have accepted additional work, the exhaustion of some of their natural resources, and in many cases a reduced standard of living in order to provide us with supplies that are required in order to win the war.

Commodity	Per cent of total United States supply that must be imported	Per cent of total United States *imports* coming from Latin America	Per cent of total United States *new supply* coming from Latin America
Quartz crystals	99.9	100.0	99.9
Tantalum	99.0	66.5*	66.0
Tin	99.9	67.5	67.5
Mica (good, stained, or better)	95.0	24.0	23.0
Beryllium	83.0	84.3	70.0
Manganese (metallurgical and battery)	85.0	35.5	30.0
Tungsten	62.0	54.5	34.0
Zinc	40.5	57.0	23.0
Copper	26.0	93.0	24.0
Fluorspar	9.4	65.0	6.0

* Including almost all of the vital high-grade material.

The picture can well be summarized by trade figures. In the year 1938, the United States and the United Kingdom imported $169 million more from Latin America than Latin America bought from these two countries. In 1941–1943 the excess of exports to the United States and the United Kingdom from Latin America was no less than $1,700 million, of which approximately $1,100 million went to the U. S. and $600 million to the United Kingdom. This excess of exports in these 3 years of $1,700 million ($740 million in 1943 alone) measures well the contribution that Latin America has made toward winning the war, and if the war should last through 1946 the contribution might very well be of the order of $4 billion.

Why then have Latin American countries exported $1,700 million more to the United States and the United Kingdom than they imported in these 3 years, and why may they export anywhere from $2 to $4 billion in excess of imports to the United States and the United

Kingdom before the war ends? The answer is that we created a demand for these products and urged these countries to cooperate with us in the production of supplies necessary for waging war. These countries, on the other hand, have been unable to obtain adequate payment in goods because of shipping shortages and the need of allocating scarce resources by countries involved in a vigorous war. What these countries will receive in exchange for this excess of exports will be an excess of imports in postwar years—at a time when goods will be plentiful anyhow. The value of what they will receive, however, will depend upon the price level in the years 1946, 1947, 1948, etc., and also to some extent on the rate at which they use their accumulation of dollars and pounds. The best index of what they have received so far is the excess of dollars and pounds which are now at their disposal. Apparently the increase of gold, dollars, pounds, etc., has been from three- to fourfold since the war started. In short, in exchange for vitally necessary war materials we have provided these countries with paper credit, with dollars that are manufactured by our banking system, and with gold for which we have no use. In the postwar period it is hoped that they will obtain adequate compensation for their natural resources, for their additional work, and for the reduced standard of living which they have encountered during the present war. In short, Latin America has provided goods when they were scarce, and it looks as though we shall return them, at least in part, when they are more plentiful. It does seem that on the whole the United States has had the better of the bargain, despite the fact that in many cases we have had to pay high prices (though generally lower than the last war) for these products, and despite the fact that we have made every effort to provide Latin America with whatever we could at relatively reasonable prices.

XIII. SUMMARY

In this introductory chapter the emphasis has been put on international equilibrium and the sensitivity of the Latin American economies to external forces over which they have virtually no control. Their low standard of living is explained only in part by this victimization. Scarcity of capital and (related to this factor) persistent inflation continue to plague the masses. We have commented on the causes of capital scarcity and the contributions that might be made by a controlled inflation. Against this background of deficiencies in capital, technology, education, and management, social legislation cannot make a major contribution. It is also made clear that independent investment policies in Latin American countries will soon be stopped by the unavailability of exchange and monetary resources. They can be justified only on the grounds that alternative uses of labor and capital will yield less favorable returns in a world which will not or cannot buy Latin American products. They may then be tested on the same criteria as a protectionist policy. If Europe, the United States, and Asia will not or cannot buy, can Latin America afford to sell? Latin Americans may have to weigh the advantage of fuller employment, better terms of trade, and increased stability against the losses of a diminished volume of international trade. Temporary palliatives are to be found in exchange depreciation, exchange control, and the courageous use of excess supplies of gold and foreign exchanges. In the absence of a healthy foreign trade more fundamental measures will be required: a reallocation of labor and capital to domestic industries; more saving; increased sanitation and education; increased imports of capital under carefully guarded conditions. Much will depend on the liberal trade policies of the major powers.[1]

[1] *Cf.* the very able appraisal of postwar trade policy by Dr. Waring in Ch. II.

Part II

GENERAL CONSIDERATIONS

Chapter II

Economic Problems of the Latin American Republics

by FRANK A. WARING

THE Latin American republics, 10 in South America and 10 in North America, occupy an area more than 2½ times as great as that of continental United States and have an estimated population of 128 millions. The American countries south of the Rio Grande, however, cannot be considered or studied as a unit because of the marked differences among them in resources, climate, industries, and trade and in peoples and languages. Each of these countries has its own peculiar economy, and in the postwar period each will be faced with its own peculiar economic problems, many of which will have arisen out of the war or will have been intensified as a result of it.[1]

The economy of Mexico is based chiefly on mining and agriculture. Minerals customarily constitute more than three-fourths the total export trade; they include silver, gold, petroleum, zinc, lead, copper, antimony, mercury, and graphite. The principal agricultural exports are bananas, henequen, chicle, coffee, fresh vegetables, and cattle.

Sugar and its derivatives are the chief products exported by the three island republics;[2] others are tobacco, coffee, and sisal. The Central American countries[3] ship principally bananas, coffee, cacao, and gold.

[1] Much of the material in this chapter pertaining to the prewar period has been drawn from recent reports of the United States Tariff Commission. The writer was author or co-author of these reports.

[2] Cuba, Dominican Republic, and Haiti.

[3] Costa Rica, El Salvador, Guatemala, Honduras, Nicaragua, and Panama.

In the northern South American countries,[1] the leading exports are coffee and cacao. Each country, however, produces certain other major export products. Petroleum is an important export commodity for Venezuela (accounting for as much as 90 per cent of total exports); platinum, gold, and petroleum for Colombia; and petroleum and gold for Ecuador. Brazil is also a very large exporter of coffee and cacao. In addition, it ships cotton, oil-bearing seeds and nuts, manganese, iron ore, and rubber.

The economies of the west coast countries of South America[2] are influenced greatly by the production of minerals, principally for export. The chief export for Bolivia is unrefined tin; for Peru, petroleum and copper; and for Chile, copper and nitrates. About 90 per cent of Bolivian exports customarily consist of minerals; the proportion is 75 per cent for Chile and 65 per cent for Peru. Chile also exports wool, meats, and vegetables, and Peru ships long-staple cotton, sugar, wool, and other fine animal hair.

The countries in the Temperate Zone[3] on the east coast of South America are dependent largely upon the production of pastoral products and cereals; their principal exports are customarily meats, wool, hides and skins, wheat, corn, and flaxseed. Argentina and Paraguay are the world's only suppliers of quebracho extract (a tanning material); and they are becoming increasingly important producers of cotton.

The economies of the Latin American republics have at least one common characteristic. These countries are all engaged in the production of raw materials and crude foodstuffs for export, and they all import a wide variety of manufactured goods and prepared foodstuffs. In most of these republics manufacturing activity is confined chiefly to the processing of commodities for export and to the production of certain types of consumers' goods, notably cotton textiles. In a few, manufacturing is more highly developed; these include Argentina, Brazil, Chile, and Mexico. In others, especially Venezuela, Colombia, and Cuba, efforts are being made to stimulate domestic manufacturing and to promote the diversification of productive enterprise in both industry and agriculture. Among the Latin American republics these seven are the leading nations in foreign trade. In 1938

[1] Colombia, Ecuador, and Venezuela.
[2] Bolivia, Chile, and Peru.
[3] Argentina, Paraguay, and Uruguay.

they accounted for 85 per cent of total exports from the Latin American republics and for 84 per cent of total imports.

Prior to 1939, when war broke out in Europe, the trade of the Latin American republics had been adversely affected by the world-wide depression and the widespread imposition of rigid trade and exchange controls, particularly in continental European markets. The war has multiplied and intensified these and other economic problems. The trade of the Latin American republics has been diverted from many of its customary channels because of the loss of markets in continental Europe and the increased demand for certain strategic or essential materials, particularly in the United States and the United Kingdom. The inability of the United Nations to obtain required supplies from usual sources has intensified the demand within the Western Hemisphere for rubber, tin, cinchona, fibers, and a number of other commodities. Moreover, the inability of certain other areas to obtain consumers' goods from long-established sources has stimulated the export trade of the Latin American republics, especially to South Africa and among themselves.[1] Some commodities, however, are not in great demand, notably wheat, corn, and flaxseed; for these, prices have been depressed by the loss of markets.

The urgent demand for materials required by the United Nations has operated to raise the prices of many export products. Furthermore, the scarcity of consumers' goods caused by the preoccupation of the United States and the United Kingdom with the war and the recent shortage in shipping have tended to increase sharply the prices of such goods in the Latin American republics. Increased employment and wages have intensified the inflationary trend in many of these countries. High prices and the curtailment of imports have stimulated industrialization in a number of the Latin American republics, particularly in Brazil, Mexico, Argentina, and Chile, where marked developments have occurred. In addition, a number of industries producing strategic materials have been expanded to meet the war demand.

In the postwar period major adjustments will be required in the economies of most of the Latin American republics. These will include the reestablishment of their trade in peacetime channels, the relaxation of economic controls necessitated by the war, the realignment of prices and of production in certain industries because of the probable

[1] *Cf.* Ch. VIII by Mr. Chalmers.—EDITOR.

decline in demand, and the renewed competition in world markets from established producers of raw materials and in local markets from foreign manufacturers of consumers' goods.

Trade Relations

TRADE BEFORE THE WAR

In 1938, the last full year before the outbreak of war, the United States took approximately 33 per cent of all exports from the Latin American republics; continental Europe also accounted for about 33 per cent, the United Kingdom for 19 per cent, the Latin American republics themselves for 6 per cent, and all other countries for 9 per cent.[1] Of imports into the Latin American republics, the United States supplied about 33 per cent; continental Europe, 35 per cent; the United Kingdom, 12 per cent; the Latin American republics themselves, 10 per cent; and all other countries, 10 per cent. Among the continental European countries, Germany was both the most important market (11 per cent of exports) and the leading supplier (16 per cent of imports). During the decade 1929–1938 the United States maintained fairly well its position in the trade of the Latin American republics, Germany increased its participation, and the United Kingdom declined in importance.

Trade with the United States (imports and exports combined) is most important to the Caribbean countries;[2] prior to the war, the United States usually accounted for about 50 per cent of their total trade. Among these countries, Panama sold to the United States 89 per cent of its exports in 1938 and Cuba 76 per cent. In that year Cuba also took the largest part of its imports from this country (71 per cent); Honduras was second with 62 per cent. In Brazil, the United States accounted for about 30 per cent of total trade, in the west coast South American countries for nearly 25 per cent, and in the east coast countries in the Temperate Zone for 10 per cent. In the Caribbean countries and Brazil, exports of merchandise to the United States (in terms of value) customarily exceeded imports from it; but, in the

[1] The 9 per cent represented principally exports of petroleum from Venezuela to the Dutch West Indies for refining. In 1938 the refined products were exported chiefly to the United States, the United Kingdom, and continental European countries. The ultimate share of these countries in the export trade of the other American republics, therefore, would be somewhat larger than that shown by official trade statistics as recorded above.

[2] Including Colombia, Ecuador, and Venezuela.

trade of the west and east coast South American countries, imports from the United States generally were larger than exports to it.

The prominent position occupied by the United States in the trade of the Caribbean countries has been due to a number of factors. Except for northern Mexico, the countries bordering the Caribbean Sea are located in the tropics. Consequently, the agricultural and forest commodities which they produce are largely complementary to, rather than competitive with, those produced in the United States. The outstanding exception is sugar, the largest export from this area, in terms of value. Exports of sugar, however, supplement United States production, which has always been inadequate to supply domestic requirements. Exports of tobacco differ from, and are complementary to, the principal types grown in the United States.[1] Most of the other important agricultural products exported from these countries are not produced in the United States and enter this country free of duty.

Gold and silver are also important products of some of the Caribbean countries, and all, or nearly all, their output is sold in the United States. Indeed, the United States is the principal export market for each of the Caribbean countries, except Venezuela, which ships its crude petroleum (the principal export product) chiefly to the Dutch West Indies for refining and export. Other factors which have operated to make the United States important in trade with the Caribbean countries are the capital invested by United States citizens in these countries, their proximity to the United States, the direction of the principal trade routes, the availability of shipping services, and the formal or informal relationship existing between their currencies and the United States dollar.

The proportionately large trade of Brazil with the United States has been chiefly the result of the great demand in this country for coffee and also for such other tropical products as cacao and oil-bearing seeds and nuts.

Because of the character of their mineral products the trade of the west coast South American countries with the United States has been proportionately less than that of countries to the north. The United States is customarily on an export basis for petroleum and copper, and

[1] United States imports of sugar come in large part from Cuba, chiefly because of preferential tariff treatment. United States imports of tobacco from the Western Hemisphere enter almost entirely from Cuba, largely because of the preference in this market for tobacco of the Cuban type.

these minerals, when entered for consumption in the United States, are subject to import excise taxes.[1] Sodium nitrate from Chile (free of duty) meets the competition of synthetic nitrates produced in the United States. Before the war, tin ore from Bolivia was refined in the United Kingdom because the complex character of the ore necessitated its being smelted in conjunction with Malayan ore, and this ore could not be obtained economically by the United States because of the imposition of an export tax by the British.

Among all the other American nations, the east coast South American countries in the South Temperate Zone found trade with the United States least important. These countries are exporters of those foodstuffs which the United States produces in large volume. From the standpoint of location, they are as close to Europe as to the United States, and trade routes are favorable to the development of European commerce. Moreover, United States investments in these countries are small in comparison with European investments and with United States investments in the other Latin American regions. Another important factor affecting the trade of this area is the large immigration into these countries from Europe and their close cultural ties with that continent. Argentina, for example, which has had the largest foreign trade of any of the Latin American countries, carried on about three-fourths of its commerce with Europe; in 1938, it sold to the United States only 9 per cent of its exports and purchased from this country 17 per cent of its imports; in that year it had an import trade balance with this country of about $40 million.

TRADE IN 1939–1940

During the first 15 months following the outbreak of war (September, 1939), total exports from the Latin American republics declined. By the blockade of continental Europe, these countries lost markets which had accounted for about one-third their sales abroad. The United States and other Hemisphere countries increased their purchases, but this did not offset the loss, and exports of the Latin American republics dropped from $1,925 million in 1939 to $1,762 million in 1940. It might be expected that commodities which customarily were sold in continental Europe would be the most adversely affected. But for some of these products the demand increased as a

[1] Copper and petroleum, when entered under bond for refining and export, are free of duty.

result of the war, and prices advanced; for others, principally agricultural products, such as cereals, coffee, cacao, sugar, and bananas, no substitute markets were developed, and consequently prices declined.

Before the war, the United States usually took about one-half of all exports of coffee from the Latin American republics; the second largest market was in continental Europe. As a result of the blockade of Europe, stocks of coffee accumulated in the Western Hemisphere, and prices declined. A similar situation prevailed for cacao, large stocks of which were available to the British on the Gold Coast and in Nigeria. For bananas, European markets were closed, and British purchases were greatly reduced. The price of sugar was depressed because of the inability of the Dutch East Indies and (to a lesser extent) Cuba to dispose of their stocks in customary markets. Some commodities were indirectly affected by large supplies of competing products. For example, henequen from Mexico declined in price, even though 85 per cent of the exports were ordinarily shipped to the United States, because of large purchases by this country of sisal from the Dutch East Indies, which could not market its product in Europe.

For a number of commodities, however, the increased demand of the United States and the United Kingdom offset either in part or in whole the loss of exports to continental Europe. Most of these commodities were minerals, such as copper, tin, zinc, lead, antimony, manganese, mercury, and nitrates, but they included also wool, hides and skins, and meat. For example, large purchases of copper and nitrates by the United States resulted in increased exports of these commodities, despite the loss of European markets. In 1940 the United Kingdom purchased large quantities of meat, and exports of wool and hides to the United States rose sharply.

The varying effects of the war upon the major export products of the Latin American republics were naturally reflected in their total trade and in their trade with different areas of the world. The total exports of some of the countries were materially reduced; for others, the reductions were slight; for a few, there were actual increases. From 1938 to 1940 exports from Argentina (in terms of value) declined about 9 per cent; those from Brazil, about 11 per cent. In Argentina the commodities most severely affected were wheat, corn, and flaxseed; in Brazil they were coffee, cacao, and cotton. Sales abroad by Cuba declined 11 per cent and by Mexico 4 per cent, chiefly as a result of the loss of markets for sugar, tobacco, and petroleum. But exports from Chile increased 2 per cent because of the greatly expanded purchases by the United States of copper and nitrates.

Imports into the Latin American republics were actually larger in 1940 ($1,411 million) than in 1939 ($1,328 million), but not so large as in 1938 ($1,492 million). Increased imports from the United States ($495 million in 1938 and $729 million in 1940) were more than counterbalanced by the inability of the Latin American republics to secure commodities in usual volume from European countries. In 1940, the United States supplied about 52 per cent of all imports into the Latin American republics, a much larger proportion than in the prewar years.

TRADE IN 1941–1943

In 1941 the United States undertook a gigantic defense program and in December of that year became a belligerent following the attack on Pearl Harbor. Purchases of strategic materials by the United States from the Latin American republics increased sharply. Total exports from these countries advanced from $1.6 billion in the year 1938 to $2.4 billion in 1943. Exports to the United States rose from $575 million to $1,340 million, and the share of this country in the total export trade of the Latin American republics increased from 33 to 56 per cent. A considerable part of this increase reflected a rise in prices, but the volume of the trade rose also, despite the shortage in shipping that prevailed in most of 1942 and a part of 1943. In the period 1938–1943 the sharpest increase occurred in 1941, when exports to the United States were $300 million greater than in the previous year. This advance was due to the large purchases arising out of the defense and war programs of this country. A second sharp increase occurred in 1943, when exports were $200 million greater than in 1942. In this instance the rise was in large part the result of increased exports of products for civilian consumption, such as coffee, cacao, and bananas, made possible by improved conditions in shipping.

Unable to obtain products from customary sources, the Latin American republics have expanded trade among themselves about threefold. Such exports rose from $99 million in 1938 to $295 million in 1943, and the share of the Latin American republics in their own export trade increased from 6 to 12 per cent. Sales to the United Kingdom, however, remained fairly constant (in terms of value) throughout the 6-year period; and, as a result, its share in the export trade declined from 19 to 12 per cent. Exports to all other countries (as a group) declined sharply in relative importance; valued at $693 million in 1938, such exports amounted to $466 million in 1943, and their share of the total declined from 42 to 20 per cent. This reduction reflects the loss of markets in continental Europe. The fact that trade with certain countries in the group, such as South Africa, Canada, and Spain, increased in the 6-year period serves further to emphasize the importance of the loss of sales to continental Europe.

Imports into the Latin American countries have remained fairly constant in terms of value. Because of the increase in prices of most imported goods, this resulted in a substantial reduction in the volume of trade. Imports valued at $1,492 million in 1938 declined to $1,328 million in 1939. Thereafter, imports rose to $1,469 million in 1941, and then declined to $1,409 million in 1943. As in the case of exports, the increase in imports from the United States and the Latin American republics operated to offset in part the loss in imports from the United Kingdom, continental Europe, and Asia. Imports from the United States rose from $495 million in 1938 to $915 million in 1941. In that year, export controls had not been imposed by the United States, and as a result the Latin American republics, unable to obtain supplies from usual sources, increased their purchases in this market. When the United States entered the war, its productive capacities were diverted from the manufacture of consumers' goods; export controls were imposed, and, in consequence, imports from the United States into the Latin American republics declined to $771 million in 1943. In that year the share of the United States in this import trade was 55 per cent, as compared with 62 per cent in 1941. But even in 1943 the United States supplied a much larger proportion of imports than in 1938, when the percentage was 33. Imports from the other American republics also advanced sharply in the period 1938–1943, their participation in the trade rising from 10 to 27 per cent. The United Kingdom and all other countries (considered as a group) declined in both absolute and relative importance. The share of the United Kingdom dropped from 12 to 7 per cent; that of all other countries, from 45 to 11 per cent.

The total exports from and total imports into the Latin American republics are shown in the table on page 51. The distribution of the

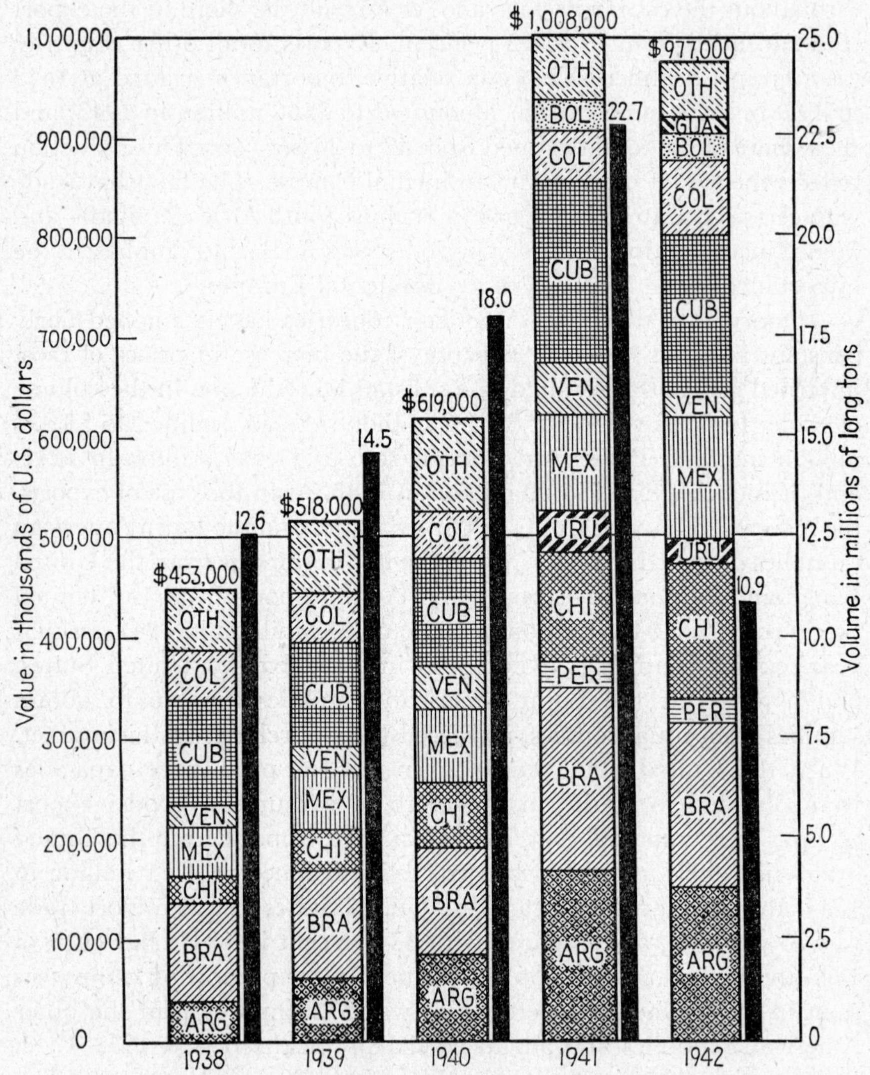

CHART 2.—United States imports from Latin America, 1938–1942. (*Source: Coordinator of Inter-American Affairs.*)

trade to the United States, the Latin American republics, the United Kingdom, and all other countries is also shown.

Chart 2 gives further indication that United States imports from Latin America have expanded greatly in dollar value since 1938; but the volume of imports has declined. A careful examination of Chart 2 will reveal changes of varying proportions for different

FOREIGN TRADE OF THE LATIN AMERICAN REPUBLICS, 1938–1943*

Country	1938	1939	1940	1941	1942	1943†
	Value in millions of dollars					
Exports to:						
United States	545	646	763	1,091	1,138	1,340
Other American republics	99	100	120	186	271	295
United Kingdom	306	323	304	364	315	280
All other countries	693	856	575	478	402	466
Total	1,643	1,925	1,762	2,119	2,126	2,381
	Per cent of total value					
United States	33	33	43	55	53	56
Other American republics	6	5	7	9	13	12
United Kingdom	19	17	17	13	15	12
All other countries	42	45	33	23	19	20
Total	100	100	100	100	100	100
	Value in millions of dollars					
Imports from:						
United States	495	534	729	915	786	771
Other American republics	142	121	174	214	334	379
United Kingdom	187	146	167	116	121	108
All other countries	668	527	341	224	186	151
Total	1,492	1,328	1,411	1,469	1,427	1,409
	Per cent of total value					
United States	33	40	52	62	55	55
Other American republics	10	9	12	15	23	27
United Kingdom	12	11	12	8	9	7
All other countries	45	40	24	15	13	11
Total	100	100	100	100	100	100

* The statistical data in this table represent a preliminary compilation from official trade statistics of the Latin American republics. It will be observed that there is a wide divergence between exports to the Latin American republics and imports received from them. This divergence may be explained in part by the addition to the recorded imports of shipping, insurance, and handling charges; the major cause, however, is probably the different methods of assessing and recording values employed by the exporting and importing countries.

† Estimated.

Source: International Economics and Statistics Unit, Bureau of Foreign and Domestic Commerce.

countries. United States exports (Chart 3) have also expanded greatly in dollar value. The rise, however, has not been so large as for imports.

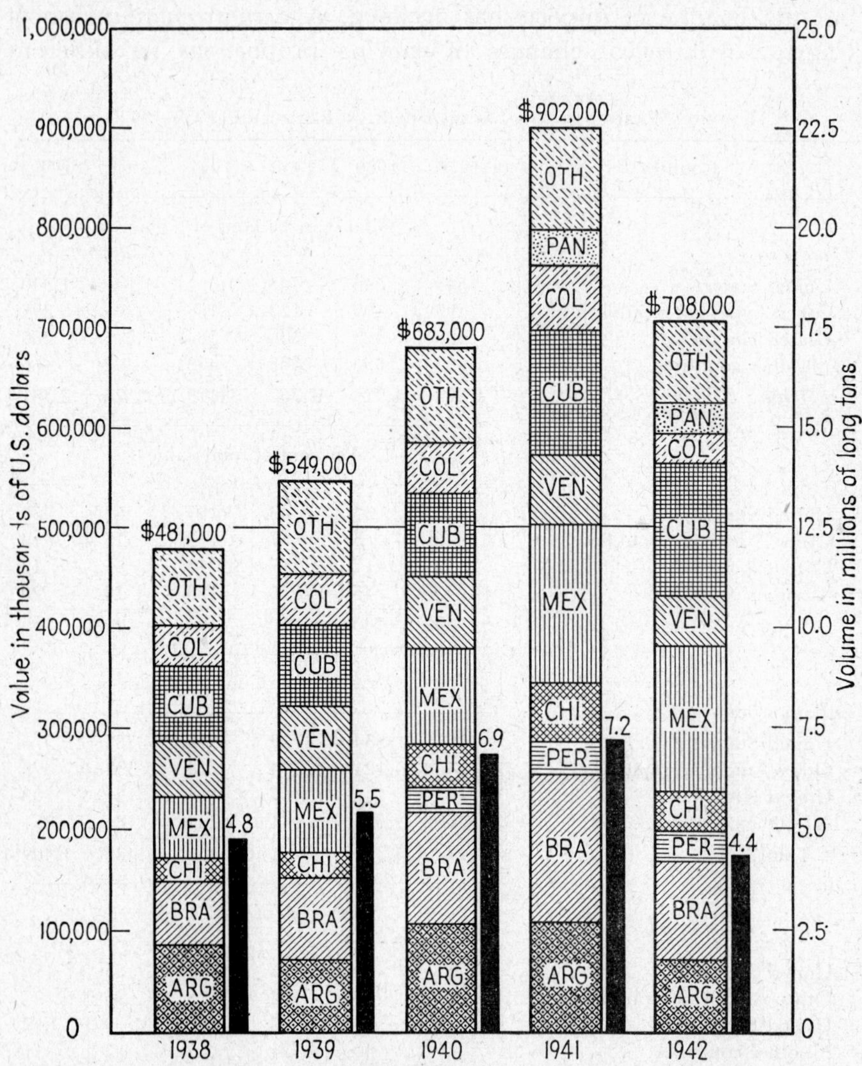

CHART 3.—United States exports to Latin America, 1938–1942. (*Source: Coordinator of Inter-American Affairs.*)

THE POSTWAR PERIOD

It appears likely that in the postwar period trade among the countries of the Western Hemisphere will not be so important as it has been during the war. But their participation in their total trade will doubtless be greater than in the prewar period. The United Kingdom and continental European countries will again become important markets for many minerals produced in the Latin American republics, such as petroleum, copper, tin, lead, and zinc, and for many agricultural products, such as cereals, meat, coffee, cotton, sugar, and tobacco, although for some of these, particularly petroleum, coffee, sugar, and tobacco, the United States will probably be the largest market. European countries are certain also to regain a part of their former importance as suppliers of imports. A major problem will then be: How rapidly can former trade channels be reopened?

During the war most of the Latin American republics have agreed to export exclusively to the United Nations, particularly the United States, a great number of essential commodities, some of which were formerly marketed largely or entirely in continental Europe. After the war, if European countries are unable immediately to absorb these products in substantial quantities, the economies of the Latin American republics will be subjected to severe strains unless the United States extends assistance during the transition period. Some industries have been overexpanded by war demands, and curtailment will be required for many of them. The task will be to integrate the need of the Latin American republics for markets, with purchases by Europe and the United States.

Economic Controls

CONTROLS BEFORE THE WAR

Before the war the Latin American republics utilized most, if not all, of the various types of trade control employed by other nations; in addition to customs duties, these included exchange and quota controls, bilateral agreements, official valuations, export taxes, and export subsidies. All these controls were not employed by each of the Latin American countries, and some of them were enforced more rigidly and were more inclusive in certain countries than in others.

There was no uniformity in the commercial policy of the Latin American republics. After 1929, customs duties, in general, were increased. In most countries they provided a large part of governmental revenue. In some, they constituted the principal source of governmental income, having been designed primarily for that purpose. In others, additional sources of governmental income were developed, and tariffs became less important from the standpoint of revenue. In certain countries where the tariff was designed to protect and promote domestic industries, the application of the protective principle operated to reduce customs receipts.

During the depression the decline in the value of the export trade of the Latin American republics made it difficult for them to meet the service on their foreign debt and to obtain imports essential to their economies. Inasmuch as many of these countries are principally producers of agricultural products and raw materials, their situations were aggravated by the fact that the prices of their principal export commodities declined more rapidly than those of the manufactured goods which constituted a large part of their imports. Because of these adverse circumstances, several of the Latin American countries, early in the decade 1930–1939, adopted exchange controls and other trade restrictions in an effort to protect their financial resources and to maintain the value of their currencies.

During the decade 1930–1939 nearly all the countries of Europe imposed additional trade barriers which were severely restrictive, and some embraced the policy of economic self-sufficiency. Most of the European countries, in their effort to control and restrict imports, adopted such devices as exchange and quota controls and bilateral agreements. This action served to accentuate the difficulties of those American republics which customarily sold substantial quantities of their products in Europe and was largely responsible for their imposition of increased trade restrictions in an effort to maintain their export markets, to secure payment for products sold, and to safeguard their financial structure.

In general, more South American countries maintained exchange controls than did other American countries. The latter undoubtedly found such restrictive devices less necessary because a very large part of their export trade was destined for the United States, where free exchange was readily available. Exchange controls as administered in the Latin American republics varied widely in the extent and rigidity with which they were applied. In some countries the rate at which foreign exchange could be bought or sold was fixed by law or decree; in others, there was a multiplicity of rates, official and unofficial, the rates varying as between commodities or countries, or both; in still others, the exchange was allocated among supplying countries and the types of commodities imported. Frequently, an attempt was made to allocate exchange to a given country on the basis of its importance as an export market. In similar fashion, imports of specific commodities were favored by providing adequate exchange at minimum rates. Thus the device was often used to protect or encourage domestic industries as well as to favor trade with particular countries or in specific commodities.

Many of the Latin American republics entered into bilateral agreements with foreign countries; these included compensation, clearing, or barter arrangements of various kinds designed to maintain certain exports and obtain payment for them, to equalize the import and export trade between signatory countries, or to provide for the exchange of surplus products. Such agreements were used most extensively by the South American countries which customarily had export trade balances with European countries and found it necessary to agree to take an increased quantity of goods from the other country participating in the agreement. Such arrangements generally operated to reduce the opportunity of third countries to sell their products in the Latin American republics.

Quotas, customs duties, and official valuations were employed by a number of the American countries as concomitant parts of their trade-control systems. Quotas were frequently imposed in connection with the allocation of exchange to specific commodities; they were utilized for bargaining purposes in the negotiation of commercial agreements and to limit the imports of certain products. By giving the Executive authority to modify rates of duty, to reclassify articles for duty purposes, and to alter fixed valuations, the tariff also became an important bargaining power in the negotiation of agreements.

The Latin American republics, like many others, were burdened with a surplus of certain commodities and, like others, resorted to export subsidies in an attempt to alleviate distress or meet competition in world markets. Export taxes were also utilized for various purposes. Such taxes were imposed to provide governmental revenue; they were also employed to discourage the export of raw materials which could be processed within the country and to recapture for the government profits arising out of increased prices for export products created by currency depreciation.

Before the war many of the Latin American republics either operated monopolies or granted certain monopolistic privileges to private enterprise. Conspicuous examples of commodities affected by such special arrangements included tobacco, alcoholic beverages, petroleum, nitrates, and quebracho. Bolivian tin interests were participants in the International Tin Committee, and Chilean producers of copper were members of the International Copper Cartel. In general, the object of these arrangements was to realize maximum profits through the regulation of price achieved by the control of production. Thus, they usually operated to restrict trade by the curtailment of supply and the maintenance of high prices. In some instances, the governments felt obliged to grant monopolistic rights to either foreign or domestic interests to ensure the development of national resources.

In the decade 1930–1939 some of the Latin American republics were concerned with mounting stocks of certain commodities for which markets at profitable prices could not be found. At various times and in varying degree the supply of these commodities exceeded the effective demand. Coffee and sugar were prominent examples. Other commodities, such as wheat, corn, and cotton, encountered similar problems in international markets, but interested countries among the Latin American republics, being low-cost producers, had less difficulty in disposing of their crops than did most others. To increase the price of coffee, Brazil undertook to destroy a part of each crop and to reimburse the producers for their loss; moreover, it sought by government regulation and control to improve the grading of coffee. The program of crop destruction was not a conspicuous success, inasmuch as other coffee-producing countries did not participate; indeed, they increased their production under the price stimulus afforded by the Brazilian action. In the case of sugar, Cuba, the largest source in the Western Hemisphere, exercised strict control over the quantities produced, probably to the benefit of the industry.

CONTROLS DURING THE WAR

As a result of the war, economic controls in the Latin American republics have been increased markedly in both number and scope. These controls have been concerned chiefly with trade, production, prices, and distribution. In 1940–1942, a number of the American countries, including Brazil, Chile, and Mexico, concluded agreements with the United States to sell exclusively to this country or its nationals many strategic commodities essential to production for war. For the United States, such agreements accomplished two major purposes:

(1) They gave assurances of ready access to available supplies in the Western Hemisphere, and (2) they checked direct or indirect shipments to the Axis Powers. By these contracts, the Latin American countries received assurances for a definite period of a market for fixed quantities of specified commodities (usually in excess of previous production) at stated pricse. To implement the contracts, they agreed to impose effective systems of export control. Thereafter, the commodities included in the agreements were exported only to the United States or to other destinations of which it approved. Most of the commodities specified in the contracts were minerals, such as copper, tin, lead, zinc, manganese, tungsten, and platinum, but other products were also included, among them rubber, henequen, cinchona, and wool.

In addition to the control of exports, most of the Latin American republics found it necessary to exercise increased control over imports. The shortage of supplies and shipping and the export control system of the United States forced the imposition of stringent import regulations. Although generally employed to aid in the more effective distribution of inadequate supplies, such regulations have occasionally been utilized to afford added protection to domestic industries, particularly those fostered by war-born scarcities.

Shortages induced by declining imports or expanding exports and enlarged purchasing power resulting from increased employment and wages have combined to cause sharply rising prices and living costs in most of the American countries. The inflationary trend in many countries, notably Bolivia, Chile, and Mexico, has caused them to fix prices (especially for commodities of major significance in living costs), and, in a few instances, to ration important commodities in short supply. Although these measures have not always been fully effective in preventing a rise in prices and the growth of "black" markets, they have doubtless been instrumental in checking unbridled inflation.[1]

Because of the war, more attention has been given to the control of production in the Latin American republics than ever before. Restrictions have been imposed on the production of those commodities for which adequate markets or shipping were not available, for example, wheat in Argentina, cotton in Peru, and coffee in Brazil. Special payments, often in the form of government purchases at

[1] See Ch. VI, Price Stabilization Programs in Latin America, for a consideration of price controls and rationing in the Latin American republics.

stabilized prices, have been made to producers. For other commodities, some intended for export to meet the war demand and others for domestic consumption to offset the decline in imports, the Latin American governments have encouraged production. Incentives have included the payment of premiums for increased production, the extension of credits, the gift of seeds, and the loan of equipment and technicians. The necessary wartime expansion of some of these commodities appears likely to create serious problems in the postwar period.

SURPLUS COMMODITIES[1]

In prewar years, a number of commodities were produced in quantities which exceeded the world's effective demand at prices satisfactory to producers. Some of these commodities, such as rubber, quinine, tin, and copper, were controlled almost entirely by a few large producers. Because of their small number, the interested producers could enter into international agreements to control production, allocate markets, and regulate price. Organized primarily to benefit producers, these international combines accorded little attention to the interests of consumers.

Before the war other commodities were also in surplus supply; these included cotton, wheat, coffee, and sugar. Producers of such commodities were numerous and therefore were unable easily to organize for mutual benefit. A number of the Latin American republics were vitally interested in the production and marketing of these crops. Brazil is one of the increasingly important sources of cotton, which is produced also in Peru, Argentina, and Paraguay. Argentina is a large producer and exporter of wheat. Brazil is the world's largest source of coffee, a product in which Colombia, El Salvador, Guatemala, Venezuela, Mexico, and a number of other Latin American republics are also interested. Cuba is the largest producer and exporter of sugar in the Western Hemisphere. The product is also important in the export trade of the Dominican Republic and Peru; Brazil, Argentina, and Mexico are substantial producers of sugar but largely for domestic consumption.

Latin American countries producing coffee have been adversely affected during the war by the loss of their markets in continental

[1] For further analysis of surplus commodities, see Ch. III on War and Postwar Agricultural Problems of Latin America.

Europe. Distress in the industry was alleviated in part by the Inter-American Coffee Agreement, which operated to control exports and prevent ruinous competition. To the extent that the agreement has achieved its objectives, it has proved beneficial to both the producing countries and the United States, although it has probably been instrumental in increasing the price of coffee to United States consumers.

In May, 1937, the principal producing and importing countries concluded the International Sugar Agreement, designed to stabilize the production and international marketing of that commodity. For a 5-year period exports of sugar to the free market[1] were limited, and the principal importing countries agreed that they would not reduce the extent of that market or prevent participation by exporting countries in an increased demand for sugar in that market. The agreement also contained provisions for the control of stocks and for the protection of consuming countries against excessive increases in price.

In 1942, wheat was also made the subject of an international agreement between the United States, Canada, Australia, Argentina, and the United Kingdom. The agreement provided for the control of production and the establishment of export quotas, maximum and minimum stocks, and maximum and minimum prices. All these provisions, however, are being held in abeyance during the war. The signatory countries have agreed to call a second conference in the postwar period, when wider representation will be invited. In the draft convention for which the agreement provides, these countries recognize that a solution of the world wheat problem will require the general reduction of trade barriers for the benefit, not only of producers of wheat, but also of consumers of wheat whose goods move in international trade.

In September, 1939, the principal producing and consuming countries met in Washington, D.C., to consider a proposal for an international cotton agreement to stabilize production and prevent destructive competition. The outbreak of war in the very week that the conference convened prevented the conclusion of any agreement at that time, but it is probable that further efforts will be made after the war.

[1] A term used to designate international trade in sugar which does not receive preferential treatment.

Whether these four agricultural commodities, as well as others, will be produced in quantities exceeding effective demand in the postwar period will depend upon a great many special factors which will operate to determine the extent of that demand. Among these may be mentioned the degree of economic activity in the large industrial nations, particularly the United States and the United Kingdom, the extent and character of the operations to be undertaken by the United Nations Relief and Rehabilitation Administration, the rapidity with which European agriculture and industry are rehabilitated, the type and extent of that rehabilitation, and the commercial policies of the principal trading nations, particularly the United States, the United Kingdom, and the countries of continental Europe. If, in the postwar period, these developments are all favorable to an expansion in purchasing power, it appears likely that, for many commodities, surpluses will disappear. It is uncertain, however, that sufficient increase in demand will be effected to make possible the consumption of all the cotton, wheat, sugar, and coffee that can then be produced. Problems of surpluses, therefore, appear likely to confront certain of the Latin American republics, in addition to other problems of adjustment in the postwar period.

Minerals—Purchase Contracts

During the war the United States has purchased and utilized in its manufacture of munitions large quantities of minerals from the Latin American republics. These minerals, purchased under contracts which forbid their sale to other consumers, were formerly marketed largely in the United Kingdom and continental Europe. Mining operations in the Hemisphere have been expanded to meet the wartime demand of the United States, and prices have increased, although not as much as during the First World War. In the postwar period, therefore, two major problems will confront the industry, (1) the reestablishment of markets and (2) the adjustment of production and prices to peacetime demand.

Before the war, Chile sold its copper chiefly to the United Kingdom and the countries of continental Europe. Important quantities were also shipped to the United States, but these were for refining and export to European markets because the United States import excise tax of 4 cents a pound prevented its domestic consumption. Production in Chile ranged from 114,000 short tons (copper content) in 1932 to 455,000 in 1937, and the price from 5.6 cents a pound to 13.2 cents. Currently, production is at the maximum capacity of about 500,000 tons, all of which is shipped to the United States, where it is purchased at 12 cents a pound, a price very much lower than in 1918, when it averaged 26 cents. Copper is also being secured by the United States from Mexico, Peru, and Cuba.

Faced with the competition of synthetic nitrates, a drastic reorganization of the Chilean nitrate industry, resulting in lower costs and prices, made possible the maintenance of exports at about 1.5 million long tons in the years immediately preceding the war. For a short time the war demand operated to increase exports, which rose to 1.75 million long tons in the fiscal year 1939–1940, but thereafter declined to 1.25 million in 1942–1943. In that year the United States accounted for about 65 per cent of the total. Increased sales to the United States partly offset the loss of European markets, and increased prices operated further to minimize that loss. In the postwar period, however, competition with the synthetic product will be resumed, and adjustments of production, markets, and prices will doubtless be required.

Under the stimulus of war demand, Bolivia has increased its production of tin from about 25,000 long tons in prewar years to about 40,000 tons, approximately one-half of which goes to the United States and the remainder to the United Kingdom, the principal prewar market.[1] The price paid for this metal has also increased from an average of 50 cents a pound in 1939 to 60 cents in 1943. After the war the consumption of tin may be reduced because of recently developed substitutes and economies in utilization. In any case, Bolivia is a high-cost producer of tin, and the ore is complex and expensive to refine. Bolivian production, therefore, will face postwar readjustments, and prices seem likely to decline, unless the International Tin Committee is able to adopt policies sufficiently restrictive to maintain them.

Other minerals are being purchased by the United States from the Latin American republics in greatly increased volume. These include manganese from Brazil, Chile, and Cuba; lead and zinc from Mexico, Argentina, Peru, and Bolivia; mercury and graphite from Mexico; tungsten from Bolivia, Argentina, and Peru; chrome ore from Cuba;

[1] Before the war the United States received its tin from the United Kingdom, which mixed the Bolivian ore with that from Far Eastern sources for smelting.

antimony from Mexico, Bolivia, and Peru; mica from Brazil; and petroleum from Venezuela, Mexico, Colombia, and Peru. Before the war the United States imported practically all its manganese from the Soviet Union, the Gold Coast, and India. Lead and zinc were supplied by domestic mines protected by the tariff. Mercury came from low-cost producers, particularly in Spain and Italy; antimony, tungsten, and graphite were imported from China, chrome ore from Turkey and Africa, and mica from India. It appears likely that these former sources will supply a substantial part of United States requirements in the postwar period. The United States, however, will probably continue to be a large purchaser of petroleum from Western Hemisphere sources because of its declining reserves and its great and increasing demand.

New or Expanded Export Industries

The Latin American republics, assisted by the United States, have expanded their production and exports of certain commodities (other than minerals) that are vital to the prosecution of the war. Among these are rubber, abacá (Manila fiber), henequen, sisal, cinchona (the source of quinine), kapok, balsa wood, and mahogany. Some of these commodities, especially rubber, abacá, and cinchona, are customarily obtained in large volume from sources in the Far East which presumably will resume production after the war. Moreover, two of the products, rubber and cinchona, will then be faced with a measure of competition from synthetic products. Exports from the Latin American countries of certain consumers' goods have also been stimulated by the war, and substantial export industries have been developed, notably in cotton textiles and leather goods. All these industries will be subject to major adjustments in the postwar period, adjustments which will affect the economies of a number of the Latin American republics.

In 1940, world production of rubber was 1,622,000 long tons. Of this amount, 83 per cent came from the Far East, and only 3 per cent from other growing areas; the remainder was obtained from synthetic production (7 per cent) and reclaimed rubber (7 per cent). In that year the United States consumed 648,000 tons, although net imports were 811,000. After the war, the United States will be a large potential producer of synthetic rubber, with an annual plant capacity of about 850,000 long tons, or considerably more than prewar consumption. At that time it appears likely that, despite estimates of enlarged world consumption, the gathering of wild rubber and the cultivation of the cryptostegia vine will be economically unprofitable. Whether plantation rubber from South America will be able to compete with natural rubber from the Far East and the synthetic product from the United States will depend not only on their relative costs of production, but also on the policy of the United States regarding protection for its war-born industry.

Loss of the Philippines turned the attention of the United States to Central America as a source of abacá, the raw material for Manila rope required for marine and other uses where great tensile strength is necessary. In 1942 the Defense Supplies Corporation concluded a number of contracts with the United Fruit Company for the planting and cultivation of abacá in Panama, Costa Rica, Honduras, and Guatemala. These contracts involve about 40,000 acres with an anticipated maximum annual yield of 9,000 tons of fiber, when the plants reach maturity, or about 20 per cent of United States prewar imports. After the war the Central American plantations will face the competition of abacá from the Philippines unless the contracts which expire in 1948 are renewed.[1] Sisal from the Dutch East Indies will also reenter world markets; and this, together with Philippine abacá, will have an effect on the sale of henequen from Mexico and of sisal from Haiti.

Most of the cinchona bark now being gathered in South and Central America is from wild trees. A few nurseries and plantations, however, are being established. Even though such trees may produce bark high in content of quinine and other alkaloids, Hemisphere production will encounter severe competition from the Kina Bureau, the quinine trust of the Dutch East Indies, and, what is more important, from synthetics, notably atabrine, which is now being produced at a cost very much below prewar prices of quinine.

The postwar demand for kapok from the Latin American republics will probably decline because supplies will again be available in the Dutch East Indies, by far the principal source. Production in the Western Hemisphere, however, has never been large; and although it has expanded somewhat during the war, the product is not of great importance in the economy of any of the Hemisphere countries. Currently, balsa wood from Ecuador is used largely in the manu-

[1] Abacá enters the United States free of duty; Manila rope, however, is dutiable.

facture of airplanes, and mahogany from Mexico, Central America, and the island republics, for boat decking. After the war, maintenance of trade in these commodities will be dependent on the development of new uses or the expansion of former ones.

In view of their inability to obtain cotton textiles in required quantities from customary sources (Japan, the United Kingdom, and the United States), the industry has expanded in most of the Latin American republics. Since additional machinery could not be obtained from manufacturers, existing equipment has been operated for two or more shifts. Because of the war, the industry has supplied a larger proportion of domestic requirements than ever before, and exports have increased sharply. This development has been most apparent in Brazil, Mexico, and Argentina, but other countries with sizable industries include Colombia, Peru, Chile, Venezuela, and Cuba. Handicapped frequently by obsolete equipment, it is unlikely that many of the Latin American republics will be able to retain important export markets in the postwar period, and some difficulty may be experienced in maintaining their present domestic markets. Postwar adjustments could be minimized by increased efficiency and the introduction of modern equipment.

New Industries Producing for Domestic Consumption

Within the limits of its capacity restricted by production for war, the United States has encouraged industrialization in the Latin American republics. This it has done with a threefold objective:

1. To increase in these countries the production of materials essential to the prosecution of the war.

2. To conserve productive capacity in the United States and save shipping space by helping some of the Latin American countries to meet their own requirements.

3. To raise the purchasing power of the people in the Latin American republics and thus increase the foreign trade of the United States in the postwar period.

The trend toward industrialization has, of course, been further stimulated by the inability of the Latin American republics to secure supplies essential to their civilian economies from customary sources, by the high domestic prices for products in short supply, and by the large amounts of capital available for investment. A part of these funds is refugee capital from Europe, and a part is derived from the unusually large exports to the United States and the United Kingdom, for which the dollar or pound sterling credits have been largely converted into bank credits in local currencies and are seeking profitable employment.

Many of the new industries are basic to the economy of the country in which they have been established. The Volta Redonda steel plant in Brazil, with an annual capacity of 350,000 tons, will fill a large part of that country's requirements for steel and basic steel products. Mexico is expanding its steel plant at Monterrey and erecting a new one at Altos Hornos. Plans have been advanced to increase the production of steel in Chile, and consideration is being given to the problem in Colombia and other countries. In addition, metal-working industries have been expanded and new ones founded in Brazil, Mexico, Chile, and Argentina.

The cement industry in Mexico has developed plans for new plants, and similar steps are being taken in a number of other countries. The chemical industry has expanded during the war in Mexico, Brazil, Argentina, and Chile. Brazil has nearly completed a paper mill to produce 40,000 tons of newsprint and 40,000 tons of pulp, an important quantity in relation to its prewar consumption of about 190,000 tons of paper and pulp, and other countries are interested in the production of at least a part of the paper they require. A logical development of the chemical and pulp industries is the erection of plants to manufacture rayon fiber. Such plans are being considered in Mexico, Brazil, Argentina, and Chile, stimulated by their inability to secure adequate supplies from the United States. A number of the countries are also encouraging sericulture, and in 1942 Brazil produced 500,000 pounds of silk.

Most of the countries, realizing the importance of power to industrial growth, are concerned with the development of hydroelectric projects; such projects, or plans for them, are under way in Mexico, Brazil, Chile, and Colombia, as well as in other countries. Moreover, coal deposits and oil fields are being reexamined in the search for power. Plans for the development of hydroelectric power frequently include the establishment of irrigation districts so that more land may be brought under cultivation. All these industries and plans for industries, if they are soundly conceived and executed, can add to the national wealth and ease the economic transition from war to peace.

Economic Aids in the Postwar Period

It appears abundantly clear that the Latin American republics, like all nations, will be faced with major economic adjustments in the postwar period. For some, the problems will be graver than for others. There is no single, simple, prompt solution. Many factors, which will vitally affect the transition in the postwar period, are beyond the control of these countries, the welfare of which, like that of all nations, is dependent upon the ultimate adoption of sound international economic policies. Certain things they may do for themselves, but even these offer no immediate panacea; instead, time will be required for their effective application. Each country, however, can make a contribution; and all these contributions, when taken together, can have an appreciable effect. In such a program, United States industry and the United States government can render assistance which will prove profitable to both the United States and the Latin American republics.

In the postwar period, the degree of economic activity in the Latin American republics will be conditioned in large part by international action. The full utilization of the economic resources of any country for the benefit of its people cannot be realized under the disruptive influence of constantly recurring wars. It is therefore essential to the economic development of all nations that a permanent international organization be established with power to ensure international security. The economies of the Latin American republics will also be affected by the activities of the United Nations Relief and Rehabilitation Administration in assisting the war-torn countries of Europe and Asia. If the program is undertaken promptly and is comprehensive in character, it will prove beneficial to the American nations in the transition period and will hasten the restoration of normal channels of trade.

Inasmuch as the Latin American republics are principally producers and exporters of raw materials, the economic activity in the large industrial nations is a matter of primary concern to them. If the large consuming countries, especially the United States and the United Kingdom, adopt policies designed to promote full employment, the effect will be to increase greatly the demand for minerals, foodstuffs, and other raw materials. This, in turn, will provide purchasing power in the American nations that can be utilized in acquiring the manufactured products which the large industrial nations will then be anxious to export.

If the Latin American republics are to achieve the maximum development of their resources, they must have the benefit of stable currencies, the maintenance of which can be assisted by international organization and action. In addition, protection against drastic fluctuations in commodity prices and the disruptive effects of alternate periods of inflation and deflation are essential to sound economic development and growth. This also is a problem which will require international cooperation if a solution is to be effected.

The Latin American republics cannot obtain the maximum expansion of foreign trade unless the countries of the world (including themselves) adopt liberal trade policies and take counsel together regarding the general reduction of tariffs and other barriers to international trade. Should nations again seek to promote policies of economic self-sufficiency, the markets of the world would be either closed or greatly reduced for the commodities which the Latin American republics must export to maintain prosperous national economies. These countries will also be dependent, to a considerable degree, upon the policy of the United States and of other capital-exporting countries toward foreign investments and the development of natural resources outside their own boundaries.

The Latin American republics, however, may take a number of positive steps to promote the full utilization of their economic resources. Industrialization, soundly conceived and executed, will assist in achieving this objective. In most of these countries new industries can be established which will serve to strengthen the various economies, and existing industries can be expanded and their equipment modernized. To the extent that industrial expansion will operate to create better balanced economies and that modernization will contribute to increased efficiency, these countries will be more able to withstand the impact of postwar adjustments.

Moreover, industrialization can be stimulated by permitting foreign capital to participate on equal terms with domestic capital and by granting to foreign technicians the essential rights and privileges accorded nationals. This does not mean the granting of special privileges to foreign interests, but rather the adoption of a policy of nondiscrimination. Foreign investment will also be encouraged by the adoption of sound fiscal policies and the regular servicing of foreign debt.

The economies of the Latin American republics are primarily agricultural, and the export trade of several of them is composed largely of a very few agricultural products. When it can be undertaken economically, the diversification of agriculture in such countries and the improvement of their agricultural techniques and practices will promote a more balanced economy and provide increased stability in the postwar period.

Private industry alone cannot be expected fully to develop the natural resources of any country. Various types of public works must necessarily become the concern of governments. The economies of the Latin American republics can be enriched by the development of hydroelectric and irrigation projects to increase the supply of power and land. Transportation is also an important part of any program to expand the utilization of natural resources; adequate highways are essential to the improvement of undeveloped areas and the movement of goods. But resources cannot be fully developed or machinery efficiently operated unless the education and health of the people are adequate to permit it. Like most countries, the Latin American republics have a major task in promoting public health and sanitation, adequate housing, and an expanded educational program.

Chapter III

War and Postwar Agricultural Problems of Latin America

by L. A. WHEELER

WHILE the agriculture of Latin America has its own problems, which are many and varied, those which are most important can best be considered in their relation to the agricultural economy of the rest of the world. Even under a policy of extreme hemispheric self-sufficiency, Latin American countries could not escape the impact of global agricultural problems.

It is these broader aspects of Latin American agriculture that are to be considered in this chapter. Emphasis will be placed on commodities rather than on countries, as economic problems are not limited by political boundaries. Other chapters in this volume will treat of the economies of individual countries and will refer to the role of agriculture in these economies.

The General Situation before the War

Before taking up the war and postwar problems of Latin America it is necessary to have in mind certain general aspects of the prewar situation.

The first of these general aspects concerns the position of the Western Hemisphere as a whole and of Latin America in particular as a surplus producer of agricultural products. For more than three centuries the Western Hemisphere as a whole has produced certain agricultural commodities over and above its own requirements. In the years just preceding the war, the great surplus agricultural products of the Western Hemisphere as a whole were cotton, wheat, coffee, sugar, tobacco, and chilled and frozen meat. In addition, there were usually large net exports of certain fruits, particularly citrus fruits, bananas, apples, and pears.

The only great staple products in which the Hemisphere was deficient were rubber, edible vegetable oils, soft fibers, tea, and rice. Rubber and rice together with cacao, cinchona, and vanilla were among the products formerly exported; but, with the development of production in the Far East and Africa, the Hemisphere had for many years been on a net import basis.

While Latin America as a whole in prewar years produced larger quantities of agricultural products than it consumed, many individual countries were far from self-sufficient, and all these countries were net importers of some farm commodities. Even Argentina, the most self-sufficient of all, was deficient in tobacco and certain fruits and undoubtedly would have imported farm products in even greater volume and variety except for substantial restrictions on their importation. Tropical America imported large quantities of wheat flour, lard, and other Temperate Zone products, but there, too, imports would have been larger if import restrictions had been less.

In Latin America generally, the characteristic situation was one of basic cash crops selling in foreign markets, with a low standard of consumption of food and fibers. The most important exception to this rule was in Argentina, where food consumption, particularly of meat, was very high on any basis of comparison. Even there, however, consumption was characterized by lack of variety.

A second general aspect of the prewar situation concerns the governmental policies in Latin American countries, affecting agriculture. In view of the numerous surplus commodities, together with the generally low standard of consumption, it might be supposed that Latin American countries would have been pursuing in prewar years policies calculated to liberalize and expand international trade. But this was hardly the case. Like countries in other parts of the world practically all Latin American countries pursued policies of high restrictions on imports, usually in the form of import duties. While it was ordinarily claimed that such duties were imposed primarily for purposes of revenue, the duties were often, if not usually, too high to provide a maximum revenue return. The conclusion is inescapable that the import restrictions were directed primarily at building up national agricultural production even though a large part of Latin America, lying within the tropics, is not suited to the economic production of a long list of Temperate Zone crops.

To a large extent this policy of attempting to build up agricultural production through high import barriers was self-defeating. This was true particularly in those tropical countries which endeavored to expand production of such commodities as wheat and cotton in areas where the soil and climate were not well adapted to such crops. The main result was to increase the prices at which the products were sold in the domestic market and thereby to diminish total consumption.

Unlike the generally applied policy of using protective import duties as a means of building up domestic production of commodities on a deficit basis, there was no generally applied policy with respect to products on a surplus basis. There are, however, a number of conspicuous examples of attempts on the parts of individual governments to deal with surplus situations.

Outstanding among these was the Brazilian valorization scheme for coffee. A second outstanding example was the restriction on the grinding of sugar cane in Cuba. While both the Brazilian coffee and Cuban sugar control schemes were effective to some extent in raising world prices of these commodities, or at any rate in preventing them from falling as much as they otherwise would, one of the outstanding results of these unilateral policies was to give encouragement to the expansion of production of the same crops in other parts of the world. It is interesting in this connection to note that at the same time Brazil was destroying coffee the Venezuelan government was granting export subsidies in order to permit its coffee industry to compete in world markets. It may also be recalled that at the time Cuba was limiting the grinding of sugar cane various other countries in the Hemisphere, including the United States, were pursuing policies designed to make their countries more self-sufficient in respect to sugar.

A somewhat different kind of governmental program to deal with surplus situations is found in the Argentine government program of supporting prices of corn, wheat, and flaxseed. This program took the form of guaranteed prices to producers, with losses made up out of government funds. The Argentine program was noteworthy in two respects. In the first place, the program did not, as a practical matter, involve any governmentally imposed restriction of production. In the second place, the prices which the government agreed to guarantee were, in general, considerably under the prices at which the governments of other important exporting countries were attempting to maintain prices and were not generally at a level sufficient to induce any significant expansion of production.

A third general aspect of the prewar agricultural situation in Latin America concerns the direction of its foreign trade. In general, the export trade of Latin America has been directed toward Europe. The basic reason for this is, of course, that the great surplus-producing region in Latin America is in the South Temperate Zone, including Argentina, southern Brazil, Uruguay, and Chile; and the products of this zone are of a kind directly competitive with the products of the North Temperate Zone, including the United States and Canada, which were producing many of the same products also for export. There was no basis for a large exchange of these competitive products within the Hemisphere. The facts are that certain Latin American products, such as meat, wheat, and cotton, actually displaced a considerable quantity of United States exports to European markets.

On the other hand, there was a very considerable intrahemisphere trade in the products of the tropical and subtropical zone, consisting mainly of imports from the American tropics into the United States. Among these products the outstanding ones were coffee, of which the United States absorbed more than one-half the total Latin American exports, and sugar, for which the United States was by far the greatest market.

The General Situation during the War

With this dependence on European markets the outbreak of war in Europe threatened to be a major disaster for Latin America. As the war spread to the Far East, the submarine menace increased and the shipping shortage was intensified. A second preoccupation of the tropical Latin American countries was the danger of a shortage of some foods ordinarily imported from North America.

Contrary to general expectations, however, production and market shifts during the war, particularly in respect to increased demand on the part of the United States for certain products, have prevented much of the anticipated distress. For example, Cuba was not able to ship all its sugar crops during 1942 and 1943 because of shipping difficulties, but the entire crops were purchased by the United States at prices well above the average of those of the preceding 10 years.

Cuban tobacco has sold at high prices with no interruption in shipment. Banana producers have suffered severe losses, but these have been compensated in part by shifts to other crops and the employment of labor on defense projects. A rapid development of textile manufacturing in Latin America has absorbed much of the cotton surplus, and a considerable volume of Brazilian cotton has been exported in spite of the shipping shortage. Brazil has been unable to market all its coffee, but the producers in the Caribbean area and Central America have been able to meet most of their marketing quotas under the commodity agreement. Peruvian cotton has been purchased by the United States and stored for postwar needs.

Of all the countries of Latin America, Argentina has felt the loss of prewar markets most, but this loss has been confined almost entirely to cereal products—corn, wheat, and flaxseed. To some extent the loss of markets for cereals has been compensated for by their use as fuel to replace coal, which Argentina has been unable to import because of shipping difficulties.

EMERGENCY FOOD SITUATIONS

The fear of food shortage has, fortunately, not been realized except in isolated instances and for temporary periods. Perhaps the most serious shortages have been of wheat flour in the Central American countries. In several instances shipments from the United States have failed to arrive until local supplies were nearly, if not quite, exhausted. Cuba, Haiti, the Dominican Republic, and Venezuela have also experienced temporary shortages of other products usually supplied by the United States. Substitute products were, however, available, and there was no acute distress. The most serious aspect of the food situation in the Caribbean area has been the inflationary tendency, which has raised the cost of living and retarded any possible advance toward better nutrition.

Another aspect of the wartime agricultural situation to which reference should be made concerns attempts to increase production of certain strategic nonfood products, such as rubber, cinchona, and insecticidal plants and fibers. These efforts have been strongly supported and encouraged by the United States with a view to securing supplies from Latin America to take the place of supplies formerly received from territory in the Far East now occupied by the Japanese. While these efforts have not yet resulted in any marked commercial production of these products in Latin America, there are numerous local instances where commercial production has already begun and more cases where a basis for future production has been laid. Certain examples which may be cited include experimentation in the production of roselle (kenaf) fiber in Cuba, abacá in Central America, cinchona in the Andean countries and Guatemala, and rubber in Haiti and Ecuador.

On the whole, the shifts in agriculture in Latin America resulting from war conditions have been of nothing like the same proportions as have occurred, for example, in the United States, Canada, and the United Kingdom. Nevertheless, shifts have occurred to a degree sufficient to raise a number of postwar problems.

Postwar Readjustments

The extent to which agricultural readjustments will be necessary in Latin America in the postwar years will depend to a considerable extent upon the time the war ends in Europe and in the Far East. Any evaluation of these possible readjustments necessarily presupposes certain predictions, a timetable of future events.

It is generally assumed that Europe will be freed from Nazi domination a year or more in advance of the final defeat of Japan. In Europe it is probable that at least 1 or 2 years will be required after an armistice before normal agricultural production is restored. In the Far East, at least a year will be required after the termination of hostilities before full agricultural production can be achieved.

During the early reconstruction period there will be a market for all the food and fibers that Latin American countries can produce and ship. This period, however, will be comparatively short because purchasing power will be limited and relief funds will not be available indefinitely, and also because agricultural production will revive rather quickly as soon as the armies are disbanded and the peasants can return to their farms. After perhaps 2 or 3 years, European import requirements will be sharply reduced and about the same time large supplies of vegetable oils, tapioca, sugar, and coarse fibers probably will become available in the Far East. This unfavorable market situation could coincide with the maximum agricultural production in the Western Hemisphere.

Every effort is now being made to increase agricultural production in the Americas to provide for the needs of postwar reconstruction.

The products of Western Hemisphere farms will certainly be needed and needed quickly after the liberation of Europe, and these products should be made available. But a catastrophic collapse of markets at the peak of production would have very serious repercussions.

On the other hand, the timing may be different. Europe may be torn by internal conflicts for months or years after the defeat of Germany, with consequent disruption of production plans. This would mean reduced demand for overseas products, but they would be needed for a longer period. Then the Far East may not have any large exportable surpluses for some years. The war in the Pacific area may last 2 or 3 years after the collapse of Germany, and the productive capacity of the Far East may be so reduced that it could be restored only after many years. Still another possibility is that under more favorable conditions the standard of living in the Far East may be raised to such an extent that the products of East Indian and East Asian agriculture may be needed and consumed in the Far East, leaving little for export to Europe.

In view of all these uncertainties, producers should be prepared to make quick adjustments to changed conditions, and they should never become too optimistic about the future of any particular crop. Governments should also be prepared to assist their farmers in case of unexpected loss of markets. In all countries farmers should be encouraged to diversify production so that the loss of one crop would not be an overwhelming disaster.

POSTWAR COMMODITY PROBLEMS

In the event that European markets are sharply curtailed in the course of 3 to 5 years, all the agricultural products produced in Latin America for export will be seriously affected. In the case of some of these products there will be no more than a reversion to the chronic surplus situation which so often obtained in prewar years. In the case of others, especially those the production of which has been stimulated by government aid to meet wartime needs, the situation may be far worse than before the war. The probable position of the various export commodities in the postwar world will be examined in some detail in the following pages.

WHEAT. While wheat is an important crop in several Latin American countries, Argentina is the only large exporter. It is one of the four great wheat-exporting countries, the others being Canada,

Australia, and the United States. In recent years the volume of Argentine wheat exports has usually been second only to that of Canada. Since 1925, Argentine wheat production has averaged about 240 million bushels yearly, of which nearly 60 per cent has been exported.

During the war, wheat production in Argentina has been fully maintained despite some reduction in area and the loss of most of the overseas markets. Above average yields have been obtained in 3 of the past 4 years. The result has been that, while fairly substantial quantities of Argentine wheat and flour have been exported to near-by countries and certain quantities to Europe, and also large quantities used for nonfood purposes, notably fuel, there has been an accumulation of large stocks of wheat in that country.

This accumulation has a favorable, as well as an unfavorable, aspect. On the favorable side is the fact that Argentina will be in a position to participate in the supplying of large requirements that may be demanded as European countries are liberated from Axis occupation. The Argentine government has recently indicated that it was prepared to make available a total of 200,000 tons of wheat for relief.

The unfavorable aspect of the situation lies in the fact that after the immediate postwar relief requirements are met the world position on wheat is likely to revert to one of excessive supplies. When that time arrives, the position of Argentine wheat in world markets will depend, on the one hand, upon the extent to which wheat production is maintained in the great deficit area—the British Isles and western Europe—by tariffs and subsidies and, on the other hand, upon the production and price policies of the governments of the other exporting countries.

Fortunately in this case a considerable step has been taken toward bringing about a closer balance between world wheat supplies and requirements than existed prior to the present war. In 1942 an interim wheat agreement was accepted by the governments of Argentina, Australia, Canada, the United States, and the United Kingdom, which looks toward a comprehensive world agreement after the close of hostilities. Agreement has already been reached, however, on one important feature of this comprehensive arrangement, *viz.*, the shares of the total market which will be allotted to the principal exporting countries. The Argentine share is placed at 25 per cent, as compared with 40 per cent for Canada, 19 per cent for Australia, and 16 per cent for the United States. Provision is also made for agreement as to the level of prices at which wheat will be sold in the world market. In the particular case of wheat, therefore, progress has been made toward preventing cutthroat competition in world markets after the war.

CORN. Corn is also an important crop in the trade of Latin American countries, but here again Argentina is the only important exporter. The wartime history of corn there has been similar to that of wheat. Production has been maintained, except in 1943, when a serious drought and reduced plantings led to the smallest crop in many years, but exports have been very small. Millions of bushels have been burned as fuel. A large exportable surplus seems certain to be coming in from the crop harvested in 1944, and there seems no reason to doubt that Argentina will continue to be the principal supplier of world markets. If strong efforts were to be made after the war both in the United Kingdom and western Europe to expand the production of dairy, poultry, and other livestock products, corn may again have an important export outlet. Corn is a relatively cheap and efficient feed which cannot be economically produced in countries with a short growing season, and Argentina is undoubtedly one of the world's most efficient producers.

COTTON. In the world of cotton one of the outstanding developments of recent years has been the rapid rise of exports from Brazil. As recently as the period 1925–1929 Brazil produced only 500,000 bales of cotton, ranking at that time sixth among cotton-producing countries, and was of negligible importance as an exporter. In 1940 Brazil produced 2½ million bales, ranked fourth as a world producer, and exported over 1 million bales. This development of Brazilian exports has been particularly significant for the United States since it presented for the first time serious competition in the world markets for the upland type of cotton of medium staple length, the kind of cotton of which the United States traditionally had had almost a monopoly. Of the other Latin American countries Mexico and Argentina produce upland cotton, while Peru is a producer of other types less competitive to the cotton produced generally in the United States. Several other Latin American republics and the British West Indies produce some cotton but do not figure appreciably in world trade.

Since the outbreak of war Brazilian cotton exports have declined, but a part of the loss has been absorbed by exports to other Latin

American countries and for a time by exports to Canada. Furthermore, the consumption of cotton in Brazil itself has been substantially increased, and Brazil has become an exporter of cotton textiles, contributing not only to near-by countries but to South Africa and other overseas countries which in prewar years imported textiles from Europe. For the first few years after the war the prospects for Brazilian cotton producers seem very good, but beyond these few years it is doubtful if cotton production can be maintained in present volume on a profitable basis. Competition from other producing areas and, what is even more serious, competition from synthetic fibers may be expected at least to limit the expansion of the Brazilian cotton area.

As for other Latin American countries, Argentina is now in a phase of expansion and may be expected to promote further production increases both to supply the demands of its own consumers and for export. In Peru, production is rather definitely limited by the available area of suitable irrigated land; but in Mexico expansion has been proceeding rapidly in the face of contracting world consumption. Given a return in postwar years to a level of world consumption of cotton approaching that of 1937, Latin America as a whole might look forward confidently to a continuation of cotton production in something like the present volume, but further expansion in the immediate postwar years would probably be unwise.

The future world outlook for cotton is somewhat similar to that for wheat. In fact, prospects are even poorer for the maintenance of a large world trade in cotton. On the one hand, there has been a substantial development of cotton production in some parts of the world which formerly relied on imports. Cases in point are to be found in Russia, China, and certain Latin American countries as already referred to. But still more important is the development of substitute synthetic fibers, particularly that type of rayon known as staple fiber. Such substitutes have been produced in greatly increased quantities in European countries since a few years before the war. Certainly considerable significance must be attached to the fact that during the years of the war the countries of continental Europe, which together provided the largest of the world's cotton import markets, have had to get along without cotton and have relied upon synthetic substitutes.

In the face of this situation, however, there has as yet been little progress in the direction of reaching any international understanding as regards production and trade in cotton. One attempt was made in this direction in the fall of 1939 at a meeting in Washington of cotton-exporting countries, but this attempt had to be abandoned because of the outbreak of war in Europe. There is, however, fundamentally a strong need for international collaboration in cotton in the face of the general threat of competition from synthetic substitutes, and in the face also of direct intervention of national governments in the support of prices and regulation of production and trade in most of the producing countries of the world.

COFFEE. Coffee has been the "green gold" of Latin America. In tropical America it has traditionally been the great cash crop and the basis of fortunes of the estate owners. Brazil alone supplies half the coffee entering international trade, and Latin America as a whole around 85 per cent.

Coffee production, however, has not been consistently profitable. The demand has always been strong, and consumption has increased steadily, with only slight declines in periods of depression, but production has more than kept pace with demand. The difficulties of the coffee industry in Brazil and the measures taken to support prices have already been referred to. Suffice it to say that long-continued price supports finally broke down during the depression. While exports from Brazil were restricted, Colombia, El Salvador, the Dutch East Indies, and other countries took advantage of the situation and rapidly increased production. Under the Inter-American Coffee Agreement completed in 1941 the industry seems likely to survive the impact of the war in fairly good condition. When European markets are reopened, it is quite possible that there will be a period of prosperity. Whether or not this prosperity continues, however, depends upon whether there will be sufficient control to hold the various surplus-producing countries in line. There is still a capacity for coffee production in most of the countries participating in the Inter-American Coffee Agreement far in excess of postwar demand. Failure to cooperate in an international control scheme would probably result in cutthroat competition, which Brazil, alone, would be helpless to control.

CACAO. Cacao, native to the coastlands of the Gulf of Mexico and Tropical South America, makes a substantial contribution to the economy of several Latin American countries. It is the principal agricultural export of Ecuador, second only to coffee in Venezuela, and third after coffee and cotton in Brazil.

Prior to the twentieth century, Latin America supplied most of the cacao entering world trade, but extensive production in West Africa has overshadowed Latin America's position. During the immediate prewar years, about two-thirds the world's cacao exports originated in West Africa and one-third in Latin America. Ecuador, Venezuela, Costa Rica, and Nicaragua, however, continue to supply most of the world's fine cacao, as West African production is confined to ordinary grades.

Prewar surpluses of cacao were not excessive, as was the case with coffee; and while world production during the war has been in excess of consumption requirements in the United and neutral nations, there has been no serious surplus problem in Latin America, since its proximity to the United States has enabled movement of surpluses. World supplies in the immediate postwar period may be short of consumption requirements; and if Europe is able to finance cacao imports, the industry will have a period of prosperity. Continued prosperity in Latin America's cacao industry, however, may depend upon the creation and effective operation of a marketing program in which the major producing countries would participate. In the absence of such a program, it is quite possible that the combined production of West Africa and Latin America will be far in excess of effective world demand.

SUGAR. In Latin America, Cuba leads in sugar production and trade. Brazil ranks second, followed by Argentina, the Dominican Republic, Peru, and Mexico. The production of British West Indies taken together is usually about equal to that of the Dominican Republic or Peru. Farther down on the list are British Guiana, the French West Indies, Colombia, Guatemala, Haiti, Venezuela, and Ecuador. In exports of sugar, Cuba ranks first not only in Latin America but in the world, while, in this hemisphere, the Dominican Republic and Peru are second and third. Brazil, Argentina and Mexico produce mainly for their own domestic markets.

International trade in sugar, like that in coffee, has been controlled by a commodity agreement. In addition, imports into the United States, the leading importing country, are limited in peacetime by marketing quotas, which in turn tend to limit the grindings of sugar cane in Cuba. The United States does, however, allow a tariff preference to Cuba. This has the effect of channeling about two-thirds the Cuban exports to the United States, while those of the Dominican Republic, Peru, and the British colonies go mainly to the United Kingdom. Under war conditions the United States has purchased the entire exportable sugar crop of Cuba for the past 3 years, while the Dominican and Haitian crops were purchased in 1942 by the United Kingdom and in 1943 and 1944 by the United States.

Cane sugar has some of the characteristics of an industrial product. The output is measured by the grindings of cane and production of sugar at the *central*, or mill, rather than by the growth of cane. Production thus may be limited by prospective markets and a considerable part of the production cost can be eliminated when markets fail, simply by shortening the grinding season. As in the case of most export crops the immediate postwar market is expected to be good, with a decline in demand later as European beet sugar areas and Far Eastern cane sugar areas resume prewar levels of production. If an international sugar agreement is in effective operation, postwar conditions in the Latin American sugar areas will probably be much the same as in recent prewar years.

If international collaboration in world sugar production and marketing does not continue, a chaotic scramble for world markets within a few years after the end of the war is to be anticipated.

RICE. Although a rather minor crop in the Western Hemisphere, rice is produced in every Latin American country and is consumed in relatively large quantities in practically every country. The production and consumption of rice in Latin America have been expanding over the past two decades, and the war has greatly accentuated this trend.

During the relatively prosperous period 1926–1930 the net imports of rice into Latin American countries averaged over 1 billion pounds a year. Of the 20 American republics only Brazil, Ecuador, and Mexico during that time produced more than enough rice for their own requirements. During the depression years of the 1930's, however, many of these countries increased their import duties on rice to encourage national self-sufficiency. As a result the net imports of rice into Latin America by 1939 had fallen to 600 million pounds.

With the occupation by Japan of the great rice-exporting countries of the Far East, Burma, Thailand, and French Indo-China, the main sources of Latin American imports were closed. As a result, efforts to increase domestic production were redoubled. The intensive submarine activities in the Atlantic in 1941 and 1942 gave a further stimulus for expanded production. By 1943 net imports into Latin American countries were less than 150 million pounds, and 13 countries were producing sufficient rice to meet their own requirements. Among these were Argentina, Chile, and Colombia, which previously had been, with Cuba, the largest importing countries of Latin America.

The consumption of rice has also been increasing in Latin America but not so rapidly as production. The larger consumption has been due in part, no doubt, to an increase in population; but the main reason, in view of the fact that rice has always been a staple item of diet in most Latin American countries, is the increased purchasing power resulting from war conditions.

This reversal of the position of Latin America from a net importer to a net exporter of rice when taken with an expansion in the production and exports of rice in the United States presents the possibility of a serious postwar surplus problem. No doubt the demand for Western Hemisphere rice will continue strong until after major European relief needs have been met and possibly for a year or two after the great surplus rice areas of the Far East have been liberated. When that time comes, large surpluses of rice from Burma, Thailand, and French Indo-China will soon be offered on world markets at low prices. Not only will that development greatly reduce the export possibilities for Western Hemisphere rice, but it will also raise questions in many countries as to the expediency of increasing import duties or otherwise restricting the importation of rice from the Far East, in order to maintain rice production at somewhere near wartime levels.

FATS AND OILS. Fats and oils production and consumption problems in Latin America are directly related to those of the United States, Canada, and other parts of the world. Events of the past 4 years have greatly enhanced the difficulties of marketing surpluses, such as that of Argentine flaxseed, and of importing fats and oils from other continents. But the outstanding feature of the fats and oils situation of Latin America, as of the Western Hemisphere as a whole, has been the marked expansion of production of oilseeds in surplus- and deficit-producing countries alike.

Following Pearl Harbor and the Japanese conquest of the rich vegetable-oil-bearing areas in the Far East, the United Nations, and the United States in particular, soon realized that the supplies of fats and oils would shortly become inadequate. The Western Hemisphere, prior to the outbreak of the war in the Pacific, had been importing about 2½ billion pounds of vegetable oils and oilseeds, primarily from the Far East.

Beginning in the spring of 1942, plans to expand oilseed production were developed in several areas in the Western Hemisphere. In the United States, oilseed acreage goals were revised upward, and price-support measures were announced. Canada encouraged increased production of flaxseed, soybeans, sunflower seed, and rapeseed. United States government agencies explored the possibilities of obtaining larger quantities of oilseeds in several Latin American countries. A program for increased production was inaugurated in Brazil, which has resulted in a substantial increase in castor bean output and some increase in the peanut production. The results obtained from expanding the output of other oilseeds and oil-nut crops have been somewhat disappointing, because of local labor shortages and transportation difficulties. Several Latin American countries initiated oilseed expansion programs of their own in order to provide in part for imports formerly obtained from abroad. In 1943, the United States agreed to buy the Argentine surplus of sunflower and peanut oils at specified prices. This information was widely disseminated in the rural areas of Argentina, with the result that record acreages were planted to these two crops.

It is difficult to determine how far these expansion programs have been effective, but a tremendous expansion in production is known to have occurred in peanuts, soybeans, and flaxseed in the United States, flaxseed in Canada, and sunflower seed and peanuts in Argentina. In addition, oilseed acreages have increased in Brazil, Mexico, and several of the smaller Latin American countries. Expanded hog production, primarily in the United States and to some extent in Canada and Argentina, has materially increased lard production.

The only surplus problem in the field of fats and oils that has existed in Latin America during the war has been of flaxseed in Argentina. Stocks of flaxseed in that country began accumulating soon after the outbreak of the war in Europe. With the shortage of coal and oil and of corn from the crop of 1942–1943, the Argentine government authorized the use of flaxseed for fuel. This drastic measure resulted in some decrease in the huge surplus during 1943.

The demand for Latin American fats and oils should continue strong until toward the close of the major European relief-feeding period, and for some months after the Philippines and the Dutch East Indies have been liberated. It may take at least 2 years to restore normal livestock and oilseed production in Europe and probably two seasons before whaling operations will result in prewar production levels.

After normal world fats and oils production has been restored, the demand for such products will continue strong as long as the leading consuming countries remain prosperous. The chances are, however, that this demand will taper off within a few years. If such a decrease in demand should come at a time when Latin American fats and oilseeds are at a high peak of production, these commodities will be forced to a lower price level. Even with continued prosperity, competition from the surplus areas of Asia and Africa and the availability of Mediterranean olive oil will tend to decrease the demand for Latin American oils and oil materials.

MEAT. One of the outstanding developments of world trade in the last 50 years has been the expansion in meat exports. This expansion may be attributed primarily to the introduction of refrigerated shipping around the turn of the century. This development made it possible for meat to be shipped long distances from the Southern Hemisphere to industrial Europe, primarily the British Isles.

Argentina was the principal export beneficiary. By 1910 Argentine beef had entirely replaced beef cattle shipments from the United States to Britain; and frozen mutton and lamb from Argentina, as well as from Australia and New Zealand, became important commodities in international trade. Argentina has always led in beef exports and among the Latin American countries has also been the chief source of frozen lamb and mutton. Uruguay and Brazil have also shared in the beef trade and Uruguay and Chile in that of mutton and lamb.

Probably the outstanding feature of the export trade of Argentina and other Latin American countries in meat has been the predominant importance of the United Kingdom as a market. More than 70 per cent of all the exports of beef and 90 per cent of all the exports of mutton and lamb from South America in the years immediately preceding the war were destined for the British market.

During the depression the demand in the British market, as well as the much less important markets in continental Europe, seriously declined. An interesting development growing out of this situation was the conclusion in 1937 of an international beef-marketing arrangement which became known as the International Beef Conference. This arrangement was brought into operation under the leadership of the British government to regulate the importation and prices of beef brought into the United Kingdom from Southern Hemisphere countries and Eire. The other participants, in addition to the United Kingdom and Eire, were Argentina, Australia, Brazil, New Zealand, and Uruguay. The primary function of the conference was to get agreement upon the quantities of each category of beef which each country could bring into the United Kingdom during each quarter of the year. The rules of the conference required unanimity, and during the 3 years of its operation it never failed finally to achieve such unanimity. No doubt this was due largely to the fact that the United Kingdom government retained its freedom to regulate imports unilaterally in the event agreement was not reached. But the conference did have a great advantage over such unilateral action in providing a common forum at which every participating country was given an opportunity to be heard.

Since the outbreak of war in Europe there has been a considerable revival in the exportation of meat from South America to the United Kingdom. Since 1940 the British government has purchased under contract all the South American meat that could be shipped. Since 1942 this procedure has continued under a joint agreement between the British Ministry of Food and the United States War Food Administration, with the understanding that such quantities of canned meat as may be needed by the United States armed forces will be made available by the Ministry of Food. The United States, as a matter of policy, has been importing no meat from South America other than the canned meat needed by the armed forces. One reason for this is that the United States during the war has resumed large exports of meat, primarily pork, to the United Kingdom. Under these conditions there would be a considerable loss in shipping efficiency if the United States were to import meat from South America and then export its own production overseas. There is, however, another deterrent to imports of meat from South America into the United

States: our quarantine restrictions prevent the importation of fresh meat into the United States from any country in which foot-and-mouth disease prevails; but foot-and-mouth disease is prevalent in all the South American meat-exporting countries: in Argentina, Uruguay, Brazil, and Chile.

The probable position of South American meat in world markets after the war is difficult to appraise. The chances are, however, that these meat exports from the Southern Hemisphere to western Europe will not expand in postwar years beyond the higher levels reached during the 1920's, and they may be substantially lower. This possibility is suggested by the fact that European countries will undoubtedly attempt to direct their agriculture more definitely into the production of livestock than was the case before the war. From an economic point of view there is much to be said for greater production of livestock in Europe, and less emphasis should be laid on the production of such crops as wheat and other grain which can be produced much more effectively in countries overseas, including, incidentally, Argentina. On the other hand, it is conceivable that industrial production and the standard of living in western Europe could be maintained in postwar years substantially above the more prosperous years between the First and Second World War. In that case there would undoubtedly be a demand for meat considerably in excess of the possibilities of domestic European production to supply.

FRUITS AND VEGETABLES. Fruits of one kind or another are produced for foreign markets in nearly every country of Latin America, and in Mexico and Cuba a wide variety of fresh vegetables are produced for winter markets in the United States. Because of their perishability, these fresh products present special marketing and transportation problems, and the market itself is characterized by extreme elasticity.

Of the tropical fruits, the banana is by far the most important in export trade. In prewar years the banana trade was dominated by two great companies, one American and the other British. These companies maintained plantations throughout the Caribbean area and operated great fleets of refrigerator ships. Of all the strictly tropical fruits, the banana alone has become so inexpensive in northern markets that it can no longer be classed as a luxury, but rather as a staple food. The war has greatly limited the banana trade in the United States and has practically eliminated imports into the United

Kingdom. After the war, however, it may be expected to revive rapidly and continue to grow in volume.

Most of the other exported fruits of tropical America, particularly limes, grapefruit, pineapples, and avocados, have to meet competition in United States markets either from the Southern States and California or from Hawaii. Their production is, however, important, particularly in the Caribbean area. Other tropical fruits either cannot successfully be shipped to northern markets or are excluded from the United States by quarantine regulations. There is always the possibility, with the development of air transportation, that a greater variety of tropical fruits may be made available in the United States and Europe.

A promising prewar development was that of deciduous fruit exports from Argentina and Chile to United States markets. These fruits, mainly grapes and pears, were marketed in the season when few northern-grown fruits were available. There was always some competition with domestic pears which have been held in cold storage, but there was a rapidly growing market for the fruit from the far south, and in postwar years this trade will undoubtedly be revised. Another important development before the war concerned the exportation of Brazilian oranges to Europe, where they competed with shipments from the United States and South Africa.

The winter vegetable trade from Cuba to the east coast cities of the United States, and from Mexico to the west coast and middle western states, had grown rapidly in the years before the war. During the war, the Cuban trade has faced serious transportation difficulties, but after the war this trade will undoubtedly again become important.

Here then at last we find a group of products which, given reasonably satisfactory world economic conditions, may be expected to enter increasingly into international trade. But even here the market at any particular point will not be unlimited, and the possibility of serious temporary gluts in particular markets resulting from overshipments from many sources of supply should not be ignored.

RUBBER, CINCHONA, AND INSECTICIDES. Production of each of these strategically important products in Latin America has been stimulated by guaranteed higher prices and by technical and financial assistance from the United States, designed to establish wartime sources of these commodities virtually "at any cost." Nevertheless, with the initial, high-cost stages well behind them, these countries may be in a position to compete with the older established areas of production in other regions, when and if these areas reenter world markets after the war. The newer production of Latin America may have one important, even if temporary, advantage. To a considerable extent this new production is being started with recently developed high-yielding strains. The importance of this fact in cases of tree crops such as rubber and cinchona should not be minimized. It takes 5 to 7 years for such trees to get into production, but once production has started the yield should be much higher than the average production of the older established plantations in the Far East. The ability of the American tropics to compete with the Far East in postwar markets will depend to a considerable extent on having high-yielding stock. But it also depends on the possibility of establishing commercial production on what amounts to a family-farm basis. This would involve individual families having their own plots of trees and, in addition, sufficient land to permit the production of a large part of their food requirements.

There is, however, an additional serious element in the postwar situation. This concerns the development of more or less satisfactory synthetic substitutes. In the case of synthetic rubber, for example, a substantial expansion in productive capacity has been developed both in the United States and in Europe. Relative costs of production of the natural and synthetic commodities, coupled with postwar policies in consuming countries with respect to the protection of the synthetic industries, will play a major role in determining the size and extent of the world surpluses of these materials.

The extent to which synthetics may replace the natural products will be determined not only by cost differentials but also by the uses to which these products are put. With respect to rubber, for example, at the present stage of development some natural rubber apparently must be mixed with the synthetic for the more important uses such as the manufacture of heavy-duty truck and bus tires. For some other uses, new elastomers have been developed which provide entirely satisfactory substitutes for natural rubber. Quinine seems to have certain natural advantages for the treatment of malaria over its new chemical competitor, atabrine. The latter is not universally suitable for self-treatment, particularly as certain individuals seem to have a natural or acquired intolerance to the drug. In the insecticidal field, certain types of insects as yet can be adequately controlled only by the organic insecticides.

There is likely to be a greater aggregate demand for all these products, both natural and synthetic, than before the war. World markets for automobiles, other rubber-borne equipment, and a wide variety of other uses will probably see great expansion. Similarly, the use of quinine will be greatly increased by a greater incidence of malaria, as a consequence of the exposure of soldiers and civilians to the disease in malarial regions and of a wider and deeper concern with public health. For similar reasons, insecticides specific for mosquitoes and flies will find wider distribution. Insecticides for agricultural uses will depend on the level of agricultural production, but it should be recalled that organic insecticides, in the usual concentrations, were gaining in popularity before the war because of their effectiveness and nontoxicity to warm-blooded animals.

From the standpoint of national self-interest and security, as well as of healthy competition in world production, there is much to be said for a policy that gives Latin America at least equal opportunity with the other areas of production for access to the technical knowledge, capital resources, and markets of the United States. Certain areas of Latin America, at least, apparently can compete favorably under such equal treatment. Certain advantages, in terms of trade and political stability, may be expected to result from a greater world dispersion of the production of these products. Such dispersion would tend to prevent any one area or coalition from using a position of dominance for political or economic exploitation of the consuming nations.

General Postwar Considerations

It is evident from the preceding review that Latin America has great and varied resources for the production of agricultural commodities. It may safely be assumed that these resources, lying within both the Temperate and Tropical zones, will continue for many years to be capable of producing far more of most of those commodities than will be needed within the region. In other words, Latin America will continue to have large surpluses for export.

Will world demand for these surplus products be sufficiently great to permit the full utilization of existing resources in production for the world market, or will it be necessary that some part of those resources be diverted to production of other commodities for home use? If not, what are the best alternative uses for excess land and labor in order that they may make the greatest possible contribution to national well-being and provide protection against the perils of a one-crop economy? What is the proper role of government intervention as a directing force along these lines in the postwar world?

It is not possible to explore these questions in detail here. It seems fairly clear, however, even assuming a generally higher level of industrial activity in the world at large, higher even than that which prevailed during the 1920's, that for a considerable number of products it will be difficult to find world markets commensurate with the potential productive resources of Latin America and other surplus regions of the world.

For products such as wheat and sugar, which can be produced in the more highly industrialized regions of the Temperate Zone in the Northern Hemisphere, much will depend upon the extent to which the countries in those regions continue to maintain relatively inefficient production with the aid of import tariffs and quotas or other forms of subsidy. The resources of most of the industrial countries for producing cotton are less than for sugar and wheat, but in that case a great deal will depend upon the extent to which synthetic fibers are produced either with or without subsidy and substituted for products made of cotton. The problem of coffee will probably continue for many years to be principally one of keeping production in Latin America in line with the world trend in coffee consumption. Judging by the past, consumption trends are likely to continue upward; but, also judging by the past, the productive resources of Latin America are more than ample to keep up with this trend.

The products just mentioned represented the principal prewar commodity problems of Latin America and the Western Hemisphere. It is quite possible that postwar years will see the rise of an entirely new set of commodity problems arising out of the stimulation of production in the Western Hemisphere when the resources of the surplus areas of the East had been cut off. Rubber is a case in point. Before the war, rubber was considered by the producers in the Far East to be a surplus problem. Now the war has caused a great expansion in the production of synthetic rubber in North America and Europe and has also encouraged a start toward the establishment of the commercial production of natural rubber in the American tropics. Even though allowance is made for a considerable increase in world consumption after the war, it requires little imagination to visualize a total production capacity in excess of effective world demand. The problems of rice and of vegetable oil materials may be even more serious than that of rubber when the Asiatic sources of supply are once more open to world trade. These potential problems suggest the advisability of international cooperation to prevent serious dislocations in national economies and to permit orderly readjustments.

There is a further aspect of the postwar situation to consider. Just as in other parts of the world, owing partly to the depression of the 1930's and partly to the war itself, governments in Latin America have found it necessary to intervene unilaterally in economic affairs in attempts to ameliorate the situations facing them. In too many cases these attempts have operated to stifle trade by the erection of tariffs and quota barriers. These tendencies are not likely to be reversed after the war and may actually be accentuated unless a satisfactory basis for international cooperation can be established as an alternative to national action.

There is, therefore, a strong argument for increased cooperation on an international basis in respect to particular commodities, not only within the Hemisphere, but in the world as a whole. The experience of Brazil with coffee, of Cuba with sugar, and of the United States with cotton shows conclusively that even the predominant producers of particular commodities are unable through their national efforts to correct serious surplus problems. In fact, it may well be argued that such national efforts merely lead to worse international situations since they tend to encourage other producers to enter the field.

In short, there is much to be said for an approach to the solution of these world-wide commodity problems, based not on unilateral competitive national programs but on international cooperation, aimed at an expansion in world consumption along with a balanced expansion of world production.

Chapter IV

Central Banking and Monetary Management in Latin America

by ROBERT TRIFFIN

THE popularity which central banking enjoyed in the twenties as a field of study and as a prospective panacea for business booms and depressions was put to a hard test by the great depression that ended the decade. The failure of monetary management to pass that test turned the attention of economists in other directions. Monopolistic competition and, later, saving-investment theories took the center of the stage.

The current discussions about international monetary stabilization and postwar lending are again bringing central banking out of oblivion. The time has come to review the monetary experiments of the interwar period and to learn from their failures as well as from their successes. Most urgent is a new inventory of the old arsenal of central-banking weapons for monetary control—discount rates, open-market operations, etc.—with a view to determine whether it will suffice for the tasks ahead or whether it is in need of a bold rearmament policy.

The question, of course, does not lend itself to any general or uniform treatment. The nature of the essential monetary problems, the present level of development reached by national monetary institutions, and the availability or efficacy of various techniques of control are fundamentally different from country to country. A full understanding of these differences and of these national characteristics is an indispensable prerequisite to any intelligent approach toward international monetary cooperation. The futility of many of the League of Nations' undertakings in the economic and financial field cannot be explained away as merely due to the stupidity or wickedness of national statesmen. The League's advice, however good in general, was primarily derived from the experience of the more stable and diversified economies of industrialized nations and could often be rightly regarded by less developed countries as impracticable or even irrelevant to their problems. It is worth noting that the best achievements of the League were scored in those cases in which it extended its help to individual countries, such as Hungary and Austria, and was perforce compelled to tackle regional and national problems in their full complexity.

The success or failure of our present stabilization plans will depend in no small degree on our willingness to abandon generalizations and recommendations of supposedly universal validity and to build up our future institutions for economic and monetary cooperation along truly "inter-national" rather than merely "a-national" lines. In order to do so, one of our most urgent tasks will be to familiarize ourselves with the functioning of the Latin American money markets. Few areas of the world present a greater challenge to monetary and banking theory in devising ways and means to promote a reasonable degree of monetary stability. At the same time, few areas have been as consistently neglected by economic students.

The purpose of this chapter is to outline, in very general terms, the present central-banking structure of Latin America and to discuss briefly the characteristic aspects of Latin American monetary problems and the techniques which would appear best adapted to their solution.

I. Silver, Gold, and Paper Money

The countries of Latin America inherited their first monetary system from the former Spanish administration. Gold and silver monies circulated side by side, with all the difficulties inherent in a bimetallic standard, until the latter third of the nineteenth century. After 1873, silver metal declined sharply in value, and most Latin American countries gradually discarded bimetallism in favor of the gold standard. Under both regimes, the regulation of the money supply was left, at least in principle, to the automatic mechanisms associated with the operations of the national mints.

In addition to gold and silver monies, however, there developed, especially in the second half of the nineteenth century, a fiduciary circulation in the form of banking deposits and paper money. The latter was issued either by the treasuries or by private banking institutions and would, in times of difficulty, be granted the privilege of inconvertibility. Paper-money regimes appeared especially early in the Rio de la Plata region, owing to the long civil wars which marked the first period of Argentine independence and to the lack of domestic gold and silver mines. The monetary stock of gold and silver had to be imported, and the young Argentine nation experienced great difficulties in building up a sufficiently favorable balance of payments to acquire those metals abroad in the amounts necessary to satisfy the needs of monetary transactions. At a later stage, the issue of paper money and the depreciation of the currency became at times a conscious policy, forced upon the authorities by the pressure of debtors' and exporters' interests. This was conspicuously true of Chile in the period 1898–1907.

II. The Exchange Offices

Such periods of inconvertible paper money usually ended with the institution of an exchange office—*caja*, *oficina*, *fondo*, or *junta*, *de conversion* or *de cambios*. The exchange office was supposed to exchange, upon demand, gold or foreign monies and deposits for domestic paper currency. In practice, however, the exchange office often proved to be a one-way street. In favorable years, the office followed the rules of the game religiously and expanded the domestic money supply through the purchase of foreign exchange balances. An inflationary situation would develop, the balance of payments would become strongly unfavorable, and the ensuing sales of foreign exchange by the office would withdraw local currency from the public, enforcing a sharp deflation in monetary circulation. The breaking point would then be reached, and the pressure of public opinion or of special groups, coupled with insufficient reserves in the office, would lead to a suspension of the system and a return to inconvertible paper. Thus, the net effect of the exchange office was to prevent an external appreciation of the domestic currency in times of prosperity, substituting for it an internal inflation. This would aggravate the exchange problem when the balance of payments became unfavorable; and, at that point, instead of maintaining the stability of the currency and enforcing an internal deflation, the authorities would close the exchange office and deflect the consequences of the unfavorable balance of payments from internal deflation to currency depreciation.

III. The Present Structure of Central Banking in Latin America

The rigidity of the exchange-office system of currency management finally led to its decline and to the adoption of central banking throughout most of Latin America. The central banks of Latin America, however, present the most diverse pattern from country to country, far more diverse than is the case, for example, on the European continent. They offer to the student of central banking an ideal laboratory for judging the efficacy of various techniques and their adaptability to different environments.

A. The Discount Banks

The central banks of the west coast, of El Salvador, and of Venezuela may be classified into one group. They are characterized by an extreme degree of orthodoxy which deprives them of any real control over the supply of money and credit.

1. THE WEST COAST: BOLIVIA, CHILE, COLOMBIA, ECUADOR, AND PERU. All the countries of the west coast received their organic central-banking laws from the famous Kemmerer missions of the 1920's. The first Kemmerer bank was organized in Colombia in 1923 and was followed by similar institutions in Chile (1925), Ecuador (1927), Bolivia (1928), and Peru (1931). The capital of a Kemmerer bank was subscribed in various proportions by the government, the associated banks, and private shareholders. The representation of these groups on the board of directors was made independent of their relative contribution to capital. The government usually received one third of the voting power, and the banks another third, the last third being divided between the representatives of private shareholders and of various commercial, agricultural, or industrial associations.[1] The leading power of the bank was narrowly circumscribed by rigid eligibility requirements as to the origin of the paper offered for discount or collateral, the number of signatures which it should

[1] The Central Bank of Bolivia, which had taken a major part in the financing of the Chaco War, was completely taken over by the government in 1938.

bear, and its maximum maturity. Advances to the treasury were allowed only up to very small amounts. On the other hand, the bank could lend, on eligible paper, not only to the banks but also to the public.

As lenders of last resort, the central banks created by Kemmerer proved helpful in the avoidance of the bankruptcies which used to accompany a financial panic. Their role, however, and certainly their effectiveness, did not extend much further. Monetary management, in particular, remained outside their sphere of action. The money was tied to a rigid gold or gold exchange standard, the only way in which the bank could influence it being the manipulation of the discount rate. Eligible paper, however, was scarce, and the discount rate soon proved a very illusory weapon of control, even more than in the older industrial countries with well-developed financial markets.

In fact, the Kemmerer banks constituted only a minor advance beyond the exchange-office system. They were unable to offset to any significant extent the tremendous inflationary expansion of money and credit induced during the 1920's by the prosperity of export markets and by the inflow of foreign capital. Between 1924 and 1927, for example, the money supply in Colombia increased by about 36 million pesos, but the maximum fluctuations in the credit money of the Central Bank[1] did not exceed 1 million pesos for the whole period. When, in 1929, the pendulum swung in the other direction, the central banks were similarly unable to control the sharp deflationary impact of the adverse balance of payments and of the domestic contraction in private banking credit. For a time they fought bravely against overwhelming odds in an effort to save both the gold standard and their own statutory structure as received from the Kemmerer missions. Between 1929 and 1931, they sacrificed most of their reserves in an attempt to maintain the stability of the currency, and they enforced, in conjunction with the private banks, a strong deflationary pressure in their respective countries.

By 1931, however, the public outcry against deflation had become irresistible and the reserves of many central banks had fallen to such a low point as to make the continuance of an orthodox gold-standard policy more and more difficult. A radical reversal of policy was adopted, and expansionary policies were embarked upon behind the

[1] For the definition of credit money, see p. 105.

protection of exchange depreciation and exchange control,[1] isolating in part the domestic economy from external monetary pressures.

The domestic-credit expansion, at first, took the form of an outright increase in the loans and investments of the central bank, under piecemeal and haphazard legislation of a frankly opportunistic type. The loans went primarily to the government, to development (*fomento*) institutions, to official and semiofficial agricultural and mortgage banks, to various producers' associations, etc. This brought about a gradual expansion of the means of payment and of bank reserves and served as a basis for the succeeding revival of other banking credit, side by side with central-banking credit.

These credit injections, coupled with more favorable conditions abroad, lifted the national economies stage by stage from the depths of the depression. The inflationary consequences of the policies adopted varied a great deal from country to country, ranging from about 14 per cent in Peru to 45 per cent in Colombia, 100 per cent in Chile, and 690 per cent in Bolivia[2] between the years 1931 and 1940.

Little remains today of the spirit of the Kemmerer legislations. In every country, the central bank was forced to expand its credit operations greatly in order to support the reflationary policies of the government and to assume new and important functions in connection with the management of exchange rates and the administration of exchange controls. These changes, however, took place over a period of years through a long succession of laws and decrees, hurriedly adopted under the pressure of various emergencies. A growing desire is now manifest for a systematic revision, simplification, and modernization of the legal maze through which the operations of the central banks must now be channeled. In Chile, the problem was recently debated in Congress and is receiving at the present time a considerable amount of attention.

2. EL SALVADOR AND VENEZUELA. Somewhat similar to the Kemmerer banks are the Central Reserve Bank of El Salvador, founded in 1934, and the Central Bank of Venezuela, founded in 1939, following respectively the reports of F. F. Powell of the Bank of England and of Herman Max of the Central Bank of Chile.

[1] Peru abandoned the gold standard in 1932 but did not introduce exchange control.

[2] These calculations are based on official price indices available for the whole period under study. These indices are not strictly comparable, and the resulting increases shown are given only as a very vague indication of the scope of the price rise in the various countries.

The Central Reserve Bank of El Salvador is an even more orthodox institution than the Kemmerer banks. Its ownership is entirely private, and the government's influence is limited to the confirmation of the president of the bank after his election by the shareholders. Operations with the public are also very limited. The bank is run in a very modern and efficient fashion but lacks real control over the money market. By legislative decree of April, 1940, however, the bank was authorized to buy and sell cédulas of the Mortgage Bank of El Salvador, guaranteed by the government, and Salvadoran government bonds quoted on the New York and London markets. The bank was also allowed to sell, to the banks or to the public, participation certificates in those investments. This power clears the way for open-market operations, which are likely to assume a growing importance in El Salvador in the future. The maximum amount of these obligations which the bank may hold is now limited to about 7 million colons, but this limit will increase gradually up to about 9.5 million colons, *i.e.*, about 15 per cent of the present circulating medium. The effective use of these powers for counteracting an expansion, however, still depends on the creation of a market for government bonds, which does not exist so far but the development of which does not seem very far off in El Salvador.

The statutes of the Venezuelan Bank do not allow open-market operations, but are in all other respects more liberal than those reviewed so far. The bank is allowed to extend credit to the banks up to 270 days and to the public up to 180 days. It may, in addition, recommend to the Executive changes in the reserve requirements of the private banks, and it is allowed to rediscount, buy, or sell treasury bills up to a maximum amount equal to twice its paid-in capital and surplus in order to help the Treasury in times of temporary budget deficits. In contrast to this the original central-banking law in Colombia permitted loans to the Treasury or other official entities only up to a maximum amount of 30 per cent of the bank's paid-in capital and surplus.

B. MODERN CENTRAL BANKS: ARGENTINA AND MEXICO

The most modern and powerful central banks of Latin America are the Central Bank of Argentina and the Bank of Mexico.

The Argentine legislation was prepared by Otto Niemeyer of the Bank of England, whose draft was adopted in 1935 with relatively few modifications. It remains true to tradition and is even stricter than the Kemmerer laws in outlawing direct relations with the public. On the other hand, the bank was allowed open-market operations up to the amount of its capital and surplus plus 400 million pesos, corresponding to consolidated government bonds in the portfolio of the bank at the time of its foundation. The bank was also vested with supervision of the private banks and with exchange control. The gold standard had been suspended in Argentina in 1929, and the bank was free from the outset to adjust exchange rates and administer the exchange-control system.

The government appoints the president and the vice-president of the bank and one of its directors. One director is elected by the government-owned bank of the nation, and the other 10 by the shareholding banks, with the stipulation that among those elected there must be one agriculturalist, one livestock producer, one merchant, and one manufacturer, selected after consultation with the proper representatives of these groups. The bank started with an original paid-in capital of 20 million pesos, 10 million of which was subscribed by the government and 10 million by the shareholding banks.

The open-market powers of the bank were further expanded in the following years. In 1936, the bank was allowed to negotiate special treasury bills up to 100 million pesos and, in 1937, gold and foreign exchange-holding certificates. The latter are direct obligations of the bank, secured by corresponding gold and foreign exchange assets. Thus the central bank could neutralize the funds which it created when buying exchange from the banks, by selling the banks certificates of participation in consolidated bonds, special treasury bills, and foreign exchange-holding certificates. The funds absorbed in this manner reached a maximum of 741 million pesos in August, 1937, *i.e.*, an amount approximately equal to the total cash holdings of the banks at the time. Since 1940, treasury bills can be placed directly with the public by public tender; and, since 1942, the certificates of participation in consolidated bonds can also be sold directly to the public, as well as to the banks.

In the short period since 1935 the Central Bank of Argentina has developed into an outstanding institution among central banks not only in Latin America but in older countries as well. Credit for this achievement is due largely to the brilliant leadership of Raoul

Prebisch, general manager of the bank during most of this period, and to an extremely able staff of executives and research workers.

The Bank of Mexico was organized originally in 1925. Its statutes were considerably modified in 1931, 1936, and 1941. The private banking system of Mexico had been nearly wiped out during the years of the Mexican Revolution, and the Bank of Mexico first devoted most of its attention to commercial lending and to loans to the state and to official and semiofficial institutions. The monetary system continued to be dominated by the government's issue of coins.

In 1931, Mexico abandoned the gold standard, the operations of the bank with the public were made subject to stricter limitations, and rediscounting with the banks began to assume a growing importance.

The present organization of the bank results from the law of 1941, which confers upon it extremely wide powers for the management of the money supply and the regulation of exchange rates. The bank has substantial open-market powers and may now vary the reserve requirements of the private banks between a minimum of 5 per cent and a maximum of 50 per cent of their deposits. The government owns 51 per cent of the capital and elects five of the nine councilors on the administrative board of the bank.

Although comparable in theory, actually the open-market powers of the central bank do not play as yet the important role in Mexico that they play in Argentina. The difference is due to the weaker credit standing of the Mexican government's obligations and to the undeveloped character of the Mexican financial market.

C. THE ALL-PURPOSE BANKS: GUATEMALA, PARAGUAY, HAITI, URUGUAY, COSTA RICA, AND NICARAGUA

Previous to the importation of orthodox central banks into Latin America by British and American experts, there had developed in a number of countries state banks of a heterogeneous character, mixing traditional monetary and central-banking function with commercial, agricultural, and even mortgage-banking activities.

The state banks of Guatemala, Paraguay, and Haiti still belong to that category. The Guatemalan Central Bank was founded in 1927, the Haitian National Bank was founded in 1911, and, in Paraguay, an Oficina de Cambios, established in 1916, developed into a state bank during the Chaco War—largely in order to finance the war expenditures of the government—and changed its name to Banco de la República in 1937. A new central-banking project is now under consideration by the Paraguayan government and will probably be put into operation in 1944.

A somewhat similar situation exists in Uruguay. The Banco de la República Oriental del Uruguay was set up in 1896 in an effort to cheapen credit and make it available to small traders and farmers. The bank was given the privilege of note issue, and this privilege became exclusive in 1911. The bank, however, is primarily a commercial one and accounts for a considerable portion of the total commercial bank loans in the country. Its activities are extremely varied, including not only short-term agricultural and commercial credit but mortgage loans, supervised credit, loans for the development of rural industries, operation of a pawnshop, and, outside the credit field proper, the construction and administration of official granaries, the marketing and export of some agricultural products, the supervision of minimum price legislation, etc.

In 1935, the note-issue functions of the bank were separated from its other functions and placed under an issue department, which operates as an autonomous section. This division, however, as now conceived, leaves much to be desired. There is some agitation in Uruguay for a clearer separation of functions and especially for the separation of central-banking functions from the other activities of the bank.

The National Banks of Costa Rica and Nicaragua, organized in 1937 and 1941 by Herman Max, are also divided into an issue department, vested with central-banking functions, and a banking or commercial department which is similar to the private commercial banks operating in the country. The National Bank of Costa Rica includes, in addition, a mortgage department.

The division, however, between those departments is much more significant than it is in Uruguay, where it is hardly more than a mere accounting device. The departments are under a common management and board of directors (except that the main powers of the issue department are reserved to a special monetary council), but each has a separate capital and presents separate balance sheets. This departmentalized system seems to offer a working compromise between the orthodox "bankers' bank" and the mixture of functions characteristic of the indigenous system of state banks evolved in some Latin

American countries before the foundation of more traditional central banks by foreign experts.

The banking or commercial department of the Max banks is given broad powers as to the maturity of its lending operations and is intended to promote agricultural and industrial development through short-term and medium-term loans on chattel or real-estate mortgages, with maturities extending up to 5 years. On the other hand, the direct weapons of monetary control in the hands of the issue department appear inadequate, with no provisions for open-market operations or for flexible reserve requirements. Max relied heavily for monetary management on flexible exchange rates to be administered more or less in the spirit of Irving Fisher's commodity dollar, but this part of his projects was never put into actual operation so that the present monetary controls of the national banks of Costa Rica and Nicaragua are extremely weak. As indicated elsewhere in this chapter, additional control measures were put into effect in Costa Rica in 1942, largely through voluntary agreements between the national bank and the private banks and, in October, 1943, the issue department was authorized to raise reserve requirements above the basic levels of the Max law.

D. ABSENCE OF CENTRAL BANKING: BRAZIL, CUBA, PANAMA, DOMINICAN REPUBLIC, AND HONDURAS

Whatever state banks exist in the other countries of Latin America cannot be properly considered as real central banks.

Brazil has a government bank, the Banco do Brazil, which acts as fiscal agent of the government and carries out discounting operations and ordinary commercial banking functions. The power of monetary issue, however, still lies with the Treasury. Various projects have been discussed for some years (one was presented about 8 years ago by Niemeyer) for the foundation of a Brazilian central bank. The question was recently debated again in a semiofficial Economic Congress, which recommended that active studies and preparations be made looking to the creation of a central bank and that an interim commission be set up at once to coordinate monetary and credit policies.

The National Bank of Panama is primarily a commercial and mortgage bank with no monetary functions; domestic metallic coins are issued by the Treasury. In Cuba, silver certificates are now issued by the Treasury and circulate side by side with the dollar, which in both Cuba and Panama has a wide circulation. An American mission recommended in 1942 the withdrawal of the dollar currency and the setting up of a central bank in Cuba; a bill embodying most of the proposals of the mission is now under consideration in the Cuban Congress.

The monetary unit of the Dominican Republic is the United States dollar. Late in 1941, the Dominican government acquired a local branch of the National City Bank and organized it into a state bank, the Reserve Bank of the Dominican Republic. The bank, however, remained an ordinary commercial one without any monetary or central-banking functions.

The responsibility for monetary issue in Honduras is divided between a government commission, which issues lempira coins, and two private banks, which may issue notes up to 175 per cent of their capital and legal reserves. In recent months, Honduras has also resorted to the importation of United States silver coins to supplement its monetary stock. An American mission was sent to Honduras during the summer of 1943 to investigate the advisability of creating a Honduran central bank. The report of the mission is now under consideration by the government in Tegucigalpa.

IV. The Special Problems of Latin American Monetary Management

The problem of monetary management in Latin America is determined by the following characteristics of the economies:

1. The dominating influence of international trade and capital movements on economic activity and especially on the money supply.
2. The erratic nature of fluctuations in the international balance of payments of those countries.
3. The chronic dependence of the Treasury on central-bank credit and the resulting conflicts between monetary and fiscal policy.
4. The lack of well-developed financial markets and the resulting unavailability or inefficacy of traditional central-banking weapons.

A. The Determinants of Money Supply in Latin America

While domestic savings and investments are the main determinants of economic activity in the older industrial countries, such a role is usually played in Latin America by the inflow or outflow of foreign exchange. Domestic savings and investments are on a relatively minor scale, and the business cycle is dominated by the international movements of capital and by the fluctuations of imports and exports. A net inflow of foreign exchange brings a multiple expansion and a net outflow of foreign exchange a multiple contraction in the volume of the means of payments through the operation of a fractional reserve system of central and commercial banking.

The magnitude of these external influences on the supply of money may be gauged from a brief review of Colombian monetary history since the foundation of the Banco de la República in 1923.[1]

In the 3 years 1925–1927, the reserves of the Banco de la República increased by about 21 million pesos. The secondary monetary expansion by the private banks amounted to another 14 million pesos, bringing about an expansion of about 35 million pesos in the total money supply, *i.e.*, an increase of about 58 per cent. Throughout this period, the central bank played a purely passive role, the increase of its monetary liabilities exactly corresponding to its acquisition of gold and foreign exchange.

In the last year of prosperity, 1928, the central bank cut its own credit money by about 6 million pesos, in the face of a further increase of 20 million in its international reserves and of 4 million in the private banks' credit money. Thus the circulating medium increased by another 18 million pesos, bringing the total expansion since 1923 close to 90 per cent.

The following deflation was as drastic as the preceding expansion had been. International reserves fell by 52 million pesos—from 65 to

[1] The following analysis is based on a statistical breakdown of the total money supply (notes and coins in circulation plus private and official checking deposits in national currency) into three components:

1. The part which corresponds to net acquisitions of international reserves by the central bank.
2. The credit money of the central bank and Treasury, *i.e.*, the total of notes and coins outside the central bank, plus total (including banks') checking deposits in the central bank and minus the net international reserves of the central bank.
3. The credit money of all banks other than the central bank, *i.e.*, their checking-deposit liabilities minus their cash reserves and balances with the central bank.

A certain degree of precision has been sacrificed for the sake of simplicity. A more detailed analysis should carry out a more complete breakdown, distinguishing, for example, between the central bank and the Treasury and between various classes of banks, and should also take into account the cash assets and liabilities of the banks (other than the central bank) in foreign currencies.

The purpose of the breakdown and its relevance to the problems of monetary control are sufficiently obvious. I hope to have occasion to discuss more fully in a forthcoming article the implications of the method and the results yielded by it when applied to the various Latin American money markets.

13 millions—and the credit money of the private banks dropped by an additional 16 millions. This potential contraction of 68 millions (60 per cent) in the money supply was offset to the extent of only 12 millions through central-banking expansion, 10 millions of which were effected only in the last year, concurrently with the abandonment of the gold standard.

Thus, during its period of orthodoxy, the Banco de la República proved to be little more than an exchange office, unable to protect the money supply from the disrupting influences of fluctuations in the balance of payments. The automatic mechanism of the gold standard merely brought about an inordinate inflation in the 1920's, followed in 1928–1931 by a drastic deflation which was still insufficient to prevent the devaluation of the currency.

The reflation period 1931–1939 is one of continuous expansion in all three components of the money supply. International reserves increased by 20 million pesos, the credit money of the central bank by the record figure of 55 millions, and the credit money of the private banks by 27 millions, bringing a total expansion of 101 million pesos in the total circulating medium, which thus stood at 160 million pesos at the end of 1939, as compared with 59 millions in 1931 and 115 millions in 1928.

In the first 2 years of the European war, domestic credit money was expanded, counteracting the decrease in net international reserves[1] and leaving a net increase of 30 million pesos in the money supply.

The great inflationary impact of the war took place in the following two years, 1942 and 1943. International reserves soared at an unprecedented pace from 20 million pesos at the end of 1941 to 178 millions in September, 1943, an increase of 158 million pesos, or 800 per cent in 21 months. The credit money generated by the banks increased in the same period by about 48 million pesos. If the central-bank credit money had remained even, as it did in the 1920's, the circulating medium would have more than doubled, rising from 190 to 396 million pesos. Actually, the credit money of the Banco de la República decreased by 73 million pesos, leaving a net increase of 133 millions in the circulating medium—from 190 to 323 millions.[2]

[1] Gross international reserves were maintained about even, through the granting of a $10 million loan by the Export-Import Bank.

[2] The hypothetical method of reasoning followed here is based on the heroic assump-

Part of this relative success is due to the anti-inflationary legislation of 1943. Although a sufficient control of the money supply by the bank is still very far distant, the reforms of the summer of 1943 may be expected to reinforce considerably the anti-inflationary powers of the monetary authorities. This legislation was extremely drastic, however, and has been attacked from various quarters. Later reforms have eliminated some of its defects but have also weakened to some extent its effectiveness. In spite of this, the Colombian experiment is a most interesting one and constitutes the most intelligent and comprehensive attempt made by any Latin American country to combat the inflationary impact of war conditions. It may suggest to the monetary authorities of other countries new instruments for monetary control, not only for wartime but for peacetime as well.

This problem of the fluctuations in the balance of payments and of their impact on the money supply has assumed an unprecedented magnitude in Latin America during the present war. The initial reaction to the war varied from country to country; but, by 1941 or 1942, the war had drastically reduced Latin American imports from outside areas and provided at the same time an abnormally high demand for exports. The loans of the Export-Import Bank, the investments or subsidy programs of other United States agencies in Latin America, and the inflow of refugee capital added a favorable balance on capital account to the favorable balance of payments on merchandise account.

A new inflationary situation, similar to the one experienced in the 1920's, developed once more under the impact of the inflow of foreign exchange. The scale of the inflow, however, and of the corresponding expansion in domestic currency reached truly extraordinary proportions within a few months.

Gold and foreign exchange balances of Latin America have about doubled in the last 2 years, and the pace of the increase nearly doubled in 1943 as compared with 1942. One of the most spectacular cases is that of Costa Rica, where the international reserves of the banking system rose from December, 1941, to June, 1943, from 14.5 to 92.8 million colons, bringing an increase of 90 per cent in the domestic money supply.

---

tion that monetary expansion by the private banks is independent of the line of action followed by the central bank. The removal of the assumption would strengthen, rather than weaken, the argument but would preclude any quantitative estimates of what would have happened if the central bank had behaved differently.

B. THE INAPPROPRIATENESS OF AN AUTOMATIC READJUSTMENT SYSTEM

The automatic adaptation of the money supply to the fluctuations of the balance of payments was, of course, considered as perfectly normal and desirable in the orthodox gold-standard theory. A favorable or an unfavorable balance of payments was taken as a sign of a fundamental disequilibrium in international price and cost levels, and it was assumed that the disequilibrium would be corrected by the domestic expansion or contraction brought about by the inflow or outflow of exchange. If the gold standard were abandoned and if exchange rates were allowed to fluctuate, the same results would be obtained through the increase or decrease in the external value of the currency.

The essential weakness of the theory is that the fluctuations of the balance of payments in Latin America are determined only to a minor extent by international cost comparisons. The inflow or outflow of foreign capital in Latin America obeys largely other influences of a more purely speculative nature, and most Latin American exports are generally accounted for by one or a few agricultural products or industrial raw materials, the supply of which may be determined by the vagaries of the weather and the demand for which is predominantly influenced by the state of the business cycle in the buying countries. Whenever this is true, the proper policies to be followed should be to offset and neutralize the effects of such erratic fluctuations of the balance of payments on the domestic money market rather than to magnify them through cumulative contraction or expansion.

C. THE DEPENDENCE OF THE TREASURIES ON CENTRAL-BANKING CREDIT

The third complicating factor in Latin American monetary management is the dependence of the treasuries on central-banking credit. The checkered budgetary history of most Latin American countries and the popularity of landholdings and mortgage certificates as an investment outlet make it in general impossible for the treasuries to have recourse either to the public or to the private banks to finance their operations. Fiscal deficits thus have to be covered through foreign borrowing or through borrowing at the central bank or through direct issue of paper currency. As long as such a situation persists, there exists little possibility for a sound coordination of fiscal and monetary policies. The provisions of many central-banking laws which limit severely the right of the central bank to lend to the government have proved uniformly to be mere paper protections, which are necessarily removed whenever an emergency arises. The realistic solution lies not in denying, on paper, all access by the treasuries to the central banks, but in providing for alternative methods of financing the expenditures of the government through a revision of the fiscal apparatus and through the development of a market for government bonds.

The tax structure in Latin America relies heavily on custom duties. Owing to decreases in imports, these revenues have dropped considerably in 1942–1943, creating in most countries a difficult fiscal situation and adding to the inflationary problem. Most countries, however, had already in existence a skeleton structure of income taxation, and some attempts have been made to increase revenue from this source so as to offset the decrease in custom receipts. A spectacular shift in this direction is noticeable, especially in Argentina and in Colombia, where custom receipts dropped by 50 per cent or more between 1939 and 1942, while income-tax revenues increased by nearly 100 per cent in the first country and 50 per cent in the second, now outstripping by far the total amount of custom collections. Colombia introduced, in addition, in the summer of 1942, a program of compulsory investments in government bonds which is discussed elsewhere in this volume (see pages 333 to 334).

D. THE NEED FOR NEW APPROACHES TO MONETARY MANAGEMENT

The magnitude of the problem of monetary management in Latin America makes it all the more necessary to endow the monetary authorities with adequate weapons of control. The absence of developed capital markets makes the task difficult of achievement and forces us to look in new directions, as yet untried in traditional central-banking practices.

1. The most traditional instrument of monetary management—the discount rate—has long proved inadequate even in the most developed financial centers. Discountable paper has always been lacking in Latin America, where bank credit is mostly extended through the use of the current account or overdraft method. The discount market is an extremely narrow one, and the result of the Kemmerer legislation on the west coast was to flood that market with

credit facilities, bringing about a general lowering of interest rates on commercial paper, but leaving practically unaffected the rates on all other forms of banking credit.

2. The most influential commercial banks are often branches of powerful foreign institutions. The banking system, as a whole, is now in an extremely liquid position as the result of the expansionary policies of the 1930's and of wartime inflation. As a result, the banks are largely independent of the central bank. The first and most obvious step would be an increase in reserve requirements. As has already been mentioned, this weapon is still unavailable to the Latin American central banks, except in Mexico and Costa Rica and, to a very minor extent, in Ecuador. To be effective, changes in reserve requirements would, in most cases, have to be extremely drastic, and such a step might be difficult, whenever the liquid position of the banks is very uneven. The willingness of the central bank to order an increase in legal reserves would be limited by its desire not to embarrass unduly the least liquid banks in the system. The solution might lie in the adoption of the measure recommended by the American mission which studied the establishment of a central bank in Cuba—allowing the bank to increase reserve requirements up to any ratio on any *future* increases of deposits. This could be used, in times of inflation, to eliminate effectively the vicious secondary expansion made possible under a system of fractional reserve banking.

3. An even more effective alternative to this method would be the direct quantitative control of banking loans by the central bank. This was adopted in Costa Rica and Mexico by agreement between the central bank and the private banks. Such a rigid control, however, would probably prove difficult in larger countries and would have to be supplemented by qualitative controls to avoid undue hardship on some classes of producers.

4. In Chile and Colombia the banking superintendents are now advocating such qualitative controls. These might range from merely negative controls, such as a limitation on loans for speculative purposes, to more extensive, and also more dangerous, controls over the distribution of bank credit among commercial, agricultural, and industrial loans or even over a more concrete and detailed classification of all productive loans. The first method is the one now advocated in Colombia, while the latter is the one contemplated in the Chilean proposals.

5. Direct lending by the central bank to the public was already included, although with very stringent limits, in the Kemmerer laws. Such direct operations with the public have proved necessary in new countries, unequipped with a well-developed financial market and where the private banking system is largely in foreign hands.[1] In many Latin American countries, official or semiofficial credit institutions have been established in order to promote medium- or long-term lending for agricultural or industrial development. In the smaller countries such functions are better carried out by the central bank itself, under a departmentalized system of the Costa Rican type. In larger countries, separate institutions will generally assume this type of responsibility but should be brought into close contact with the central bank in order to ensure a unified and efficient monetary and credit policy. As far as possible, the development of this type of credit should be accompanied by a comprehensive program designed to raise the necessary funds from domestic savings rather than resorting to inflationary injections of credit through mere money creation.

6. This brings us to the next point—the development of open-market operations and of a market for government bonds or other types of securities. Wherever the government's credit standing is too weak for the purpose, other instruments could be used, such as the mortgage certificates (cêdulas) so popular in Latin America, or even direct obligations of the bank itself or privately issued bonds of high standing. Short-term notes of the central bank or the Treasury, backed by gold or foreign exchange reserves, might constitute a first step in this direction.

7. The offsetting policies recommended in an earlier part of this chapter might conceivably take the form of flexible exchange rates. Such a view has been advocated by Herman Max and is strongly defended by some Latin American economists, especially in Mexico.[2] Personally, I doubt both its feasibility and its adequacy. Exchange rates move easily in a downward direction, but any appreciation of the currency is likely to meet strong opposition on the part of exporters and of finance ministers.[3] Any rigid automatism, such as foreseen in

[1] See A. F. W. Plumptre, *Central Banking in the British Dominions* (University of Toronto Press, 1940), pp. 65, 97, 152–154, 425, and *passim*.

[2] See Victor Urquidi, "Los Proyectos monetarios de la postguerra," *El Trimestre economico*, Vol. X (1943), pp. 539–571.

[3] The case for currency appreciation is especially strong today, in view of the extraordinary inflows of foreign exchange which war conditions have brought about throughout

the commodity-dollar theory, would moreover require much more statistical sophistication than is now possible in most Latin American countries. I should also question the efficacy of a devaluation in bringing about an equilibrium readjustment of the balance of payments, especially in the case of a highly specialized economic area, the international transactions of which are dominated by a few exports faced by an inelastic demand. A devaluation by Argentina would probably be followed in short order by devaluations on the part of her main competitors, and the final increase in Argentine exports would not compensate Argentina for the lowering of unit prices in terms of the buying countries' currencies. The situation recalls the case of oligopolistic competition in which none of the sellers are usually able to profit for very long from price-undercutting policies.

8. From an international as well as from a national point of view, I am inclined to think that some direct quantitative controls on exchange transactions would, in most Latin American countries, be preferable to exchange depreciation. I realize that such a suggestion is extremely controversial. Any system of exchange control is difficult to administer, and the temptation is great to use it in discriminatory fashion or for purposes which bear little relation to those which might legitimately warrant its adoption. Instead, however, of taking the rigidly dogmatic view advocated at least implicitly in many circles,[1] that anything is preferable to exchange control, I should prefer to examine the question in more concrete and detailed fashion and devote the energies now wasted in a futile condemnation of all forms of exchange control to a fight against these discriminatory practices which have proved most damaging to international trade and good relations.

The disequilibrating effects of the fluctuations of the balance of payments may, in some cases, reach such fantastic proportions that

---

Latin America. Currency appreciation so far, however, has remained extremely moderate and has mostly taken an indirect form through the liberalization of exchange controls, the lowering of the curb rates and of the higher selling rates attached to "unessential" transactions, and a reshuffling of exchange-control classifications widening the field of application of the more favorable exchange rates to transactions formerly subject to less favorable ones.

[1] The position taken by many economists on this point appears to be inspired, to a considerable degree, by the study of European exchange-control regimes, in which aggressive or political considerations and discriminatory practices often played a much more important part than was the case in most Latin American countries. Latin American controls themselves were far from blameless, and I do not defend, any more than I reject, all controls *in globo*.

nothing short of quantitative controls can ensure a reasonable degree of stability in the domestic economy. The complete wiping out of all banking loans in Costa Rica would have remained insufficient to offset the tremendous increase in the money supply fostered by the inflow of foreign exchange in the 18 months following the United States' entry into the war. Under such circumstances, I should favor the type of controls introduced in Colombia and freeze into certificates of deposit or other similar instruments a portion of the exchange entering the country. On the other hand, in times of abnormally severe exchange shortages due to temporary factors, I should recognize the principle that all the foreign exchange resources of the country should, as far as possible, be controlled by the monetary authorities and rationed among the buyers according to some system of priorities in a nondiscriminatory manner and only for the period of the emergency. To avoid profiteering by the importers, such rationing may have to be complemented by other measures; price control of essential import goods, higher exchange rates—possibly through a system of public tender similar to the one used in Argentina—for luxury imports. All this tends to make exchange control a most delicate weapon, the introduction of which may lead to further and further departures from a free economy. Exchange control should be used only in cases of dire necessity and should be surrounded with all possible guarantees and limitations against an undue extension of the controls or their use for ends other than general monetary policy.

V. Conclusion

To conclude this review of central-banking problems in Latin America, I should like to return to the point at which I started—the problem of international monetary cooperation and of the postwar institutions which may help in this task. Among the proposals that have been most widely discussed so far, three are of particular interest to Latin America. International commodity agreements have been suggested in order to prevent wide and disruptive changes in the price of the most important foodstuffs and raw materials. A second group of measures relates to long-run development loans, designed to increase production and living standards and to diversify the economy of undeveloped areas. Such measures will be of fundamental importance to monetary stability by lessening the dependence of those economies on one or two export products, the supply of or the demand for which may vary in a most erratic fashion, bringing havoc in the balance of payments and the economy. They will also help to prevent wide fluctuations in export prices and demand. A third group of measures aims directly at exchange stabilization: by making available to the member countries additional international reserves in times of need, they may avoid recourse to currency depreciation or exchange control or even to internal deflationary policies in the event of a temporary deficit in the balance of payments. It must be noted, however, that the avoidance of deflationary pressures, in this case, would by no means be automatic. The international reserves so placed at the disposal of the central bank would still be sold to the importers, withdrawing domestic money from the public as long as the balance of payments remains unfavorable. In the opposite case of a favorable balance of payments, leading to inflationary increases in the domestic money supply, the operations of Keynes's Clearing Union or of White's Stabilization Fund would be of no help. On the contrary, they would tend to perpetuate the disequilibrium by permitting the buying countries to continue their purchases despite the fact that their own balance of payments is unfavorable.

Moreover, the plans would limit severely the use of exchange control and restrict recourse to exchange depreciation and aim to shift at least part of the burden of readjustment policies to internal credit expansion or contraction. This again emphasizes the fact that, ultimately, the achievement of stability will depend essentially on efficient monetary management within each country, rather than on mere international agreements or machinery.

The Clearing Union or the Stabilization Fund would advise member countries on the internal monetary and credit policies which it deems desirable. Its main influence in enforcing the adoption of such policies would, however, emerge only in cases where the country is short of reserves and has already exhausted a considerable portion of its quota with the union or the fund. This would presumably indicate that the country's competitive position has been allowed to deteriorate to such an extent that, barring exchange control or currency devaluation, drastic deflationary policies would have to be recommended. Such policies are, of course, unpopular and politically distasteful. They may, in addition, be very difficult to carry through successfully in economies predominantly agricultural and dependent on world markets for a wide range of consumption and production goods. Monetary policy is more likely to be effective in neutralizing the inflationary pressure of a favorable balance of payments than in reinforcing the deflationary impact of an unfavorable one. The first case, however, is precisely the one in which a country would be least dependent on the fund.

The insistence placed in White's proposals, on exchange stability has met with considerable criticism in many quarters. Personally, I have little anxiety on this score. I think that exchange flexibility has been overemphasized in recent years as a weapon of readjustment and that it would often prove unwise or futile in Latin America as a matter of practical politics. On the other hand, the insistence on stability in terms of gold goes too far in the other direction. In the case of small countries whose balance of payments is largely dominated by one or two currencies, external currency stability might be defined in terms of those currencies rather than in terms of gold, at least as long as currency devaluation by the big countries is not entirely ruled out. Some such system, similar to the composite exchange standard recently adopted by Paraguay, might be suggested as a workable and realistic scheme of international currency stabilization and might be used in bridging the gap between the world approach of White and Keynes and the key-currency approach proposed by John Williams.

These plans would be of immense value to the Latin American economies; but no matter what international scheme is adopted, be it a world stabilization fund or a world clearing union, an inter-American bank or a world bank, the task of domestic monetary stabilization will remain primarily the responsibility of the national monetary authorities, and especially of the national central banks. Stabilization loans or long-term loans will be invaluable or worthless, depending on whether they operate in a domestically stable or unstable monetary environment. Success in this latter field will require primarily a full interchange of information and of technical assistance between the various Latin American countries as well as between Latin America and the United States. The same type of information will be sorely needed by any international agency for an efficient administration of its own responsibilities. Among the functions of the inter-American Bank which received most emphasis from its promoters was its prospective role as a central bankers' club. The current discussions about an international stabilization fund have placed, so far, little emphasis on this aspect of the new institution. It may yet prove to be of more importance than many other and more spectacular features of the fund.[1]

[1] During Dr. Triffin's absence in Latin America, new versions (April, and July, 1944) of the stabilization plans were announced. They go further in the direction of exchange flexibility than was anticipated when Dr. Triffin wrote this essay. The need for deflationary monetary policy is to that extent reduced.—EDITOR.

Chapter V

Fiscal Policy and the Budget

by HENRY C. WALLICH

CONSIDERABLE progress has been made by many of the Latin American republics in the use of fiscal policy as a means of moderating economic fluctuations. Under the impact, first of the depression, which cut off foreign loans, and later of the war, which curtailed foreign supplies, the republics have developed new fiscal techniques to finance their budgets and to stabilize their economies. Chief among these is the growing use of corporate and personal income and excess-profits taxes and the improvement of domestic facilities for government borrowing. In spite of these advances, however, an independent fiscal policy still encounters severe limitations in most of Latin America, and it is perhaps not unfair to say that for a long time to come many of the republics will be more dependent upon the fiscal policies of their great trade partners than upon their own.

The main obstacle to a successful policy of stabilizing the economy by fiscal means lies in this heavy dependence upon foreign trade. What investment and savings are to the United States as determinants of national income, exports and imports are to the Latin American republics.[1] Exports rather than investment are the chief stimulus to income, while imports, rather than savings, constitute the main

[1] Exports and investment both give rise to additional income, in the form of wages, profits, etc., without causing an equivalent volume of consumable goods to appear on the market to absorb this purchasing power. The secondary repercussions of this excess purchasing power cause income to rise beyond the amount due to the original export or investment. Imports, on the other hand, like savings, unless they lead to additional real investment, cause purchasing power to be diverted from the domestic market and bring about a shrinkage of income.

"leakage" from the domestic money flow. If exports are lagging and the government then attempts to raise shrinking national income through domestic expenditures, its endeavors, if successful, will cause a rise in imports and, given the low level of exports, a loss of foreign exchange. Carried too far, the process must lead to the exhaustion of reserves and a depreciation of the currency, resulting first in a rise of import and export prices, and eventually in general inflation.

It is possible, of course, to block the rise in imports and the outflow of exchange by imposing foreign exchange control, as a majority of the Latin American republics have done. In that case, however, the government's endeavors to stimulate national income are likely soon to meet a second obstacle in the insufficient elasticity of supply in local industries. A limited capacity and, in some fields, a complete absence of domestic production facilities are the counterpart of a heavy dependence upon imports. Hence, if imports are restricted through foreign exchange control, the rise in national income induced by government spending will lead, at a fairly early stage, to a rise in the price of domestically consumed products rather than to a continued increase in output. Rising costs create new difficulties for the export industries and may force the exchange-control authorities to depreciate the currency. With or without control, therefore, an attempt to make up for lagging exports through deficit spending is likely to lead to inflation and depreciation. The financial history of Chile since 1938 is perhaps the most striking demonstration of this process. Thus the classical economists' horror of government deficits—which in the United States, with its different economic structure, has proved rather exaggerated—finds a good deal more justification in the Latin American environment.

Apart from these structural obstacles, Latin American fiscal policy also is handicapped by the relative inadequacy of revenue systems and, frequently, of borrowing facilities. In spite of recent advances in these fields, a great deal remains to be done. It is in this more limited sphere of taxation and government credit, rather than in that of broad fiscal policy, that the efforts of Latin American governments hold out some promise of success.

In all but a few of the republics, corporate and personal income taxes constitute a very minor part of total revenues, and the traditional dependence on administratively simpler indirect taxes, chiefly tariffs and excise levies, is still very much in evidence. The principle underlying this tax policy is not so much the individual's ability to pay as the government's ability to collect. This relatively antiquated revenue system is called upon to meet the demands of expenditures which, in many instances, arise from the assumption of entirely "modern" responsibilities, particularly in the field of social services, including education, public health, and public works. The result of this combination of antiquated revenues and modern expenditures is an inherent tendency toward unbalanced budgets. This tendency was very much in evidence during the 1930's, although the depression more than the structural weakness of government finances must primarily be held responsible for the deficits of that period.

In earlier years considerable difficulties were encountered in the financing of deficits, unless foreign loans were available. Not infrequently the printing presses had to be used. Recently the advent of central banks in most of the republics has done away with the immediate financial dilemma, but not, of course, with the inflationary consequences of money creation. Some countries, notably Argentina, have developed excellent capital markets through which the savings of the public are made available to the government at moderate rates of interest. Elsewhere, however, the market for government securities still is narrow. Owing to the great liquidity induced by wartime trade surpluses, however, many investors are beginning to look upon government securities with a less jaundiced eye than previously, a development which should be of lasting benefit.

I. BUDGETARY PRACTICES

In some instances the budgetary difficulties mentioned above are aggravated by the conditions under which the budgets are produced and the manner in which they are executed. Owing to the instability of many sources of revenue, particularly tariffs and income taxes, as well as to the lack of comprehensive statistics, Latin American treasuries do not have an easy task in estimating revenues. To meet this problem, the Colombian budget law discourages excessively sanguine expectations by limiting the maximum estimate of revenues from existing taxes to the average of such revenues during the 3 preceding years. This method, however, although sound in many respects, nevertheless ties the hands of the authorities to an unnecessary degree.

Budgets, once adopted, are not always strictly followed. Shifts of funds from one item to another are made frequently, and extraordinary expenditures, occasionally without allocation of funds, are authorized by the legislature or the executive. The Chilean Congress has in recent years indulged in these practices to such an extent that, in view of the inflationary consequences of its generosity, it decided to abrogate its constitutional prerogative to initiate appropriations and turned this power over to the President.

A familiar feature of many Latin American budgets is the profusion of extraordinary, special public works and other revenues and funds and the practice of earmarking the revenue from certain sources for specific purposes. This practice of breaking up the unity of the budget, which of course is not entirely confined to the Latin American republics, is sound if it involves merely the segregation of state-operated enterprises, such as railroads, utilities, and similar services, from the general budget. In other respects, however, a lack of budgetary unity is clearly undesirable. In Cuba, for example, over 30 special funds were reported to exist in 1939,[1] and devices like the allocation of an increase of 10 per cent in the cigarette tax to the purchase of serum for cattle have not been unusual. Such methods frequently serve no better purpose than to protect appropriations dear to certain interests from having to run the annual gauntlet of congressional discussion. Even where continued appropriations are justified, the yield of the earmarked taxes is almost invariably too small or too large. In the first instance the service to which the tax is allocated suffers, while in the second it tends to expand beyond need, to the detriment of other services. It is interesting to note that the constitution of Venezuela prohibits the earmarking of revenues for particular purposes.

A similar quasi permanence of appropriations results from the practice of extending the life of the budget, which is sometimes resorted to when political deadlocks arise. In Latin America, as elsewhere, the passage of the budget by the legislature frequently is delayed until the very last moment. If no agreement can be reached among the political parties, or between the latter and the executive, the existing budget is renewed. The Costa Rican budget now in force, for example, was originally passed in 1937 and has since been extended annually. The embarrassing rigidity of such budgets is tempered only by the practice of interim supplementary appropriations, and at times by a certain unconcern with budgetary provisions. The delay in the

[1] Roswell Magill and Carl Shoup, *The Cuban Fiscal System* (1939), pp. 103–108.

legislative dispatch of budget bills occasionally also brings it about that new expenditures are voted, while time runs short before new taxes can be agreed upon. The simple reenactment of existing taxes must then be resorted to, leaving a gap between appropriations and revenues.

II. REVENUES AND EXPENDITURES

Although the Latin American republics have come a long way since they ceased to be colonies of Spain or Portugal, certain of their basic economic and political features have remained unchanged and have continued, in varying degrees, to exert marked influence on their public finances. Foreign trade, now as then, is a dominant commercial activity, and the tariff therefore has not ceased to be an important source of revenue.[1] A change has taken place only in its nonrevenue aspects; its aim no longer is to safeguard the trade monopoly of the motherland, but to protect domestic industries. The dislike of the people for direct taxes, as well as the lack of developed administration, now as then, make easily administered indirect taxes the best method of raising internal revenues. The dispersal of population, although not so pronounced as formerly, likewise favors indirect taxation. The government of many of the republics, now as then, rests in the hands of a small minority—then the Spanish bureaucracy and some favorites of the Crown, now a native landowning aristocracy, which has understandable misgivings about levying taxes against its own interests. This accounts for the relative absence of land taxes now, as during the colonial period, and for the contemporary resistance to strongly progressive income taxes. The regressive character of the resulting revenue system is sharpened by great inequalities in the distribution of income.

An analysis of the revenues and expenditures of the republics is by no means easy. The reasons are numerous if not the same for all countries. The questionable practice of breaking up the budget is perhaps the greatest obstacle. A second difficulty is the delay in the final liquidation of budgets, because accounts sometimes are held open long after the end of the fiscal year. Third, the reconciliation of

[1] For many countries, and particularly for the great regions in the interior of the continent, foreign trade has increased in importance since colonial days, owing to improvements in transportation. During the early period the economic activities of the interior, however, were largely of a noncash character and not easily amenable to taxation.

budget results with movements in treasury balances and in the public debt occasionally meets with difficulties. Finally, the classification of revenues is guided, as it must be, by administrative considerations, which sometimes conflict with economic criteria. An excise tax, for example, levied on a commodity which is imported *in toto* is naturally classified as an internal revenue, although in an economic sense it constitutes a tariff levy. Thus a comprehensive statement of revenues and expenditures, and their breakdown into economic categories, frequently can be only approximations.

a. TARIFFS. Ease of collection constitutes, of course, the most attractive feature of the tariff from the government's point of view. Where a large stream of goods, all of them neatly labeled, flows through the narrow channels of a few ports, the government has little difficulty in sluicing off its share. The tariff, however, is not a reliable revenue producer. The foreign trade of most of the republics probably fluctuates more widely than their national incomes, and certainly more than the governments' financial needs. Export tariffs, which in varying degrees are levied by practically all Latin American governments, are particularly unreliable, because, in addition to undergoing cyclical fluctuations, they are exposed to the danger of crop failures and to sudden shifts in international demand. Haiti's experience with the export tax on coffee and Chile's experience with nitrate are cases in point. This disadvantage of export taxes from the revenue standpoint is, however, sometimes made up for by the fact that they frequently can be levied upon large foreign corporations rather than against domestic producers. In the light of the dictates of fiscal policy, of course, any tax on exports is undesirable during a depression, inasmuch as it is the equivalent of a tax on investment.

During the last quarter of a century many of the republics have shifted from a pure revenue tariff to one providing both revenue and protection. A mild movement in this direction began immediately after the last war, when a sudden flood of foreign goods threatened to inundate some of the war-created industries. During the depression the trend was greatly accentuated. Cuba, Mexico, and Brazil have been in the vanguard of the more recent movement. Partly owing to this change in the character of tariffs, but much more as a result of new internal taxes and an expansion of the domestic economy vis-à-vis a stagnant foreign trade, tariff revenues have declined in relative importance. Whereas in 1923 Argentina, Colombia, and Mexico derived 48.4,[1] 61.7, and 37.2[1] per cent, respectively, of their ordinary revenues from tariffs, in 1937, the last prosperous prewar year, the approximately corresponding figures were 39.1, 44.0, and 30.0 per cent. The impression produced by these data, however, is somewhat exaggerated because there has meanwhile been a growth in the importance of other forms of taxation on foreign trade, such as consular fees, excise taxes on commodities of foreign origin, port charges, and revenues from foreign exchange control. The latter, whether in the form of exchange taxes or of a margin between buying and selling rates, have proved particularly fertile sources of revenue. Argentina, for example, in 1939 derived 112 million pesos in special revenues from exchange profits, equal to 12 per cent of ordinary revenues. In 1940, such profits amounted to 201 millions. The vested interest in foreign exchange control which some governments have thus acquired presents a serious obstacle to the reestablishment of free exchange markets.

Although the tariff is an indirect tax, it is not inevitably regressive. If only luxuries and capital goods were thus taxed, its effect might even be progressive. In actual fact, however, although rates on luxuries may be high, stiff duties frequently are also levied on basic necessities, such as foodstuffs and textiles. Thus the lower income classes are forced to contribute disproportionately to the support of the government or of tariff-protected industries.

b. INCOME TAXES. Taxes on personal and corporate income have been in existence here and there for a considerable period, although the revenue raised through them was insignificant. Brazil, Chile, and Colombia, for example, all passed personal income-tax laws before 1924. Corporate income taxes have existed in Bolivia since 1886, in Cuba since 1900. In recent years, and particularly since the war began to cut into tariff revenues, new income-tax laws have been introduced and old rates stepped up.

A permanent income tax was not established in the United States until 1913, and the Latin American republics may therefore be said to have turned to this desirable but administratively difficult tax at an earlier stage of their economic development than this country. Since governmental expenditures in Latin America undoubtedly absorb a greater share of national incomes than they did in the United States at a comparable stage, some kind of direct taxation certainly

[1] Budget estimates.

was needed. It is less certain, however, that all the republics are psychologically and administratively ready for a personal income tax. It is commonly stated that there is a great deal of evasion, particularly in the higher brackets. This is facilitated by the fact that Latin American corporate stocks are largely in bearer form, so that the recipients of dividends cannot be traced. The Argentine Finance Minister stated a few years ago that the recipients of 80 per cent of all dividends paid out failed to pay the surtax.[1] Apparently as a result of similar difficulties, El Salvador has shifted from regular income taxes upon coffeegrowers to a tax upon exports.

Most Latin American income-tax laws apply differential rates to income from various sources, such as salaries, rents, dividends and interest, and professional income. The Mexican tax law, for example, employs five schedules of rates. The war has brought increases in income-tax receipts which have surprised even the most optimistic treasuries. Brazilian receipts from this source, for example, rose from $50.5 million in 1942 to $79.8 million in 1943. Gains have been due, not only to higher rates and to the assessment of excess-profits taxes, but more particularly to the rise in business activity and prices, both of which have swelled incomes in the upper brackets. The new revenues have helped to fill the gap left by declining customs revenues.

c. OTHER TAXES. Apart from customs and related levies, the bulk of revenues usually is derived from internal excise taxes. Income from stamp taxes also is important. Some governments obtain substantial income from national properties and nationally operated services. A number of countries, finally, derive revenues from the national lotteries. The evils of this institution have been conclusively demonstrated many times; the claim sometimes made in defense of lottery levies, that the public "enjoys paying them," seems to make no more sense than if made for an excise tax on luxuries.

Urban real estate usually is subject to tax, but other landholdings frequently are tax-free or assessed at insignificant rates. The absence of a general land tax tends to delay agricultural development, because it enables large owners to carry their sometimes vast holdings at little cost, in peaceful contemplation of the slowly growing unearned increment. In many cases the failure to levy substantial land taxes reflects

[1] Ministerio de Hacienda de la Nacion, *Proyectos financieros y economicos* 1941–1942 (Buenos Aires, 1942), p. 77. This loophole was partly plugged through the 1943 tax decree, which imposed a withholding tax upon dividends on domestically owned securities at the maximum rate of 25 per cent, subject to recovery upon declaration by the recipient.

the power of the landowning aristocracy or of big foreign corporations. Venezuela, however, has introduced a special type of tax with its recent petroleum legislation, which penalizes the continued holding of undeveloped oil lands.

While some governments have a well-organized and efficient tax system, others have devoted more resourcefulness to devising new taxes than to getting full value out of existing levies. The result sometimes is a bewildering variety of small taxes which yield little and are relatively expensive to administer. Such tax systems often also throw an unnecessarily large administrative burden upon the taxpayer; a simplification of procedures and elimination of nuisance taxes probably would not only facilitate business, but also yield larger revenues. The suggestions and comments which various experts have made on Cuban public finances, for example, are a case in point.[1]

d. EXPENDITURES. In Latin America a career in the public service attracts a proportionately much greater following than it has found in the past in the United States. The general desire to be on the public pay roll often leads to a considerable inflation of administrative personnel. Commenting on this problem, the conservative *Prensa* of Buenos Aires recently remarked that "there were employees who had instructions to show up at their offices only at the end of each month to collect their salary, because in this way they were less of a nuisance."[2] It is true that salaries often are pathetically small and rarely are in line with the rising cost of living. Efficiency naturally is not improved by this. The insufficiency of regular salaries is to blame in large part if public employees sometimes turn to irregular sources of income. Nevertheless, the overexpansion of personnel is a heavy drain on the treasury and must be held partly responsible for the high cost of public administration in many republics.

Expenditures for the armed forces frequently are also considerable. For the year 1939, for example, Argentina budgeted 19.5 per cent of her aggregate regular expenditures to the army and navy, Peru 14 per cent, Cuba 22.9 per cent. These military establishments, of course, are needed to protect national sovereignty, but they also play an important role in domestic politics. The government relies upon the armed forces to restrain unsettling political movements and must

[1] E. R. A. Seligman and Carl Shoup, *A Report on the Revenue System of Cuba* (Havana, 1932). Foreign Policy Association, Inc., Commission for the Study of Cuban Affairs, *Problems of the New Cuba* (New York, 1936), p. 373. Magill and Shoup, *op. cit.*

[2] In an editorial of Aug. 11, 1943.

in turn restrain the forces by means of generous appropriations. The relative ineffectiveness of naval artillery in dealing with internal disputes explains in part the fairly general neglect of navies, which, as the present war has shown, might be of greater usefulness to some of the republics than their armies.

Adequate expenditures for public works naturally are of considerable importance for a growing country. In former years such programs were financed in good part out of foreign loans. When the latter fell victim to the depression, some countries endeavored to finance their public works out of current revenues, frequently with discouraging results. Others, among whom Argentina is outstanding, have systematically financed development projects through internal bond issues. Argentine internal flotations for such purposes, in 1939 and 1940, amounted to approximately 15 per cent of the regular budget. It is hardly necessary to mention that public works expenditures often are heavily loaded with politics. At times this otherwise questionable aspect may become a useful means of preserving political stability. The Venezuelan government, for example, skillfully employed a rising public works program to smooth the critical transition from the dictatorial Gomez regime to a more liberal system.

In their social legislation, and in the social services provided in the budget, some of the republics are ahead of the United States, not only relative to their stage of development, but also in an absolute sense. Chile, for example, introduced a comprehensive program of social reform as early as 1924. It must be admitted, however, that legislative aims have not always been fully translated into tangible results. Moreover, the motives connected with the establishment of social insurance schemes which yield a revenue surplus in the short run may sometimes be suspect, since their financial aspects cannot fail to be attractive to the government. Social services which are not supported by direct contributions, on the other hand, frequently strain the finances of the republics.

Whereas most classes of expenditures have generally tended upward, public debt services, in many cases, weigh less heavily upon budgets than they did at the end of the twenties, because a number of the republics have unburdened themselves through the reduction or suspension of foreign debt services, followed sometimes by a settlement at lower rates. Internal financing, of which more will be said later, usually has been arranged at low cost to the government.

III. SOME CHARACTERISTICS OF THE BUDGET

The foregoing discussion reveals a disproportion which is characteristic of many Latin American budgets: the contrast between an antiquated revenue system and an advanced expenditure program containing provisions for liberal social services and other needs. The result is a steady pressure which makes it necessary to work existing sources of revenue for all they are worth, with little hope of tax reductions at any time. During a depression, taxes are increased in order to bolster shrinking receipts. When recovery brings unexpectedly large returns from these levies, expenditures tend to expand to the limit of available funds. Of course, these characteristics are not the exclusive property of Latin American public finances, but they appear there with particular force.

The effects on business enterprise of the tax systems already described cannot, on the whole, be regarded as depressive. It is true that in some instances the multiplicity of taxes and the complexities of their administration are a drag upon enterprise. Taxes on profits, however, are light, and excess-profits taxes, a very restrictive form of business taxation, began to appear only after the war raised profits to very substantial levels. Even the new Brazilian excess-profits tax, with its fairly impressive maximum rate of 50 per cent, is not so severe as might seem, since this rate applies only to profits in the top bracket and since, in addition, it contains several escape clauses. Business taxation may, however, become depressive in cases where a large and well-established industry has become a fiscal wheel horse which can always be relied upon to pull the budget over the hump. The sugar industry in Cuba, which has been made to suffer at times because it was always good for a little extra revenue, exemplifies this situation.

Owing to the regressive character of the revenue system, which is obvious in view of the predominance of consumption taxes and the low level of income levies, savings go largely untaxed. In a mature economy this would be bad fiscal policy, and a redistribution of income through progressive taxes would be advisable, in order to raise the propensity to consume, quite apart from considerations of equity. In a developing country, however, savings call for stimulation rather than discouragement, and a steeply progressive income tax would be undesirable from this angle. Nevertheless, the matter cannot be stated in quite such simple terms. A regressive and inadequate tax system may, for example, be a cause of political or monetary instability and thus indirectly discourage capital formation. The lack of tax consciousness which results from predominantly indirect taxation may likewise be regarded as an obstacle to political and economic progress. Hence, while taxation of savings at rates similar to those which have been applied for some time in the United States would be undesirable, even if feasible, the need for capital formation is no conclusive argument against some degree of progressive taxation.

IV. BORROWING

A great change in the borrowing practices of Latin American governments was brought about during the thirties by the collapse of the international capital market. It may be hoped that in the postwar period this market will once more revive, and a few considerations connected with foreign loans therefore require attention.

a. FOREIGN LOANS. Only a few Latin American governments were able to meet their foreign obligations fully, or almost fully, during the difficult period of the thirties. Those who succeeded did so at a considerable sacrifice, and it is of some interest to inquire whether their efforts have in any sense been rewarded. Ethical considerations aside, the maintenance of debt service is worth while in a financial sense only if the borrower thereby maintains a credit standing which allows him to raise further loans as needed. It is discouraging, therefore, to note that during the thirties Argentina was the only Latin American country able to float a loan in New York. Countries like Cuba and Uruguay, whose record of debt payment shows only minor blemishes, were unable to borrow in the American capital market. It is a characteristic of this market that it looks primarily to the earning power of the borrower, *i.e.*, in the case of a nation, to its fiscal capacity and its potential supplies of foreign exchange. During the depression the earning power of most Latin American countries was low, and the honest effort which some countries put forth to meet their obligations could not remedy that shortcoming.[1] Since the outbreak of the war, however, Latin American countries have been able to borrow from United States government agencies practically regardless of past debt performance. It appears, therefore, that up to the present at least, special efforts of particular debtors have not been "rewarded." In the postwar period past performance may yet be made to tell, but it

[1] Domestic borrowers whose credit rating had gone down experienced similar difficulties in their attempts to raise funds in New York.

must be feared that the lessons which borrowers are likely to draw from recent experience will unfavorably affect international credit relations for some time to come.

Latin American borrowing policies during the twenties almost universally neglected an important consideration which since has gained recognition and has been embodied in the United States Treasury's draft for a Bank for Reconstruction and Development.[1] It was not sufficiently appreciated that there is no need to raise abroad funds which are to be spent domestically, *i.e.*, for local labor and materials, except insofar as local expenditures may generate additional demand for imports, which would require foreign exchange. If such funds are raised abroad, they must be converted into domestic currency through sales to the local market or to the central bank. The resulting credit expansion will be no less than if the funds had been borrowed directly in the internal market or, if not available there, from the central bank. The latter method therefore is less burdensome, always keeping in mind the qualification with respect to additional demand for imports. Private borrowers and political subdivisons naturally cannot be expected to take this into account; they will borrow wherever money is cheapest. The monetary authorities, therefore, must see to it that the balance of payments is not burdened with additional debt service beyond what is necessary.

b. DOMESTIC BORROWING. All but a few Latin American countries, among which Argentina is the outstanding exception, encounter considerable difficulty in borrowing from their own nationals. The weakness of local capital markets, and of markets for government bonds in particular, can be traced to various roots. In the first place must be mentioned the paucity of savings, the great inequality in the distribution of income notwithstanding. The basic cause of this paucity is of course the low level of national incomes as a whole. In part, however, the deficiency of savings must also be attributed to political and monetary instability and to the tendency toward dissaving evident among some members of the wealthy classes, which is attested by heavy unproductive mortgages resting upon many great estates. A second major reason for the weakness of domestic capital markets is the lack of confidence which native capitalists, more than foreign investors, have felt toward the governments of the republics and

[1] *Preliminary Draft Outline of a Proposal for a Bank for Reconstruction and Development of the United and Associated Nations* (Nov. 24, 1943), IV-8-*b*.

which has been sharpened by the external defaults of the thirties. This attitude toward internal obligations has been much less justified than it would have been in the case of the external debts, for defaults on internal obligations have been comparatively rare, although they did occur once in a while. Instances are the defaults on the older Mexican internal bonds, on the Paraguayan internal bonds of 1935, and on various Colombian internal bonds. It is true, of course, that a country with a central bank or even a printing press need never default on its internal debt, but the inflationary consequences of maintaining service by these means may be very grave. In a situation where default and inflation are the sole alternatives, a country with an undeveloped internal debt structure may be well advised to sacrifice government credit in favor of price stability, although a country like the United States, whose monetary system would utterly collapse if the government defaulted, probably would have to choose the other alternative. A final obstacle to the domestic placement of government bonds is the fact that these bonds compete with real-estate mortgages and business investment on distinctly unfavorable terms. The yield on mortgages is frequently in the neighborhood of 10 to 12 per cent—a return higher than any government can afford to offer. Earnings in a successful enterprise usually are far above what is customary in the United States and not infrequently a multiple of what the government can offer. Under the new Brazilian excess-profits tax, profits equal to 25 per cent employed capital (not identical with capital and surplus) are regarded as "normal." Average profits of a group of representative Mexican industries in 1941, an admittedly prosperous year, were 17.9 per cent, profits of Mexican commercial banks 22.5 per cent.

Some governments have by-passed these obstacles to internal flotations by the simple device of turning over bonds to contractors in payment of public works. Although the response of these reluctant holders, who are likely to sell out at a discount, does not help a government's credit standing, it does help to create a market. In Mexico, where road contractors frequently are paid in this form, their bankers have sometimes made a market for the bonds.

Direct borrowing from central banks has been the main recourse of many hard-pressed finance ministers. Most Latin American central banks hold large blocs of government debt, although this is not always evident from their published statements. In some instances, part of the debt antedates the establishment of the respective central bank. Although the statutes of practically all such banks contain provisions against excessive lending to the government, these restrictions, like similar restraints in the case of the Federal Reserve System, have had to be relaxed when the pressure became too high. The portfolio of the Banco Central de Bolivia, which contains 99.5 per cent of the internal public debt, is an example, although an extreme one, of this type of financing.

Borrowing from central banks has been cheap, because governments can name their own rates, and can usually recoup part of the interest paid via their participation in profits. Some central banks, among which that of Argentina has done pioneer work, have undertaken to offset the inflationary consequences of government borrowing (and of the recent foreign exchange inflow) by the sale of certificates of participation in government bondholdings. This procedure substitutes a short-term instrument, which is attractive to banks and business firms, for a long-term one, which perhaps cannot easily be marketed. The credit of the government is replaced by that of the central bank, which in some countries is reported to rate more highly. In this way, a market may gradually be built up, first for short- and later for longer term securities. The careful nursing of money and capital markets, wherever they are not adequately adopted, should be one of the primary concerns of the monetary authorities, since weak capital markets limit the potentialities of fiscal and particularly of monetary policy.

V. PROBLEMS OF FISCAL POLICY[1]

The basic problems of Latin American fiscal policy were briefly summarized at the beginning of this paper, and particular reference was made to the significance of imports and exports, which assume the roles played by investment and saving in the United States. This exchange of roles has important and rather discouraging consequences. In the United States only a very minor part of a rise in income is spent on foreign goods, and hence there is no great difference between the marginal propensity[2] to consume home-produced plus foreign goods and that to consume home-produced goods alone. In Latin America,

[1] In view of the somewhat technical character of the discussion which follows, the non-economist reader might prefer to skip this section.

[2] The marginal propensity to consume any particular type of good is defined as the increase in the consumption of that good associated with a given rise in income.

however, the difference is decisive; for while the marginal propensity to consume both types of goods is high, that to consume home-produced goods alone is relatively low. Although the absence of satisfactory statistics on national income for the Latin American countries makes numerical comparisons difficult, it is probably safe to say that for at least a good number of the republics the propensity to consume home-produced goods is lower than for the United States; their income multiplier, therefore, is also lower.[1] Their economies, in other words, require a larger stimulus in order to attain a given rise in income.

A low multiplier, while inconvenient from the viewpoint of effective deficit spending, ordinarily has at least the advantage of endowing the economy with greater stability.[2] In the case of the Latin American countries, however, this potential advantage is more than offset by the extreme width of fluctuations in exports. Cyclical swings in volume are large enough, but even wider are fluctuations in prices, since exports consist mainly of raw materials. Whereas in the United States such swings in the price of a large part of national output would produce changes primarily in money income, leaving real income relatively unchanged, in Latin America the effect on real income is also substantial, owing to the great importance of imported goods, the price of which is relatively more stable. The effect of cyclical fluctuations upon income, in other words, is aggravated by parallel changes in the terms of trade.

Another element detrimental to Latin American stability remains to be mentioned. In the United States, the effect of investment is to raise national income above a certain equilibrium level at which saving and investment are both zero; and national income is maintained, because it is consumed in its entirety.[3] While the prospect of "bumping along the bottom" is not attractive, it conveys at least the relative assurance that income will not fall further. Most of the Latin American economies do not have this floor under their income. Although income may easily fall to the point where savings become zero, it would have to drop much further before the demand for

[1] For a discussion of the multiplier, with special reference to foreign trade, see F. Machlup, *International Trade and the National Income Multiplier* (Philadelphia, 1943). The formulation of the multiplier theory relevant to the present discussion is that which regards total exports and investment as autonomous factors.

[2] A low multiplier also causes the adjustment in the balance of payments to any given change in exports to take place more rapidly than would otherwise be the case.

[3] *Cf.* Alvin H. Hansen, *Fiscal Policy and Business Cycles* (New York, 1941), Ch. XIII.

imports had disappeared or could be offset by investment and dishoarding. This dilemma is made less acute but is not quite eliminated by the fact that exports are less likely than investment to fall to zero. In any case, moreover, depreciation or exchange control could and undoubtedly would be resorted to in order to reduce the leakage of income into imports and to equilibrate exports and imports, but the absence of a basic level below which income cannot fall is nevertheless a disadvantage. The extreme income shrinkage during the depression in Cuba, where depreciation and exchange control were not feasible, illustrates this.

In brief, then, it may be said that in spite of the relative stability provided by a low multiplier, the great volatility in the size of the stimulating factors and the character of the leakages make the income of the republics highly unstable. With this in mind, we may proceed to survey the influence exerted upon national income by exports and investments, or, what is more interesting for our purposes, by government spending. This influence makes itself felt through three distinct chains of causation: (1) the multiplier, (2) induced investment, (3) rising liquidity.

It follows from what has already been said that the multiplier effect must be relatively small. A large part of the government's expenditures is drained away into imports and does not stimulate the domestic economy. Rising imports imply, of course, that other economies are being stimulated, but the thought that American or British exports have been raised by a small fraction of 1 per cent is little comfort and less profit to a Latin American government.

Induced investment is likely to appear at an early stage, because the capacity of domestic industry is small and expansion soon becomes necessary in the face of rising national income. Its importance as an income-generating factor, however, will often be small, since a large part of the funds to be invested must be spent abroad. The acceleration effect of government spending, in other words, like its multiplier effect, probably will not be very great.

There remains the effect associated with a rise in liquidity. A budget deficit is virtually certain to involve an increase in the supply of money, since the chances of financing it exclusively out of savings are practically nil. It is true that in the United States during the thirties the rising supply of money failed to act as a major stimulus; the new money simply entered into idle balances. In Latin American countries, however, an increase in the quantity of money appears to be more effective. One may suggest that the simple quantity theory of money, which has been rejected by most of its former adherents on the basis of recent experience, still holds good to some extent in Latin America. This seems to be particularly true with respect to the volume of currency, which in Mexico, for example, appears to be closely correlated with the price level, whereas the influence of deposits seems to be minor. One can do no more than speculate as to what makes Latin Americans less willing to hold idle money than North Americans have been during the last 15 years. Probably it has something to do with past experience with monetary instability, with high interest rates and a low volume of saving, with the absence—usually—of well-organized money and securities markets, and with the greater proportion of currency employed relative to bank deposits. Perhaps it also is not unconnected with the state of the spirit of enterprise in the respective parts of the Hemisphere.

The sum total of the effects exerted by government spending, via the multiplier, induced investment, and greater liquidity, is likely to be quite large, although each effect may be relatively small. A substantial expansion of national income through government spending, however, meets with two grave obstacles. The first of these is the lack of a sufficiently well-rounded industrial system. In the United States, rising expenditures would tend to draw idle factors into the productive process, and no serious inflationary consequences need be expected until full employment was being approached. Not so, however, in most Latin American countries. There the economy is geared to absorb idle resources only in one direction—toward the export industries. These, however, are usually little affected by rising domestic demand, whereas the industries whose products are in demand cannot expand and absorb factors as rapidly as necessary. The channels through which monetary demand must flow to become effective in raising output are simply not there. Thus the limits of expansion in the domestic industries are likely to be reached even while there is still large-scale unemployment in the export industries. If government spending takes the form of purchases of export products, the latter industries will indeed provide the economy with substantially full employment. But since goods that cannot be sold are of small value, such government purchases add little more to national income than a straight dole.

The second obstacle, which is financial in character rather than structural, is the loss of foreign exchange reserves, which must be expected when imports rise and the balance of payments turns passive. As long as the outflow of exchange is tolerated, nothing worse will happen than a decline in the liquidity of the banking system, which can be offset by appropriate monetary policy. The country then is simply adding to its current income by consuming accumulated reserves. If credit contraction or a cessation of government spending does not reverse the passive balance, however, depreciation and foreign exchange control eventually become the only alternatives. Either will serve to bring about equilibrium in the balance of payments, but the enforced decline in imports shunts part of the income stream, which had previously gone abroad, back upon the domestic economy. The inelastic supply situation prevailing there meanwhile is aggravated by the scarcity of foreign raw materials and supplies, which now begin to hamper the domestic industries. Under the impact of rising demand and incipient shortages, therefore, prices will begin to rise. If exchange control, rather than depreciation, was first resorted to, the latter measure may now also become necessary, in order to protect the already stagnant export industries against an increase in costs. If depreciation was the original solution, it now may have to be supplemented by exchange control, because the rise in domestic prices soon begins to counteract the favorable effects of lower exchange rates upon the balance of payments. Different paths thus lead into the same blind alley.

It is worth while to trace some of the effects of depreciation upon national income. Generally it is assumed that under all but very exceptional circumstances depreciation is likely to bring about an increase in exports and a decline in imports. National income then gains because (1) it is stimulated by rising exports and (2) this stimulus again is made more effective by the rise in the marginal propensity to consume home-produced goods, which increases the multiplier.[1] These basic tendencies are present, of course, in Latin America, but they are frequently counteracted, and even obliterated, by other factors. If the public, and particularly importers, expect depreciation to continue, imports will rise, because they now become a profitable

[1] The unfavorable effect which depreciation usually has upon the terms of trade must be taken into account, however, in estimating real income gains from depreciation. The extent of this effect depends chiefly, though not exclusively, upon the importance of the depreciating country as a buyer and seller on the world market.

speculation. While inventory buying by importers does not directly reduce the domestic-income stream, indirectly it may have this effect in more ways than one. To carry larger stocks, importers need bank credit. Where the supply of credit is not unlimited, the accommodation available to producers of export goods is reduced and their output suffers. The attention of businessmen becomes increasingly absorbed in speculative trading operations, and the more humdrum job of production tends to be neglected. Exporters, finally, endeavor to delay their sales, and hence, also, some of the expenditures which are connected with the liquidation of the crop. If these effects are strong enough, we have the paradoxical result that depreciation for a while encourages imports and discourages exports, thereby contributing to a further drop in the currency. Ecuador, for example, seems to have been caught in a vicious circle of this sort during various parts of the thirties.

It is evident, then, that although large-scale government spending will not remain ineffective, its ability to produce an expansion of real income nevertheless is limited by the size of foreign exchange reserves and the capacity of the domestic industries. Expenditures which take account of these limits will probably be beneficial, but larger ones are likely to produce nothing more than a rise in prices and a decline in the currency. By purchasing unexportable surpluses, the government can maintain approximately full employment without inflation, as long as its exchange reserves permit a sufficient volume of imports. Thereafter, expenditures would have to be cut down to a level compatible with the capacity of domestic industries. With a given volume of exchange reserves in hand, therefore, the government has the choice of large expenditures for a short period or of smaller ones for a longer period.

Small expenditures, however, while better than a drop in the bucket, are hardly more than a cupful during a major depression. Because of the large shrinkage in exports, government expenditures frequently would have to be on a very substantial scale. In the absence of enormous exchange reserves, therefore, most of the republics will not be able to escape the effects of a prolonged depression abroad, no matter how skillful their fiscal policies.

Only a few words need be said here of measures to curb a boom—which at present are of great topical interest—as they are being dealt with in other chapters of this book. The point already made in connection with depression policies applies here as well: since the disturbing element is large, the government's countermeasures likewise have to be on a substantial scale. Chief emphasis must be placed upon income taxation, accompanied, if possible, by sterilization of part of the proceeds, because in most of the republics the main expansionary force is the immediate impact of large exports upon incomes and profits, rather than the secondary effect of credit expansion. Adequate monetary measures, such as sales of government securities to absorb purchasing power, nevertheless are also important. The tools for carrying out such a stabilization program—a progressive tax system and a broad market for government bonds—are gradually being forged. In most of the republics, however, they still are far from attaining the effectiveness which they need in order to deal with the present explosive situation. Once the instruments are at hand, fiscal policy in Latin America would be approaching the point at which monetary policy in the United States appears to have arrived some time ago: it can prevent overexpansion, but it cannot equally well cope with a depression.

VI. WARTIME AND POSTWAR FISCAL POLICIES

Before the war, Latin American fiscal policies were concerned mainly with public works and, in some instances, with operations to support the price of export products. These fiscal measures were undertaken chiefly to cure specific ills, and their effect on national income in general was a secondary aspect in most instances. The expansion of the United States arms program soon eliminated any need for general income stimulation, but simultaneously it intensified the necessity of supporting individual commodities. This burden, however, was largely taken over by the United States, through purchase and storage operations. The biggest operation of this type, however, the financing of Argentina's grain surpluses, was carried out by that country with its own resources.

In the course of the war, emphasis has shifted from antidepression measures toward techniques of controlling a boom. Within the realm of fiscal policy, the problem has been attacked chiefly through income taxes and sales of securities. Details regarding these and other measures will be found in Prof. Harris's chapter on Price Stabilization Programs. A few words may be said, however, concerning the public works policy of some of the republics. It is obvious that one of the first moves in putting the brakes on a boom should be a reduction in the government's own investment activities. This, however, has not been the rule in recent Latin American fiscal policy. Mexico did indeed announce its intention to reduce public works expenditures in 1943. Brazil likewise indicated that such expenditures would be cut down. The latter country's regular public works appropriation in 1943, however, has remained unchanged from the 1942 budget, and other governments also have continued, or even increased, public works expenditures. To some extent, the maintenance of these programs is justified by the desire to prevent sectional unemployment, which would result from their suspension. It must also be remembered that in a developing country public works, besides being a stimulus to income, are ordinarily needed for their own sake. More significantly, however, the continuance of these expenditures reflects the still prevailing view that the time to spend money is when the money is there. A sound compensatory policy should follow the opposite principle, but the idea of sterilizing the proceeds of bond sales and particularly of taxes still meets with considerable resistance. There can be no doubt that government spending and credit policies have aggravated the inflationary situation in several of the republics.

In the postwar period, fiscal policy will be facilitated by the wartime growth in domestic industries, which has somewhat lessened dependence upon foreign trade, by the improvement in income-tax systems and by better government-bond markets. A fundamental change from the prewar pattern, however, need not be anticipated in these respects. Another of the factors governing the scope of fiscal policy, however, has undergone a very substantial modification as a result of the war—the reserves of foreign exchange. The exchange resources of almost all the republics have grown tremendously. At the present time the aggregate is more than $2 billion and it continues to rise. This phenomenon is due in part to abnormally large exports and in part to subnormal imports, and has been intensified, in some countries, by an inflow of capital. Hence the accumulation of delayed demand, in conjunction with the availability of foreign exchange, has led to the belief that a great Latin American buying wave is in prospect, once goods become available. It has even been suggested that this reversal of the wartime flow of purchasing power might come to be a sustaining factor in the United States economy, if a postwar slump should develop.

These optimistic forecasts must be received with some skepticism. It may be suggested instead that the intensity of Latin American demand for our goods will depend not so much on the mere existence of large exchange reserves as upon the level of national income in the republics, which in turn depends upon exports, investment, and fiscal and monetary policies. If business is good, Latin American buying will be heavy. If business is bad, the chances are that the new reserves will remain in large part unused.[1] Hence, if exports or investment is insufficient to produce prosperity, the use or nonuse of reserves will largely depend upon fiscal and monetary policies.

The conclusion that a large volume of reserves and even a heavy backlog of unsatisfied demand will not by themselves induce large imports is supported by several considerations. It is true, of course, that many acute shortages must be made good and that imports, therefore, will not be determined exclusively by national income. A certain amount of delayed-demand buying can confidently be expected. But it is probably wrong to assume that the exchange reserves accumulated during the war have as their counterpart an equivalent accumulation of savings and that the size of these reserves can hence be taken as an indication of the demand that will develop. Although new money has been created against incoming exchange, much of it has gone, not into idle balances, but into active circulation, where it is needed because of higher prices and rising activity.[2] Part of these active funds would no doubt be set free if business declined, but that condition would hardly encourage the placing of larger orders abroad.[3] If national income shrinks, Latin America will find out, as we did during the thirties, that demand once delayed can be delayed again.

Any voluntary curtailment of purchases in the face of falling business activity is likely to be accelerated by governmental measures

[1] If capital flight is permitted to proceed unchecked, reserves may dwindle although imports remain low.

[2] While some economists would define this new money, however held, as savings, it does not represent savings available for the purchase of imports.

[3] This view need not be regarded as conflicting with earlier remarks concerning the relative unwillingness of Latin Americans to hold idle balances. This unwillingness probably will have a certain stimulating effect upon imports when a fall in prices and activity makes presently active funds idle. Barring a very severe deflation, however, one must expect a permanently higher price level in Latin America, which will limit the volume of funds to become idle. Their amount will further be reduced by repayments of bank loans, and perhaps by capital flight. Finally, the desire to hold idle balances is likely to increase at least temporarily, when a depression sets in.

aimed at protecting domestic industries (some degree of protection for war-created industries must be expected in any case). Higher tariffs, more rigid foreign exchange control, and depreciation are then likely to be resorted to. All these gloomy reflections apply, of course, only to slump conditions, resulting from a depression experienced by the republics' major trade partners. If the latter are prosperous, the exports of the republics will be large, and so will their imports, but there will then be little need to call upon accumulated exchange reserves.

Given, then, the conclusion that the use or nonuse of exchange reserves will in large measure depend upon fiscal and monetary policies, it is important to note that the existence of these reserves is in itself an inducement to pursue liberal policies. A shortage of reserves, as already pointed out, constitutes the chief limiting factor for an expansionary fiscal policy. From this limitation the republics have now been freed to a considerable extent. For the first time since fiscal policy came into their purview, the republics can pursue a large-scale expansionary program for an extended period without having to fear that a passive balance will soon confront them with the choice between contraction and inflation. It is to be hoped, therefore, that the monetary authorities will not yield to the temptation to hoard gold, as some of them have done during earlier depressions, but will make full use of their new reserves if a postwar slump should develop.

Chapter VI

Price Stabilization Programs in Latin America

by SEYMOUR E. HARRIS

INFLATION control is one of the serious economic and political problems of Latin America. Price or inflation control assures an equitable distribution of goods in wartime. Moreover, any group which suffers from rising prices—because its income does not rise so rapidly as prices—becomes disgruntled, and therefore the group becomes a political liability. Price control is therefore necessary both on political and economic grounds. All groups will gain—even the business entrepreneur who, though he may temporarily gain through rising prices, would pay the bill in the later, inevitable period of collapse.

This chapter is divided into two parts: (1) some broad generalizations which apply more or less to all Latin American countries; (2) individual studies of five countries. In the latter the peculiar problems of each country are considered in detail. Some readers may wish to read only Part I and particular sections of Part II.

I. THE GENERAL PICTURE[1]

Inflation is a vital economic problem of common interest to the Americas. Inflationary forces have been at work on a hemispheric

[1] This section is largely based on the introduction of a "Report on Anti-inflationary Programs in the United States." That document, which includes reports to four Latin American governments, was put together for the use of several agencies of the United States government. The introduction of that report has been published in *Foreign Commerce Weekly*, October, 1943, and in numerous Latin American journals.

scale. This is reflected in the sharp wartime rise of living costs in the Latin American republics, the same as in the United States, particularly during the period of shortage in shipping facilities, with the consequent decline in imported supplies from the United States. Rising living costs in the United States are induced by current wartime conditions—tremendous war spending, disruption of normal trade, shortage of shipping, concentration of industry upon arms production, shift of manpower into the armed forces and arms factories, and loss of raw material from the sources of supply, such as rubber and tin from the Far East.

The battle against rising prices transcends national borders to become a problem international in scope. In the Western Hemisphere it is in truth an inter-American problem. The inter-American aspects of the problem have been recognized officially both in the United States and in the other Americas. At the Rio de Janeiro Conference of American Foreign Ministers in January, 1942, the basis was laid for Hemisphere cooperation in price control. In the cooperative spirit of that conference, the United States has extended, insofar as possible, the protection of its own price ceilings to goods moving into export channels for the other Americas. Cooperation in price control also has been manifest in the request for and assignment of representatives of the Office of Price Administration to aid some of the other Americas in working out price control mechanisms and integrating these mechanisms with United States price controls.

SERIOUS PROBLEMS REVEALED. As one of these representatives recently sent to Latin America, the author can speak at first hand of the cooperation and of the serious problems revealed. The main objectives of this visit were to see what could be done to integrate more effectively our price policies with those of the other Americas and to be available for consultation on price control measures. Brazil, Chile, Bolivia, Peru, and Colombia were visited. Keen interest was found in these countries in anti-inflationary measures and proposals for moderating the domestic rise in prices of goods imported from the United States.

Prior to this trip the Office of Price Administration made a study of prices of United States products in Latin America. The study revealed serious problems in the pricing of United States products in the other Americas. In general the rise in prices to the ultimate consumer was excessive when compared with United States f.o.b. port of exit or Latin American prices c.i.f. port of entry. This discrepancy obviously was due in large measure to speculation for higher prices in scarce imported goods.

The Latin American countries are very much interested in stopping the speculation which is rampant in the area of imported commodities and have taken measures to deal with these problems. In Brazil, for example, the government, under the Ministry of Economic Mobilization, has taken very strong measures to control the number of middlemen, determine the resale prices of the importers, and eliminate excessive demands for imported commodities.

To ensure the sale of imported commodities at reasonable prices to the final consumer, it is necessary to fix prices at the point of embarkation and at the port of entry and to fix the resale prices by the importers and any other distributors who are involved. Where—as has happened in at least one country—the one who purchases, presumably as a consumer, holds private auction sales at highly inflated prices, it is desirable that these sales be prohibited. When a consumer purchases, he should be required to consume and not to act as a middleman.

Unless this control is carried through at every stage of distribution, some middlemen will make large profits. For example, the refrigerator that is sent to South America may cost $150 at the port of entry; but if only one-quarter as many refrigerators are sent as are demanded at a reasonable price to the ultimate consumer of, say, $200, the price will rise greatly in the absence of a thoroughgoing control. In a free market under present supply-and-demand conditions, the price may well rise to $500. It is up to the government to ensure a price of $200 and not to allow an importer or distributor to absorb the extra $300; to eliminate unnecessary middlemen; to control the prices of resale at every stage; and to eliminate demand which is based merely on capacity to pay and not demand which is based on urgency of need.

PRICE RISES LARGE. There can be no mistaking the rise of prices in Latin America: these rises have been large. They are discussed more fully later in a chapter on exchanges and prices. As a general rule, the increases have occurred at a more rapid rate than in the United States. This is rather unexpected in view of the fact that in the United States we are spending at the rate of $90 billion annually for war, whereas in the Latin American countries war expenditures have been relatively small. The more rapid rise of prices in these countries has become a matter of concern to the governments involved—all are initiating strong measures to deal with the situation.

Unfortunately, many of these countries lack the experienced personnel to administer thoroughgoing price control programs. They are therefore inclined to rely rather heavily on decrees and not sufficiently on administration and enforcement. These governments are aware of the saving to consumers and to their own budgets that will result from effective price control. They are, therefore, expanding their programs and personnel in an attempt to bring about, through price control, a better distribution of scarce supplies.

In some cases these governments—like ours—have made mistakes in the area of price control. They have attempted to write sweeping laws without adequate enforcement. In some cases they have encountered difficulties resulting from division of responsibility, conflict of interests between ministries, and an unwillingness by the legislature to grant adequate authority to the executive. Yet, despite these difficulties, the countries of Latin America are making progress. Certainly the record of the United States in the area of price control is not so unblemished as to warrant strong criticism of the Latin American price programs.

THE PATTERN OF INFLATION. The general picture of inflation is similar in each country. There is an excess of Latin American exports, which is explained by insistent war demands, by favorable selling agreements for important crops, and by restrictions on exports by selling countries, particularly by the United Kingdom and the United States. Although in many cases the United States has been able to fill the gap where usual sources of supply for Latin America could not be tapped, nevertheless the excess of exports of Latin American countries has continued to be large.

This excess, plus the inflow of capital, has flooded Latin American countries with dollars and with sterling. These dollars in turn are converted into local currency. An exporter who sells copper obtains dollars. He is required to turn over a certain percentage of his dollars to the central exchange authorities. In return he receives pesos. These pesos are represented by a deposit of the banks. The banks in turn obtain cash with the central bank for the dollars turned over by the exporter. The central bank now holds more dollars, and against this asset it has a liability, *viz.*, deposits belonging to the banks.

Under these circumstances, both the commercial banks and the central bank have increased their cash as much as their liabilities. Since ordinarily their liabilities are several times the amount of their cash, both the commercial and the central banks are in a position to expand their liabilities—*i.e.*, create more money. As the recipients of income in the prosperous export industries now spend their money, they increase demand and output in other industries, and these industries in turn are favored by new loans, which are made possible by the original inflow of dollars. This expansion of money, then, is accompanied by a larger expansion of income and output and further increases in the supply of money.

Ordinarily an importation of capital results in an increase of imports for the borrowing country and a reduction of exports. In this manner, the borrowing country obtains its capital by obtaining more goods. In the present war, however, the inflow of capital brings about, for the most part, not an expansion of imports and a reduction of exports for the borrowing country, but rather an inflow of dollars. In other words, a large part of the capital that is exported to these countries is used to pay for domestic resources and labor in the Latin American countries and not to purchase machinery, raw materials, engineering services, and other requirements from the United States.

Another peculiarity of the present situation is this: the more rapid rise of prices in Latin American countries is not having the effect of discouraging exports and encouraging imports for the country that suffers from the more rapid rise of prices. This failure of exports to decline and of imports to be encouraged is explained by the unimportant role played by price movements in wartime. In view of the insistent demand for Latin American products, exports are determined by considerations of political and economic warfare and not by price considerations primarily. The United States pays whatever is necessary for essential supplies. And, despite unusual demand and higher incomes in Latin America and relatively low prices in the United States, these countries are unable to purchase additional supplies as they would have been able to do in more normal times. What goes abroad from the United States is determined by allocations and available transportation and only to a small degree by price movements.

Increased wages do not contribute so much to inflation in Latin America as in the United States. First, wages there have not risen as much as in the United States. Second, there has not been the large rise of employment that has been experienced here. It should be observed, however, that because wages in Latin America *follow* the rise of prices—and generally with considerable lag and frequently with smaller rises—the increase of prices brings serious distortions in the distribution of available supplies of goods.

GOVERNMENTAL PARTICIPATION. In Latin American countries, the governments are now playing a larger part in the economic life of the communities. Even if this increased participation did not involve deficit financing, the effects on prices would still be serious. This follows both because there is very little unemployment in these countries, and therefore any additional demand, *e.g.*, through absorption of idle savings, is likely to bring about higher prices, and because the governments rely heavily on indirect taxes. The more they spend, the greater the burden of taxes on commodities. Therefore, even with balanced budgets, prices rise with increased government spending.

In many cases the increased participation of the government makes it more difficult to obtain supplies of strategic materials, since the government competes for available transportation, labor, and other economic factors. On the other hand the government, in this manner, also builds roads, irrigates farms, and performs other tasks that may be considered part of the general program for the development of the economic resources of these countries. One might, however, raise the question as to whether a larger part of these development programs should not be postponed for the postwar period when unemployment of economic resources may be a serious problem.

Countries in Latin America have had considerable experience with price control and in some cases have had price control previous to the United States. Several of them have put into effect a general freeze of all prices. Others have concentrated on a limited number of the necessities of life. In general, price control has not been over-successful. The freeze technique does not work well unless all factors that contribute toward prices of products are stabilized more or less. The freeze will not be successful in the absence of a high degree of regulation unless indirect taxes are stabilized and excess purchasing power is siphoned off through adequate direct taxes and borrowing programs and unless wages are stabilized.

WHAT IS THE WAY OUT? Before suggestions are made, it must be remembered that a tax program of the proportions attained in the United States is not possible in these countries—first, because participation in the war is limited and, second, because the tax systems are not so flexible as ours. Where countries are not heavily industrialized, where governments are dependent largely on indirect taxes, and where tax collection is beset with many difficulties, an expansion of total taxes, for all governments, of three to five times—as in the United States' experience—will not be forthcoming.

Another difficulty with price control in these countries is that they have not been able to introduce comprehensive rationing programs. Rationing is difficult of attainment because of the administrative complexities and also because many of the products that are scarce are not consumed widely enough to justify rationing. The net effect is that these countries, confronted with high incomes and insufficient supply of goods, are unable to reduce demand through the introduction of rationing programs and to that extent are faced with very difficult problems of price enforcement. They have, however, reduced the demand for imports through licensing of imports and allocation of exchange.

The general prescription for these countries is more or less the same: Concentrate price control on a limited area and, in particular, on the necessities of life and the indispensable machines and raw materials. Introduce price control all along the line for the vital commodities. As administration improves in this limited area, as the excess purchasing power gradually spills into uncontrolled areas, and as economic resources move into the uncontrolled areas (in response to more favorable, *i.e.*, uncontrolled, prices) controls are gradually extended. Wherever possible, prices should be fixed in pesos and centavos and regional differences in prices allowed for. This last is particularly important, because transportation costs are so high in Latin America. (The peso is used here only for convenience of expression and not as the currency of all Latin American countries.)

Where commodities are numerous, and where the cost of acquisition varies greatly, it may be necessary to use a markup system rather than a specific peso and centavo price regulation. Where the markup system is used, the governments should be careful to allow an adequate markup. An insufficient markup results in wholesale evasions, as has been proved by experience. The markup system is more difficult to enforce and, therefore, should not be used except where absolutely necessary. Since most of these countries are not far advanced in manufacturing, as compared with the United States, and have relatively few products, it may be possible for them to fix manufactured prices on the basis of costs and not use the elastic and difficult-to-enforce formula ceilings that are used in the United States. Above all, emphasis must be given to administration and enforcement because the greatest weakness of price control in Latin America lies in this direction.

In general, Latin American price authorities have been given more than adequate authority on paper. They generally may obtain necessary information on stocks, prices, costs, and capital invested; they may requisition; the government may buy and sell, determine prices and markups, and classify commodities and stores. Even where price control has been none too successful (*e.g.*, in Bolivia), the powers granted have been adequate. Adequate powers are available in other countries: Chile, Brazil, Colombia, etc. In some respects Latin American countries have gone much further than the United States. A Brazilian program provides for the manufacture of an adequate proportion of cheap textiles: prices are to be based on direct costs only, the overhead costs to be covered in the prices for more expensive textiles. In this manner, the well-to-do consumer subsidizes the poor consumer. In Peru a large part of the distribution of foods has been taken over by the government; in this manner, official prices are ensured. Where speculators tended to increase the price of imported machinery excessively, the Colombian government took over the trade. In Bolivia the police stand guard in the Indian markets of La Paz, thus preventing any gouging at the expense of the lowest income groups.

Despite these advances, the results so far have frequently not been satisfactory. Too much paper authority; too little administration; too many new middlemen; excessive reliance on freezes where the possibility of a success is even less than in the United States; recourse to rent control on the basis of investment, which is difficult of enforcement; a tendency to introduce control over too large an area; the setting of margins that are too low to enlist cooperation of the law-abiding middlemen; excessive reliance on cost studies instead of simple formulas—these are the more important shortcomings of price control in Latin America.[1]

SUMMARY. As has already been noted, not only is demand on the increase, but supply conditions are less satisfactory. Exports are up

[1] *Cf.* Ch. I and VII for a discussion of attacks in the international field.

and imports are down, with resulting unfavorable effects on supplies. Production and distribution have suffered also as a result of the unavailability of raw materials and the breakdown of transportation. Almost every Latin American country has suffered serious effects from the reduction of available shipping and of motor transportation. Not only is there a scarcity of raw materials and especially of imports, but in addition all these countries suffer from higher costs, which, in turn, affect supply adversely because they have to substitute domestic products for supplies formerly obtained abroad—or else have to substitute supplies from other countries which produce at higher costs than the former sellers. For example, in Colombia reliance is had on Brazilian tires, on wool yarn from Argentina, and on Colombian rice, which is now substituted for Asiatic rice. All these products are obtained at higher costs and greater effort than in 1939 and earlier years. We have, then, a reduction of supply and an increase of demand. This rise in demand results from the international factors already considered, from increases in wages and profits, which have been universal in Latin America, and also from the increased participation of the government in economic life. The government contributes toward rising prices not only because it indulges in deficit financing, but also because Latin American governments rely heavily on taxes on commodities and, therefore, any expansion of government spending is likely to be reflected in a rise of prices.

In addition to these factors that account for higher prices, there is always present the speculator who takes advantage of scarce supplies and inordinate demand. He helps bring about higher prices by withholding supplies from the market, by charging what the traffic will bear, and also by increasing the number of turnovers of the scarce commodities. This particular phenomenon has been especially evident in the import trade, where scarcities have been great. Despite the measures taken by the various governments, there has been a large increase in the number of middlemen in the area of distribution of imported commodities. Strong measures are required to control this situation. The governments must get rid of the new middlemen who have just come into this field, and they must control prices of these commodities all along the line if the cooperative action of the United States in controlling export prices on behalf of Latin American consumers is to be effective. Unless strong measures are taken in Latin America, the saving made as a result of the controls at this end will be absorbed by speculators at the other end—in the Latin American republics, to the great disadvantage of their peoples.

In sum, the Latin American price situation is serious. Supplies are down, and demand is up. Short of very vigorous price control, the only means of dealing with this situation, if a further sharp rise of prices is to be avoided, is to increase supply and reduce demand. Numerous measures (*e.g.*, a strong tax and loan program, moderation in profits)—these are all required. Any expansion of supplies, through improvement of transportation or reallocation of resources to more productive fields, and bans on exports of necessary commodities are helpful. But even the strongest practical measures in the area of income control, exchange measures, fiscal measures, and the like, will not be adequate. There will remain an excess of income over supplies at current prices, and the only means that will ensure price stability will be a combination of all these measures, plus a strenuous price control program. And this control should be continued in the postwar period until normal supply and demand conditions are reestablished.

II. STUDIES OF INDIVIDUAL COUNTRIES

As has already been said, the pattern of inflation has in general been similar for all countries. In this section the high lights and deviations of several countries from the general pattern are noted.

1. COLOMBIA. A few figures on trade changes will throw some light on the inflationary picture. The exports of coffee, which declined modestly in 1940 and 1941, actually rose from 83 million pesos in 1941 to 144 million pesos in 1942, whereas total exports rose by 65 millions in the years 1940–1942. During this same period petroleum exports declined from 40 million to 14 million pesos. This increased importance of coffee in the export trade accounts for the very favorable balance of trade of Colombia and, from the viewpoint of postwar changes and readjustments, is significant in that the termination of the war is not so likely to affect adversely the Colombian export trade and exchange position as might be true in the case of other countries. Another interesting aspect of the Colombian trade situation is the much larger part now played by the United States in Colombia's export markets. The most significant change from 1941 to 1942 was a rise from 92 million to 155 million pesos in exports to the United States and a reduction of 20 millions in exports to Canada. In this year the United States took about 90 per cent of total Colombian

exports. Even in the years 1939–1941 export trade to North America, and particularly to the United States, increased almost as much as trade to Europe and to other non-American areas declined. In 1942, coffee accounted for 75 per cent of total Colombian exports, gold 11 per cent, and petroleum 7 per cent (in 1938, coffee exports were 54 per cent of the total, petroleum 23 per cent, gold 11 per cent, and bananas 5 per cent).

It is evident then that the increased participation of the United States in Colombian export trade has enabled Colombia to maintain its trade and exchange position and to accumulate vast resources in dollars. In the import area there have also been very significant changes. From 1939 to 1941, the increase of imports from the Americas almost made up for the reduction of imports from Europe. In 1942, however, the United States reduced its exports to Colombia from 125 million to 60 million pesos. This was exactly the reduction of total import trade for Colombia. In other words, war restrictions and scarcity of shipping had deprived Colombia of much needed import commodities. Imports from other Latin American countries, however, increased from 18 million to 28 million pesos.

This reduction of imports and the change in the distribution are significant, not only because there is a reduction of supply involved, but also because the net result has been a change of country of purchase—from countries that produce under very favorable conditions, to countries that produce under less favorable conditions. For example, from 1937 to 1939, Colombia imported 15 million kilos of rice, but in 1941 and 1942 imports were negligible. The result has been the substitution of domestic production, which is costly compared with the low-cost rice previously imported from Japan. A similar tendency is to be noted in imports of sugar and wheat.

This tendency on the part of the country to produce at home products that had previously been obtained from abroad or to obtain alternative supplies in alternative and higher cost markets naturally results in higher unit costs. Exports to other Latin American countries account for more than twice as large a percentage of total exports as before the war. One result of the war throughout Latin America has been growth of protectionist sentiment nurtured by their inability to obtain foreign supplies. An example of this is illustrated in the history of the textile industry. In 1938, the total consumption of cotton in Colombia was 8.6 million kilos. By 1942, total consumption had risen to 17 million kilos. The textile industries have been very prosperous and prices very high.[1]

A second feature of the Colombian situation has been the large rise of gold and *Devisen* held by the central bank. The amount in millions of pesos is as follows:

1940	43
1941	39
October, 1943	183

The rise from 1941[2] was almost 370 per cent.

An indication of the reasons for the imports is given by Table 1. One important consideration is the large amounts of imports by foreign companies for which payment in foreign exchange is not made; this is a form of capital import.

TABLE 1
(In millions of pesos)

Year	Gold and exchange inflow	Authorized payments abroad	Licenses for imports
1939	98	107	115
1940	86	93	81
1941	100	100	117
1942	131	87	109

A third aspect of the Colombian inflationary pattern has been the strong measures taken to neutralize the effects of the inflow of foreign currencies. These are discussed in the chapter on foreign exchanges.

Fourth, the fiscal pattern is relevant. Like most Latin American countries, Colombia has had some serious budgetary problems in the last few years. She has, for example, suffered greatly from a reduction of customs duties. Whereas her receipts from customs accounted for 41 million pesos in 1939, the yield in 1942 was only 19 million pesos. This serious reduction of revenue from customs duties has resulted in a reduction in receipts of all taxes. What has followed therefore has been a deficit, although that deficit has not been a serious factor in the price situation. The main budgetary picture is presented in Table 2.

[1] All figures are obtained from the *Informe del Departmento de comercio y industrias*, 1941–1942 and 1942–1943.

[2] *Revista del Banco de la República*, November, 1943, pp. 438–39. *Cf.* W. Ward, *Foreign Trade, Post-war Plans and Prospects* (1944), p. 9.

TABLE 2.—COLOMBIA: RECEIPTS, TAXES, EXPENDITURES AND DEBT 1939–1943*
(In millions of pesos)

Year	Total receipts	Customs	Income, inheritance, and excess profit	Total taxes	Ordinary expenditures	Internal consolidated and floating debt
1939	91	41	19	80	88	89
1940	77	28	22	67	84	107
1941	81	30	22	72	78	122
1942	77	19	27	62	87	126
1943 (1st 6 months)	33	10	12	29	41	158 (June)

* *Revista del Banco de la República.*

The rather large rise shown by internal consolidated and floating debt can be explained in part by the extraordinary measures taken by the government to contend with inflation. The government has also been very successful in the increase in the yield of direct taxes. Unlike most Latin American governments, there has not been a very large rise in total expenditures, and, furthermore, the contribution of direct taxes is probably larger than in most Latin American countries. The fact that the government, through necessity in part, has to rely on direct taxes more than in earlier years has helped rather than hampered the struggle against inflation: the greater the dependence on direct taxes, the less the pressure on the price structure. For the year 1943, for example, direct taxes of the government are estimated to yield about 25 millions as compared with ordinary taxes and expenditures of 85 million pesos. In addition, however, the government expects to collect about 34 millions of special taxes, and roughly 15 millions of these special taxes are direct taxes.[1] In addition, large levies are made on the stabilization fund for coffee, but these are turned back to the growers.

Fifth, an examination of Tables 3 and 4, increases in reserves and assets and liabilities of central and commercial banks—suggests that the potential expansion of deposits and money had not been realized. Production has risen only moderately, and in some areas (*e.g.*, gold, petroleum, and exports) actual declines are registered. In view of the substantial rise of deposits and money accompanied by a small expansion of output, the rise of prices has been moderate. By *October*,

[1] Figures are taken from Report: *Ministerio de hacienda y crédito público* (1943).

1943, however, the cost of living in 18 *cities* was almost 30 per cent in excess of the level in 1942.

COST OF LIVING, BOGOTÁ

1937	100
1940	115
January–May, 1943	137

A summary statistical view is given by the following:

TABLE 3.—ASSETS AND LIABILITIES OF THE BANK OF THE REPUBLIC
(In millions of pesos)

Year	Gold and devisen	Credit operations	Notes in circulation	Deposits—sight
1940	43	77	62	51
1941	39	101	74	50
1942	108	74	104	69
October, 1943	183	61	111	115

It will be observed that as the central bank has obtained more cash and as the banks of the country and the government have increased their deposits, the credit operations of the central bank have tended to decline. In other words, the inflow of dollars has enabled the money market to repay part of its loans to the central bank. To that extent, the inflow of dollars has not been inflationary. Notes have increased greatly, however, with resulting pressure on the price structure; and, furthermore, the deposits of the banks and the Treasury with the central bank have also increased significantly. In short, the major part of the inflow of gold and *Devisen* has been used to increase the deposits of the central bank and also to increase the notes in circulation.

Sixth, the effects on the commercial banks are evident in Table 4:

TABLE 4.—ASSETS AND LIABILITIES OF COMMERCIAL BANKS
(In millions of pesos)

Year	Loans, discounts, etc.	Deposits	Cash and deposits with Bank of the Republic
1940	158	132	28
1941	167	146	26
1942	179	187	42
June, 1943	203	217	57

Cash, which includes deposits at the central bank, has increased by more than 100 per cent; deposits by approximately two-thirds; and loans, discounts, etc., by 30 per cent. In other words, in the light of the large increase of cash, commercial banks have expanded with moderation. Yet the rise of deposits has been large, and to that extent the favorable balance of payments has contributed toward inflation.

According to the *Memoria de hacienda*, 1943, pages 25 to 26, the index of total means of payment in May, 1943 (1939 = 100) for the country was 185; velocity of circulation, 70; commercial bank loans, 149; loans to be gradually amortized, 112. Observe that the large increase in the means of payment has to some extent been cancelled or nullified by a reduction in velocity of circulation to 70. The net increase of active purchasing power since 1940 has been roughly 30 per cent, *i.e.*, 185 times $^{70}/_{100}$ equals 130.

Seventh, let us briefly survey the origins of recent price control measures.

In presenting to Congress in 1942 the Economic Plan, the Minister of the Treasury and Public Credit emphasized recent inflationary trends.[1] The reduction of imports, the expansion of bank notes associated with the favorable balance of trade, and the increasing activities of speculators were held to be responsible for rising prices. Increasingly, markets were becoming inaccessible to the poor, with resulting menace to their health. The minister commented on the Maximum Export Price Regulation of the United States, which protected foreign consumers against exorbitant markups in the United States; but prices of these products actually were much higher than might be justified by the f.o.b. price in the United States plus shipping costs and reasonable markups in Colombia. After citing some of these increases, the minister emphasized the need of integrating the export price regulation of the United States with the control of import prices in Colombia and that it was not fair that Colombia should intervene to obtain priorities in the United States and in shipping facilities in order that speculators in Colombia might profiteer.

Law 7-A provided for a relaxation of exchange control in the hope that the inflow of dollars and the resulting expansion of domestic supplies of currency would be reduced. Interests of exporters were to

[1] The *Exposición de motivos* and Law 7-A of Mar. 2, 1943, and later legislation are to be found in *Suplemento al No. 186 de la revista del Banco de la República*, May, 1943, pp. 23–38.

be protected, however. In other words, serious exchange appreciation was not to be tolerated. The government was also to found and support cooperatives, which were to facilitate the program of price stability. Again, where speculation was rampant, the government might import directly, thus eliminating the speculator. I shall not discuss Colombia's price control as provided by Decree 928 of May 11, 1943, because it is discussed fully and well in the chapter on Colombia.

2. PERU. In general, the supply situation in Peru has been unsatisfactory. There has been a serious shortage of rice. The slaughter of meat has declined perceptibly. In Callao, for example, where 40 per cent of all meat is generally slaughtered, there was a reduction of about 20 per cent in the amount of meat slaughtered in the early months of 1943. There are 44,000 hectares of land available in the provinces of Lima and Callao for the production of food, but actually only 20,000 hectares are used for food, and 134,000 hectares are needed. Yet in this area population has doubled in the last 10 or 12 years. Total imports of food into Peru in 1942 were but 16 per cent of the amount imported in 1940. There had also been a very serious decline in the production of foodstuffs in the Sierra area, where production in the early months of 1943 was roughly one-third less than that in the corresponding period in 1942. The net result of this shortage of food is, of course, a serious strain on the price structure in the deficient areas. These scarcities have been aggravated by the inevitable shortage in shipping space that comes with war, making the lack of a north-south railroad a particularly unfortunate factor at this time in the distribution of supplies. It has also been unfortunate that the scarcity of rice appeared at a time when the supplies of wheat and meat were also inadequate—and to make matters worse there have been periodic shortages of potatoes.

Supplies are then inadequate, both because imports are down and exports are up, and also because of the peculiar difficulties of production and distribution within the country. That the government controls the distribution of a large part of the foodstuffs will, undoubtedly, contribute toward a better distribution of the supplies and, to that extent, will alleviate the supply situation. The best system of distribution, however, can never quite correct serious deficiencies of supplies.

The country has not suffered from an unemployment problem for many years and particularly since the introduction of large public works programs. Since there has been no significant unemployment problem, it might well be assumed by many that there has been no increase in employment. This does not necessarily follow. It is possible that many have moved from activities where their output is small or negligible (*e.g.*, some types of farming, peddling, begging) to more productive work. In this sense, there has been a reduction of "disguised" unemployment and a rise of employment. Furthermore, the population has increased, and to that extent more workers have become available. In short, there undoubtedly has been an increase in the number of workers in industry and in the mines, partly at the expense of farming and partly at the expense of some very unproductive forms of employment or activity. Total wages rise in part because more men are at work, particularly in productive enterprises.

A rise in the wage bill accounts for an increase in the demand for consumption goods. This rise of demand on the part of workers for commodities stems from a rise of the average productivity of workers (and hence an increase of wage rates), from a rise in the wage rate not associated with higher productivity, and from any rise in employment.

In the woolen textile industries there has been an increase in wage rates from July, 1940, to July, 1943, of 66 per cent for the lowest paid workers and 12 per cent for the highest paid workers. The increase for the workers who earn an average wage (*i.e.*, approximately 4 soles, or 60 cents, per day) has been about 34 per cent. Wage increases of similar proportions have occurred in the other textile industries, the wage increase for the average workers, however, being 28 per cent in the woolen textile industry and approximately 23 per cent in the other textile industries. It should be observed, however, that the textile workers are probably the best paid workers in the country. The wage rise for these workers has on the average been not substantially less than the increase in the cost of living. Their standard of living has not suffered, therefore, as a result of rising prices. Their failure, however, to improve their position in a period when the textile industry has had its most prosperous period is worthy of comment.

Let us consider some of the less fortunate recipients of income. The Army, for example, has received no increase in pay during the period 1931–1939. In 1939 the lowest paid soldiers were granted an increase in pay of 20 per cent, and the others up to 15 per cent. Since the Army is paid largely in kind, one should not infer from these figures that its standard of living has deteriorated to the extent indicated by these figures. It may actually have improved.

Workers in commercial houses have suffered a reduction of their money wages in many cases and probably in all cases a serious reduction of their standard of living. Public employees other than the Army obtained an increase of 20 per cent in 1942, if their salaries were less than 120 soles, or $18, per month, and up to 5 per cent for those earning 800 soles, or $120, per month. It is obvious then that the economic status of important groups of workers has suffered under rising prices.

Some indication of the occasion for the inflow of dollars on the Peruvian market will be afforded by the export picture. The excess of exports in millions of soles has been as follows:

Year	Millions of soles
1935	127
1939	126
1940	87
1941	137
1942	158

A puzzling feature of the export-import figures is revealed when one considers the very large rise in the price of imports as compared with the price of exports. If the prices of imports have risen so much, why should the volume of exports relative to imports have increased? The explanation is, of course, that import prices are not the prices paid by the Peruvian importer, but rather the prices of resales of import commodities, and these resales have been at notoriously high levels.

The increase of gold and *Devisen* in 1942 was 60 million soles for the central bank and 36 million soles for the commercial banks, and the percentage of rise for 1942 was 103 per cent. This increase in cash naturally resulted in significant changes in the position of the central bank. These changes are evident in Table 5.

Note in particular that in 1942 the cash of the central bank was more than three times as large as it had been in 1933; its earning assets six times as large; its notes in circulation four times as great; deposits of associated banks six times; and the deposits of the Treasury approximately ten times. At the end of 1942, cash was about three

TABLE 5.—MAIN CHANGES IN CENTRAL-BANK POSITION 1933–1942
(In millions of soles)

Date	Cash	Earning assets	Notes issued	Deposits of associated banks	Deposits, treasury
Dec. 31, 1933	44	49	67	20	27
Dec. 31, 1940	51	153	143	47	130
Dec. 31, 1941	62	205	209	46	182
Dec. 31, 1942	143	289	283	115	258

times as great as in 1940, earning assets and notes about two times, and all deposits (last two columns) had risen more than 100 per cent since 1940. Observe that from 1933 to 1940 the tendency was for the activities of the central bank to increase much more rapidly than its increase of cash. Since 1940, however, the reverse has been true. The central bank has expanded its earning assets and its deposits and notes considerably less than its cash. The effects of large supplies of cash are evident in the following: a 1 per cent rate for Treasury bills, 2 per cent for loans to the Treasury, 3 per cent for loans on minerals, 4 per cent for loans to industry and agriculture, 5 per cent to associated banks, and 6 per cent to the public. Another feature of the statement of the central bank is the marked increase in the participation of the Treasury in the activities of this organization.

For commercial banks, the expansion in earning assets and deposits has not been in proportion to the increase of cash. This holds both for the period 1931–1942 and for the period 1940–1942. In the latter period, for example, the increase of cash has been about two-thirds, of earning assets 20 to 25 per cent, of sight deposits about one-half. It should be observed that in 1942, despite the very large rise of cash or disposable funds, the expansion of earning assets of commercial banks was moderate; and the rise of cash was accompanied by a corresponding rise of deposits. Commercial banks remain, therefore, in a very liquid position. In short, the inflow of dollars has contributed to a substantial expansion of banking activities and, therefore, of deposit money and to that extent toward higher prices. This expansion, however, has not been so great as was possible, in view of the very large inflow of cash.

Finally, we present a table of prices.

The main conclusion to be drawn from Table 6 is that there has been a significant rise of prices. The increase from 1940 to *April*,

1943, (not given in Table 6) in wholesale prices has been roughly 50 per cent. What is particularly interesting is that the rise has been only roughly 30 per cent in export prices, 40 per cent in domestic prices, and about 140 per cent in import prices. Import prices have risen 3½ times as much as domestic prices. A more moderate rise in the export prices than in domestic prices is an unusual phenomenon in periods of inflation. Since 1913, in fact, the rise of import prices has been more than twice that of export prices.

TABLE 6.—PRICES[1]

Year	Wholesale				Cost of living	
	Total	Domestic	Export	Import	All	Food
1935	176	170	146	225	152	147
1940	204	188	197	267	183	174
1941	230	206	213	412	198	197
1942	274	235	253	551	222	220
December, 1942	290	251	266	599	229	225
Percentage rise, January-November, 1943	10.5	...	10.5	8.9	10.3	12.3

[1] In the Peruvian budget of 1943 the author unfortunately failed to note the base year. These data were obtained while in Latin America.

In discussing the inflationary problem, one should not, however, leave out of account the government's finances. It has been observed that the government relies much more heavily on the banking system than it did in earlier years. Furthermore, the increase of the governmental budget has been roughly from 100 million to 400 million soles in recent years. This increase is very large, even if one allows for the transfer in 1941 of the receipts under the special laws to the ordinary budget. This very large rise in government expenditures is bound to have a significant effect on the price level. This conclusion rests on two considerations. First, the government relies very heavily on indirect taxes, which are passed on in higher prices to consumers of products. In the Peruvian budget of 1943 direct taxes account for only 40 million soles, or about one-tenth the total tax revenue. There may be a few additional direct taxes collected under the special laws, but they are not very important. Since the government raises most of its revenue through indirect taxes, the net effect of large increases of government expenditures is that the more the government expends, the greater the pressure toward higher prices for commodities. In addition, one has to take into account the fact that there has been a government deficit, and a government deficit is likely to be financed through borrowing from banks, with a resulting expansion of monetary supplies.

The second factor is that the government spends large sums of money on development programs. These programs increase the demand for scarce factors of production and especially labor and machinery. Insofar as the government becomes an important buyer on these markets, they contribute toward higher prices in these markets. Demand for these scarce factors increases, and their prices rise. If the net effect of these government activities were an immediate flow of consumption goods, the increased pressure on economic resources would be offset by an increased supply of consumption goods, and the effects on prices might not then be unfavorable. Unfortunately, however, the flow of consumption goods will be felt in the future rather than in the present. In the meanwhile, scarce resources are being used to produce capital goods, roads, etc., and not primarily consumption goods in a period when consumption goods are scarce.[1]

I shall summarize here very briefly the more important price measures taken by the Peruvian government since the outbreak of the war. The first important measure apparently was Law 8951, issued soon after the outbreak of the war in Europe. A rise in the price of necessary articles is prohibited; no increase in the price of manufactured products or in the price of construction materials will be tolerated without previous authorization; exports of necessaries are to be subject to previous authorization; monopolies directed toward increasing prices are forbidden; reductions of wages and dismissals without sufficient cause are not to be tolerated. The price history since 1939 is adequate evidence that this particular regulation did not prove to be very effective.

On Dec. 5, 1941, the government created the post of Official Inspector of Prices. His task was to prevent unjustifiable rises in prices of indispensable consumption goods and to prevent the hoarding and speculation of raw materials. On Dec. 8, 1941, it was announced that the Inspector General was to take an inventory of construction material and indispensable consumption goods. He was empowered

[1] The author is not unaware of the fact that in many instances (*e.g.*, roads and irrigation works) the yield in consumption goods will be felt in the immediate future.

to survey the distributive system; take inventories; study the import situation, the state of production, and in general to consider the economic activities of concern to the price fixer. It was further announced that undeclared and hidden stocks would be requisitioned by the government.

In February, 1942, the factory and retail price of soap was specifically fixed, and in May, 1942, the price of skins was set. In June, 1942, the authorities moved with vigor into the import area and published a long list of commodities which had been subject to serious speculation. In August, 1942, provision was made for the creation of commissions to control the price of construction materials, indispensable consumption goods, etc., not controlled by the Director of National Foodstuffs and the Director General of Health.

In November, 1942, the government once more restricted the volume of exports and particularly stressed that imports were not to be reexported and that the exporter or manufacturer of the article must prove that the proposed exports were not inimical to the internal consumption. In April, 1943, measures were taken to coordinate transportation as a means of improving the supply of subsistence and, in that manner, keeping the price of subsistence down.

In April, 1943, also, the Peruvian government authorized the Minister of Agriculture to buy the whole rice crop and took over control of distribution and price, indicating the spread between farmers and distributors, and distributors and consumers. In June, 1943, wholesale prices and the price to consumers for beans were set.

From this brief survey, it is evident that the government has issued decrees which cover most commodities. Virtually all food commodities are subject to control by the Director of Foodstuffs. His control provides specific prices, which allow rather moderate markups for wholesalers and retailers.

The area in which the least seems to have been done is in textiles and clothing. As the government's control in the future is strengthened, it will undoubtedly be necessary to close the remaining speculative areas and to introduce price control for the more important kinds of clothing and textiles. Adequate control in the import area will take care of prices of machinery and other imported commodities.

3. CHILE. The price increase has been serious in Chile. In the year 1942, for example, the cost of living rose by 26 per cent and

wholesale prices by 32 per cent. The latter increase may be compared with a somewhat similar rise of wholesale prices in the *last* 3 *years* for the United States. A somewhat longer period may be studied with advantage. The cost of living was 43 per cent higher in January, 1943, than in January, 1938. Or compare the cost of living in Santiago in 1941 and 1942 with that in 1928:

(1928 = 100)	
December, 1941	275
December, 1942	343

or a rise of 25 per cent in the year ending December, 1942. For necessaries, the rise was somewhat greater. From 1939 to the latter part of 1943, the cost of living rose by 93 per cent, a larger rise than for any other important country of Latin America.

As incomes rise, the pressure on commodity markets grows. Available figures do not indicate that there has been a corresponding rise in output. Had there been such a rise, the increase in money income would have been offset by a corresponding increase of supplies. Inflation would not necessarily be averted in such a case, for money earned in the production of copper and other industrial materials will be inflationary when disbursed on consumption markets, if the increase in money incomes thus earned is not offset by an expansion of consumption goods. But at least to some extent the pressure would have been reduced.

The inflation of wages undoubtedly contributed toward the expansion of demand. Daily wages in 10 industries were 75 per cent higher in 1942 than in 1938; and the rise in December, 1942, from December, 1941, was 35 per cent. From 1938 to 1942 a rise of wages and salaries, which was absorbed in no small part in social-security payments, was 3.7 billion pesos. This figure is to be compared with one of 5 billion pesos for profits.

It is clear that the excess of income has not been absorbed through additional demands by the government. Ordinary receipts of the government rose by 850 million pesos in the years 1940–1942, or about 40 per cent of total receipts in 1940. This has indeed been a substantial increase; but since taxes are less than 20 per cent of the total income of the country, an increase in receipts of 40 per cent is not enough to counter the inflationary forces. An increase of tax receipts of 40 per cent in these 2 years would absorb but an 8 per cent rise of national income. Its actual rise was several times that amount. In the United States, for example, the rise in the Federal tax receipts of nine times and in all tax receipts of about four times has not been adequate to eliminate the inflationary effects of a rise of income of more than 100 per cent.

Savings may also siphon off part of the excess. But, according to the Estadística Chilena, savings had increased only from 819 million pesos in 1940 to 1,077 million pesos in 1942. This increase is equivalent to a very small percentage of the rise in national income. Undoubtedly the quoted figures on savings do not include all savings and can therefore be taken only as a rough guide of the expansion of savings.

From 1932, attempts have been made to control prices in Chile. The initial attempt in 1932 went for naught. In 1939, another program was introduced, this time by the Popular Front government, which now provided for a Commissariat of Subsistence and Prices. The resulting freeze of prices is generally admitted to have been unsuccessful. At various times from 1939 to 1942, items became specifically subject to price control. These articles included the more important foods, certain industrial products, fuels, some textiles, construction materials, and miscellaneous items (*e.g.*, matches and brooms). These items covered a fairly wide area.

The establishment of yardstick stores which could be used as a guide and also a threat directed against violators of price regulations has been an interesting innovation. In one case (tea), the government took over control of the major part of total supplies. Another measure which tends to induce a more favorable price situation, since it prevents the excessive diversion of supplies to foreign countries, has been the increased control of exports. Yet all these measures have not sufficed to prevent serious rises of prices. And it has not been for lack of authority, on paper, that the price control program has failed. The commissariat can control the production, sale, transportation, importation and exportation, and the retail and wholesale prices of necessaries of life, which cover a large part of total consumption. It can also create monopolies, intervene in rationing of exchange in order to encourage the importation of necessaries, require reports of stocks, make cost-of-production studies, condemn production of adulterated products, obtain preferential transportation where deemed necessary, and requisition and sell directly the necessaries of life. These are indeed adequate powers.

On Apr. 26, 1943, the President asked Congress for exceptional economic powers. In particular, the message recognized the inflationary effects of the rise of wages, the reduction of imports, the excessive level of profits, and the conversion of foreign exchange into domestic currency. It was necessary first for the government to offset the inflation resulting from the accumulation of dollars and the resulting conversion into domestic currency. The proposed technique was to induce the public to purchase dollars and gold in anticipation of needs, thus sterilizing a corresponding volume of domestic currency. In the government's program, a stabilization of wage rates was to play a prominent part. Adjustments were to be allowed only to compensate for a rise in the cost of living, to raise substandard wages, and to compensate for an increase in productivity. It was also proposed to refuse foreign exchange and licenses to importers who raised prices excessively. Again the government proposed to ration commodities (particularly imports), limit profits to 15 per cent of investment, and compel the investment of the remainder in the Fomento (Development Program). These measures, inclusive of price control, comprise a well-rounded program. A substantial part of this program of stabilizing wages, profits, and prices was enacted, though not exactly in the form desired by the government.

4. BOLIVIA. Bolivia is a small country with a population of 3 or 4 millions, largely dependent upon neighboring countries for foodstuffs and upon the United States for necessary industrial materials. She is therefore not in a strong position to protect herself against rising prices in other countries. When prices rise abroad and when foreign countries restrict exports, Bolivia necessarily suffers greatly; and at the very best she must accept this rise in foreign prices and try to moderate the increases within her own boundaries. Although, in general, Bolivia's success in the field of price control is limited by these considerations, nevertheless, the fact that she is so dependent on imports from abroad gives her a weapon for the control of markups within Bolivia. Through the control of import licensing and foreign exchange, Bolivia is in a strong position to control the speculative propensities within the country.

A unique feature in the situation of Bolivia is that she is a one-product country in a very important sense. More than 80 per cent of her exports are metals, and tin alone accounts for approximately three-quarters her total exports. It follows therefore that unless the price of tin is satisfactory and the volume of tin exports at a sufficiently high level Bolivia will not be able to pay for her necessary imports. Depreciation of the exchange will then be inevitable, with the resulting upward pressure on prices within the country.

A third peculiarity of the Bolivian economy, in wartime especially, is the weakness of the transportation system. Adequate supplies of particular commodities may be available in one part of the country, but, because of the deficiency of transportation, they may not be made available in another part of the country. In a period of scarcity of supplies, this inadequacy of the transportation system is especially serious.

Fourth, Bolivia has had a long history of inflation. The country is inflation-minded. It does not require a formal education in economics to become aware of the fact that the longer one waits in a country infected by rising prices, the less the monetary unit will buy. The masses of Bolivians are now well aware that if they buy today, their bolivianos will purchase more than if they wait until tomorrow. In other words, the country is now on the verge of what one economist has called the era of galloping inflation. Because price stability is a matter only of memory and the distant past, the stabilization of prices at the present time is very difficult.

Another peculiarity of the Bolivian situation is the great expansion in the number of middlemen and intermediaries in the distributive process. The entrenchment of unnecessary distributors is a phenomenon of inflationary periods. Each seller attempts to profit by placing himself between the buyer and seller. In doing so, he does not perform a productive function and contributes greatly to the rise of prices. All evidence shows that the spread of these speculative practices is a great evil in the Bolivian economy—and apparently the speculators are strongly organized. It is unfortunately true that, unless strong measures are taken to drive out the unproductive middlemen who perform no legitimate function, stabilization of prices will be impossible.

A few figures will indicate the extent to which inflation has progressed in Bolivia. I present therefore a table of figures since 1929 which gives the main outlines of inflation in Bolivia (Table 7). It should be noted, moreover, that the exchanges have depreciated greatly since 1929. For example, the boliviano was worth about 36 cents in 1929 and by 1934 was worth less than 25 cents, by 1939 a little more than 3 cents, and at the present time is worth about 2.4 cents. In a period of 13 years the boliviano in terms of dollars has depreciated to but 1/15 its value at the beginning of this period of 15 years. This fall in the value of the boliviano of 15 times is to be compared with an increase in money in circulation of 19 times, of bank deposits of 43 times, of total gold and deposits in New York and London of about 20 times, and an increase in the total earning assets of the central bank of about 9 times. These figures are included in Table 7:

TABLE 7.—BOLIVIA: MONETARY STATISTICS, 1929–1943*
Rows 1, 2, 5, 8 = indices = July, 1929 = 100.
Rows 3, 4 = millions of bolivianos.
Rows 6, 7 = percentage.

		July, 1929	December, 1934	December, 1939	December, 1940	December, 1941	December, 1942	March, 1943
1	Notes in circulation	100	184	812	1,048	1,413	1,802	1,917
2	Deposits	100	684	1529	1,905	2,939	3,925	4,267
3	Gold	19	0.9	31	102	377	497	462
4	Total gold and deposits in New York and London	35	9.7	144	158	567	707	691
5	Indices	100	27.9	413	455	1,633	2,037	1,991
6	Percentage legal reserves to circulation	53	4.3	21	18	46	44	40
7	Total cash reserves—percentage of circulation	94	6.3	23	34	61	58	51
8	Portfolio of central bank—percentages	100	186	455	893	611	952	907

* *Central Bank Bulletin*, January–February, 1943.

Actually, the reserve percentage declined despite the increased value of a given weight of gold or dollar reserves following successive devaluations of the currency. It will be observed, for example, that the reserve ratio was smaller in 1943 than it was in 1929. This reduction occurred despite the increase in the value in bolivianos of each dollar of gold, as the government successively depreciated its currency. The expansion of central-bank liabilities was then at a greater rate than the expansion of reserves in Bolivia.

An indication of the recent increase in the cost of living is to be had in Table 8.

It will be observed from this table that the cost of living in La Paz rose by about 75 per cent in the 2 years ending in December, 1942.

From January to November, 1943, the cost of living index of La Paz reveals a further rise of 8 per cent. Since 1931, the increase in the cost of living was about twelve to thirteen times, an increase that roughly parallels the depreciation of the exchanges. In other words, the higher cost of foreign currencies, which partly reflects the expansion of monetary supplies in Bolivia and also, in turn, contributes toward higher prices, has played an important part in the upward movement of prices. As more money is issued in Bolivia, the value of the local currency falls and its value declines in terms of foreign currencies which have remained relatively stable in value at home; and the increased prices of foreign currencies result in an increase in the prices of exports and imports; and domestic commodities are affected.

TABLE 8.—COST OF LIVING*
La Paz, 1939–1942.
(1936 = 100)

December	General index	32 necessaries of life
1939	343	287
1940	401	357
1941	542	514
1942	701	609

* *Estadística Bancaria.*

In 1935, the Bolivian government formulated a price control program which covered primarily the field of imports. The prices of 10 necessaries of life were fixed at both wholesale and retail. These items included watches, fuel, meat, rice, gasoline, flour, and sugar. Importers were allowed to bid for the privilege of purchasing and selling at stipulated prices; and if their bids were acceptable to the government, they were allowed to obtain exchange. These products, which were bought at relatively low prices, soon found their way into the black market, and the experiment has not been held to have been successful.

This emphasis on control in the import area rises largely from the great reliance of the country on imported foodstuffs. Bolivia produces potatoes, vegetables, and fruit and only a little meat, milk, and corn.

This particular program, as I have indicated, did not work well, and it was ultimately given up. The continued depreciation of the exchanges and the numerous violations of the regulation contributed to the failure of this experiment. A more far-reaching approach was attempted under the decree of July 24, 1941. The main provisions of this decree were that profits were not to exceed normal level; unnecessary middlemen were to be eliminated; the central bank and commercial banks were to give preference in the allocation of exchanges for the purchases of foodstuffs; local authorities were to favor the production of necessaries; they were also to fix the price of necessaries and, where crises arose, were to encourage importation; the sale of imported commodities was to be free, especially for necessary commodities; a committee to control prices was provided; sellers were to present their costs to the departmental committees, who, in turn, must accept or reject these applications in 10 days; any increase in prices required the permission of the Commerce and Economic Ministry, and the decree provided for possible subsidies on imports. In addition, the decree calls for certain sanctions in case of violations. Investigators are to study costs, inspect books, indicate where speculation takes place, and denounce violators of the regulation.

It is generally agreed, now, that this particular regulation has not had a great success. Very few of the sellers presented their costs to the government; and, in general, little attention was paid to this very comprehensive attempt to deal with the inflation of recent years.

A final attempt was made in the promulgation of the decree of May 19, 1943. This particular measure bestows full powers in the area of price control on the fiscal *interventor* of prices who operates under the Ministry of National Economy. He is to catalogue the articles of consumption, determine their costs, fix their prices, ration articles of import, and determine the prices of services. The government also now classifies commodities in several categories, fixing, for each category, percentage markups by wholesalers and retailers, as well as importers. For example, in the case of foods which are absolutely essential, the markup for wholesalers is 8 per cent plus 3 per cent for expenses and for retailers 10 per cent and 4 per cent. In other categories, where the commodities are not so essential, the markups are higher. For example, in the fourth category, the markups are as high as 25 per cent, plus 10 per cent for expenses. More recently (1943–1944) Drs. Neiswanger and Nelson of the OPA have advised the Bolivian government on price control.

5. BRAZIL. This is a brief statistical summary of the Brazilian economy, which reveals that inflation is progressing in Brazil. A cursory examination of Table 9 provides adequate evidence that the

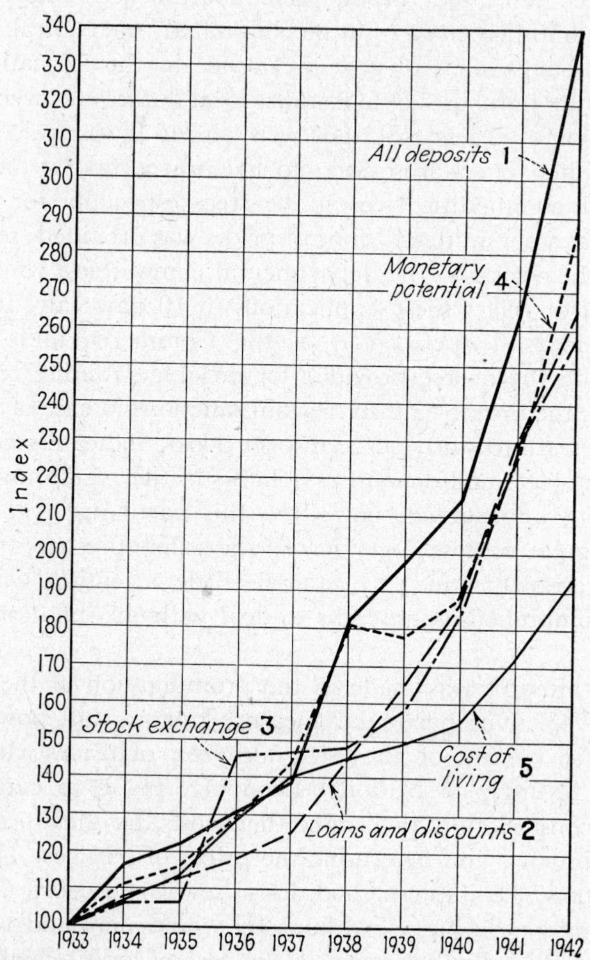

CHART 4.—Brazil. Expansion of money, bank assets, transactions, and prices, 1933–1942. (*Source: Based on material in Banco do Brasil S.A., Relatorio de* 1942.)

situation is becoming serious. Note the increase of loans (1939–1942) of the Bank of Brazil (65 per cent), of its deposits (56 per cent); of bank turnover, which gives an indication of total spending (67 per cent); of all bank loans (61 per cent), currency in circulation (67 per cent), and potential money (an inclusive variable covering all money)

66 per cent. In view of these changes, the increase in the cost of living of but 30 per cent seems moderate. Added supplies of money may have spilled into markets other than those that enter into the cost of living. All prices may well have risen much more than is indicated here. In fact, a later study of export and import prices suggests that the rise has been greater than 30 per cent. Real estate has, moreover, been rising rapidly. According to one report, land in Rio has risen in price by 6 times.

TABLE 9.—BRAZIL: INFLATIONARY VARIABLES, 1939–1942*

	Per cent change	
	From 1939	From 1941
A. Bank of Brazil:		
1. All loans	+65	+36
2. Loans to public authorities	+33	+37
3. Deposits	+56	+27
4. Deposits of public—total	+56	+21
5. Deposits of public—demand	+36	+27
6. Payment orders and collections	+101	+30
7. Bank turnover	+67	+20
B. All banks—inclusive of Bank of Brazil:		
1. Loans	+61	+14
2. Deposits—other banks	+67	+24
3. Currency in circulation	+66	+24
C. Potential money	+66	+30
D. Cost of living—Federal District	+30	+12

* *Banco do Brasil, Relatorio de* 1942.

Further evidence of inflationary pressure is to be found in Chart 4. All indices of monetary supplies have been rising rapidly. Stock-exchange transactions (not prices) reflect inflationary forces. The rise in the cost of living has been moderate in comparison with the monetary expansion.[1]

[1] Since then, what scanty figures are available (*Bulletin* 98 of the Departamento de Imprensa e Propaganda, Feb. 12, 1944) show a small further increase in loans (agricultural loans from 1,105 to 1,305 million cruzeiros, industrial loans from 219 to 369 million cruzeiros) but a threefold increase in so-called discounted "titles" (evidently bills or commercial paper) from 660 to 1,860 million cruzeiros. Deposits of the Federal government and other public authorities have gone up about 20 per cent; those of other banks around 10 per cent; but the demand deposits from 1,591 to 2,104 million cruzeiros, and time deposits from 820 to 1132 million cruzeiros. Cash reserves declined from 1,000 to

Prices rise in Brazil as they do elsewhere when demand exceeds supply at existing prices. Demand is excessive in this sense because imports have been reduced relative to exports, because there has been a large influx of dollars to cover expenditures of the United States government and those of refugees, and because there is more employment and at higher wages. Free conversion of dollars into local currency tends to increase the pressure on domestic markets.[1] Whereas the United States exports capital (dollars) to Brazil, the usual accompaniment of such importation of capital, a rise of imports and a reduction in exports for the receiving country, does not follow. In truth the United States provides Brazil with dollars, and the resulting expansion of notes and deposits in Brazil in exchange for dollars increases the inflationary pressure on Brazilian markets. Brazil in short provides the United States with an excess of exports over her imports from the United States and thus provides the latter with the real resources required to win the war. Her accumulation of dollars and sterling will be used to repay debts for goods received in the past or to purchase goods in the postwar period (when it is hoped that current restraints on exports will be lifted) and, in part, for purchase of goods currently.

It is no matter for comment, then, that dollar and sterling balances of Brazil have been rising at a very rapid rate; that the excess of exports in 1942 was at the high figure of 140 million; that the amount

---

678 million cruzeiros. Unfortunately, currency in circulation is not mentioned in our source. It has admittedly gone up (see *Bulletin* 88, Nov. 19, 1943), but, says the government, not more than the increased transactions would require. Gold reserves rose 120 per cent (see *Federal Reserve Bulletin*, April, 1944, p. 400).

The increase in the cruzeiro value of transactions is, of course, partly due to inflation; prices continued to rise, and it is still to be seen whether a recent price freeze order of November, 1943, which fixed prices at their Nov. 10 level, will prove effective. Wages, too, were increased as of Dec. 1, 1943 (see *Foreign Commerce Weekly*, Jan. 15, 22, 1944). Taxes, too, were raised significantly and are expected to bring 46 per cent more than in 1943; the budget for 1944 is balanced, but it does not contain any expenditures strictly in relation to the Second World War (*Foreign Commerce Weekly*, Feb. 5, 1944). Income taxes for individuals and forced subscription to war bonds, as well as the new excess-profits tax (see *Bulletins* 95 and 96 of the Departmento de Imprensa e Propaganda, Jan. 15, 26, 1944) should siphon off some of the money being created as a result of a constantly rising favorable balance of trade. For, although in 1943 imports rose as a result of the eased shipping situation, exports rose in value (manufactures were 19 per cent of exports, as compared with 13 per cent in 1942), and the balance of trade for the first 10 months of 1943 shows an active balance of 2 billion cruzeiros. Participation of the United States in both exports and imports rose.

[1] The recent marked change in the relative values of exports and imports is revealed in Chart 5.

of money in circulation and deposits (minus till money) had risen by about 66 per cent by the end of 1942; that the large profits being made as a result of rising prices are finding outlets in a vast building boom. Priorities are not a serious obstacle to further building, as in the United States, for most building supplies are obtainable in Brazil.

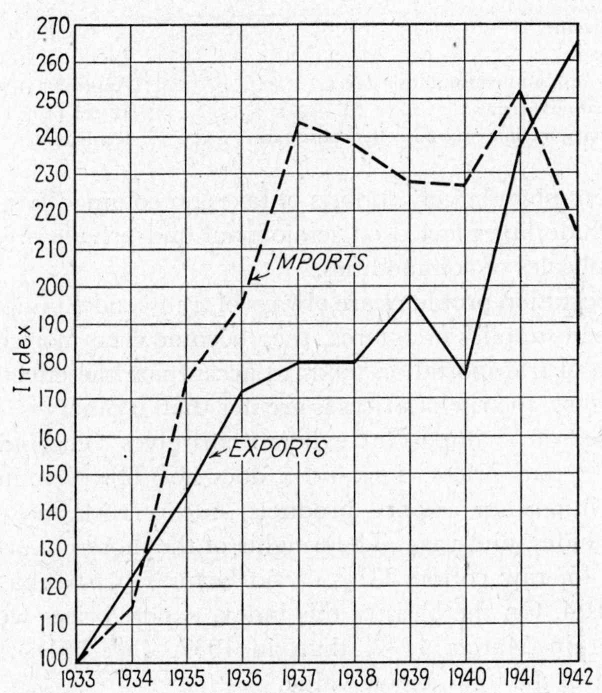

CHART 5.—Brazil's foreign trade, 1933–1942. (*Source: Based on series in Banco do Brasil S.A., Relatorio de 1942.*)

The Brazilian fiscal system is less flexible than ours. Unfortunately, Brazilian revenues are obtained largely at the expense of consumers' sales taxes, excise taxes, etc. These taxes are not raised easily, and increased yields from direct taxes meet strong opposition from business interests. Though the excess purchasing power is of small proportions compared with the amount in the United States, the problem of siphoning it off may be just as serious. These generalizations are still valid despite substantial increases in direct taxes in 1943–1944.

The pressure of the government tax program on the price level is evident from the following: (Taxes have recently been raised—these recent increases have not been included or taken into account here).

1. Consumption taxes as percentage of product:	
Tobacco	41
Salt	30
Matches	22
Beverages	21
Alcohol	20
Cement	18

2. Federal revenue, 1939	3,795 million cruzeiros
Income taxes	Less than 10 per cent
Import, stamp, and consumption taxes	Approximately 60 per cent
State-owned enterprises	12 per cent
Extraordinary income and miscellaneous taxes	Remainder

The tax system largely consists of taxes on commodities, and these do not include taxes levied on semiofficial and private organizations that control sales of commodities.

Transportation problems are always of transcendent importance in Brazil. When supplies are scarce, they become even more important. Breakdown of transportation tends to accentuate the effects of shortages; therefore, the rise of prices is greater than it otherwise would be.

An index of 15 important export items gives some indication of the rise of export prices. This index does not, however, include the following important export products: meat, rock crystal, mica, diamonds, hides, and yarn. The weights of the more important items are coffee 45, raw cotton 22½, cacao beans 7, carnauba wax 6½, castor seeds 4. On the basis of this index, export prices were 50 per cent higher in March, 1942, than in 1937. This index represents 61 per cent of the total export value.

An import index includes the following commodities and weights: wheat 30, coal and coke 16½, gasoline 14, tin plate 10, cellulose for paper making 8½, newsprint 4, caustic soda 3½, kerosene 3. The others included are of less importance. In the first half of 1942 approximately one-third of total imports were covered by the index. By that time import prices had risen by 48 per cent over the level of 1937.

One explanation of the rise of export prices is undoubtedly the government policy of restricting supplies available for export markets, selling through cartel arrangements abroad, and to some extent using the large profits as a means of depressing domestic prices. In a recent year, for example, there was in effect a production limit for sugar, quotas for the export of cocoa, an institution for regulating the sale of maté, more favorable prices for export of meat than allowed at home, a rice institute that controls exports, control of coffee quotas and coffee prices, minimum prices for exportation of oranges and limited sales abroad, similar provisions for bananas, a 10 per cent export tax on rock crystal, which was available only for export markets, limitations on the exportation of yarn, price control of rubber all along the line. In short, through a control of supplies made available for export markets and a control of the selling price, the government and private cartel arrangements have been able to exact higher prices from foreigners, which in turn to some extent has eased the price situation at home. Prices at home have been depressed because more export commodities were made available to the domestic market and also because sellers were able to sell at lower prices at home as a result of their ability to extract higher prices from foreign buyers.

Inflationary pressures have, moreover, found an outlet in a vast building boom and much speculation in commodities. Profits are very high and profit taxation relatively low despite a rise under a decree of September, 1943.[1] (The tax has accounted for only 10 per cent of Federal revenue.) Annual profits in excess of capital investment are frequently obtained. These profits are in no small part invested in real estate. A recent program (early 1944) of excess-profit taxation will reduce the pressures only a little. It is planned to relieve the entrepreneur of the tax if he invests in 3 per cent certificates, the proceeds to be used by the government to import machines and materials to modernize Brazilian industry.

Rising prices in Brazil follow the usual pattern of all Latin American countries.[2] Reduced imports, increased exports, inflow of capital, conversion of the resulting increased supplies of dollars into local currency, increased government spending and a concomitant use of indirect taxation, a rise of wage rates—these are the outlines of the inflation picture. In Brazil the rise of prices has been moderate in comparison with the expansion of monetary supplies. The fact that Brazil is more nearly self-sufficing than most Latin American countries has kept down the rate of rise of prices because the loss of imports has not been so serious as it otherwise would have been.

[1] *Foreign Commerce Weekly*, Nov. 27, 1943.

[2] I have not discussed the control measures taken to moderate the rise of prices. Dr. Edwards (see pp. 286–294), which discuss these fully.

6. SUMMARY. Price control has not been too successful. The pattern is similar everywhere. Latin American inflation is serious. Reduced supplies and increased demand, which has not been cut or controlled adequately, is to be found everywhere. Inflation is serious in Chile and Bolivia and in other countries but has been relatively under control in Argentina and Colombia.

The survey of individual countries reveals similar patterns for all countries: an excess of exports; reduced supplies; monetary expansion, inadequate controls; and rising prices. In one country, *e.g.*, Peru, the breakdown of transportation is especially important; in another, *e.g.*, Chile, the large excess of exports and ambitious public investment programs stand out; in another, *e.g.*, Colombia, courageous stabilization programs help to moderate the rise of prices; in another, *e.g.*, Brazil, relative self-sufficiency keeps the rate of price rise down.

Chapter VII

Exchanges and Prices

by SEYMOUR E. HARRIS

INTRODUCTION

Exchange problems are dealt with incidentally in several chapters in this volume.[1] It seems necessary to treat them somewhat more fully here. They are, of course, technical problems, but in this chapter the treatment is as nontechnical as it can be made without being inadequate.

In recent years Latin American countries have not been disposed to allow their exchanges to fluctuate freely in response to supply and demand. They have not, on the other hand, adhered to fixed exchanges. When demand for their exports has weakened seriously, exchanges have frequently been allowed to drop. Dollars (used interchangeably for world currencies) become more expensive and pesos (here used for purposes of exposition as the Latin American currency) cheaper. When, on the other hand, exports have been greatly in demand and capital has flowed in, the authorities have not been inclined to allow the exchanges to find their free level. Appreciation has not been so popular as depreciation. Governments have found ways of holding appreciation in check.

Exchange policy has also been directed toward (1) encouraging exports; (2) discouraging imports; and (3) improving the terms of trade, *i.e.*, obtaining more units of imports for *X* units of exports.

Exchange depreciation is, of course, a simple technique for the encouragement of exports and discouragement of imports. Assume

[1] See especially Chs. IV on Central Banking and Monetary Management and X, XII, XIV, and XVIII on Bolivia, Chile, Cuba and Venezuela.

that the peso falls from 10 pesos = $1 to 20 pesos = $1. On the assumption that prices in the United States and (say) Chile are unchanged, the Chilean exporters obtain more pesos, and the Chilean importer pays out more pesos. Chilean goods become cheaper because pesos are cheaper and prices in Chile have not risen proportionately. Actually, prices will rise in Chile; and the bounty on exports will be measured by the relation of the increased cheapness of the peso (in dollars) and the drop in the purchasing power of the peso in Chile relative to that of the dollar in the United States.[1]

Most Latin American countries have advanced beyond exchange depreciation, which, as a rule, has the effect of giving a lift to all export industries whether the stimulus is needed or not. It furthermore imparts the stimulation irrespective of need and at the expense of the terms of trade. Exporters may gain, and those who buy foreign commodities or make payments abroad lose. Depreciation can be justified, then, only on grounds of ease of administration and the distress of exporters. World prices (*e.g.*, in dollars) of the Latin American exports fall, *i.e.*, more is given for *X* imports.

In applying exchange control, the government controls supply and demand. It may, for example, maintain the exchanges above an equilibrium level. It then restricts demand and forces an accounting for incoming exchange upon all recipients. If, on the other hand, the peso tends to rise too much, the government may intervene through purchases of dollars. Against the rise in demand for pesos is introduced an induced rise in demand for dollars, *i.e.*, increased offers of pesos.

Through exchange control, governments offer favorable prices (many pesos for a dollar) for dollars obtained in sale of commodities of elastic demand (*i.e.*, a small reduction in the dollar price elicits large additional sales) and an unfavorable price (few pesos) when demand is inelastic (in popular language, price is not a major consideration). In this manner, the authorities are enabled to charge what the traffic will bear. They can obtain maximum revenue from a given volume of exports. They can, moreover, make the most effective use of foreign exchange by denying exchange to purchasers of nonessential commodities and exporters of capital and by offering dollars at low prices to purchasers of commodities badly needed by

[1] See my *Exchange Depreciation* (Chs. 1 and 2) and also H. S. Ellis, *Exchange Control in Central Europe*.

the economy and at higher prices for less essential commodities and services.

In this chapter the main subjects discussed are: (1) the relation of exchange rates and prices, 1939–1943; (2) the limits put on exchange appreciation; (3) kinds of appreciation; (4) techniques of varying rates.

PRICE MOVEMENTS

Prices have risen greatly in Latin American countries. The extent of the increase has varied from country to country. At best the results given in Table 1—based on the index numbers of the various countries—should be accepted with reservations. Those who have followed the index-number controversy in the United States are well aware of the pitfalls, although many of the criticisms are not fully merited. Critics frequently expect index numbers to reveal more than they are constructed to reveal. For example, index numbers measure changes in the cost of a sample of goods consumed by low-income groups in a recent period. They are not supposed to measure the rise of costs of an improved standard of living in wartime. The BLS cost-of-living index number has been attacked on various grounds: that it is not representative (*e.g.*, expenditures and prices in public dining halls have risen disproportionately, but these prices are not considered in the index number); that deterioration and black-market prices are not adequately measured; that the index does not allow for the disappearance of cheap items; that it measures the prices of goods currently obtainable, not the goods obtainable in 1938, etc. Unfortunately, no index number can deal adequately with deterioration and the disappearance of cheap articles; nor can index numbers perform the many tasks which their critics demand.

Latin American measures of prices can be similarly criticized. In addition, they are much more crudely constructed than our index numbers. Frequently they are unweighted and are based on a very small sample (*e.g.*, 12 commodities). Technically they are not so acceptable as the BLS index numbers. Regional differences in prices are even more important than in the United States, and the price quotations in one large city or even in several are less representative of national prices than the quotations of numerous cities recognized by the BLS. In short, the prices given in Table 1 at best can be accepted as a very rough guide of price history.

We have had an increase in the cost of living from 1939 to the third quarter of 1943, of over 90 per cent for Chile; of 86 per cent for Bolivia (until 1942); of 72 per cent for Mexico; and of as little as 20 per cent for Colombia. More recent figures reveal more rapid rises in Colombia and serious movements in Mexico City. These significant rises indicate that prices have risen much more rapidly in Latin America than in the United States where, during 5 years of war, wholesale prices have risen by only about one-third and the cost of living by about one-fourth. This unusual increase of prices in Latin America in the face of only moderate governmental expenditures and relatively moderate disturbances brought on by the war, as compared with those in the United States, gives evidence of strong inflationary forces in these countries. It further reflects the fact that prices of imported commodities have risen greatly there. In many of these countries, a large proportion of all commodities consumed or used for capital purposes is obtained from foreign countries; therefore, any given rise of national prices is explained, in no small part, by the increased prices of imports. This would, for example, be particularly true of countries like Bolivia, Peru, Colombia, and Chile, which depend heavily on imports. In Argentina, a country self-sufficient in food and possessing well-developed transportation facilities which have suffered little as the result of the war, the rise in the cost of living has been relatively moderate. The volume of imports, especially from customary sources, has declined greatly. Prices are higher not only because imports from given countries generally are high-priced but also because inferior sources abroad or at home must be tapped.

Perhaps the most interesting feature of price movements in recent years is their failure to respond along expected lines to fluctuations in the exchanges. In 1939–1940, for example, the Latin American exchanges in general depreciated in relation to the dollar. The explanation was frequently not what might be expected, *viz.*, a greater rise of prices in these countries than in the United States. Substantial declines in Latin American exchanges occurred in the middle of 1940 which clearly must be associated with speculative influences. The major explanation of exchange depreciation seems to be the relatively large decline in export values, actual and anticipated. In 1942–1944, however, Latin American exchanges rose in value. Yet, in this period, prices generally rose more than in the United States. On the principle that the currency varies in value abroad according to its *relative*

TABLE 1.—PERCENTAGE CHANGES OF WHOLESALE PRICE AND COST-OF-LIVING INDICES, 1939–1943 *

Name of country	Cost of living	Wholesale prices
United States	25.0	34.0
Argentina	7.4	
Haiti	18.0†	
Colombia	20.0	18.0
Brazil	30.0	
Peru	45.0	100.0
Costa Rica	53.0	56.0
Ecuador	56.0	
Cuba	60.0	
Mexico	72.0	52.0
Bolivia	86.0†	
Chile	93.0	94.0

Name of country	Percentage rise January–November, 1943	
	Cost of living	Wholesale prices
Bolivia	8	
Colombia	19	17
Peru	10	10
Venezuela	..	3
Mexico (October)	30	23

* 1939 to latest period available—July to October, 1943. Basic figures have been put at my disposal by the Foreign Information Branch of the Office of Price Administration. I have, however, adapted them to my use.

† 1939–1942 only but see second part of this table.

change in purchasing power at home as compared with the variation in the internal purchasing power of the foreign currency, one would not expect this.

Over short periods, the large rise of exports (absolutely and relative to imports) of Latin American countries and the inward movement of capital account for the appreciation of their exchanges. As pesos become more expensive, Latin American exports should fall and imports rise and then prices in Latin America should decline and their exchanges should weaken as they buy more and sell less abroad. On both counts, exchanges and prices would move toward equilibrium. The dollar should appreciate, and prices in Latin

America rise. But Latin American exports and imports are not determined primarily by price considerations. Latin America may wish to import more; but the United States and the United Kingdom impose export restrictions, and shipping is limited. Latin American countries, furthermore, are not disposed to import as much as they are able to obtain abroad: they conserve exchange and protect their industries. In short, prices do not move in relation to exchanges as they would in a free market.

EXCHANGE RATES

Exchange appreciation has been the general tendency since 1941, but the rise has not been so great as might be expected from the favorable balance of payment of Latin American countries. On the other hand, it has been greater than might be expected from an examination of price movements in the United States and in these countries. A few examples of the rise of exchange rates is given in Table 2. It will be observed from this table that the tendency in Chile has been downward rather than upward; this is particularly noticeable in view of the fact that the government in 1943 recognized the free market rate, which had been a more depreciated rate than the official one. Other currencies, in general, have risen in value. Thus the Ecuadorian currency rose from 18 to $1 in June, 1940, to 14.10 to $1 by November, 1943;[1] the Cuban dollar from 88 cents in June, 1940, to $1 by November, 1941; the Mexican peso from 5.99 to $1 in May, 1940, to 4.85 to 4.86 in 1942–1943. Bolivianos had been sold at 40 to $1 for certain foodstuffs and at a compensatory rate of 55 to $1 for other imports available in limited quantities. By the early part of 1942, a single rate of 46 to $1 was established. This represented, of course, depreciation for the importers of foodstuffs and appreciation for others. Early in 1943 the price of dollars was reduced from 46 to 42 bolivianos.

A history of Argentine, Brazilian, and Chilean rates since 1939 is given in Table 2.

In general, Latin American exchanges were weak in 1938–1940 and strong in 1942–1944. The favorable balance of payments in the latter years may be associated with an intense demand for Latin American products, restricted outflows of goods from other United Nations, price control of United States exports, and exportation of

[1] That is, rose in value from 5⅔ cents to 7 cents.

capital to Latin America. In addition, numerous production control programs and price measures were taken to keep up the prices of Latin American exports.

TABLE 2

Argentina

(Pesos = $1)

Date	Official *A*	Official *B*	Bid	Free
1939	3.70	4.32	....	4.33
1941	3.73	4.23	4.24	
November, 1943	3.73	4.23	4.94	4.00

Brazil

(Cruzeiros = $1)

Date	Official	Free	Special free	Curb
1938	17.64			
1939	16.83	19.87	21.54	20.83
1941	16.50	19.72	20.68	20.30
November, 1943	16.40	19.63	20.30	

Chile

(Pesos = $1)

Date	Official	Export drafts	Curb	Free	Gold exchange	Mining	Agriculture
1938	19.37	25.0	27.48	.....	25.00		
1939	19.37	25.0	32.47	31.04	29.86		
1941	19.37	25.0	31.78	31.15	31.15	31.35	31.15
November, 1943	19.37	25.0	32.47	31.00	31.00	31.00	31.00

Weakness of Latin American currencies in 1938–1940 (or 1941) was accompanied by an increase of controls and, in free exchange markets, by depreciation. Even where the exchanges are controlled, moreover, recourse was had to depreciation. Variations in exchanges are frequently found in a change in the free rate, which is generally a lower—*i.e.*, a more depreciated—rate than the official rate, or sometimes in a reclassification of rates applicable to particular transactions. Again, exporters may be allowed to convert their exchange at the free—*i.e.*, the depreciated—rate and importers of nonessential commodities may not be allowed access to exchange at the high official rate, *i.e.*, the low dollar price. In both cases, the effect is a relative depreciation of the exchanges.

In general, appreciation of Latin American currencies after 1941 has been held in check by authorities. An appreciation of the exchanges has been especially popular with price administrators in these countries. They argue that an appreciation would result in a reduction in the prices of imports, since dollars, etc., would be cheaper, and also in a reduction in the prices of exports, since the local seller would get a smaller number of units of domestic currency for his foreign currencies. He would therefore be more disposed to sell in the domestic market than at home. I shall return presently to the explanation for the failure of the currencies of Latin American countries to appreciate more than they actually have.

In general, Latin American currencies are still, in 1944, at a lower value in dollars than in 1937–1939. The downward course clearly has been stopped for the time being, and there has been a slight movement upward. Appreciation has been the stronger movement in 1942–1944 despite the relatively greater rise of prices in Latin America (*i.e.*, relative decline in value at home) than in the United States.

In short, the balance of payments is related to price movements; but, in the short run and in controlled markets, prices are not so decisive as in the long run and in free markets. The low prices in the United States, for example, would be more significant if the Latin American importers could purchase freely in this market. That they cannot contributes toward weakness in the external value of the dollar, despite the high value of a dollar as reflected in what each dollar might buy in goods, relatively to what a peso buys.

That there has not been an even greater rise in the dollar value of Latin American currencies since 1941 is explained by the following considerations:

1. The willingness of the central authority to absorb excess dollars at a given peso, milreis, etc., price. This policy has had the effect of sustaining the demand for dollars and also of inducing monetary expansion at home and thus reducing the value of local currencies and maintaining the value of the dollar in these currencies. Unlimited purchases of dollars result in the issue of pesos at a fixed ratio for excess dollars offered to the central authority.

2. In general, because of the fear of adverse effects on export industries, Latin American countries have not been disposed to allow

the exchanges to rise to a point given by the peculiar supply and demand situation of wartime. Finance ministers generally fear the effects of appreciation on exports. When, as in Chile, exports account for a substantial part of national income and also of the Treasury's revenue, opposition to exchange appreciation is strong, for national income in pesos would suffer and receipts from taxes on exports would be reduced following a depreciation. If a ton of copper yields X pesos at an exchange of 25 pesos to $1, it will yield only $X/2$ if the rate becomes 12½ to 1. If, however, the price of copper in dollars rises, the adverse effects to that extent will be offset.

3. Pressure has been exerted by foreign interests against a policy which would reduce the value in Latin American currencies of capital sent into Latin America.

4. Many Latin American authorities are fearful of the postwar situation. The more depreciated their exchanges, the more, they assume, will their accumulations of dollars, sterling, and gold grow and therefore the greater the cushion when the balance of payments once more becomes adverse. This argument is of doubtful validity. Many countries would probably increase their receipts in dollars and gold if they appreciated their exchanges more. Exporters confronted with a reduction in the peso yield of dollars would increase the dollar price of their exports and would not suffer a corresponding decline in sales. Demand for most Latin American exports in war is highly inelastic. A related point has greater validity: in the postwar period it is increased competition with foreign nations that is to be feared. It is admitted that current exchanges are too low-priced in dollars: *i.e.*, the peso is undervalued. In the postwar period, however, when competition will have revived, the current values will not be too low: the bribe of cheap exchange will be required to induce foreigners to buy.

5. Opposition to a reduction in the price of dollars arises also from those who fear that the effect will be an encouragement of imports of unnecessary commodities.

SPECIAL ASPECTS OF APPRECIATION

First, note that the Latin American countries and particularly Argentina have had to accumulate large balances in London as a result of a favorable export trade with the British Empire. These accumulations of sterling are not freely available, although they may be transferred among the Latin American countries. Insofar as the accumulation of foreign exchange is in blocked balances, as is true in this case, the local Latin American country is not favored by an increased demand, and therefore its currency does not tend to appreciate. The British pay not by buying pesos but by depositing sterling in London. By 1942 Argentina could report a credit balance of 340 million pesos in free exchange and, after repayment of debt, a growth of balances subject to clearing agreement of 207 million pesos in sterling and a reduction of similar balances of 43 million pesos vis-à-vis Brazil.

Second, it should be noted that exchange appreciation may take place, not through any change in the official rate or even in any of the free or relatively free rates, but rather through a reclassification of transactions in terms of the applicable rate. Thus a rate of 10 pesos to $1 may now be the appropriate rate for 60 per cent of all transactions and 40 per cent for the rate of 15 pesos to $1. If the former respective percentages were 20 and 80, then there has actually occurred an appreciation of exchanges. This may be brought about by a reclassification of transactions in terms of the applicable exchange rates or even by changes in the relative importance of different kinds of transactions. In the latter case, the appreciation would result merely from the fact that the transactions that yield foreign currencies convertible per unit of dollar, pound, etc., into relatively small number of local currencies have become more important.

EXCHANGE POLICY

It should be observed that there are perhaps three different approaches to the exchange problem. First, the exchanges may be strong, and reconversion of foreign exchange into local currencies would then follow. The result is inflationary, and the tendency of prices to rise in Brazil (say) should depress the cruzeiro, since demand for it would fall as prices in Brazil rise. This may not happen, however, if foreign prices continue to rise and if the demand for local currency increases in response to intensification of war demands for Latin American products. A second approach is to allow a rise in the value of the local currency when the exchanges are strong. In this manner it is hoped to reduce the demand for the local currency and increase the demand for dollars etc., relatively because exports become more expensive, because the importation of capital is discouraged, and also because imports become cheaper. Finally, there is what might be called the *Colombia technique*, which largely aims to exclude both appreciation and domestic inflation. The technique is to siphon off the additional purchasing power which results from the conversion of foreign into domestic currencies. This technique is discussed below.

In general, Latin American countries have followed the first policy. Price rises since 1941 have generally been more rapid than in the United States and the United Kingdom. Strong demand for the Latin American currencies and the ensuing expansion at home have persisted, nevertheless, because of restrictions of exports by the United States and the United Kingdom and the intense demand for Latin American commodities. Appreciation and sterilization of the newly acquired dollars (*e.g.*, taxation of copper companies) or of the resulting new pesos, etc., have played a secondary role in Latin American policies.

Colombia's technique (in the last year the sting of the legislation cited has been substantially reduced[1]) is evident from the following:

In presenting Decree 1148 of 1943, the Colombian government emphasized the large accumulation of exchange, the danger to exchange stability, the need of stabilization to protect export industries and to ensure the development of domestic industries, the increasing pressure on prices, the need for exchange reserves in order later to purchase imports not now available, and the need of exchange reserves to avoid a debacle like that of 1929.

This decree and a supplementary decree of July 3, 1943, are in many respects the most advanced anti-inflationary measures taken in the Americas. The decree required that business units should invest 20 per cent of their profits and 50 per cent of their depreciation reserves in government certificates (domestic currency, gold, or dollar certificates); that importers should invest to the extent of 10 per cent (in some cases 5 per cent) of their imports; and that other institutions also should invest in these certificates. In addition, by the end of 1943, banks were required to increase their cash reserves by 100 per cent. It was anticipated that in a period of 2 years this legislation would absorb 100 million pesos of cash, which was estimated to be the excess inflow resulting from the favorable balance of payments. In other words, as dollars come in and are converted into pesos, pesos are sterilized *pari passu*. This is indeed a remarkable bit of legislation and

[1] *Cf.* Ch. XIII on Colombia.

goes far in the direction of offsetting inflationary effects of the favorable balance of payments.[1]

In addition, there has been a considerable relaxation of exchange control, which has tended to encourage the exportation of capital. Other measures also tend to have the effect of discouraging exports. There is, for example, the important law which provides that a certain proportion of dollars are to be converted into government bonds. For example, exporters of coffee were required to invest, in some cases, 10 per cent of their exchange, in others, 20 per cent, in government bonds. Importers of new capital were also required to invest 20 per cent of their dollars in government bonds. It was anticipated that in 1943 exporters of coffee would have invested 7 million pesos in these bonds; other exporters, 1 million; importers of new capital, 5 million; and the total investments in these bonds in 1943 would come to 30 million pesos. The government also requires various institutions to put a certain portion of their assets into these bonds, thus assuring a market for them when they are sold by those who are forced to purchase them.

VARYING PRICES FOR FOREIGN CURRENCIES

Exchange policy has generally been directed toward maximizing the dollar receipts from Latin American exports. Where appreciation of the exchanges, *i.e.*, the reduction in the price of dollars, and other currencies, has been allowed or introduced, it has frequently been restricted to foreign currencies obtained through exports and in particular to exports for which the demand abroad is strong. In this manner the Latin American exporter who is now offered fewer pesos might be compensated by charging a higher dollar price.

An action taken in January, 1944, according to *Circular* 348 of the Exchange Department of the Argentine government, gives an excellent example of the technique of limiting appreciation to given fields. Pointing out that whereas in 1933 only 2 per cent of exports had been negotiated at the preferential (*i.e.*, more depreciated) rate as compared with 40 per cent currently, the government announced that exchanges arising from the most important exports of raw materials and manufacturing products would now be sold at the

[1] This summary of the legislation has been paraphrased from *Suplemento al No.* 186 *de la Revista del Banco de la República*, May, June, and July, 1943. This legislation is discussed more fully in Ch. XIII on Colombia. Later concessions by the government under pressure are there noted.

official rate of 335.8 per $100. This rate equals 29.773 cents per peso as compared with the preferential rate of 25.125 cents. If the exporter now charges the same price in dollars, he will obtain approximately 3.35 pesos per dollar instead of almost 4 pesos, or 15 per cent less in pesos. The net effect then will be that the Argentine exporter who sells at the same dollar price will be deprived of 15 per cent of his peso proceeds. Naturally, one assumes that in these markets where the Argentine position is strong the exporter will compensate himself by charging a higher dollar price. In other words, this is a technique for exacting higher dollar prices from foreign buyers. Thus, virtually all exports of cattle products, meat, and skins now go either to the United States or to the United Kingdom or to both. In these particular markets and also in the wool market Argentine exporters are in a very strong bargaining position.

In his chapter on Venezuela, Dr. Bennion has also given an interesting example of the preferential technique. In 1940, dollars were convertible into bolivars at the following rate:

	Per Dollar
Petroleum	3.09
Copper and cattle	4.30
Cocoa	4.60

These rates reflect the competitive position of Venezuela: the petroleum exporter can be compensated by a higher price in foreign currencies, whereas the cattle exporter would have greater difficulties. Dollars obtained from the exportation of petroleum are then convertible into relatively few bolivars.

In general, the governments concerned are inclined to allow the exporter to exchange his dollars for a large number of local currency units where the additional stimulus of higher prices is required. However, in cases where the position of the exporter in foreign markets is strong, he is encouraged to charge a higher *dollar* price and thus obtain more local currencies; or else he is forced to turn over to the local government a given proportion of his dollar receipts and obtain in exchange a relatively small number of local currency units. In this manner the Chilean exporters, of copper and nitrate, for example, are forced to convert at a low peso price, and the government in turn thus obtains necessary supplies of foreign currencies, which are used to pay its own bills, or thus puts foreign exchange at the disposal of importers of very essential imports.

The government is also inclined to allocate foreign exchange at prices that are dictated by the essentiality of the use for which the exchange is purchased. Where the commodity is very necessary, exchange may be obtained at a lower rate, *i.e.*, at a more appreciated price for the local currency and a lower price for the foreign currency.

EXAMPLES OF DIFFERENTIAL EXCHANGE RATES

Numerous examples may be given of the tendency on the part of governments to allocate exchanges at prices determined by essentiality. In addition to the Argentine and Venezuelan cases discussed above, I shall now discuss briefly the treatment in Colombia and Brazil.

Before April, 1943, the exchange rates for dollars (number of Columbian pesos = $1) were 1.75, 1.79½, 1.87, and 1.95. Corresponding rates since April, 1943, are 1.75½, 1.76½, 1.77½, and 1.78½. These rates necessarily reflect the importance of the commodities to be imported. Where a commodity is considered necessary (*e.g.*, raw materials and machinery), the importer has to pay only the lowest rate, *i.e.*, 1.75 or (later) 1.75½; where the commodity is less important (*e.g.*, typewriters, sewing machines, biscuits, shoes), he has access to the second rate; where it is deemed essential to encourage domestic output (*e.g.*, rice), the importer is frequently forced to pay the third rate, *i.e.*, 1.87 before April and 1.77½ afterward. Finally, where the import is a luxury and production may be encouraged at home (*e.g.*, whisky and wine), the importer has to pay the highest rate. The classification of rates undoubtedly had some importance in determining the kind of imports that were brought into the country before April, 1943. Differences in exchange rates have been so small since April, 1943, and the market for commodities so speculative that it is undoubtedly true that variations in rates have played a relatively insignificant part in determining imports.

Until April, 1943, the availability of exchange at the cheapest rate made a difference of more than 10 per cent in the price of importation (as against the most expensive rate) and therefore, for commodities for which demand was elastic, variations in rates might have had some effect on the volume of imports. Actually prices had risen so much (and in particular to the ultimate user) that even in 1942 and early 1943 the differentiation of rates might be considered a factor of secondary importance. By April, 1943, and later, the maximum difference in exchange rates has been but a few per cent, and by that time the rise of prices of imports associated with restricted flows of goods, speculative influences, etc., had become much more important than any rise associated with the payment of the expensive rate for dollars. If the importer has to pay 2 per cent less, some speculator makes 2 per cent less or (less likely) prices may go up somewhat. By that time, price differences of even 10 to 20 per cent will have little effect on the amounts purchased.

Let us consider the Brazilian structure of rates. There were four rates in vogue in Brazil in the summer of 1943. The rates were as follows: (1) the gold buying rate 20.45 cruzeiros = $1; (2) the official exchange buying rate 16.50 cruzeiros = $1; (3) free exchange buying 19.47 cruzeiros = $1, selling 19.63 cruzeiros = $1; (4) special free exchange buying 20.00 cruzeiros = $1, selling 20.50 cruzeiros = $1.

(1) The gold rate is used for diamond purchases and dollar purchases from the diplomatic corps. (2) The official exchange related to about one-third the export bills. These must be sold to the Bank of Brazil at that rate, the profits being used for governmental expenditures abroad. This rate is fixed and does not fluctuate. (3) The free exchange rate is the relevant rate for the conversion of foreign exchange received for the remainder of exports and for all imports. There is also a 5 per cent exchange tax on the purchases of foreign currencies in this market. The rate fluctuates, but the Bank of Brazil has been responsible for relatively stable exchanges in this market. (4) The special free exchange market is used for noncommodity purposes, *e.g.*, maintenance, remittances, capital transfers, tourists, etc. There is a 5 per cent exchange tax on all purchases of foreign exchange in this market. This rate (special free exchange) has been maintained on an even keel during the past year. Control is exercised by making all sales of foreign exchange subject to the prior authorization of the government. In fact, no commodity import or export of checks or currency can be made without informing the government. Purchases of foreign exchange must be reported to the government, and banks are limited as to the amount of their holdings. Finally, through the operation of censorship the black market has been largely eliminated.

The net effect of the varying exchange rates is of course to provide the government with exchange at a cheap rate to cover its own expenditures and also to discourage to some extent the transactions in exchanges which are considered contrary to the public interest.

In general, the differences in rates are not great enough to have any serious effect on the movement of goods and services. Exporters, on the average, obtain less local currency for each dollar available than importers or other purchasers of dollars are required to pay for each dollar. A substantial proportion of exports are paid for at the rate of 16.50 cruzeiros = $1, whereas purchasers must pay from 19.65 to 20.50 cruzeiros and, in addition, a 5 per cent tax.

CONCLUSION

We have now surveyed the exchange history of Latin America in 1939–1943 and in particular have indicated the reasons for controlled appreciation. In the postwar period, Latin American exchanges once more are likely to be weak, although at least for a year after the war in the Far East there may be elements of strength. Undoubtedly demand for basic materials will then be greatly reduced from war levels, and imports will greatly rise. How weak the exchanges will be will depend on the success in reallocating economic resources, the improvements in productivity in new industries, the tariff policies of the major buying countries, the extent of international monetary cooperation, the resumption of international financing, and the progress made in international commodity agreements. A cushion of perhaps $3 billion or more in reserves will be very useful in the transition period when the balance becomes adverse and the necessary longer run adjustments have not yet been made. The prospects for the elimination of exchange control do not seem very bright. Much will depend on the leadership of the United States and the United Kingdom.

Chapter VIII

Inter-American Trade Policy

by HENRY CHALMERS

The Setting of the Current Problem

WHAT has happened in the trade relations of the American republics during this war is reminiscent of the Maeterlinck play in which the characters go through various adventures in far-off lands in search of the Bluebird of Happiness, only to find it in the end in their own back yard. Similarly, it seems to have required the exigencies of war for the American republics fully to realize and to utilize the possibilities of supplying their import needs from each other. During this emergency, when most of the continent of Europe and the Far East were closed off by military developments, there has been much gratification over the extent to which the countries of the Western Hemisphere have been able to obtain from each other the essential raw materials and manufactured products for which they used to be largely dependent upon Europe or the Orient.

During the early period of the war, doleful prophecies were heard about what was going to happen to the Latin American countries, with their $500 million market on the continent of Europe cut off. Yet, for the third successive year, the increased purchases by the United States of Latin American commodities, new and old, are practically offsetting in value—if not in full range—the loss of those European markets. Far from the depression predicted for them in 1940, most of the countries of Latin America are now prospering. In a number of the southern republics, the United States procurement and development programs have simulated local business conditions to the dimensions of a boom.

On the other hand, the fact that the Latin American countries have been beyond the reach of producers in Germany and other European countries, whom they had come to regard as the preeminent suppliers of certain classes of goods, has not meant that they have been suffering seriously from the lack of these goods. The record shows that, by assiduous search within each other's territories for alternative sources of supply, and particularly by dovetailing their trade programs with that of the United States, the countries of Latin America have in fact been fairly well supplied with the imported products most essential to their economic life. What curtailment of supplies there has been in the southern republics—varying with the current availabilities of shipping—has not been much different from what the citizens of the United States have been subject to, under the imperative prior demands of the war.[1]

Yet, despite the remarkable degree to which the American republics have been able, under stress, to meet deficiencies in each other's import requirements, the indications are strong that they are all looking forward to the day when they can again form part of the general world trading community. Only in the very darkest days of 1940, when many feared that the world might have to accommodate itself to the economic life of continental Europe being indefinitely under the centralized control of a totalitarian government—bent on a large measure of autarchy on that continent and arbitrary dictation over the conditions of all its purchases from overseas—was there much thought given to the possibility of forming a more or less closed regional economy among the countries of the Western Hemisphere. Many bold plans were then put forward for the "economic defense of the Americas," as it was termed. These usually called for radically new arrangements for the combined disposal overseas of the surplus products of the American republics and for drastic readjustments of the production and trade of the individual countries in the effort to make the Western Hemisphere as self-sufficient as possible.

Interest in such proposals has subsided, probably for several reasons: the great difficulties and dislocations involved in those programs which aimed at a system of integrated and semiclosed regionalism; the diminishing likelihood of an Axis victory; and the passing of

[1] For analysis of the methods by which these wartime developments in the commercial relations between the United States and the Latin American republics were brought about, see my article, "Wartime Controls and Stimuli upon the Foreign Trade of Latin America," *Foreign Commerce Weekly*, Apr. 24 and May 1, 1943.

the danger of forced American isolation. Most students of the situation are agreed, moreover, that the American republics do not constitute a balanced self-sufficient economic area. It is significant that, in that very period of anxiety when the foreign ministers of the American republics first met in emergency session at Panama in the fall of 1939 to recommend strong measures for continental solidarity, they made it clear "that these principles are free from any selfish purpose of isolation, but are rather inspired by a deep sense of universal cooperation." When these foreign ministers met again at Havana in the summer of 1940, after the fall of France, to work out a program of inter-American financial and economic cooperation, their abiding faith that the clouds would pass was revealed in the declaration "that the American nations should be prepared to resume the conduct of trade with the entire world in accordance with these [liberal] principles [which they were resolved to apply in their own relations] as soon as the non-American nations are prepared to do likewise."

WARTIME TREND TOWARD CLOSER INTER-AMERICAN TRADE RELATIONS

The present close integration of the trading programs and controls of the various countries of Latin America with the export control system and import procurement programs of the United States, developed during the emergency, necessarily involves a high degree of preferential treatment of each other's commerce and economy. These exceptional relations can hardly, however, be expected to carry over unchanged into peacetime. Few, indeed, would then desire that any large part of this network of war-born arrangements should continue. Nevertheless, urgings are already being heard, and are likely to increase, for some limited forms of special trade relations among the American republics, even when overseas markets and sources of supply are again accessible.

Special arrangements are likely to be urged, not only between the United States and the southern republics, but also between various pairs or groups of the countries of Latin America. During the war these countries have enlarged their sales to each other to an extent averaging more than double the prewar level, although substantial gains have been made by only a few of the countries and, as a whole, only minor portions of most export products of the Latin American republics find markets in each other's territories even now. Cotton piece goods represent probably the most notable exception. In the desire to retain and broaden these newly enlarged currents of inter-Latin American trade, some feel that official arrangements for preferential relations are desirable.

CONCILIATION OF PREFERENTIAL IDEA WITH OPEN WORLD TRADING SYSTEM

How to harmonize these proposals for customs unions or various other forms of special preferential trade relationships among the American republics as permanent arrangements, with the declared general desire of the United Nations to work back toward an expanding and competitive system of international trading, constitutes one of the central problems in visualizing a consistent program of commercial relations on the American continent for the postwar period.

A review of the principal proposals and programs in this direction, and of the extent of their progress or failure, should afford a valuable background for appraising the various types of plans and formulas currently being proposed for special preferential inter-American commercial relations.

I. Early Aspirations and Proposals for a Continental Customs Union

The idea of specially close relations between the countries on the American continent—in trade as in other matters—has been put forward in different forms by various of their leaders for more than a century. As far back as 1790, when Francisco de Miranda of Venezuela first sought the support of England in his efforts for the revolutionizing of the Spanish colonies, he placed before the British Prime Minister an elaborate plan for a union, under a single government, of all Spanish America, reaching from the sources of the Mississippi to Cape Horn, as their emancipation was effected.

BOLÍVAR'S FIRST CONGRESS OF AMERICAN STATES, 1826

The first Congress of American states that was assembled at Panama in 1826 by Simon Bolívar, to discuss the formation of a continental confederation, included among its objectives commercial cooperation among the new American republics "as allies and confederates," as well as the preservation of peace and a unified stand against the return of European domination.[1] The state of general political instability which still prevailed, however, the undeveloped means of communications between their widespread territories, and the overriding concern of each of the newly liberated countries with the organization of its internal affairs combined to prevent the realization of Bolívar's ambitious proposals. Although his central idea of organizing the erstwhile colonies into a single family of nations recurred, with variations, for several decades at succeeding conferences of various Latin American republics—even at one held as late as 1864 in Lima—nothing ever came of any of them.

HENRY CLAY'S CONCEPT OF A "SYSTEM" OF FREE AMERICAN STATES

It is notable that, although the United States was invited to be represented at several of these conferences, the aim of the sponsors was distinctly limited to bringing together the Spanish American or, at most, the Latin American countries. Probably the first suggestion of a larger relationship, which included the United States, was that put forward by Henry Clay, as Speaker of the House of Representatives, in connection with his championship of our recognition of the independence of the newly liberated Spanish American colonies. In his address of May 10, 1820, he stressed the commercial as well as the political advantages that would accrue from such a step.

Dwelling on the importance of the commerce of South America, "when freed from its present restraints," and contemplating the prospective increase in wealth and population of the American countries, he declared:

> It is in our power to create a system of which we shall be the center and in which all South America will act with us. In respect to commerce, we shall be most benefited; this country would become the place of deposit of the commerce of the world. . . . But however important our early recognition of the independence of the South might be to us, as respects our com-

[1] In view of the frequent current references to Bolívar as one of the earliest promoters of the Pan-American movement and the incorrect accounts often given of the scope of his proposed federation and of his attitude toward the participation of the United States, it is particularly timely to have a fresh documented discussion on this point. This will be found in the recent review by Roscoe R. Hill of Luis Quintanilla's "A Latin American Speaks," *Hispanic American Historical Review*, November, 1943, pp. 668–675.

For full analysis of the aims and efforts of Bolívar in convening the historic Panama Conference and of the reactions of the various American governments to it, see Joseph B. Lockey, *Pan Americanism: Its Beginnings* (1920), *passim*.

mercial and manufacturing interests, was there not another view of the subject, infinitely more gratifying? We should become the center of a system which would constitute the rallying-point of human freedom against all the despotism of the old world.[1]

The approval of the Congress of the United States to the invitations to the Congress of Panama of 1826 was so long delayed that the first meeting had adjourned before the United States delegates could have arrived.[2] They *were* present in Mexico the following spring, when the Congress was to reassemble, but that second meeting did not take place. Although they were not used at the time, the detailed instructions to that Panama Mission on the subject of commercial policy, signed by Henry Clay as Secretary of State, have historical significance. The delegates of the United States were instructed, in any trade negotiations undertaken, not to seek exclusive privileges, even as against the European powers. They were rather to urge upon the other American states concurrence in the general principle of equality of treatment for the regulation of their commerce and navigation, with no discrimination to be made because of the nationality of the goods or of the ships.[3]

[1] Many historians attribute to Clay a "grand plan" for the establishment of a "human freedom league in America," in which "all nations from Hudson's Bay to Cape Horn" would be united. In view of the apparent inconsistency with the instructions to the delegates of the United States to the Panama Congress, given by Henry Clay as Secretary of State (later cited), to avoid exclusive trade privileges among the American countries, careful research was made into Clay's speeches and writings, without finding any corroboration of this alleged plan for a continental union.

The proposal for a "human freedom league in America" appears to have been given currency first in H. E. von Holst's *Constitutional and Political History of the United States*, Vol. I, p. 179, translated from the German by John J. Lalor and Alfred B. Mason (Callaghan and Company, Chicago, 1889). The original German edition of von Holst's work (*Verfassung und Demokratie der V. S. von Amerika*, Düsseldorf, 1873, Vol. I, p. 357–358) carries a footnote giving as his source Vol. I, pp. 238–244, of the *Speeches of Henry Clay* by Calvin Colton, Clay's contemporary biographer. However, Henry Clay's speech in the House of Representatives of May 10, 1820, to which von Holst refers, does not contain such a proposal, which von Holst apparently read into it. The foregoing broader suggestion, for a "system" of free states on the American continent, is quoted from Colton's account of Clay's speech.

[2] That was the case also with the representatives of several of the South American countries. The United Kingdom and the Netherlands *were* represented at Panama.

[3] The full text of that letter of instructions, a neglected document in the history of United States commercial policy, will be found in "Documents in Relation to the Panama Mission," transmitted to the Senate and House by President John Quincy Adams on Mar. 3, 1829 (printed as Appendix to Gales and Seaton Register of *Debates in Congress* for 20th Congress, 2d Session, Vol. V, 1830, pp. 38–49; also in Historical Appendix, Vol. IV, pp. 113–150, to report on the *International American Conference*, Government Printing Office, 1890).

SHIFT OF OBJECTIVE FROM TOTAL TO COMMERCIAL UNION

It is also notable that the early proposals, both from the southern republics and from the United States, were in terms of a political union, federation, or system, with closer economic or trade relations an incidental part of the more ambitious plan. It was from the United States, apparently, that there first came the proposal for a more limited program, focusing specifically upon closer commercial relations between the American republics, cooperating as independent political states.

STEPHEN DOUGLAS'S PLAN FOR A COMMERCIAL UNION OF NORTH AMERICA

One of the earliest formulations was that of Senator Stephen A. Douglas, drafted shortly before his death in 1861.[1] He was impressed with the complete freedom of commerce between all the states and territories of the United States as a most conspicuous advantage of the Federal Union, and also with the Canadian-American Reciprocity Treaty of 1854, then in operation, which virtually established free trade in natural products between the United States and the British North American provinces. Douglas regarded that as "an important step toward the adoption of a liberal commercial system" for all North America and the adjacent islands.

He visualized a "Continental Union for Commercial Purposes Only," as he called it, along the lines of the *Zollverein* among the various German states, as affording the advantages "which would naturally result from a uniform and well-regulated system of free trade, transit, and intercourse," without the disadvantages of attempting a political federation of "countries and peoples of different systems of civilization." Douglas believed that such a commercial union of the various political communities of North America could be accomplished "on terms of equality and justice," "without . . . interfering with their respective forms of governments, or political relations, or their internal policies," and that this "could not fail to be mutually

[1] It was first published in October, 1889, as a private pamphlet, on the occasion of the convening of the first Pan-American Conference, to be later discussed. Although not made public during Douglas's lifetime, his plan acquired significance from the fact that the opposition of the Argentine spokesman at that conference to the idea of an American customs union was based upon Douglas's formulation of it. (Douglas's draft was later reprinted as *Senate Document* 61, 62d Congress, 1st Session, July 5, 1911, as a paper on "North American Trade.")

beneficial to all branches of industry, trade and commerce in each country."

BLAINE'S PROPOSAL AND THE FIRST PAN-AMERICAN CONFERENCE, 1889–1890

The only actual attempt on the part of the United States government to bring about a customs union among the American republics was that initiated by Secretary of State James G. Blaine in 1881. Blaine combined the vision of a large, unrestricted continental market with an ardent championship of a protective tariff for the United States. Eighteen countries were represented at the conference, which actually took place at Washington in the period October, 1889, to April, 1890. The act of Congress authorizing the President to convene the conference specifically named as one of its topics "measures toward the formation of an American customs union, under which the trade of the American nations shall so far as possible and profitably be promoted."[1]

The conference provoked an extended and quite outspoken discussion of the current trade positions and concerns of various American countries, even though the customs-union proposal itself was at once pronounced impracticable on a number of grounds, political and economic.[2] The conference did find acceptable the idea of tariff reciprocity among the American nations, to be approached by gradual steps. As the first step, it recommended that the governments represented conclude commercial treaties of partial reciprocity with one or more of the American countries as it might be in their interest, "upon such a basis as would be acceptable in each case, taking into consideration the special situations, conditions and interests of each country, and with a view to promote their common welfare." The Argentine and Chilean representatives were outspoken in their opposition, even to the moderate recommendations for negotiations for partial reciprocity.

In his report on the conference to President Harrison, Secretary of State Blaine declared that

[1] The committee of the conference to which this topic was referred interpreted the term *customs union* to mean an association or agreement among the several American nations for a free interchange of domestic products, a common and uniform system of tariff laws, and an equitable division of the customs dues collected under them.

[2] That discussion is still worth reading. See *International American Conference*, Government Printing Office, Washington, D.C., 1890, Vol. I, Reports of Committees and Discussions Thereon, pp. 103–264.

Fifteen of the seventeen Republics with which we have been in conference have indicated . . . their desire to enter upon reciprocal commercial relations with the United States; the remaining two express equal willingness, could they be assured that their advances would be favorably considered.

As a practical and prompt mode of testing the question, Secretary Blaine suggested an amendment to the tariff bill then pending in the United States Congress, which would authorize the President to declare the ports of the United States free to all the products of any nation of the American hemisphere upon which no export duties were imposed, whenever and as long as such nation should admit to its ports free of all taxes a specified list of commodities of United States origin. The list included what were then the principal export products of the United States. The actual provision of reciprocity which was embodied in the Tariff Act of 1890, and the experience with the series of agreements which were concluded under it before they were terminated by passage of the Tariff Act of 1894, are well-known phases of the tariff history of the United States.[1]

ABANDONMENT OF CONTINENTAL CUSTOMS UNION IDEA AFTER 1890

That full and forthright discussion, at what has since come to be known as the First International Conference of American States of 1889–1890, apparently disposed definitely and negatively, for at least half a century, of the idea—which had been vaguely projected during the preceding decades—of a continental customs union among the American republics.

The conferences of American states convened since that time have repeatedly urged the general desirability of facilitating trade interchanges among the American republics, and many of them have recommended specific programs to that end concerning particular aspects of their economic relations. Moreover, on various occasions during those years, aspirations from different sources have been expressed for an ultimate league or union of all the American republics or of a large part of them; and, at times, plans to implement them have been elaborated and given considerable publicity. However, no concrete proposal for a customs union of such scope in the Western Hemisphere has appeared either on the formal agenda or in the resolutions of any Pan-American conference, since the Blaine proposal of 1889–1890.

[1] U.S. Tariff Commission, *Reciprocity and Commercial Treaties*, 1919, pp. 145*ff*.

The nearest approach to it came 52 years later, in the recommendation at the Rio de Janeiro meeting of the foreign ministers of the American republics, in January, 1942, "that the Governments of the American Republics . . . study the desirability of making an exception in the commercial agreements which they conclude with nations outside the Western Hemisphere of the treatment which they extend in commercial and customs matters to all of the other American Republics." It is significant that the United States delegation recorded its reservation to the above recommendation, "on the ground of inconsistency with the traditional policy of liberal principles of international trade maintained by the United States, and as enunciated and reaffirmed" at various recent conferences of the American republics.

FACTORS OPERATING AGAINST CUSTOMS UNIONS WITHIN LATIN AMERICA

The discussions of the first Pan-American Conference in 1890 were centered upon a customs union that included the United States. As for a customs union among the other American republics, there appears to have been no strong or widely shared desire for any such large merger of their economic interests. From time to time proposals have been put forward for uniting into a single economic area the productive forces and markets of limited groups of Latin American countries, particularly in the River Plate and Bolivian regions and in Central America.

Possibly the most fully developed plan of this character was that prepared in the late 1920's by a group of Argentine and Chilean economists, which contemplated "the elimination of customs barriers between the five southernmost countries of the continent by means of a treaty of customs union or *Zollverein.*" This "Unión Aduanera del Sud" was to be achieved by "an annual reduction of 20 percent, so that all duties would be eliminated in four years," and by the creation of a single tariff for the composite area. Improved communications among the various member states and stable exchange ratios between their respective currencies were cited as essential collateral conditions of such a union.[1]

[1] This plan was publicized in Latin America and embodied in a report submitted in advance for the Fourth Pan-American Commercial Conference of 1931, by an Argentine

As will appear later, a similar plan has recently been put forward by the government of Argentina, contemplating an ultimate regional union with the surrounding countries, to be approached through a series of bilateral customs unions. Thus far, however, no such customs union has actually eventuated among the southern republics, excepting for the experimental arrangements in Central America, to be discussed later. Aside from the political considerations involved in such a project, a number of obvious economic explanations suggest themselves.

The geography of the continent itself imposes serious obstacles to easy communication between many of the southern republics. The facilities for the transport of goods between some of the Latin American countries, whether overland or by sea, are still meager. The tradition of commercial nonintercourse between the various regions of Latin America, enforced upon them during the long centuries as Spanish or Portuguese colonies, persisted as habits long after their independence. Moreover, at least in the past, the nature of their staple surplus products, as well as of their principal import requirements, operated to encourage trade with the industrial nations of the world rather than with each other.

It is striking to note that, until the recent depression, all major questions of commercial policy were noticeably absent from the agenda of the numerous inter-American conferences held during the four decades after the 1890 conference. Discussions of trade matters at these gatherings were largely limited to secondary commercial topics, such as the centralized collection and interchange of commercial and financial information; adoption of uniform customs nomenclature; simplification of consular procedures and customs regulations, and of port dues and formalities; facilitation of frontier

---

delegate. However, the proceedings of that conference record no formal discussion of this proposal at its meetings or any recommendations on the subject in its resolutions.

For a full discussion of this plan by its sponsors, see a pamphlet entitled "Hacia la unión aduanera y monetaria de la América Latina," edited by Eliodoro Yañez and issued by *La Nación* of Santiago de Chile in 1926. (Pamphlet available at Library of the Pan American Union, Washington.) See also Ch. XII on Unión Aduanera del Sud in *Una Nueva Argentina*, last work of Alejandro E. Bunge, leading Argentine economist and industrialist (Buenos Aires, 1940).

For a documented, historical review of proposals for customs unions among the American countries, from the Latin American viewpoint, see "Proyectos de Grandes Uniones Aduaneras Americanas" by Hector M. Lapriza Carrau, of Montevideo (Uruguay), in *Revista de Economía Argentina*, May, 1943. pp. 150–174.

and transit trade; uniform plant and animal sanitary regulations; extension of commercial arbitration; protection of patents and trade-marks; regulation of commercial travelers; and the broad collateral field of the improvement of inter-American transport and communication facilities.

II. Efforts for Limited Reciprocity Arrangements Prior to 1930

For a generation after the first Pan-American Conference in 1890, little progress was made by either the United States or the southern republics toward implementing its recommendation for a series of bilateral commercial treaties between particular pairs of American countries for tariff reciprocity. (Until after the First World War, import duties were practically the only important form of official control over foreign trade used by all these countries.)

EARLY UNITED STATES EXPERIMENTS WITH LATIN AMERICAN RECIPROCAL AGREEMENTS

As far as the United States was concerned, public sentiment was apparently not ready for the freer admission of various competitive Latin American products into its market. This was reflected in the limited and rather inflexible character of the reciprocal concessions which the United States Congress authorized as the basis for trade negotiations.

The experiences with the commercial agreements concluded under the changing reciprocity provisions of the United States Tariff Acts of 1890 and 1897 were unsatisfactory; some of these agreements never came into operation because of the failure of senatorial ratification. The Tariff Act of 1909 terminated all authority for reciprocal concessions; it authorized tariff changes by executive action only for penalization of the imports of those countries which unduly discriminated against United States commerce. The Tariff Act of 1913 authorized the President to negotiate agreements with foreign nations for the mutual expansion of trade, but they were not to become operative unless ratified by the Congress. In effect, there was practically precluded for several decades after 1890 any substantial progress toward the reciprocal liberalization of the conditions of trading between the United States and the other American republics.

With the exception of the special Reciprocity Convention of 1902 with Cuba,[1] it was not until the United States Congress authorized the current Trade Agreements Act of 1934 that this basic attitude was revised and the way opened up for this country substantially to implement the program for partial reciprocity recommended by the first Pan-American Conference of 1889–1890.

MEAGER EARLY INTEREST IN INTER–LATIN AMERICAN TRADE FACILITATION

Among the Latin American countries themselves, there appears to have been very little interest, until well into the twentieth century, in a policy of reciprocal reductions of their import tariffs in order to promote substantial trade exchanges between their peoples by sea, the principal important channel of commerce then open to them. Only in the comparatively recent past has such a movement become at all active among the southern republics. In part this has followed naturally from the gradual development of agricultural diversification and of industrialization in certain of the larger countries. Its main stimulus, however, appears to have been the pressure after 1929 for finding larger outlets for their surplus products within Latin America, to offset the adverse effects upon their outside markets of the great depression and of the measures to restrict imports resorted to by the United States and various of the European countries in the 1930's.

During the early decades of their independence, and sometimes carrying over into the present century, most of the Latin American republics, especially in South America, had embodied in the treaties with their neighbors provisions allowing the duty-free admission of each other's products when entering by land routes or rivers. This practice was particularly marked during the periods following their separation out of the extensive colonial viceroyalties or early federations into distinct national states, or after important transfers of territory, as after the War of the Pacific.

The full motives prompting this early series of arrangements for duty-free land frontiers between so many pairs of adjacent countries

[1] The exchange of exclusive tariff concessions between Cuba and the United States has generally been recognized as in a class by itself, in view of its close connection with the political arrangements following the Spanish-American War and the responsibility then assumed by the United States for the economic support and general stability of the new Cuban republic.

in Latin America, the actual experiences under them, and the reasons for their ultimate curtailment and termination appear to constitute an unexplored chapter in the history of inter-Latin American commercial policy. Pending fuller investigation, it seems reasonable to regard those arrangements as reflecting primarily the unsettled and unpoliced state of the new national boundaries, and the undeveloped condition of internal transportation which characterized the earlier decades, and as tapering off with the gradual passing of those conditions.

Since the duty-free privilege was not usually extended to traffic by sea, it would appear that these were either arrangements of temporary tolerance to allow gradual adjustments to the new national boundaries or simply official recognition that the inhabitants of communities in bordering provinces needed to continue to exchange their surplus products in the nearest or traditional market towns, irrespective of the differences in the political affiliation of the areas in which they lived. Before the development of modern transport facilities in Latin America, the ports or main commercial centers of a country were often less accessible to much of the rest of the country than some towns of an adjacent country. Moreover, the sheer physical difficulty of transporting bulk products great distances overland, often over mountainous or jungle territory, in itself probably limited the range of possible overland trade between most Latin American countries, mainly to the exchanges of local commodities between adjoining frontier regions, much along the lines that had developed during colonial days.

With the extension of railways during the latter decades and, in more recent years, of automotive highways and airplane routes, even outlying regions are coming within easier reach of the commercial centers of the same country, and the old duty-free tolerance for exchanges along the land frontiers, in order to facilitate the supply of those regions from the nearer communities in the adjacent country, has apparently become less necessary. The current commercial treaties between the various southern republics now usually carry simply a provision for customs tolerance for local frontier traffic between peoples living close to the common border, a tolerance which is recognized in practically all parts of the world. Certain more extensive exceptions, as in the Tacna-Arica region of the west coast, will be touched upon later.

THE PERIOD OF THE ARGENTINE-CHILEAN "FREE CORDILLERA"

Perhaps the best known early arrangement of this character in Latin America was that which prevailed between Argentina and Chile for a period of 12 years. From 1856 to 1868, the products of these two countries were permitted to move across the land frontier into the territory of the other, free of all duties or levies, federal or provincial, and the citizens of each were accorded trading privileges in the other equal to those enjoyed by its own nations. As the end of the initial period of the treaty approached, Chile proposed that it be modified so as to include also the free entry of merchandise introduced into each other's territory by sea; and when Argentina would not agree to the change, Chile declared the arrangement as expiring at the end of its term. This has come to be known historically as the period of the Free Cordillera.

There have been subsequent attempts to restore what has been described in retrospect as a highly beneficial arrangement, but no adequate account has been found in either Argentine or Chilean sources of their peoples' benefits derived from this experiment with a duty-free frontier between these two countries. Nor do we know the precise reasons for its discontinuance.

Such statistical records as are available regarding the trade between Argentina and Chile during this period indicate that the sales of the domestic products of each in the other's territory were quite small. The great bulk of the movements westward across the Cordillera appears to have consisted, at that time, of livestock from the piedmont provinces of northwestern Argentina, which were shipped overseas through Chilean ports—then much nearer and more accessible and safer than the eastern route through Buenos Aires—and, in the other direction, of miscellaneous goods from outside countries brought in through the Pacific ports for consumption in northwestern Argentina. Under the conditions then prevailing—the very limited range of products which either country had to offer to the other and the absence of railways since built, which run from both coasts and across the Andes,—it would appear that only slight benefit could have been derived from the duty-free privilege for overland trade between Argentina and Chile during the operation of the early Free Cordillera arrangement.

The idea of a Free Cordillera has persisted, however, although with various meanings, somewhat as the idea of Canadian-American reciprocity has in North America. As recently as August, 1943, the governments of Argentina and of Chile agreed to study the possibility of a revival of the old arrangement that would carry it much further, approaching the character of a full customs union and including broad economic coordination in other respects. This will be touched upon later.

CENTRAL AMERICAN EXPERIMENTS IN TARIFF RECIPROCITY

Among the countries of Central America, reciprocal free trade, or very nearly that, was agreed to several times during the first century of Spanish American independence. This was usually done as part of a general political federation of all or most of the Central American states. All such experiments have been of short duration, however, their dissolutions being soon prompted by the withdrawal on political grounds of one or more of the participating governments.

During more recent years, the principal efforts in this direction have been more modest in scope, consisting of arrangements between particular pairs of Central American countries for the waiver or reduction of their import duties on most of each other's national products. These limited bilateral trade facilities also appear to have been short-lived, however, and only one is understood to be in operation now, that inaugurated in 1918 between El Salvador and Honduras.[1] Several of the republics of Central America grant preferential free entry or reduced duties on the admission of certain natural products originating elsewhere in Central America, but without any contractual commitment.

There is record of certain other types of initiative prior to 1930 for closer trade relations between neighboring American countries, such as that made by Mexico during the middle twenties to develop markets for its manufactured articles in the countries of Central America. On the whole, however, the rarity of successful efforts on the part of the Latin American countries, until quite recently, to facilitate through trade agreements the exchange even of selected noncompetitive products, of which one of the southern republics was a surplus producer and the other an importer, is striking. This applies both to agreements embodying reductions in duties on each other's distinctive

[1] A similar wartime agreement between Guatemala and El Salvador, entered into in 1941, was curtailed in scope within a year and terminated by El Salvador at the close of its initial term in November, 1943, on the ground of unequal trade advantages and losses in revenue.

products which would be generalized also to third countries with treaty claims and to those which would be largely exclusive in character from the very nature of the products.

OVERSEAS OBLIGATIONS AS FACTOR IN RARITY OF LATIN AMERICAN CONCESSIONAL AGREEMENTS

The fact that most of the countries of Latin America were under obligation, by the most-favored-nation provisions in their commercial agreements with the United States and European countries, to extend to them the benefits of any duty reductions may have operated as a deterrent to active negotiation with each other of arrangements for the exchange of trade concessions. However, the infrequency, prior to the recent depression, of inter–Latin American trade agreements carrying concessions which might have to be generalized, but from which the neighboring country would probably be the principal beneficiary, suggests that the fear lest overseas countries insist upon also sharing somewhat in their benefits was not the prime deterrent.

In addition to the physical difficulties to easy commercial exchanges between the southern republics and the similarity of many of their major export products, previously mentioned, part of the explanation is probably to be found in the unfortunate fact that the relations between some countries of Latin America have in the past often been marked by boundary disputes and a general feeling of suspicion and, at times, by open hostilities. This naturally caused a reluctance either to improve the means of communication with each other or actively to foster increased trade between their peoples.[1]

Several Latin American countries, notably Chile, endeavored through these decades to maintain their right to grant special preferences, either to neighboring countries or to all Latin American coun-

[1] As late as 1937 the proportion of the aggregate exports of all the 20 Latin American countries that were sold for consumption within Latin America averaged about 6 per cent. During 1942, when war conditions forced them to explore every possibility of finding markets and sources of supply among themselves, the proportion of the total Latin American export products that were sold within that area averaged around 15 per cent, with only Argentina, Brazil, Ecuador, Paraguay, and Peru exceeding that average.

For analysis of the effect on inter–South American trade of the similar quickening of their trade relationships under the exceptional conditions of the First World War, see series of articles on "El Comercio entre las Repúblicas Sudamericanas" in *Revista del Banco de la República*, Bogotá (Colombia), July to September, 1941.

For a brief survey of the efforts to improve inter–Latin American trade and transport during the Second World War, see my article in *Foreign Commerce Weekly*, May 1, 1943, pp. 17*ff*.

tries. Although maintained as a matter of traditional principle, this position has not been exercised and has been only intermittently urged until recent years. Since these countries have depended so heavily upon the markets of the United States and of western Europe for the disposal of their staple agricultural and mineral surpluses, they may have been deterred from granting exclusive preferences to neighboring countries by the fear of reprisals in the form of discriminations against their standard staples in the markets of these industrialized countries.

III. Types of Closer Inter-American Trade Relations Recently Tried or Proposed

The period since the onset of the great depression in 1929 has been marked in Latin America by the advocacy of closer trade relations with each other and of various means to bring that about, including proposals for some form of preferential treatment. This movement has been developing despite repeated affirmations at various inter-American conferences during the past decade of the desirability of the general adoption of more liberal, nondiscriminatory trade policies. In fact, at the Seventh Pan-American Conference, held at Montevideo in 1933, where for the first time in many decades the broader problems of commercial policy reappeared on the agenda, the resulting resolutions carried both an endorsement of the most-favored-nation policy promoted by Secretary of State Hull in the name of the United States and a recommendation for the study of a contractual formula that would permit the granting of exclusive advantages by contiguous or neighboring countries.

UNITED STATES TYPE: BARRIER-REDUCING AGREEMENTS ON A NONDISCRIMINATORY BASIS

As one of its counterdepression measures, the United States launched, within 6 months of the Montevideo conference, what has since developed into the most extensive trade-agreements program of any country. In addition to the reciprocal reduction of trade barriers, however, one of the main objectives of this whole series of trade agreements concluded by the United States during the past decade has been to spread the general application of the most-favored-nation principle. Apart from the special case of Cuba, the United States has not granted preferential treatment in the course of these agreements, nor has it asked for it, with regard to any commodity or any form of trade control.

The program has not overlooked the desirability of ensuring that the bulk of the advantage from the concessions exchanged in this type of trade agreement should accrue to producers in the contracting countries nor the desirability of leaving sufficient inducement for other countries—even though already on a most-favored-nation status—to enter into similar negotiations, in which they would offer specific advantages in order to secure reciprocal advantages on behalf of their distinctive products. To that end the United States reciprocity program has, as a rule, confined reductions of duty to those products or types of particular products of which each country dealt with was the principal supplier or in which it expected to be the principal beneficiary of the concession, even though the prospective advantage was to be shared in some measure also by producers in other countries.

About half of the 28 agreements thus far worked out have been with governments of Latin America. Fifteen of the 20 republics have already concluded such agreements with the United States, and two additional agreements are now (early 1944) in process of negotiation. With the one exception cited, they all follow the same pattern: each country reduces and stabilizes its conditions of admission on selected products of special interest to the other, and on a general nondiscriminatory basis. Still, in these negotiations and outside of them, the desire of certain of the southern republics to leave the way open for special preferential arrangements with other countries of Latin America has been expressed with increasing frequency during the last few years. Various methods of giving concrete expression to the preferential idea have been experimented with or proposed.

How to harmonize this persistent if vague desire with the declared broader program of the United Nations, to work back toward an expanding and more competitive system of world trade, and on a basis of equality of access to markets and materials—to which most American governments have declared warm adherence in principle—constitutes one of the central problems for a consistent program of commercial relations on the American continent after the war.

A full analysis of the many trade agreements negotiated between the various Latin American countries during recent years is now in process, in order to make available a concrete and comprehensive picture of the various preferential provisions or tendencies that are current. While that study has not been completed, it has been advanced far enough to allow at this time a preliminary characterization of the principal types of such preferential arrangements and proposals on the part of the southern republics. They will now be briefly reviewed, in terms of significant illustrations of each. Two rather exceptional types of arrangements will first be dealt with, before considering those of more general scope and applicability.

EXCLUSIVE PREFERENCES FOR LANDLOCKED COUNTRIES

The principal result of the regional conference of the five River Plate countries, held at Montevideo early in 1941, was the agreement upon measures of economic relief for Paraguay and Bolivia, in recognition of their landlocked position and of their economic difficulties after the destructive Chaco War. Argentina, Brazil, and Uruguay signed a convention under which they agreed to refrain from invoking the most-favored-nation clause with respect to any exemptions or facilities which may be accorded exclusively to Paraguay and Bolivia. A number of special facilities for these two countries have already been initiated under this convention, partly by tariff concessions, but mainly in the form of transit and free-zone privileges for their products by their coastal neighbors and by the extension of railroads and highways into the interior on the part of both Argentina and Brazil.

This program of preferences for these two landlocked South American countries appears to have met with no expressed objection from outside countries. The circumstances in their case are unique, however, and it is thus hardly capable of extension or wide application elsewhere.

CUSTOMS FREEDOM BETWEEN BORDERING FRONTIER REGIONS

A trade preference of a special type has come into being since the settlement of the Tacna-Arica boundary dispute between Peru and Chile in 1929. Partly because of the shift of territory involved in that settlement, but also because of the geographic and transport difficulties of supplying these bordering provinces from the main portion of the countries to which they are now attached, it has come to be recognized that special trade facilities for the exchange of goods between the Peruvian department of Tacna and the northern ports of Chile have exceptional justification.

A situation somewhat similar to that of Tacna-Arica is presented by the outlying frontier provinces of Colombia and Ecuador, although the agreement concluded in 1942 for an exchange between them of special tariff exemptions on important lists of products is reported as contemplated to extend to the entire territories of the two countries. That agreement has not yet been ratified.

CONTINENTAL TRADE PREFERENCES

It will be recalled that, at the Rio de Janeiro meeting of foreign ministers in January, 1942, it was recommended that a study be made of the desirability of the American republics making trade concessions among themselves which might be denied to countries outside the Western Hemisphere. This would constitute a new type of preferential arrangement of large proportions and potentialities. It will also be recalled, however, that the United States delegation at Rio de Janeiro definitely recorded its reservation to the idea on the ground of inconsistency with its traditional trade policy.

CUSTOMS UNIONS, REGIONAL OR BILATERAL

In addition to the older experiments in tariff reciprocity among the Central American republics, the idea of working toward customs unions of other pairs or groups has been advanced from several directions in Latin America in recent years, although they do not appear thus far to have gone beyond the proposal and preliminary study stage.

At the third meeting of the Inter-American Union of the Caribbean, held at Port-au-Prince in 1941, a recommendation was adopted that the countries concerned make the necessary studies of their tariffs and customs regulations to determine the possibility of a customs union of the Caribbean. There has been no further meeting of that group, at which the results of such a study were to be presented.

At the Regional River Plate Conference of 1941, Argentina put forward a customs-union proposal; but when it appeared that what was sought was approval for the formation of such a union between single countries, and the exclusion of others from its benefits, opposition soon developed. It is reported to have been urged that customs unions should be thought of in terms of groups of countries only, lest one large power thus obtain undue influence over the resources of smaller neighboring ones. The outcome was a recommendation that the participating countries study the possibility of concluding a regional customs union and the establishment of a central office at Montevideo to examine the project more fully.

The outstanding official proposal for a customs union within recent years has been that advanced by Argentina to Chile, mentioned above. Thus far, this has been only an agreement, signed in August, 1943, for the formation of a mixed commission to study the problems involved for each in a customs union and the complementary measures to facilitate "the merging of both economies." The commission is to report within a year. The proposed union would be open to the adherence of any neighboring country and is visualized as "a first step toward a continental economic organization, including the reduction or abolition of customs barriers." Three months later, Argentina concluded a similar exploratory agreement with Paraguay.

In November, 1943, the ministers of foreign affairs of Chile and Peru issued a joint declaration expressing their intention to designate national commissions to examine the possibility of establishing gradually, between the two countries, a regime of free commercial interchange. As soon as preliminary conclusions regarding this matter have been reached, these national commissions are to unite as a mixed Peruvian-Chilean commission. These two contiguous countries have already gone far, in recent treaties, in the exchange of duty reductions on each other's chief export products.

REGIONAL TRADE PREFERENCES

Related to the proposals for customs unions are the more limited projects, for groups of neighboring Latin American countries to grant each other special trade advantages which are not to be extended to outsiders, on limited lists of specific products, with each country still maintaining its own distinct tariff and trade controls. Among the countries of the River Plate, this concept is frequently advanced when a regional customs union in that part of South America is discussed, on the assumption that regional preferences necessarily constitute an approach to customs unions.

A regional project of similar scope has recently been foreshadowed in connection with the conclusion of a new commercial treaty between Brazil and Paraguay in May, 1943, in which Paraguay agreed not to claim the benefits of any exclusive concessions which Brazil may grant to countries in the Amazon basin. In return, Brazil waived its most-favored-nation claim to exclusive concessions by Paraguay to countries in the River Plate basin. Adequate information regarding the implications of this provision is not yet available.

Of a simpler character was the arrangement which came into operation in 1942 between Haiti and the Dominican Republic, the joint occupants of the island of Hispaniola, whereby certain products of each may move under reduced duties into the territory of the other. A similar treaty providing for practically full tariff reciprocity between these two countries had been concluded in 1874 and planned to run for a period of 25 years. The facts of its actual operation are not readily ascertainable. The recent preferential agreement was expanded in its terms shortly after it came into effect, but in September, 1943, the Haitian government gave notice of its desire that it should become inoperative in March, 1944, at the termination of its initial 2-year period.

For completeness, mention should be made under this category of the possibility of additional regional preferences in Central America. The earlier close association and temporary federations of these countries have led to the settled acceptance of the idea that exclusive preferences between these countries constitute a legitimate exception to the most-favored-nation principle.

BILATERAL PREFERENCES BETWEEN CONTIGUOUS OR NEIGHBORING COUNTRIES

The most common trade arrangement among Latin American countries is that providing for limited tariff or other trade concessions between pairs of contiguous or neighboring countries. This is the type which presents probably the most difficult questions regarding the consistency of exclusive preferences with the general most-favored-nation principle.

The past decade, particularly since the outbreak of the Second World War, has been marked by curtailed access of these countries to their usual foreign markets and sources of supply and by unprecedented activity in the way of negotiations for trade agreements between pairs of Latin American countries—all in an effort to stimulate alternative sources and outlets for goods. With increasing frequency, in the last few years, these have embodied provisions for an exchange of reductions in duties or other concessions on lists of selected export products of each other. Thus far these concessions have usually been generalized and extended also to similar products from third countries to which the contracting countries were obligated to extend most-favored-nation treatment.

The principal current exceptions—apart from the old special preferences among the countries of Central America, and those recently operative for a short period between Haiti and the Dominican Republic—are contained in certain provisions of the commercial treaties between Argentina and Chile and between Brazil and Argentina. Most of these, however, are of such a character as to be hardly susceptible of generalization to third countries. Illustrative are the Chilean promise to allow so many Argentine cattle to be admitted quarterly across the land frontier without duty; or the Argentine agreement not to construct a plant for the manufacture of synthetic nitrates for a period of years and to restrict the importation of synthetic products analogous to the natural Chilean nitrate; or the Argentine-Brazilian understandings with regard to the mixing of yerba maté. This type of concession is so local in character as to be almost inevitably exclusive in its application; and while it sometimes affects the trade of outside countries indirectly, the disadvantage to them is probably slight.

The developments in connection with the reciprocal trade treaty of 1932 between Argentina and Chile well illustrate the problems of those Latin American governments which want to keep their relations with overseas countries on the basis of the most-favored-nation principle, in order to ensure that their export products would be under no discriminatory handicap in those markets, and which, at the same time, would like to facilitate especially close trade relations with their neighbors. A number of the products on which Argentina originally granted duty concessions to Chile, in that treaty, were of a kind which the United States and various European countries had customarily also sold in the Argentine market. Under their long-standing most-favored-nation treaties, several interested European countries demanded, and obtained, the extension to their products of the reduced duties granted to Chile.[1]

In some Chilean circles, this generalization of the reduced Argentine duties was regarded as largely nullifying the benefit of the concessions, although the statistical record of the subsequent Argentine

[1] The United States also requested the benefit of the reduced rates, but this was denied by Argentina on the grounds that the old Argentine-American treaty had been historically constructed as conditional in character.

imports of certain products of special concern showed sizable increases in receipts from Chile during the period following the conclusion of the agreement. This particular situation was resolved by a revision of the lists of commodities subject to concessions, so as to exclude those in which third countries had a large or predominant interest. However, the experience probably strengthened the opinion often heard expressed by some Latin Americans—possibly without sufficient analysis of its inherent soundness—that only by exclusive preferences can a country materially increase its trade with particular other countries.

As earlier noted, the Seventh Pan-American Conference, held at Montevideo in 1933, recommended the study of a contractual formula which would allow the granting of exclusive advantages by contiguous or neighboring countries. In September, 1941, the Inter-American Financial and Economic Advisory Committee, sitting at Washington and consisting of high representatives of each of the American republics, recommended the following formula, in pursuance to the Montevideo resolution:

> That any such tariff preferences, in order to be an instrument for sound promotion of trade, should be made effective through trade agreements embodying tariff reductions or exemptions;
>
> That the parties to such agreements should reserve the right to reduce or eliminate the customs duties on like imports from other countries;
>
> And that any such regional tariff preferences should not be permitted to stand in the way of any broad program of economic reconstruction, involving the reduction of tariffs and the scaling down or elimination of tariff and other trade preferences, with a view to the fullest possible development of international trade on a multilateral unconditional most-favored-nation basis.

It is of interest that the preceding formula was presented jointly by the representatives of Argentina and Brazil, and that the only representative definitely opposing it was that of Chile, on the ground that the right to extend to third countries the benefits granted to border countries contravened "an old tradition and definite position of the Government of Chile in this matter." It is also important to note that the statement of support presented on behalf of the United States was limited to tariff preferences to *contiguous* countries.

In view of the appreciable use that has already been made of this formula, attention should be called to the fact that, in presenting it, the Argentine representative related the desirability of its adoption to "the grave difficulties which have been created for our countries out of the European War" and recommended this as a means of affording reciprocal aid and solidarity, "given the circumstances in which our countries are placed at the present time."[1] Although the formula itself does not carry any specific statement on this point, the fact that it was definitely introduced as a measure of wartime aid gives it only transitory standing and leaves it open to reconsideration after the wartime conditions have passed. Its transitory nature was further indicated in the statement of support by the United States, which recognized its desirability, "in the present critical state of world affairs."

In the actual use of this reservation for special preferences which the Latin American Republics might give to bordering countries, an interesting reservation has begun to appear, which may become wider spread. Thus, the Brazil-Chile Treaty of Commerce and Navigation, concluded on Mar. 1, 1943, provides that the recognition of the right of each to grant exclusive advantages to contiguous countries, as an allowable exception to the general most-favored-nation obligation, is not to apply to certain specified products listed by Brazil and by Chile. The treaty provides that these commodities, which appear to comprise most of the important export products of each country, shall continue to enjoy in the market of the other treatment equal to that of the most-favored-nation, in an unconditional and unlimited form.

JOINT DUTY-FREE MARKETS FOR NEW PRODUCTS OF ADJOINING COUNTRIES

A new type of arrangement for special trade relations between adjacent American countries was given exceptional prominence in the Latin American press at the time of signature of the Argentine-Brazil Trade Agreement of November, 1941. Broadly, the agreement was designed to provide a wider market area for the productive forces of the individual countries than their own populations afforded, starting with the nascent industries. Specifically, these two governments agreed to foster the establishment in their countries of industrial and agrarian activities which did not yet exist in either and undertook not

[1] *Actas de las Sesiones del Comité Consultivo Económico Financiero Interamericano* (Unión Panamericana, Washington, D.C.), Vol. XII, p. 1606.

to impose any duties or other restrictions in their territories upon the products of these new industries for a period of 10 years. Similar liberal treatment was to be given to commodities now produced in only one of the two countries or of no great economic importance in the other. There was also envisaged the possible subsequent expansion of this principle to include competitive products where existing duties could be gradually reduced without injury to the respective national economies. So far as known the agreement is not yet in operation.

This idea, that the diversification and industrialization which many of the countries of Latin America are anxious to promote cannot be carried very far on the basis of the limited markets for the new products in their own territories, has been prominent in recent statements of the leaders of a number of the southern republics. During the discussions of the Inter-American Financial and Economic Advisory Committee on the formula for exclusive preferences between contiguous (and neighboring) countries, which also took place in the fall of 1941, the Argentine representative stressed the same thought, that individual American markets have a small absorptive capacity, whereas several American markets together have a larger capacity for particular products, and that the fuller development of these markets was the principal object of the proposal which the Brazilian and Argentine delegates had put forward. They did not mean, he said, that they wanted to have such an agreement solely between Argentina and Brazil.

CONCESSIONS IN COLLECTIVE AGREEMENTS ON AN OPEN-END BASIS

A quite different line of approach to the attainment of the essential objectives sought by most of the programs sketched above has recently come into the discussions of international trade policy. It contemplates a multilateral arrangement for the simultaneous reciprocal reduction of trade barriers on the part of as many countries as are ready to undertake such an obligation. The principal earlier attempt of this character—initiated by the governments of Belgium and the Netherlands at Ouchy in 1932—proposing the progressive lowering of tariffs and other trade barriers between their countries and such others as would join the group was obstructed by the rigid insistence upon their most-favored-nation rights by certain countries which were not ready themselves to participate in the program. It is not widely known, however, that the Seventh International Conference of

American States, held at Montevideo toward the close of 1933, launched a formula for overcoming that difficulty which has not yet been tried out.

With a view to "encouraging the developments of economic relations among the peoples of the world by means of multilateral conventions," the Montevideo Conference recommended the general adoption of a new attitude on this subject. It put forward a document under which all countries were to be allowed to claim the benefits derived by the parties to collective trade from agreements to reduce barriers as soon as they were ready to assume the obligations of such trade.

The characteristics of the multilateral economic conventions contemplated in this agreement are described as follows:

1. Are of general applicability.
2. Include a trade area of substantial size.
3. Have as their objective the liberalization and promotion of international trade or other international economic intercourse.
4. Are open to adoption [Spanish and Portuguese versions read "participation"] by all countries.

In accordance with the Conference Resolution of Dec. 24, 1933, this Montevideo agreement was deposited with the Pan American Union at Washington, and opened to the signature of all States on July 15, 1934. Within about a year, the agreement had been signed *ad referendum* by the United States, Colombia, Cuba, Guatemala, Nicaragua, and Panama, and by the Belgian-Luxemburg Union and Greece. It was subsequently ratified by the United States, Cuba, and Greece.

There have thus far been no further developments in this matter, either in the way of additional adhering governments, or of the formation of any group of countries ready for the simultaneous reduction of their respective trade barriers on each other's trade along the lines indicated above. However, the formula developed by the Inter-American Financial and Economic Advisory Committee in September, 1941, regarding the conditions for allowable regional tariff preferences, cited above, apparently provided for this type of collective action when it specified that such preferences "should not be permitted to stand in the way of any broad program of economic reconstruction . . . with a view to the fullest possible development of international trade. . . ."

If such a collective trade-liberalizing program should be proposed as one of the possible instruments of international collaboration toward the postwar economic reconstruction of the world, parallel to the current movement for the general stabilization of currencies, the Montevideo agreement of 1933 might well come into prominence again, as a foundation step.

The Inter-American Trade-policy Problem in a World Framework

The future orientation of the commercial policies of all the American republics, in their relations with each other as well as with the countries overseas, will be greatly influenced by the character of the general system of world trading and international financial relations which may prevail after the war. Only the broad objectives of the prospective international trading system were sketched in the Atlantic Charter of August, 1941. The series of lend-lease (mutual-aid) agreements since concluded between the United States and most of the United Nations, including 18 of the 20 Latin American republics, have given them some general definition in the identical terms of Article VII. Consultations looking to the development of specific common policies and concrete joint arrangements, to implement the objectives envisaged in the foregoing general documents, are only just being initiated among the leading Allied governments.

The precise formulation of attitude toward customs unions, regional preferences, and other forms of commercial policy among the American republics will therefore necessarily have to await further developments in the filling in of the larger postwar framework for world economic relations. In the light of the perspective of past attempts and experiences among them, however, and the analysis of current plans and proposals presented in this study, it should be possible even at this stage to begin to formulate consistent criteria and programs in the inter-American field. There is good reason to believe that it should be possible to advance the essential objective sought, *viz.*, the strengthening of the economies of all the American republics by arrangements for fuller and freer trade relations among them—without setting up precedents for action by other countries that might rebound to their own disadvantage, and without materially contravening the basic principles upon which the general postwar world trading system seems likely to be built.

Part III

SPECIAL COUNTRY STUDIES

Chapter IX

Argentina

by MIRON BURGIN

I

IN an address delivered at the Instituto Popular de Conferencias in Buenos Aires in August, 1943, Torquato di Tella, a prominent Argentine industrialist, referred to the Argentine industry as one that has "begun wearing long trousers." This characterization was not an expression of wishful thinking by an overzealous nationalist, nor was it prompted by considerations of a political order. It was rather a sober recognition of the fact that the economic development of Argentina has entered a new phase; it expressed satisfaction with the progress of Argentine industry in the past three decades; and it voiced the desires and aspirations of a large and growing sector of Argentine society. Argentine industry has come of age, and that means that this sector of the national economy demands and must receive at least as much attention and recognition as has until now been accorded only to agriculture and cattle breeding.

In most published discussions about Argentina the emphasis is on the agricultural and pastoral industries. Invariably the reader's attention is directed almost exclusively to the agricultural prowess of Argentina. He is told that Argentina is one of the world's largest producers of wheat, maize, and flaxseed, that it is the world's largest exporter of meat, and that it is an important producer of wool. And if in the mind of the reader there is still any doubt left as to the nature of the Argentine economy it is quickly disposed of by reference to Argentina's exports. Indeed, a very large proportion of Argentine exports is made up of agricultural and pastoral products.

The importance of agriculture and cattle grazing in Argentina cannot, of course, be denied. But to stop our analysis at this point would be to indulge in oversimplification that is both unwarranted and misleading. In the past twenty or thirty years the economic structure of Argentina has undergone considerable changes, and agriculture is no longer the sole or even the most important source of national income.

This shift in the economic pattern of Argentina manifests itself in a variety of ways. To begin with, the proportion of rural population in Argentina has declined markedly since 1914. The second national census of that year revealed that 58 per cent of the country's total population lived in cities and towns of 1,000 or more inhabitants. According to Alejandro Bunge's calculations for 1938, urban population as defined by the 1914 census represented 74 per cent of the total. Even more significant are Bunge's estimates of occupational distribution. In the period 1914–1940 the number of persons employed in agriculture rose by about 19 per cent, from 880,000 to 1,050,000. The number of persons who depend upon industry for their livelihood rose during the same period from 1,246,000 to 2,770,000, or by about 122 per cent. It is true that the industrial group as defined by Bunge includes artisans and persons employed in the handicraft industry. The industrial census of 1935 interprets more narrowly the term *industrial workers* and does not, as a rule, cover handicraft establishments. But even on this definition of the term the growth of industrial population in Argentina is impressive. The 1914 census listed 383,000 persons employed in industry. In 1935 the number of persons (wage earners, salaried personnel, and owners) depending upon industry was 544,000, representing an increase of 42 per cent in the intervening 21 years.

Recent data on occupational distribution reveal even more strikingly the process of industrialization of the Argentine economy. The agricultural census of 1937 registered about 300,000 agricultural laborers in addition to some 440,000 owners and operators of agricultural establishments, or a total of about 740,000 persons. Industrial statistics for the same year listed 698,000 persons in industrial employment. In 1939 the number of persons employed in industry was 747,000.

Fully as significant as the shift in the occupational distribution of Argentina's population is the change in the relative importance of agriculture and industry as contributors to the national income. In 1935 the net value of agricultural and pastoral production was estimated at 2,150 million pesos. The industry's contribution to the national income in the same year was valued at 1,300 million pesos. In 1942 the total net value of production was calculated at 5,350 million pesos almost evenly divided between agriculture and cattle breeding (2,700 million pesos) and industry (2,650 million pesos) (see Table 1).

It will be observed that, while the net value of agricultural and pastoral production in the 6 years between 1935 and 1942 increased by about 26 per cent, the value of industrial production during the same period more than doubled. Moreover, the value of agricultural

TABLE 1.—VALUE OF NATIONAL PRODUCTION[1]
(In millions of pesos)

Year	Gross value				Net value	
	Agriculture and pastoral			Industry	Agriculture and pastoral	Industry
	Agriculture	Pastoral	Total			
1935	1,850	1,050	2,900	3,330	2,150	1,300
1937	2,300	1,350	3,650	4,750	2,850	1,550
1939	1,800	1,300	3,100	4,830	2,400	1,750
1940	1,550	1,350	2,900	5,050	2,200	1,850
1942	1,750	1,750	3,500	7,000	2,700	2,650

[1] SOURCE: Banco Central de la República Argentina, *Memoria anual. Octavo ejercicio.* 1942 (Buenos Aires, 1943).

and pastoral production in 1942 was below the level attained in 1937, but considerably above 1940. The value of industrial production, on the other hand, has risen without interruption throughout the period.

No doubt a part of the increase in the value of industrial production must be attributed to rising prices. This factor has been especially pronounced since 1940. In terms of physical volume, expansion of industry was less spectacular, though none the less considerable. If 1935 is taken as a base (1935 = 100), the value of industrial production in 1942 was 210, and the volume for that year was 155.

While the origin of modern industry in Argentina dates back to the nineteenth century, its expansion has been especially rapid during the last 20 to 25 years. More than two-thirds the industrial establishments registered in 1939 were founded after 1920. These establishments employed 47 per cent of the industrial labor and produced 41 per cent of the total value of industrial output. Close to 23 per cent of the number of industrial enterprises operating in 1939 were established in the 5 years from 1931 to 1935. These enterprises employed 16 per cent of the industrial wage earners and produced 12 per cent of the total value of the industrial output.

The reasons for this accelerated process of industrial expansion are not difficult to discern. The First World War (1914–1918) with its attendant shortages of imported manufactures, the growing domestic market, the accumulation of domestic capital in search of profitable opportunities for investment, foreign funds and enterprise, the depression of the early thirties, and the resultant curtailment of imports—each contributed its share to the creation of an economic environment favorable to the growth of industry. The process of industrialization was not so much the result of a conscious and deliberate government policy as it was a consequence of a series of fortuitous circumstances over which the government had little or no control, but which at times forced the government to reexamine its commercial and economic policies.

Whatever the causes of its growth, industry has become a vital factor in the economic development of Argentina. It has helped to diversify and to stabilize the national economy to an extent never attained before, and it has at the same time opened new economic frontiers to Argentine capital and enterprise. Industrialization has reshaped the economic structure of the country; more than any other factor it has been responsible for the emergence of what Bunge so aptly calls the New Argentina, an Argentina in which the traditional concepts of economic and social relationships are no longer valid.

II

The impact of the war upon the economy of Argentina followed a familiar pattern. As in 1914, Argentina almost at once found itself cut off from important European markets and sources of supplies. In the First World War the initial shock occasioned by the loss of export markets was of short duration. The demand for foodstuffs in Allied countries more than compensated for the loss of markets that were subject to blockade; and submarine warfare, severe though it was at times, did not seriously interfere with Argentina's foreign trade. The flow of manufactures to Argentina was, of course, considerably reduced, but the shortages were at no time critical. In all these respects the effects of the present war have gone far beyond the worst conditions of three decades ago. To begin with, the area occupied by Germany, and therefore subject to blockade, extends to nearly all Europe, including Italy. All this area has been lost to Argentina as a market for foodstuffs and a source of supply of manufactured goods. Second, the relative scarcity of shipping space has been much more severe in the present conflict than 30 years ago. Great Britain, the only remaining market of any importance for Argentine exports, reduced purchases from Argentina to a minimum. Third, the flow of goods, both raw materials and manufactures, to Argentina suffered rather severe changes, partly because of diversion to war uses in countries which would otherwise have been the sources of supply, and partly also because of scarcity of available cargo space. And finally, preclusive purchases by the United Nations of strategic commodities in neutral and United Nations areas limited rather rigidly the flow of raw materials to Argentina.

There were a number of factors, however, which mitigated the full weight of these restrictions and which permitted the Argentine economy to adjust itself to war conditions with comparative ease. The loss of European markets did not occur all at once and without warning. It was not until the middle of 1940 that German domination in western Europe was completed. Until that time Italy remained neutral and was not, therefore, subject to blockade. Even after the fall of France, trade with Germany and German-dominated areas continued, although on a reduced scale. The war was still confined to Europe, and it was only toward the end of 1941 that it assumed global proportions. Again, the Argentina of 1939 was much better equipped to meet the crisis arising out of the disruption of its trade relations with Europe. The economy was more diversified than it had been before the First World War. It had an industrial plant that already supplied a considerable proportion of the country's manufactured goods and that was capable of further expansion. According to estimates of Bunge nearly 38 per cent of Argentina's annual consumption in 1914–1918 was imported from abroad. In 1936–1938 the proportion of imports in the country's annual consumption was about 26 per cent. At the same time Argentina turned to the Western Hemisphere as a market for its exportable surpluses and as a source of supplies of raw materials and manufactures.

The volume of Argentine exports fell rather sharply in 1940. The decline continued in the following 2 years. In 1942, exports amounted to some 5 million tons as compared with about 13 million in 1939.

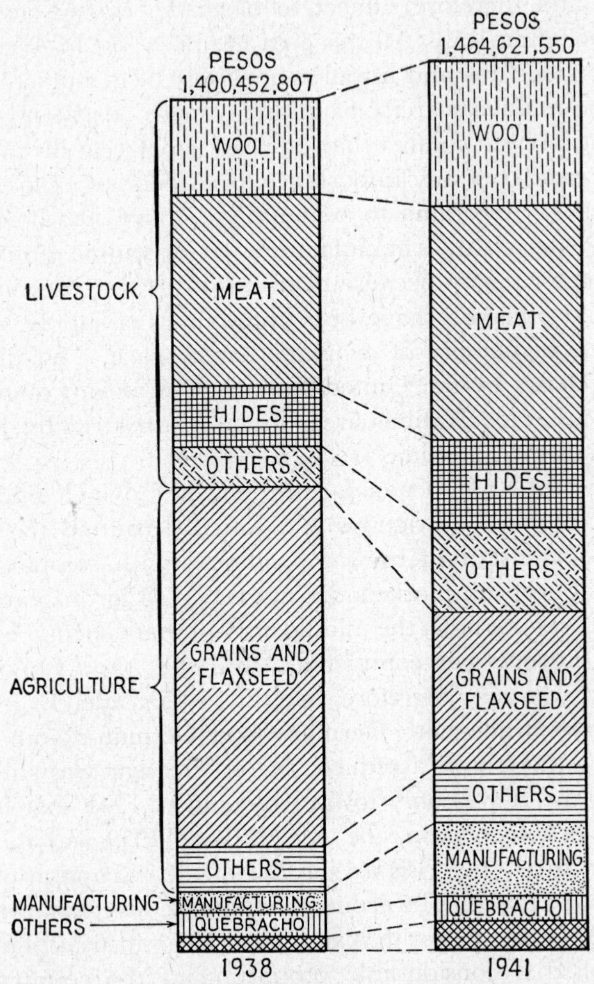

CHART 6.—Argentina. Exports by commodities 1938, 1941. (*Source: Coordinator of Inter-American Affairs.*)

The decline in the volume of overseas sales was almost entirely accounted for by a reduction in exports of agricultural commodities, especially corn and linseed. In 1935–1939 Argentina exported annually over 6 million tons of corn and 1.5 million tons of linseed. In 1942, exports of these cereals amounted respectively to 219,000 tons and 314,000 tons. The decline in wheat exports although substantial was more orderly, from an average of 3.2 million tons in 1935–1939 to 2.2 million tons in 1942.

The sharp decline in the volume of exports was not reflected in the value of Argentina's sales abroad. In fact the value of its exports in 1942 was about 14 per cent above the value for 1939. The rise in export prices apparently more than offset the decline in the volume of exports.

An examination of Chart 6 reveals the changes in the composition (value) of exports. Grains and flaxseed declined precipitously, but exports of wool, meat and manufacturing rose.

The volume of imports followed the downward trend that was observed in Argentina's export trade. From a volume of about 10 million tons in 1937, imports declined to 6.5 million tons in 1941 and 4.5 million tons in 1942. The decline in value was not nearly so drastic. In 1937 the total value of imports amounted to 1,557 million pesos. The value of imports in 1941 and 1942 amounted to 1,278 million pesos and 1,274 million pesos, respectively.

TABLE 2.—VOLUME AND VALUE OF ARGENTINA'S FOREIGN TRADE

Year	Value, millions of pesos		Volume, thousands of tons	
	Export	Import	Export	Import
1937	2,310	1,557	18,235	10,335
1938	1,400	1,460	9,119	9,905
1939	1,573	1,338	12,875	9,756
1940	1,428	1,499	9,467	8,096
1941	1,465	1,278	6,241	6,473
1942	1,789	1,274	5,303	4,516

It goes without saying that changes in Argentina's foreign trade brought about by the war confronted the country with a series of economic problems of undisputed gravity. The most urgent and immediate problem was of course that of providing a market for the rapidly accumulating surplus of agricultural commodities. The terms of the problem were simple enough. Either these surpluses were to be destroyed at the expense of the producers, or the government was to step in and assume responsibility. And since destruction of the crops at the expense of producers was tantamount to wholesale deterioration of a vital sector of the national economy, the government had no alternative but to launch an extensive program of purchases of agricultural commodities.

Late in 1940 the Argentine government announced that it would purchase wheat, corn, and linseed through the Junta nacional de granos (National Grain Board) at fixed prices. By January of 1942, the board acquired nearly 5.5 million tons of cereals. No data are available on the purchasing operations of the board after Jan. 9, 1942. It has been estimated, however, that by the end of 1942 the government spent over 1 billion pesos on purchases of cereal crops..

There can be no doubt that the grain purchase program forestalled what might have easily developed into a major economic catastrophe. It saved some 360,000 farmers from almost certain ruin. For although the prices paid by the National Grain Board (55 cents per bushel of wheat and 33 cents for corn) were too low to ensure prosperity in the grain-growing areas, they were sufficiently high to maintain agriculture on an even keel and to place a minimum amount of purchasing power in the hands of a sizable part of the population.

The second problem which confronted Argentina in the early months of the war was more general in scope. It centered around the progressive curtailment of the flow of raw materials and of manufactured goods to Argentina. Not only was Argentine enterprise called upon to supplant foreign industries that had hitherto supplied the country, but it was also confronted with the problem of finding new sources of raw materials. Moreover, increased production of industrial goods could not wholly solve the problem. It was also essential to attain greater diversification of the production of manufactures by opening up new fields of industrial activities.

There were two ways in which the problem could be attacked. One method championed by Federico Pinedo, former Minister of Finance, called for "inspired" large-scale industrialization of the country. Pinedo's proposal argued that expansion of established industries and implantation of new industries are economically feasible and socially justifiable. It argued further that intensive industrialization would reduce the country's dependence upon foreign markets and, therefore, provide a broad basis for a permanent solution of the problem of instability that had hitherto characterized the economy of Argentina. The plan proposed the launching of a large-scale program of housing construction, the creation of long-term industrial credit facilities, and the adoption by the government of economic and tariff policies that would ensure Argentine industry of continued protection after the war.

The alternative method was to dispose of the problem by a series of partial solutions. On this plan the government was to deal with the difficulties created by the war as they arose, without attempting to reshape the economic pattern of the country. This alternative was apparently predicated upon the assumption that should the war be of short duration forced industrialization was neither necessary nor desirable and that should the war last longer than expected Argentine industry and enterprise would have sufficient time and opportunity to step into the breach left open by curtailed imports. By restricting the supply of foreign manufactures and shipping facilities the war afforded effective protection to Argentine industry, and no revision of tariff policies designed to encourage industrial expansion was called for.

The solution of planned industrialization as proposed by Pinedo was rejected. The Argentines were not prepared to discard the traditional view that agriculture and foreign trade, which had served the country so well in the past, could no longer be relied upon to ensure prosperity. Many in Argentina opposed a policy of artificial industrialization at the expense of consumers. Still others saw in the plan of "inspired" industrialization a threat to all those activities that had grown and flourished when agriculture, stock raising, and foreign trade ruled the national economy. The country was willing to accept state intervention, but it insisted that such intervention be limited to emergency measures. It was satisfied that the question of supply of manufactured goods was not critical and that private initiative was capable of meeting the challenge.

The actual course of events seemed to justify the rejection of the plan of forced industrialization. The progressive drying up of sources of supply of manufactured goods, caused partly by scarcities in the supplying countries (Great Britain and the United States) and partly by shipping shortages, created conditions extremely favorable to industrial expansion. No tariff or other restrictive commercial policy short of total prohibition could offer a greater stimulus to Argentine capital and enterprise. Then, too, investment capital was rapidly becoming more abundant. These funds originated partly within the Argentine manufacturing and cattle-breeding industries, and partly also in Europe, which was seeking refuge and investment opportunities in neutral Argentina. Already in 1939 the inflow of capital exceeded outward movement by 66 million pesos. This balance increased to 79 million pesos in 1940 and to 325 million pesos in 1941. In 1942, the last year for which estimates have been made, Argentina received on balance 235 million pesos. It is true, of course, that not all refugee capital was investment capital. Much of it came to Argentina in search of security rather than profits and has been kept liquid in the form of government securities and bank deposits. But whether the influx of capital funds has been permanent or temporary, it has contributed to the general cheapening of credit in the Buenos Aires market.

These factors together with the expansion of overseas sales of Argentine meat and other strategic commodities more than outweighed the adverse effects of the war. The country entered upon a period of prosperity that has continued on an ever-ascending level. The average monthly industrial employment in 1942 was 24 per cent above the level of 1937, which was a rather prosperous year in Argentina. In August of 1943, the latest month for which information is available, industrial employment rose to 128.7 (1937 = 100). Growth of employment was especially marked in the textile, foodstuffs, chemical, oil, and paper industries. Other indices show a similar trend. Consumption of electric power, for example, increased from 1,753 million kilowatt-hours in 1938 to 2,135 million kilowatt-hours in 1942; freight transport increased from 8,701 million ton-kilometers in 1938 to 11,560 million ton-kilometers in 1942; deposits in commercial banks rose from 3,790 million pesos to 5,253 million pesos in 1942.

Economic prosperity in Argentina has been all the more remarkable in that it has not been conditioned by forces that in the past were decisive in shaping the economic destinies of the country. Neither agriculture nor foreign trade, the two traditional pillars of prosperity, have been important contributing factors in the upswing of business activity soon after the first shock of the war wore off. The honors of leading the nation to prosperity belong partly to stock raising, but above all to industry. A net rise of exports and an inflow of capital were, however, of some importance; and the expansion of industry may be associated with the appearance of new barriers to trade and, notably, the reduction of shipping.

The bright picture of the Argentine economy in the last four years has not been wholly without dark spots. While the country capitalized upon the advantages of war-conditioned demand for meat, hides, and certain strategic minerals, it could not wholly escape the strangling effects of shrinking foreign trade, increasing scarcity of raw materials, machinery, and equipment, and dwindling transportation facilities. These adverse factors became particularly pronounced early in 1942 after the United States entered the war.

One of the most perplexing problems confronting the country was the growing shortage of fuel. In normal years Argentina imported annually about 3 million tons of coal, a very large part of it from Great Britain. It became apparent soon after the outbreak of the war that Great Britain would not be able to supply even the 800,000 tons a year that were considered essential to cover Argentina's minimum requirements. Indeed, in 1942, British shipments of coal to Argentina were not much over 200,000 tons. Argentina turned to the United States in order to make up the deficiency but met with only partial success largely because of scarcity of shipping facilities. Moderate quantities of coal were obtained from Latin America (principally from Brazil and Chile) and the Union of South Africa. All these new sources of supply could not fully compensate for the loss of British coal. The Argentine government instituted, therefore, a series of conservation measures designed to reduce consumption of coal. The use of coal for nonessential purposes was prohibited, and wherever possible partial substitution of wood, corn, and linseed was made compulsory. At the same time the government encouraged a more intensive exploitation of domestic coal deposits. These measures did not solve Argentina's fuel problem; they did, however, enable the country to weather the worst consequences of the shortage.

Equally perplexing has been the shortage of iron and steel and their manufactures. As in the case of coal it became evident soon after the outbreak of hostilities in Europe that England would not be able to supply anywhere near the quantity it normally exported to Argentina. The only other important source open to Argentina was the United States. The entry of the United States into the war, however, considerably reduced the potential supply of these commodities from this source. Argentina made strenuous efforts to procure iron and steel from every other available source, including Spain and Brazil. These imports together with the scrap available in the country enabled the country to maintain production of iron and steel manufactures on an even keel.

The problem of shipping became critical toward the end of 1941. Argentina was wholly unprepared to meet the impending crisis, for in the past it had relied upon foreign, largely British, shipping for contact with overseas markets. As shortage of shipping facilities became more acute, Argentina purchased 16 Italian ships that had remained idle in Argentine ports since Italy's entry into the war. In 1943, Argentina purchased 3 French ships and 2 vessels from a German-controlled concern. In this manner Argentina acquired a merchant marine which it utilized mainly in maintaining and expanding trade relations with the American republics.

However partial were these solutions, they were sufficient to prevent serious dislocations in the economy of Argentina. Foreign purchases of meat, of minerals, and of a number of other strategic commodities at highly profitable prices were more than sufficient to overcome not only the economic effects of shortages of some raw materials but also the financial hazards of government grain purchasing programs. Sustained domestic demand for consumers' goods and the meager inflow of manufactures from abroad gave Argentine industry an impetus it had not experienced even in the stormy days of the First World War. And the general decline of overseas imports into Latin America opened up for Argentine industry and commerce new economic frontiers.

Argentina's trade with Latin America has grown remarkably since the beginning of the war. Trade with Bolivia in 1943 was more than three times larger than in 1939. With Chile, commerce increased five times during the same period; with Colombia, almost six times; with Brazil, it rose by 50 per cent and with Uruguay by more than 100 per cent. Of course, the increase in trade with Latin America could not compensate Argentina for the losses sustained as a result of the elimination of most of Europe as a market for Argentine exports or as a source of supply of Argentine imports. It is true, also, that a part of the Latin American trade, perhaps a considerable part, is of the emergency variety, conditioned by the exigencies of the war and not likely to survive restoration of international trade on a world-wide scale. But, whatever the origin or the future of Argentina's inter-American commerce, it has strengthened and extended the foundation upon which the prosperity of Argentina, and especially of Argentine industry, rests.

What is perhaps most significant about Argentina's wartime foreign commerce is the remarkable increase in the value of exports of manufactured goods. In 1939, Argentina's shipments of manufactures were valued at 45 million pesos, representing 3 per cent of total exports. In 1943, such exports amounted to 424 million pesos, or 19 per cent of the total. No less significant is the fact that most of the products shipped to Latin American countries in 1943 were new to the list of Argentine exports since 1939. About one-half the new exports to Latin America consisted of textiles; a sizable part of the remainder was accounted for by leather manufactures, and a number of chemical and pharmaceutical products appeared for the first time in the Latin American markets under the label "Industria Argentina."

It is probably an exaggeration to claim that this expansion of Argentine exports of manufactures is an "expression of the amazing vitality of the Argentine industry." A much more severe test would be necessary in order to appraise the vitality and resourcefulness of Argentina's industries. Such a test would have to measure, not only Argentina's capacity to produce, but also its ability to supply foreign markets under competitive conditions. Nevertheless, the fact that in spite of all the difficulties Argentine industry was at all able to expand production beyond domestic requirements is in itself evidence of its aggressiveness and alertness.

In its annual review of economic conditions for 1942 the Banco Central of Argentina cautioned against excessive optimism with respect to continued expansion of industrial activity. While it noted with satisfaction past performance and achievements, the review emphasized the gravity of the situation created by scarcity of raw materials. In normal years, the review points out, Argentina required approximately 1,500,000 tons of imported raw materials essential to the maintenance of industrial activity on a level adequate to ensure reasonably full employment. In 1943, not more than 500,000 tons of such materials could be expected from abroad. Nearly 60 per cent of these materials must be obtained from the United States. Even if all the expectations with respect to imports from abroad materialized, contraction of industrial activity appeared inevitable; and the Banco Central suggested, therefore, that serious thought be given to the impending problem of economic readjustment.

The Cassandra-like prophecies of the Banco Central have not materialized. The level of economic activity in 1943 was not lower than that for the preceding year. Argentina's exports of manufactured goods in 1943 were larger than ever before; industrial employment held its own throughout the year. In the face of all difficulties, economic as well as political, Argentina's national economy has survived another year by a comfortable margin of safety.

III

It is generally agreed in Argentina that after the war the country will face a serious problem of economic readjustment. Most of those concerned with the country's future realize that while it is impossible to predict in detail the scope and character of such a readjustment it is nevertheless essential to examine the broad aspects of the problem at the present time so that the difficulties of transition may be reduced to a minimum. The problem is admittedly complicated, but even now two of its broader aspects are clearly discernible. One is the question of adjustment to a peacetime world economy. The other is the problem of internal adjustments and the emergence of a new relationship of the various sectors that compose the economic pattern of Argentina.

What Argentina can do to shorten and mitigate the period of transition will, of course, depend upon the kind of world that will emerge after the war. Argentina is a relatively insignificant sector of the world economy. It cannot materially influence its organization, but it is, on the other hand, profoundly affected by the manner in which international trade and world markets function. While Argentina's dependence upon foreign markets has declined in the past 30 years, foreign trade will continue to play an important part in the economic life of the country. And the extent to which Argentina will be able to recapture its prewar foreign markets will determine to a considerable degree the pattern of allocation and utilization of the country's natural resources. Argentina may elect to revert to the prewar position of an agricultural exporting country, or it may be forced to divert a greater proportion of its land to the production of industrial crops for domestic processing. Again, it may continue the present system of extensive cultivation and production of export surpluses, or it may find it both necessary and advisable to lay greater emphasis upon colonization and the development of family farming units.

It is reasonable to assume that postwar Europe, Argentina's principal market, will be a devastated and hungry Europe. The foodstuffs that Argentina will be able to produce in the years immediately following the war will find a ready and eager market. It is likely, moreover, that at least during the period of reconstruction and relief every effort will be made to remove all barriers to the flow of commodities across international boundaries. To Argentina this would mean an almost instantaneous solution of its problem of agricultural surpluses; it would bring back prosperity to Argentine agriculture, but it would also prevent any institutional and economic reorganization of the agricultural sector of the economy.

How long the period of European reconstruction will last it is, of course, impossible to say. It may be assumed, however, that the period of rehabilitation of agriculture in Europe will not be prolonged and that the demand for Argentina's agricultural commodities will of necessity decline. The extent of the decline in demand will be determined by a number of factors over which Argentina will have little or no control. Of great importance in this connection will be the manner in which the more general question of international trade with respect to tariffs and quotas is solved. It is quite possible that the prewar tendency of European consumer countries toward self-sufficiency in basic foodstuffs may be revived, and this in turn will tend to reduce the market for imported agricultural products. Again, it is likely that for some time after the war the standard of living in Europe will be lower than that which prevailed before the war and that importation over and above the basic necessities of the European population may well be discouraged.

The stock-raising industry, which throughout the war has reaped the benefit of high prices, will in all probability enter a period of recession upon the termination of hostilities. It is entirely possible that this recession will be orderly, partly because of the destruction of livestock in Europe and partly also because demobilization in Great Britain and in Europe may of necessity be gradual. It should be noted, however, that meat is not an essential commodity above a given minimum and that therefore the demand for meat products in postwar Europe will probably be elastic. A possible decline in the demand for meat may be compensated for by an improved market for Argentine wool, which has not fared particularly well in recent years.

In general, the postwar prospects for Argentine agriculture and stock raising do not portend far-reaching changes of institutional character. Nor do they call for a revision of the basic principles of policy which in the past determined the pattern and the position of these sectors in the national economy. Given a postwar economic organization of the world in which international trade will be allowed to play its traditional role, Argentina will endeavor to revert to the position of a food-exporting country and to restore, thereby, the economic and sociopolitical *status quo*.

But successful restoration of the prewar economic equilibrium will depend to a large extent upon the position assigned to industry. This sector of the national economy will find it much more difficult to adjust itself to postwar conditions. It is generally recognized that after the war Argentine industry will face severe competition both at home and abroad, and there is reason to doubt whether it can successfully meet such competition. The growth of Argentine industry during the war has been conditioned by a series of circumstances which are not likely to persist once peace is restored and which have rendered nugatory the basic safeguards against artificial expansion. Scarcity of raw materials of adequate quality, lack of replacements for machinery and equipment, scarcity of skilled labor—all these factors have been responsible for rising costs of production. During the years of emergency Argentine industry could disregard the element of cost largely because it operated for markets, whether domestic or foreign, in which the availability of goods rather than price and quality was of importance. With the restoration of normal international trade many Argentine firms that have come into existence during the war or have expanded production on the basis of war prices will become highly vulnerable to foreign competition. This is not to say that foreign competition will destroy all the gains achieved by Argentine industry during the war. In some industries expansion has been economically justifiable, and postwar readjustment in such industries may entail nothing more drastic than the necessity of modernizing equipment and increasing efficiency of labor in order to reduce average costs of production to a competitive level.

Whatever the nature of postwar readjustment may be, Argentine industry will require considerable assistance from the government. It will demand protection of the domestic market, and it will insist upon more sympathetic consideration of its problems and postulates in matters of domestic and foreign economic policies.

The weight of industry in the economic and political equation of Argentina is already considerable and is destined to grow after the war. Unlike agriculture and stock raising, Argentine industry cannot hope to gain a foothold in the European market. It looks to the country itself and to the industrially weak economies of the Western Hemisphere for support. In order to survive it must secure the domestic market, and in order to prosper it must have an expanding market both at home and abroad. Were Argentine industry fully equipped to meet successfully foreign competition, the question of markets might have remained largely within the realm of private enterprise rather than governmental action. But in reality Argentine industry is not prepared to wage a successful struggle for markets, either at home or abroad, without continued assistance from the government. As long as industry occupied a secondary position in the national economy, government support was of necessity half-hearted and sporadic. But as industry expanded, as its contribution to the national income increased and its future was more intimately linked with the economic destinies of the nation, the need for a revision and possible reorientation of the economic policies of the central government became more insistent. That the government has at least partly recognized the need for adapting its policies to the changing pattern of the national economy cannot be doubted. The recent drive toward the establishment of a more or less complete customs union with Chile and Paraguay, the rather vigorous policy of economic penetration into Bolivia sponsored by the government, and the efforts to create within the country an adequate mechanism for the flow of long-term funds to facilitate industrial expansion are all manifestations of the government's concern for the welfare of the national industry.

Whether these measures will satisfy the needs and aspirations of Argentina's industrial interests is rather doubtful. The question of tariff protection has not been seriously raised in the past two or three years, primarily because the war in Europe and in the Pacific effectively removed all foreign competition. But demands for adequate protection of national industries after the war are already being formulated and will become more insistent as the war draws to its close.

Revision of tariff policies is, however, only one of the industry's desiderata. Protection will secure the domestic market for national manufactures, but it will not in itself ensure the expansion of such a market or create the proper economic and social environment for an expanding industry. In order to accomplish this purpose a long-range program of economic policies much broader in scope than the revision of the tariff will have to be devised. Such a program will inevitably involve a reexamination of some of the fundamental principles which had hitherto determined the economic policies of the country. Questions of colonization, distribution of land, taxation, and transportation will have to be considered anew and solved in accordance with the requirements of an economy in which industry is no longer a sector of secondary importance, but rather an equal partner of agriculture and stock raising in shaping the nation's economic life.

Thus the problem of postwar readjustment in the industrial sector extends to the whole economy. It goes beyond the realm of purely economic considerations, for it affects the position and interests of groups that have for many decades controlled and guided the destinies of the country. To this extent Argentina finds itself on the threshold of a period of transition, a period in which many of the traditional economic and social concepts will have to be discarded to make room for values that conform more readily to economic realities. The carrier of these new values in Argentina today is industry, and upon it falls the burden of leading the country through the period of storm and stress toward new economic frontiers.

Chapter X

Bolivia

by WILLIAM A. NEISWANGER
and JAMES R. NELSON

BOLIVIA is a large and potentially rich land whose mineral deposits have been worked since preconquest days. Its other resources, largely undeveloped, are capable of providing the basis for a substantial increase in the standard of living through greater food production and an expansion in imports of industrial products.

In area, Bolivia is more than twice as large as Spain, but its population is only 3,500,000. Although it is known to the outside world as a leading source of minerals, two-thirds of the population are attached to agriculture and handicrafts. Industry employs only 12,000 salary and wage earners, and mining occupies not more than 60,000 workers at peak production. In spite of this extensive occupation with agricultural pursuits, farming is mainly of the subsistence type, and food produced within the country is insufficient to feed the population. Where surpluses do exist, inadequate transportation facilities narrowly restrict the market.

From a financial standpoint, on the other hand, the mining industry quite completely dominates the Bolivian economy (see Chart 7 on her exports). It provides 95 per cent of Bolivia's export values, and taxes on minerals yield the government about 50 per cent of its revenues. Essential imports, including food, therefore enter Bolivia in exchange for minerals, and the stability of Bolivia's money and of the government itself is tied to tin, tungsten, antimony, and other less important mineral exports.

It is apparent that the original and continuing emphasis on the mining industry as a source of quick and large returns for both individual promoters and the government has produced a dangerously unbalanced economy. The basic importance of agriculture to a sound economy in an undeveloped country; the need to provide transporta-

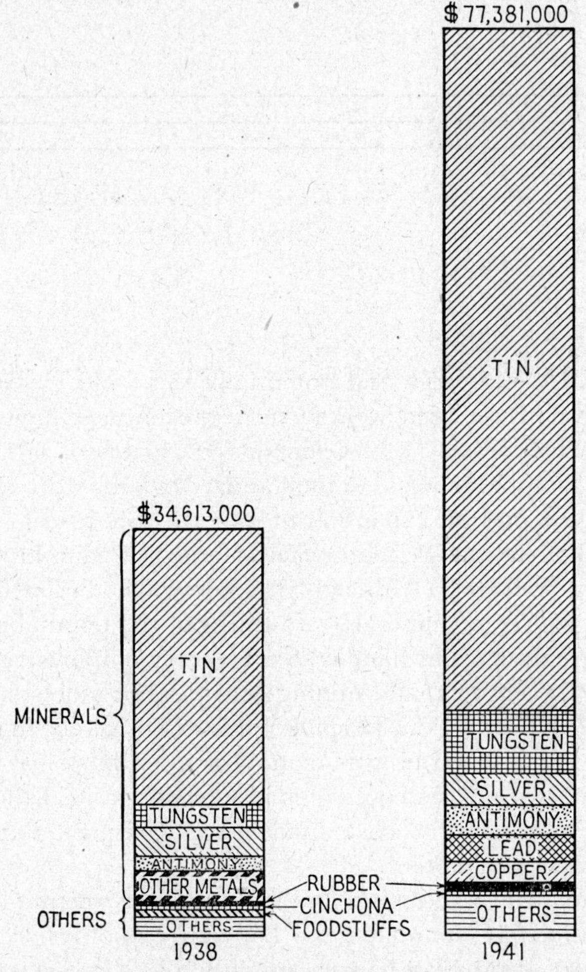

CHART 7.—Bolivia. Exports by commodities, 1938, 1941. (*Source: Coordinator of Inter-American Affairs.*)

tion to distribute agricultural produce as well as ores; the further necessity for the development of food processing plants together with the power resources to operate them—all have been neglected in favor of exploitation of rich mineral deposits. A *Corporación Boliviana de Fomento* (Bolivian Development Corporation) has fortunately been established by the Bolivian government with United States cooperation to correct the obvious and basic faults in the Bolivian economy.

The human resource offers Bolivia great promise and a difficult problem. The labor force is predominantly Indian. The Indians of Bolivia possess the usual share of native intelligence, mechanical aptitude, and managerial ability found in any cross section of mankind, as has been shown where education and other opportunities for advancement have been available. The physical remains of preconquest Indian civilizations found in Peru and Bolivia reveal a high degree of mechanical and engineering skill. Writings of the early Spanish historians indicate a well-integrated social organization featuring an agricultural system complete with "ever normal granaries" which provided a high degree of economic security for the Indian. This skill, specialized knowledge, and social organization passed with the coming of the Spanish, as did other less admirable aspects of the Indian culture.

The Indian of the high plateau and neighboring valleys has not been taught to read or write; he speaks Quechua or Aymara, the languages of his fathers, and follows customs which frequently date from the period before the Conquest. The economic future of Bolivia therefore raises ethnic and cultural questions which are both complex and important. Establishment of the Indian as an educated, responsible member of the economic community is a prerequisite for any permanent economic progress. The forms which this change should take, and the means necessary to bring it about, are questions whose answers will largely determine the future of a nation.

THE NATURAL SETTING

The landlocked country of Bolivia has been divided by nature into three principal areas: the Altiplano, the Montaña, and the lowlands.

Altiplano is the name used for the high plateau, 450 miles long and about 100 miles wide, which lies between the western and eastern ranges of the Andes. It extends from north to south, with its western edge adjacent to the Chilean border. This area, with an average altitude of about 12,500 feet, includes some 14 per cent of the national total. Although it is within the tropics, its height above sea level saves it from the diseases which make life difficult in the lowlands. Partly for this reason, the Altiplano has been a center of population in both ancient and modern times. Here are located La Paz, a city of rare beauty and the *de facto* capital of the country, Oruro, an important mining center, and Potosí, at the foot of the fabulous Cerro Rico from which the Spanish took billions of dollars' worth of silver and which is now worked for its tin. Most of Bolivia's important mineral discoveries have been in this area, mainly in the eastern cordillera. The Altiplano is said to be the original home of the "Irish" potato, which appears here in many varieties and is a basic item in the highland Indian diet. Hardy grains are also raised here, and herds of sheep, llamas, and alpacas dot the plain.

The Montaña area is the eastern side of the Andean highlands where the mountains slope away to the flat tropical lowlands of eastern Bolivia. The Montaña is, therefore, a rugged country of great beauty, with towering peaks and narrow valleys. The northern part of the area is heavily wooded, in contrast to the bleak and barren Altiplano. At present the region is industrially undeveloped, although there is an abundance of potential water power in the mountain rivers which finally empty into the Amazon. Temperatures range from temperate to subtropical, depending on the altitude. Oranges, lemons, coffee, sugar cane, pineapples, bananas, and coca grow in the lower regions; corn, wheat, barley, potatoes, and vegetables thrive at higher altitudes.

To the east lie the flat lowlands of tropical Bolivia. Rainfall is heavy in the northern part of this area; but, as in other regions of Bolivia, it diminishes in the south until irrigation becomes necessary for successful farming. The Amazon basin in the northeast produces rubber and cinchona, from which quinine comes. Sugar cane and rice are also important crops in parts of the lowlands. It is estimated that the region also supports a million head of cattle. Transportation to the Altiplano cities is not available, however, and so the producer of foodstuffs receives a low price when he is able to find a market. Except for a few articles of high value in small bulk, such as coca and alcohol distilled from sugar cane, exports from the lowlands move to the east, and the major economic interests of eastern Bolivia tend to follow this movement into Brazil. While the lowlands seek a market for their beef, the cities of the Altiplano receive their supply by rail from Argentina. As yet, the lowlands are thinly populated, conditions of life are hard, and tropical diseases abound. Civilization has touched only the fringes of this region.

Differences of climate in Bolivia are largely the result of elevation. The country produces an amazing variety of products within a relatively small area because of the many levels at which cultivation takes place. This is a potential source of strength for the economy because of the possibilities of exchange to give the entire population an ample, varied, and nutritious diet. But the physical characteristics which provide this potentiality also place a great impediment in the way of its realization. The difficulties and costs of transportation from lowlands to Montaña and Altiplano remain great. Railroad lines to Cochabamba and Sucre in the Montaña region have permitted shipments to Altiplano consuming centers; truck transportation enables the fruits of the Yungas valleys to reach La Paz and other cities. But the lowlands are almost completely inaccessible, and only a few points in the Montaña have been tapped.

A DEVELOPMENT PROGRAM

One objective of the Bolivian Development Corporation is the construction of roads and food processing plants so that the agricultural products of the Montaña and lowlands can be sold on the Altiplano, thus conserving foreign exchange now spent for foreign foods and increasing agricultural income and living standards. With exchange saved and rural purchasing power improved, Bolivian imports of manufactured goods can be increased and sent through the Altiplano cities to the agricultural areas. Thus mineral exports will pay for imports of manufactured goods, and Bolivia will produce most of its own food at a relatively low cost. Such specialization and exchange should raise living standards in Bolivia and in other countries. The program will also tend to bring financial stability to Bolivian money and commodity markets, which have been afflicted with extreme inflation since 1931. The agricultural development program is, in the last analysis, a plan to stabilize Bolivian finances, at the same time raising living standards.

The success of any such long-run program in Bolivia depends on (1) the maintenance of export markets for tin in order to pay for the immediate expenses of the program and for subsequent imports of manufactured goods; (2) the financial ability of the Bolivian government, with United States assistance, to support a program of road construction and other necessary improvements without contributing to an increase in present inflated prices; (3) the willingness of Bolivian authorities to accept certain institutional changes necessary to improve the financial position of the government and the efficiency of the productive process on the farms and in the mines; (4) the education of the Indian so that he will employ more modern agricultural techniques and experiment with newly developed varieties of grain, stock, and vegetables which the experts of the Bolivian Development Corporation find to be especially suited to Bolivia's soil, rainfall, and temperature.

The position of Bolivia's mining industry, the organization of finance and production, and the status of the Indian worker must be examined to judge the present economic position of Bolivia and to gain some hint as to trends.

THE MINING INDUSTRY

This industry is the financial mainspring of the Bolivian economy. It directly supports only about 100,000 people, or approximately 3 per cent of the population, but it is mainly responsible for the country's present development. It has maintained a relatively dense population on the barren Altiplano, and it has conditioned the construction and location of the principal railroads. Foreign sale of its output provides practically all Bolivia's foreign exchange, and taxes on the export of minerals constitute half the national tax receipts. In addition, the mining companies construct and maintain roads, schools, houses, hospitals, and recreational facilities in mining camps scattered around the edges of the Altiplano region. Mining and the industries which supply it with transportation, power, and other services are the main large-scale employers of labor in Bolivia and have absorbed most of the foreign investment made in the country. The mining industry is also the pivot of Bolivian political controversy.

This predominance dates from the earliest days of the Spanish Conquest. Discovery of silver in the Cerro Rico of Potosí in 1545 placed this region in the forefront of world producers for 200 years. The city of Potosí, entirely dependent on this one source of income, reached a peak population of 160,000 in 1650 and was one of the world's largest cities almost throughout the colonial period. Impressed labor was brought in from such distant points as Cuzco and Quito.

Silver continued to dominate Bolivian exports during the early republican period after 1825, although other mines had begun to overshadow those of Potosí. Discovery of mineral resources in Bolivia's Pacific Coast provinces in the Antofagasta region brought capital and labor from other countries, especially Chile, and helps to explain

Bolivia's loss of this region to Chile as a result of the War of the Pacific. Silver production began declining in 1870 because of low world prices and exhaustion of mines, but tin gained steadily until it was more important after 1900 than silver had been since the early colonial days.

Tin has contributed an average of approximately 70 per cent of total Bolivian exports for the past 20 years. Many other mineral exports are possible only because of joint use of transportation and other facilities originally built for tin; therefore, tin's importance is greater than the figures indicate.

Tin production expanded greatly at the turn of the century for numerous reasons—higher prices, which reflected its increasing demand as an industrial metal; abandonment of silver mines and resulting release of their labor forces; completion of the Antofagasta to Bolivia Railway from the Chilean coast to the mining regions during the 1890's; and the activities of Simon I. Patiño in developing the rich tin mines at Llallagua. Spanish prospecting, aided by promises of freedom to Indians who discovered and reported ore veins, had been thorough; therefore, discoveries of new ores played a minor part in this development. Mineral horizons remained almost constant. Economic horizons expanded overnight.

The Bolivian tin belt, which has produced between 19,000 and 47,000 tons of fine tin annually since 1920, extends along the higher levels of the main eastern range of the Andes in a north-south direction. Few tin mines are below 12,000 feet altitude, and some are located beneath glaciers at a height of 16,500 feet.

Bolivian tin operations are divided into sharply defined ownership groups. Three large companies produce between 75 and 80 per cent of total output, and the remainder is contributed by over 500 medium and small mining enterprises. The average gross value of small-mine tin production was only about $5,000 in the prosperous year 1941. On the other hand, the Patiño mines have formed the basis for one of the world's largest fortunes.

Patiño exports of tin concentrates provided almost 60 per cent of Bolivian tin export values in 1929 and almost 50 per cent in 1941. Mines in the Llallagua area, organized as the Patiño Mines and Enterprises Consolidated, Inc., a Delaware corporation, produced over 40 per cent of the Bolivian total in 1929, although this percentage dropped in subsequent years. Mauricio Hochschild, a relative newcomer who began operations in Bolivia in the early 1920's, produced almost 10 per cent of the national tin output in 1929 and over 25 per cent in 1941. The third large company, a Swiss corporation named for and partly controlled by the Bolivian Aramayo family, contributes about 5 per cent of Bolivia's tin.

Other Bolivian mineral exports display great variety. Tungsten and antimony lead the minor mineral group at present because of war conditions. Silver, copper, zinc, and lead production is on a substantial scale, and gold, sulphur, and bismuth are of minor importance.

Production of minor minerals is mainly in the hands of the principal tin mining companies. Copper, mainly derived from the American Smelting and Refining Company mines at Corocoro, and antimony, which is produced by a number of small mines, are the conspicuous exceptions.

THE OUTLOOK FOR BOLIVIAN MINING

Bolivia has always faced competition in marketing her principal minerals. Expansion in Mexico and the United States hastened the decline of the Bolivian silver industry. Even tin, which has come to be associated with Bolivia, is normally exported in larger volume from the Malay Peninsula and the Dutch East Indies.

War conditions have cut off principal peacetime sources of tin, tungsten, and antimony and have greatly strengthened the Bolivian competitive position. This change is temporary, however, and, owing to development of new supply areas, may hurt Bolivia's long-run prospects as much as it will improve them. Bolivia must be expected to sell in a highly competitive market in the postwar period unless cartel organization artificially limits production and controls prices.

World tin prices and output were controlled by the International Tin Committee in the 1930's. The governments of the principal tin-producing countries organized this central agency on a semiformal basis in November, 1930. The committee's first move was to adopt standard tonnages, which were, in general, equal to exports in 1929, and to fix production quotas for each signatory country on the basis of a percentage of these standard tonnages. The percentage of 1929 standard tonnages was the same for each producing country, but varied from time to time depending on the tin committee's judgment as to market conditions. Controls were tightened as the committee gained power and experience. Continued market declines after the committee was organized caused the creation of a buffer stock, or tin stock pile, to be purchased by the four original signatory producing areas from their domestic output and delivered to the committee for sale or holding at its discretion. This measure, which superseded two informal pools previously organized by large tin interests, further underlined the governmental nature of the cartel.

Noncartel competition was a constant threat. This was met by the inclusion of major tin producers in the original agreement, the subsequent membership of minor producing countries, and the provision that the cartel would become inoperative if noncartel output exceeded a certain percentage of the world's total. This was originally fixed at 25 per cent and was lowered in 1936 to 15 per cent.

Although the committee has been practically inoperative since October, 1939, it may vitally affect the future of Bolivian tin production after the war. But many changes have occurred since 1939.

The original committee was based on British dominance in tin production and smelting. The Malay Peninsula and Nigeria were two of the original members, and British smelting interests which receive ore from Bolivia and other producing countries were unquestionably also influential. The war has changed competitive relationships. While the Malay Peninsula, the Dutch East Indies, and Thailand have been shut off from major world markets, production has been greatly expanded in other areas and has been begun in still others. Cartel quotas may be unattractive to producers who have achieved importance during the war.

Furthermore, the United States government had the foresight to construct a tin smelter at Texas City, Tex., before Pearl Harbor. Under a United States–Bolivian tin contract this smelter now receives all Bolivian tin exports except those of the Patiño group of mines, which are still shipped to Great Britain. Therefore, United States interest in tin prices, stemming from its position as the world's chief consumer of refined tin, is reinforced by possession of an expensive fixed asset which may retain or lose its value depending on operations of a world cartel.

Political considerations also affect the cartel's position. Unlike most such agreements, that for tin is intergovernmental. Bolivia's dependence on tin for a substantial part of its government revenues and as a means of paying for most of its imports has been mentioned. Far Eastern areas which have exported both rubber and tin will be gravely affected if synthetic rubber impairs markets for the former product. Increased dependence on tin to provide employment and pay for imports may cause demands for removal of cartel restrictions to permit greater output or, at the other extreme, for curtailment of production in order to enhance gross or net cash revenues and to ensure a longer life span for tin deposits. Here, the position of governments may depend on the underlying issues of costs, prices, volumes, and profits.

Finally, changing technology may influence the decision. United States production of tin cans has provided the largest single outlet for virgin tin, and one of the most dependable. Changes in container types or specifications would strike a heavy blow at price-maintenance plans.

Thus the future of the cartel is uncertain. Bolivia's position in it is more so. Bolivian mineowners strongly maintain that their tax burden alone is equal to total production costs in the Malay Peninsula, and that Bolivia's presence in the cartel was the result of influence more than of necessity. They cite low Bolivian tin exports during the 1930's, which were far below Bolivian quotas in every year except in 1938, as proof of the relative decline of Bolivian productive efficiency. The clamor of Far Eastern producers for higher quotas during the period is presented as further proof of Bolivia's loss of competitive strength. In addition, Bolivian tin ores are mainly low grade (some mines now worked yield only 1.5 per cent recovery) and reserves are of yet lower quality; their exploitation promises to raise unit costs. Bolivia has also passed through a period of extreme currency depreciation which has operated to the short-run advantage of the mining companies because of the lag in wages and certain other costs behind increased receipts from foreign currencies when converted into depreciated bolivianos. In spite of the efforts of management to maintain low wages and costs, the advantages which the industry has enjoyed from a 12-year inflation cannot be expected to endure. Inflation obviously leads to disaster if it is adopted as a permanent national policy.

The question therefore arises: Will others who are interested in the postwar market cooperate in maintaining a price high enough to cover Bolivian taxes and costs by a severe curtailment of production under a cartel arrangement?

Not all factors are so unfavorable to Bolivia. Far Eastern tin production did not expand greatly during the growth period of Bolivia's tin industry. Choice of the year 1929 as the basis for assigning quotas favored Bolivia, which in that year achieved the highest output in its history. The Patiño interests have large investments in tin production outside of Bolivia; since they are also the largest Bolivian producers, Bolivian production should not be unduly slighted in the distribution of allowable output. The Chaco War, which greatly unsettled the entire mining industry and caused labor shortages through death and emigration which outlasted the war period, is an important explanation of Bolivian failure to meet tin quotas during the 1930's. Far Eastern producers have naturally been interested in maximizing long-run total profit from a wasting asset, even at the expense of immediate production or net return. Finally, several years may be required to restore their prewar production facilities even after hostilities end. During this period the price policies of England and the United States, as principal buyers, will be of paramount importance.

Technological changes may be significant. Lack of smelting facilities, resulting from the absence of low-cost coal or oil resources in or near the mining region, has necessitated expensive shipment of concentrates to foreign smelters. Mine operators must pay freight charges, which are mainly levied against worthless rock. They must also throw away valuable minerals in order to increase the tin content of the concentrates they ship and reduce their high transportation expenses. Experiments are now in progress with new methods of concentration which will permit the processing of lower grade ores and improve the grade of the concentrate, thereby cutting transport expenses and making available huge reserves of low-grade tin ores now unworked or discarded in dumps. Success in this experiment is problematic. On it hinges much of Bolivia's mining future, since most other important tin areas are located much closer freightwise to smelters.

Discovery of important new ore resources is not likely. Spanish prospecting was unscientific but thorough. Almost all of Bolivia's large mines were discovered before the country became independent in 1825. Experienced prospectors are pessimistic with respect to every mineral but gold, which they believe to exist in large quantities in the unexplored eastern lowlands. Even an increase in gold output, however, will require vastly improved transportation facilities to permit replacement of present manual recovery methods.

Bolivian government policy is another unknown. Present tonnage taxes undoubtedly reduce production, but the government appears reluctant to introduce high profits taxes as a substitute because of the accounting problems involved and the additional variability which such taxes would introduce into government receipts. Monetary policy will have an influence on mining operations, either to make them less profitable if the national currency unit is maintained at its present level, or possibly to increase their profitability if it is decided to continue inflationary policies and give the mining companies another temporary advantage by further currency depreciation.

Labor in the mines presents a series of problems of its own. Working conditions are on the whole unsatisfactory; the accident rate is high, and the incidence of pulmonary diseases is also high so that few Indians look to a career in the mines. Since work is at a high altitude, laborers from lower elevations are confronted with the serious problem of adjustment. According to the records of the Bolivian Workers' Insurance and Savings Fund, 20 per cent of the miners covered have received each year compensation for temporary or permanent incapacity. Miners employed in the smaller mines, not always included in the compensation plan, probably have an even higher disability rate. The fund also estimates that 8 to 9 per cent of the miners are permanently incapacitated each year by occupational diseases, primarily lung ailments. Labor turnover is consequently very high. The Indian miner characteristically signs up for a 3 months' period in the mines, in the hope that he may be able to accumulate a small amount of cash in that period to supplement his meager agricultural income. Surface workers at the mines, mostly mestizoes (Cholos), are more permanent.

Because the typical Indian miner looks upon mining, not as a vocation, but rather as a temporary employment engaged in to obtain a money wage, he has little interest in labor union organization. Nor has he the ambition to improve as a miner or to exert himself at the high altitude in order to increase output.

To these explanations of the inefficiency of the Bolivian miner must be added chronic malnutrition and unhygienic living conditions. The report of the Joint Bolivian–United States Commission of Labor Experts, issued in March, 1943, described the diet of the Bolivian worker as "low and unbalanced." The same report also states: "With a few honorable exceptions it might be said that housing facilities at the mines are inadequate in quality and inadequate in quantity to a greater or lesser degree."

In addition to these environmental conditions, which are not conducive to efficiency, the Indian miner is addicted to the characteristic Indian custom of chewing coca. The cocaine released from the leaf assuages hunger and induces an illusion of general well-being at the expense of nutrition and ambition.

Owing to the combination of these conditions and the present state of the country's developed resources, the output of the Bolivian miner is substantially below that of workers in more advanced industrial countries. The miner's real income is difficult to estimate because in the larger mining camps he is provided with free housing and medical attention and is permitted to purchase necessities at the company stores (*pulperías*) at artificially low prices. Certainly the actual money wage is low. A distribution of wages prepared by the Workers' Insurance and Savings Fund is as follows:

WAGE PAYMENTS TO BOLIVIAN MINERS, 1942
In Bolivianos

Daily Rate	Number of Miners
5–10	1,998
10–15	2,595
15–20	2,555
20–30	3,631
30–40	6,341
40–50	225
50–60	192
	17,537

Forty-one per cent of Bolivian miners received less than 20 bolivianos, or 46 American cents, per day. The lowest wages were paid mainly to women and children. Even if the value to the worker of free services and below-cost necessities is equal to the money wage paid, as managements contend, wage payments are still very low and, because of subsequent inflation, may represent considerably less purchasing power than 1929 mine wages.

The *pulperías* operated by the mining companies occupy an important place in the economic life of the Bolivian laborer. Legislation in 1937 forced them to sell necessary articles at 30 per cent below cost, and they were later given the option of selling at 10 per cent above cost if they increased wages "at least as much as prices." This practice, plus the provision of free housing and medical care already mentioned, enables management to claim that real wages are rising while labor contends that its real income is going down rather than up. The result is a very confused situation in which wages at different mines cannot be compared and no one knows what has actually happened to the level of real wages in Bolivian mines during the past decade.

It is clear, however, that the *pulpería* is a powerful economic force and is used as such to control labor. Company stores are opened at noon each day, by which time foremen have reported those who are at work. Members of workers' families are permitted to draw food and other necessities up to a fixed percentage of earnings, usually 70 per cent. No food is issued if the miner is not at work and has drawn up to his limit. The credit system is unknown in the *pulperías*. The same policy leads to the closing of company stores when a strike is called. Since mines are usually isolated and competitive stores are practically nonexistent because of the price policy of the *pulperías*, the results of closing the company store are obvious.

Furthermore, workmen's compensation and other benefits are calculated on the basis of money wages received. These are artificially low and variable because of low *pulpería* prices.

Bolivian governments have enacted much labor legislation. Early laws were aimed at abuses inherited from the colonial period. Recent measures have more nearly followed the pattern of labor legislation in industrialized nations.

Laws regulating labor contracts in order to prevent involuntary servitude illustrate the first type of enactment. Control was first introduced in 1896 for contracts in the northeastern rubber-producing area, where government action was particularly necessary. More strict regulations were established in 1935.

The modern industrial pattern has been increasingly pronounced in the last twenty years. The Busch Labor Code of 1939, originally issued as a decree and given the status of law in December, 1942, is a compilation of most previous measures, with additions. This code requires all enterprises employing 500 or more workers (*i.e.*, the larger mining companies and a few other employers) to provide free hospitalization and medical care and to maintain hospitals. It also repeats previous requirements by specifying the construction of free housing in all mining camps employing over 200 workers and located more than 6 miles from the nearest town. The 8-hour day and 48-hour week are made universal except for unusual situations; women and children under eighteen are restricted to a 7-hour day and 40-hour week and are limited to 5 hours of continuous work. Private labor-recruiting agents, the *enganchadores*, who work for mining and other companies on a commission basis, are outlawed; free, state-operated employment offices are authorized.

The code also provides for minimum wages to be set by the Ministry of Labor, double pay for overtime, a bonus of 25 to 50 per cent for nightwork, and annual vacations with pay for periods depending on the worker's length of service. Annual bonuses of 15 to 30 days' pay are also to be given by companies making a profit during the year.

Social security in Bolivia takes the following forms: (1) a system of compensation for accidents and occupational diseases; (2) compulsory savings plans for mine and transportation labor; (3) pension funds for various groups of officials or salaried employees: teachers; postal and telegraph employees; employees of the judiciary, banks, printing trades, and railroads; and journalists.

Mining companies pay 3 per cent of their pay roll to the Workers' Insurance and Savings Fund to cover their liability for occupational accidents and diseases. The worker contributes 5 per cent of wages, which is invested, 1 per cent for the compensation fund and 4 per cent as compulsory savings. Compensation payments range from 6 months' pay for partial and temporary disability lasting over 6 months to 2 years' wages for death or permanent total disability. Savings may be withdrawn under certain circumstances, subject to approval of the local labor inspector. The 1943 report of the Joint United States–Bolivian Commission of Labor Experts comments that Bolivia is the only country in the world which requires workers to contribute to their own compensation insurance, and it is generally agreed that the compulsory savings system has failed to perform a valuable function. Purchasing power of these savings has been impaired or lost because of inflation.

Enforcement of social legislation has been more of a problem than enactment. The *enganchadores* continue to supply labor for the mines. Collective bargaining, a right guaranteed by the Constitution of 1938, has been made very difficult by the 1939 Labor Code's requirement that a union must enroll 50 per cent of the employees of an establishment to have legal status and that 75 per cent of the workers must be in favor of a strike before the work stoppage can be considered legal. Management, therefore, has the frequently used opportunity to refuse to deal with individual unions on the ground that they have no legal status. The legal position of unions is therefore weak; periodic exile or imprisonment of union leaders has made their actual position even weaker.

Martin Kyne of the CIO, a member of the United States–Bolivian labor commission of 1943, has said: "The Union of Industrial Workers of La Paz and the railroad and transportation unions are the only ones which can be considered as labor organizations in the European or North American sense. . . ." Since the government does not possess the funds or personnel to enforce a complicated body of social legislation in nearly a thousand mines and numerous industrial establishments, the weakness of union organization gravely compromises the effectiveness of existing statutes. Practice will continue to lag far behind published requirements as long as no strong force exists to compel observance of government stipulations on behalf of a working population which is usually unaware of its legal rights.

PETROLEUM

Bolivian petroleum has been overshadowed by mining, but it is viewed as a natural resource of great promise.

Crude-oil output in Bolivia registered a fortyfold increase between 1926 and 1940, but even so, total production in the latter year was insufficient to supply the small domestic market. Domestic wells furnish most of the gasoline and kerosene used in Bolivia, but about nine-tenths of the Diesel and fuel-oil requirements are imported.

Part of the explanation lies in the small area of fields discovered in Bolivia. These are not comparable with the oil reserves of Venezuela and other Latin American countries in area or in output.

The major cause of deficient production, however, is a familiar one: transportation expense. Heavy oils are imported because present transport costs from the Bolivian fields in southern Bolivia to Oruro in the mining region are higher than delivered prices of Peruvian petroleum. High-priced refined products are imported into the domestic market because they can bear high freight rates.

Transportation costs are high because lowland fields connect with plateau consuming centers by very bad mountain roads, which are frequently closed in the rainy season. Although the ascent from the fields is no greater than from the Pacific Coast, the latter route has the advantage of good railroad service. Bolivian petroleum cannot supply the domestic market cheaply until good roads or railroads are constructed to the fields. This has led the Bolivian Development Corporation to place transportation development to the oil fields high on its priority list. Although fields currently being exploited are small and exploration has been fragmentary, existing reserves are known to be adequate for a long period of exploitation. Since output is likely to rise, the expense of improved transportation per barrel of oil transported should be small.

A further possibility is the construction of a pipe line from the Bolivian oil district to the Argentine frontier. This has seemed impractical in the past because of the small area and scattered location of the oil fields. But the Argentine oil deficit is large and chronic, and pipe-line construction would be relatively simple. Bolivia may benefit from export shipments as a result.

The political history of Bolivian oil has been stormy. The Standard Oil Company of Bolivia developed all present oil fields, but Paraguayan attempts to capture these reserves during the Chaco War and Bolivian complaints as to the wartime policy of the Standard Oil Company brought the foreign-ownership problem to a head in the immediate postwar years. Standard Oil properties were expropriated on Mar. 13, 1937, and turned over to the newly established government petroleum monopoly. Compensation of $1,729,375 was paid to Standard Oil in 1942. Government operations have raised an issue which is not common in larger countries: whereas the Standard Oil development never lacked capital, the Bolivian government monopoly has been gravely handicapped because of the smallness of its funds in relation to costs of expansion.

MANUFACTURING AND INTERNAL COMMERCE

Manufacturing in Bolivia is now in a transitional stage between handicraft methods and modern factory production. Hand-spun and -woven woolens compete against those produced by highly mechanized processes.

Consumers' goods of easily fabricated types dominate Bolivian manufacturing as they have for 400 years. Almost three-quarters of all recorded Bolivian wageworkers are in the textile, food processing, and beverage industries. This emphasis, similar to that of many other Latin American countries, has numerous explanations. Bolivia's mass market is restricted to low-priced, standardized essentials. Present mechanical equipment and labor skills are insufficient to permit output of most manufactures. The growth of cities has encouraged specialization in products, such as beer, whose value is low in relation to weight or volume. Production of durable goods is almost nonexistent because of the absence of cheap sources of iron and steel, oil, and coal.

Manufacturing development will undoubtedly continue along present lines, with government tariff and exchange policy as erratic factors which may promote or impede it. Agricultural advance and growth of food processing are complementary, and development in both directions is expected. Bolivia will not be an important manufacturing country in the near future because of its physical isolation from important external markets, its small population and low per capita purchasing power, and its deficiency in most of the cheap sources of power.

Present commerce is channeled by a transportation network which is mainly the result of the growth of tin mining. Bolivia's most important railroad, which is British-owned, enters the country from Antofagasta (Chile) and reaches the city of La Paz after traversing almost the entire length of the Bolivian Altiplano. This road was constructed to haul mine supplies and ores, and its main tonnage still derives from this source. Other lines, the property of the Bolivian government except for a British-owned route through Peru, connect Bolivia with the Pacific at Arica (Chile) and Mollendo (Peru) and with the Atlantic at Buenos Aires. External commerce flowing through these various routes has been a principal factor in establishing the dominant commercial importance of La Paz and in further strengthening the international nature of Bolivian trade. Competition of Brazil and Argentina for Bolivian production and markets has resulted in surveys for two rail routes, one west into Bolivia from Corumbá (Brazil) and the other from Argentina north into the Bolivian oil fields. A small section of the line from Brazil has already been constructed toward its intended Bolivian terminus at Santa Cruz.

Bolivia's largest business houses are mainly importers, and frequently their capital and control are of foreign origin. Importers also own most of the principal retail establishments in the cities.

In sharp contrast is the organization of distributive channels for domestic food production and most of the cheap essentials. This commerce flows through the hands of the mixed Spanish and Indian, or Cholo, population of the country; this group does most of the purchasing from country growers, operates the majority of trucks used for short hauls to markets, monopolizes market stalls in La Paz and other cities, and manages small retail shops. The women of the group conduct most of Bolivia's commerce in home-produced and essential articles, and their reputation for commercial shrewdness is great.

Some regions preserve a more primitive organization, with Indians bringing farm produce into the markets for sale and delivering the proceeds to the estate owner whose land they cultivate.

Bolivian commercial development hinges on the future of mining and agriculture. Cholo domination of small-scale trade shows no signs of weakening and in fact is creating a middle class much more numerous than the present Bolivian ruling group.

AGRICULTURE

Bolivia's wide variety of agricultural production has already been described. The grain, *quinoa*, indigenous to the Altiplano, is said to be richer in its vitamin content than any other known cereal. Though Bolivia has been highly favored by nature, its agricultural institutions have been a retarding factor. The organization of production in rural Bolivia has resulted in an inefficient use of labor, retardation of technological improvement, and wasteful use of natural resources.

The pattern of landownership in the country is varied. A rural population of some 2.5 million persons includes approximately 90,000 proprietors. The department of Cochabamba alone contains half this total, which is far above its proportion of agricultural production. On the other hand, the highly fertile Yungas valleys in the Montaña are owned by only 516 individuals. Bolivian land is generally divided into large estates, or *fincas*. In the Lake Titicaca region, such estates usually cover more than 2,000 acres; in the Yungas region and the lowlands they are frequently even larger, some of them containing hundreds of thousands of acres.

The buyer of such a tract also acquires the resident Indian population as a labor force. No Indian is bound to the land by contract or legal requirement or custom as in medieval Europe. He may leave if he finds a better opportunity elsewhere and can manage the expense and transportation problems of changing to a new situation. But his mobility is greatly restricted by his lack of education, specialized skills, and money.

The Indian is assigned a piece of land on the *finca*, which he and the members of his family work and from which they receive the produce. In return, the *colón* works for the *patrón* 4 or 5 days each week, his children tend the landowner's flocks, and on occasion members of the *colón's* family go to the city home of the *patrón* for a term as house servants. Clearly there is no incentive for efficiency here on the part of either *colón* or *patron*. The *colón* and his family must render a certain amount of service. They do not ordinarily share in the master's crops; their welfare is tied instead to the productivity of the small piece of land which they work for themselves on free days. The *patrón*, on the other hand, has what amounts to cost-free labor. He, therefore, has no interest in expensive farm machinery. The labor which might be saved by such innovations yields him no financial advantage. Inefficiency is to be expected from such an organization of production.

Under these conditions the welfare of the worker depends on the character of his *patrón*. Occasionally he receives supplementary cash wages. Sometimes he is assigned land for his own use in rich valleys; at other times his plot is located on a mountaintop. The law requires that schools be established on *fincas*. Schools may be organized, or on the other hand, the school building may be used as a granary. Housing conditions vary greatly; it is the rule that each family construct its own dwelling on the *patrón's* land. A one-room windowless structure with tamped earth floor and thatch roof is customary.

Indian groups, known as *comunidades*, still exist on the Altiplano. These retain independent possession of their land and cultivate it on a communal or individual basis. They maintain herds of sheep and llamas and produce potatoes and other foods; producing their own food and textiles, they possess a high degree of self-sufficiency on a subsistence level. Although the *finca* has much the same independence of the outside world, the owner often has substantial quantities of produce to sell in near-by communities.

Separate Indian landholdings are also numerous in certain restricted areas.

The present organization of agricultural production in Bolivia results in much uncultivated land. Since rural estates are practically tax-free, there is no pressure for production from this source. Cash wage payments, which might create an incentive for additional production and greater efficiency in the use of both land and labor, are rare. Cost-free labor also discourages the purchase and use of agricultural machinery, as has been noted.

The financial stability of the country is directly related to the organization of agricultural production. Present inefficiencies result in the importation of foodstuffs from other countries and create an unnecessary demand for Bolivia's already deficient supplies of foreign exchange. The economic pressures of a higher land tax and a wage system for farm labor would do much to improve the efficiency of Bolivia's agricultural production. It must be recognized, however, that the landowners of Bolivia are in a strong political position and that the *colón* system is rooted in 400 years of history.

Improvements in the efficiency of agricultural operations in large areas of Bolivia would be wasted, however, if the transportation system continued to be inadequate to transport the goods to market. The Bolivian Development Corporation has embarked upon a program of road building; it let its first contract in 1943 for construction of a highly important road from Cochabamba to the important lowland center of Santa Cruz.

This corporation is also establishing camps for the purpose of developing varieties of grains, vegetables, and animals especially suited to the climatic and geographical conditions of the various sections of Bolivia. Although Bolivia is the original home of the potato, the Bolivian potato is usually small and of inferior quality. Sheep are grazed mainly for their wool, although it is planned to introduce meat-producing animals. The hog of rural Bolivia is a scrawny creature by modern standards, and the cattle are mainly lineal descendants of those imported by the conquistadores. Possibilities of advance through introduction of more scientific techniques are enormous.

Education of the rural Indian is obviously important if he is to be expected to adopt modern practices of cultivation and husbandry. But his educational status is an integral part of the *finca* system and consequently raises acute political issues. There is danger, therefore, that the well-conceived program of the Bolivian Development Corporation may fail to achieve its long run goals in the field of agriculture because of the persistence of ancient prejudices and institutions.

FINANCIAL ORGANIZATION

Bolivian financial trends have appeared as both cause and effect of national economic problems. The causal role has been particularly important since the beginning of the Chaco War in 1932.

During the nineteenth century, silver was the chief export product, the basis of the national monetary system, and the sole currency in circulation. Private banks were run mainly by and for the silver miners. A large part of government revenues was derived from minting profits on silver, and times of stress made Gresham's law the most important element in government fiscal arrangements. "Weak" silver coins constantly drove those with higher silver content out of circulation, and the government's preoccupation with reaping the benefits from the situation alternated with its interest in correcting it.

Tin brought Bolivia into the international financial picture after 1900. Adoption of the gold standard in 1908 represented the definitive break with the silver period, and commercial banking and international loans developed as tin exports advanced. Until 1930, Bolivian government finance could depend upon foreign loans to meet chronic deficits and to pay for internal improvements. Foreign investors in tin mines and other private enterprises swelled the flow of foreign currency available to Bolivia. The financial and banking reforms of 1928—the "Kemmerer laws"—represented the high-water mark of Bolivian internationalism. These laws provided that the national currency should be placed on the gold exchange standard and that a central bank should be established to serve as the regulator of the national currency and the means of converting national into foreign money. Bolivia thus became an integral part of the world financial system.

This development came to an abrupt end in 1931 because of conditions both inside and outside Bolivia. Loans by United States investors to the Bolivian government, which totaled $60 million in the 1920's, were used to retire previous British and French loans as well as to cover domestic deficits and effect internal improvements. Service on this debt was suspended in 1930, and new loans were no longer forthcoming. Prices and production of minerals dropped abruptly with the onset of the world depression. Great Britain, the principal market for Bolivian exports and the controlling power in determining world tin prices, went off the gold standard. Mining companies had no interest in making investments in Bolivia, and private investors no longer purchased properties from Bolivians. As a final blow to the country's financial position, the Chaco War began in June, 1932, and produced an insatiable government demand for domestic funds and foreign exchange at the depth of the national depression.

This series of factors revolutionized Bolivian financial procedures and had lasting effects on the economic life of the country. Compulsory exchange deliveries by exporters, which had been required on a minor scale prior to the new legislation of 1928, were reintroduced in a stringent form in 1932 and have continued in effect up to the present. Managed exchanges appeared as soon as Great Britain abandoned the gold standard and have continued since, together with control of imports. Government expenditures, previously at a low level, were enormously expanded by war needs, while revenues dropped; the disappearance of foreign loans forced borrowings from the Bolivian central bank, which inflated the circulating medium and by 1935 made the bank little more than a government bondholding institution. Gold and foreign exchange reserves, reduced to half their 1929 high level by the end of 1931 because of an excess of withdrawals of foreign exchange over purchases, declined almost to the vanishing point by the end of 1934. The factors which caused abandonment of a "free" financial and exchange system also plagued the managed system.

The Bolivian government has never succeeded in solving these problems. The dollar value of the domestic currency unit was only about one-fourteenth as great in 1944 as it had been in 1929, in spite of a reduction of the gold value of the dollar which occurred in the interim. The total of the domestic circulating medium in the hands of the public has expanded in every year since 1931. Prices have risen steadily until they are now at least fifteen times as high as their 1931 levels. Gold and exchange holdings of the Banco Central have expanded until they are now at approximately their 1929 level in terms of dollars; but confidence in the future of the currency is not great, and reserves against circulation are about half what they were in 1929.

This failure is the result of many factors. Inexperience with the operation of exchange controls was a difficulty when they were first introduced, and control techniques still leave room for improvement. But this administrative phase was never vitally important and has become less so with the passage of time.

Loss of sources of foreign capital has been very important. Bolivian development until 1930 was accompanied, and partly caused, by a continuous influx of foreign capital which permitted payment of interest and dividends and importation of a wide range of commodities without exchange difficulties. Although Bolivia's foreign trade statistics show that import values are normally only 50 per cent of export values, this does not mean that the country enjoys a "favorable" balance of trade of this magnitude. Export values are based on prices in consumption markets, which are about 15 per cent above values of exported articles at the Bolivian borders, and import values are f.o.b. country of origin and hence understate delivered prices. Furthermore, mining companies have always paid large sums abroad in interest and dividends, and the increased weakness of the Bolivian monetary unit has caused them to hold all possible sums abroad. Therefore, the balance of payments is very different from the picture given by international trade statistics. Exports must provide virtually all foreign exchange, while previously inward capital movements supplied a large part.

Although foreign capital supplies are no longer available—except for loans made by foreign governments as part of their war program—internal demands for credit have greatly increased even in terms of stable currency units since 1929. Previous railroad building was partly financed by foreign private capital. Present road construction is necessarily for government account. Bolivian towns are united in their clamor for modern lighting, sewage, and paving, improvements which were beyond their hopes in the 1920's. The very fact of inflation has increased the demand for credit. Businessmen, who could hope for no profit from borrowing money and returning it at stable prices, are eager to contract for a maximum of loans to be repaid in a depreciated currency.

Increases in these internal demands for credit have altered the Bolivian fiscal and financial organization. Bolivian banks in 1929 included the semiprivate Banco Central, which engaged in operations with the public, two commercial banks, and two small mortgage banks. These, with their branches, still exist, while the central bank is now entirely owned by the government and the two private banks have increased their nominal capital to a much smaller degree than the national money has depreciated.

Government financial institutions have appeared since 1932. The Banco Minero was created to finance mining development in 1936 and was nationalized in 1939; the central bank was also nationalized in the same year; an agricultural loan department was created in the central bank in 1940 and transferred to the new Banco Agricola in 1942. Various special banks to receive workers' compulsory savings and pension funds have appeared, beginning with the Workers' Insurance and Savings Fund (Coja de Seguro y Ahorro Obrero) in 1935. These banks are the result, not only of increase in demand for and decrease in foreign supply of loans, but also of increased government intervention in all phases of national economic life. The development banks have been created to intervene in national capital markets; the workers' banks, a by-product of labor legislation, perform a similar function.

A newer trend is toward the financial invasion of Bolivia by banks of other countries. A branch of a large Peruvian private bank was opened in La Paz in 1942, and it soon achieved an important position in the commercial banking field. Negotiations concerning establishment of a branch of the Banco de la Nación Argentina are continuing, and Chilean banks have also displayed an interest in the Bolivian money market.

Neighboring Latin American countries have necessarily become more important suppliers of Bolivian imports since 1942; Argentina in particular has expanded its share of the Bolivian market to almost three times its prewar percentage and may now have wrested first place from the United States as a source of Bolivian imports. Part of this change is temporary. Part is a permanent alteration which reflects growth in inter-Latin American trade and resultant increased complexity of both commercial and political relations among Latin American countries.[1]

Government tax and expenditure patterns raise further problems. Although government surpluses have been recorded for numerous years since 1935, these figures do not reveal the essential problem, which is the continuous excess of government cash expenditures over government cash revenues. Only in 1941 was this relationship reversed, and in that year extraordinary receipts and artificially low expenditures combined to create an exceptional situation. Since government external credit disappeared with the depression and internal credit

[1] *Cf.* Ch. VIII.

with the Chaco War, deficits are met through borrowing from the central bank and the money supply is increased annually as a result.

This perpetual unbalance is only partly the result of the lack of foreign loans already discussed. It is also a consequence of the growth of state intervention and of the concept of the welfare state. Government employees are estimated to have trebled or quadrupled in numbers since 1929. Some of them are engaged in providing additional educational and health services. Others are employed to draw up and enforce a constantly increasing body of laws dealing with all fields of national life.

Still more important as a budgetary factor is the inadequacy of the present Bolivian tax system. Bolivian inflation, the result of many factors, is the cause of still others which continue to feed it. Many Bolivian taxes are on a specific basis. These were either not increased as the money in which they were paid lost its command over goods, or they were increased tardily and by inadequate amounts. Mining taxes form the one major exception to this generalization. These were originally increased during the Chaco War by the simple expedient of forcing delivery of foreign exchange at a price favorable to the government for sale at a much higher price. Exchange profits, which provided about 40 per cent of national government revenues in 1936 and 1937, were replaced by additional tonnage export taxes in 1939. These taxes now account for some 50 per cent of national government revenues. Other taxes, especially those on land, have declined to nominal levels as the currency has depreciated. The income-tax revenue, which might have been expected to increase, is negligible.

Not only are taxes inadequate and unbalanced because of their extreme dependence on mining activity, but also they are unnecessarily numerous. Surcharges, special taxes for special funds, and other arrangements which began in the Chaco War and have constantly expanded since result in payment of as many as 14 separate levies before some goods can even be released from customhouses. This adds to the expenses of both the government and the governed.

Exchange controls have also followed an erratic pattern, partly because of the frequent changes of government which followed the Chaco War and partly because of pressure by different groups. Requirements as to compulsory exchange deliveries have varied enormously, although they have tended toward much greater stability in recent years. The whole exchange-rate system has been changed as often as four times in 3 months; "official" rates have frequently differed so much at the same time that the cheapest was four times as favorable as the most expensive; at one time immediately after the Chaco War 13 separate buying and selling rates were in use. This technical problem has become less important with the disappearance of the desperate financial conditions of the Chaco War period, but it has left a legacy of reliance on rather arbitrary exchange manipulation as a governmental device and of distrust in the future value of the monetary unit.

The program of the Bolivian Development Corporation at present offers the most hope for escape from this impasse. Through it, Bolivia has an opportunity to improve its internal economy without resort to inflationary expansion of the domestic circulating medium or unwarranted mortgaging of exchange reserves. Outright contributions of $10,500,000 to the corporation by the Bolivian government are to be supplemented by United States funds extended through the Export-Import Bank on specific developmental projects in an amount not to exceed $15,000,000. These loans, to be made by a United States government institution and not by American private investors, differ from those of the 1920's in other important respects; their use is to be limited to self-liquidating projects, with the Bolivian government contribution earmarked for road building and other internal improvements which may not yield allocable cash returns; specific loans are to be made for particular projects, with revenues earned as security for interest and principal; the Export-Import Bank is to appoint half the corporation's directors and its manager as long as any loans remain outstanding; projects are primarily directed toward conserving Bolivian foreign exchange by increasing Bolivian output of agricultural and other products which can be efficiently produced within the country.

These provisions show the impact of experience. The repayment burden placed on the Bolivian economy is minimized, and loans are safeguarded so as to guarantee their use in directions which will fortify the economy of the country and provide domestic revenue and foreign exchange for delivery to the lender. This represents a highly important change in the nature and terms of foreign lending to Bolivia. Its consequences will be important in determining the future course of Bolivian public finance.

The recent financial history of Bolivia has been conditioned by the inheritance from the Chaco War. The depletion of foreign exchange reserves and gold holdings left the currency in a weak position which could be rehabilitated only by high domestic taxes and reform of the tax system, sharp curtailments in imports to conserve exchange, and tight financial controls over bank credit expansion and currency issues. This difficult path, however, was not followed. Governmental deficits were recurrent, bank credit expansion was encouraged, public works projects were sponsored and paid for by paper-money issues, and the impatience to consume after the war led to excessive imports, especially in 1938, when exports dropped off sharply, so that the opportunity to bring stability to the money and commodity markets was lost. Instead, the period after the Chaco War is characterized by successive devaluations of the currency and a progressive inflation which threatens to become worse. Inflation came, as it always comes, with unequal emphasis on the various commodity markets; some have benefited, others have been pushed to the edge of starvation, and there has as yet been no period of stability which will permit the inequalities to be corrected. Political unrest, labor agitation, and an atmosphere of insecurity were the inescapable consequence of the use of inflation as a disguised method of taxation. However, Bolivian officials made a statesmanlike move in establishing the Bolivian Development Corporation in 1942. From this the people of Bolivia should receive real and lasting benefit.

CONCLUSION

The Bolivian economy moves on two distinct levels, the subsistence level of the Indian farm laborer, and the commercial and industrial life organized around the mining industry. Each has its own problems. The integration of the two is perhaps the most important long-run task facing the country.

A program has been evolved and implemented in Bolivia with a substantial sum of money, which is intended to change subsistence farming into commercial farming so that the foodstuffs of rural Bolivia may be used to satisfy the demands of the Altiplano cities and mining communities. The foreign exchange created by the sale of minerals to the outside world, at present used to a considerable extent for the purchase of foreign foods, can then be spent for other imports, with a resulting substantial increase in the standard of living and welfare in Bolivia.

This program is obviously desirable and should achieve many of its goals in spite of difficulties. Alone, however, it cannot ensure the future economic security of Bolivia.

A substantial decline in either the price or the volume of tin exports from Bolivia will create a critical condition since it is from mineral exports that the Bolivian government obtains (1) half its tax receipts, (2) the reserve for its banking and monetary system (in the form of dollar and pound sterling balances in New York and London), and (3) the means of importing goods. Further, a collapse in the metal markets may deprive rural Bolivia of a part of the food market it is to be organized to serve. Although the number of wage earners in the mines is relatively small, collateral economic activities, transportation, banking, and power generation, employ additional numbers.

The ancient and continuing emphasis on mining has created an unbalanced economy which cannot be corrected by the building of all-weather roads, introducing improved types of agricultural products, and constructing sugar refineries and canning and packing plants, important as these are. More basic changes which are difficult to make in view of the antiquity of certain institutions and attitudes may or may not be attempted.

Nor can any country without foreign investments expect to consume more than the value of its annual output per worker, and the surest route to prosperity is to improve the productivity of the workers. Elementary education for workers in mines, factories, and farms is basic to any long-run program. In the mines, modern safety controls, personnel management, and reasonably sanitary living conditions would seem to be prerequisite to the building up of a stable group of skilled workmen. In rural Bolivia, a fundamental change in land tenure and the reorganization of a system of production in agriculture which is 400 years old would contribute to efficiency.

Twelve years' experience with inflation has demonstrated the ease with which mining revenues can be increased by changing the ratio of the boliviano to the dollar. It has also shown that wages are not promptly adjusted to new and lower values of the boliviano on the foreign exchanges. The government, too, has found that it can profit from the establishment of differential exchange rates and enjoy large windfall gains by depreciating the currency.

This inflationary program has brought its whirlwind of revolution and discontent, but the pressures to continue, once an extreme inflation is under way, are great. Continued reliance on revenues from mineral exports may force further currency depreciation even though the Bolivian government sincerely desires to renounce inflation as a method of financing the activities of the state.

Chapter XI

Brazil's Economy in the War and After

by CORWIN EDWARDS

BRAZIL in 1939 was in an early stage of development from a colonial agricultural economy to an industrial one.[1] Her natural resources were adapted to modern technology, for she possessed rich bauxite and magnesium ores and great possibilities for the development of hydroelectric power in the region which already contained most of her population and industrial activity. Nevertheless, throughout most of her history she had been primarily dependent, except for foodstuffs, upon foreign trade. Prosperity had been derived from a series of export booms in tropical agricultural commodities—sugar, tobacco, cotton, rubber, and coffee. Most manufactured durable goods, industrial equipment, metallic raw materials, and even fuel had been imported. A plantation system, operated by slave labor until 1888, had delayed the development of internal trade, of a domestic market, of a mobile working class, and of an entrepreneurial group.

With population and economic life concentrated upon the seacoast, Brazil's economic life in 1939 was still regional rather than national. (In this connection Chart 8 is of some interest.) Lines of traffic ran inland from the ports toward nowhere, some without interconnection and others joined only to other transportation routes

[1] The information upon which this chapter is based was obtained by the author while serving as Chief of Staff of the American Technical Mission to Brazil between September, 1942, and March, 1943. Insofar as it is derived from published sources, these are indicated by footnotes. Otherwise it is based upon interviews with and data supplied by a considerable number of expert observers, both Brazilian and American.

within the same region. There was no practicable means of land transportation between the capital and the largest cities of the northeast. Domestic trade between regions moved chiefly by sea.

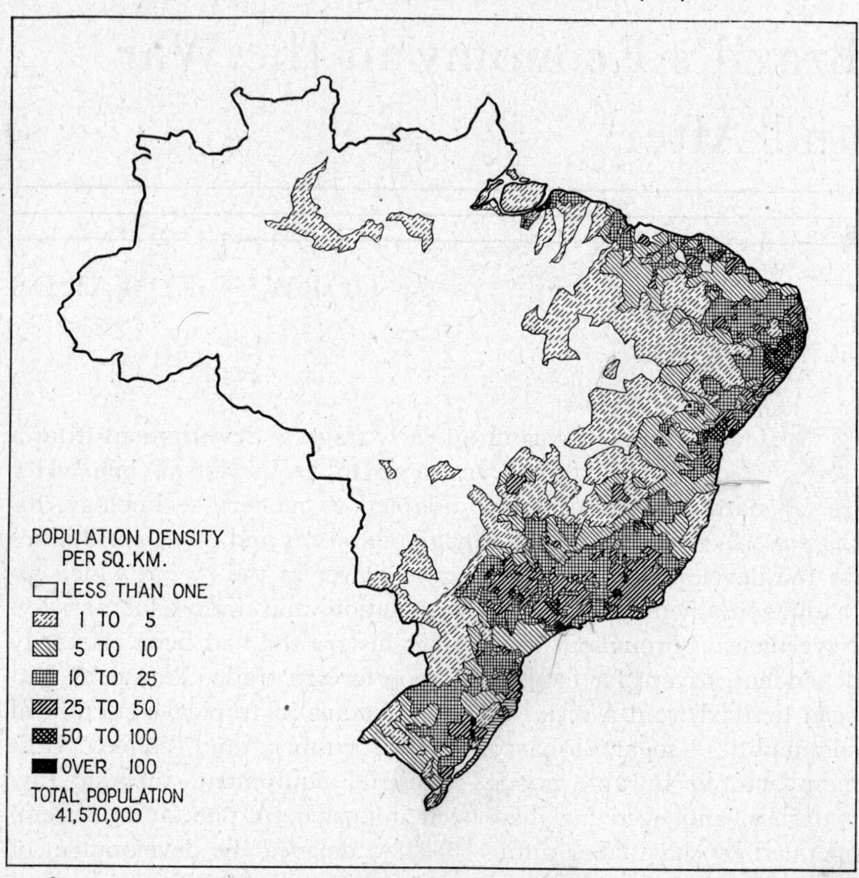

CHART 8.—Brazil. Population density, 1940. (*Coordinator of Inter-American Affairs.*)

THE REGIONAL ECONOMIES

Three regional economies are recognizable in Brazil. The first, covering more than two-thirds of the total area, is an undeveloped back country with a population of one to three persons per square mile.[1] It contains the tropical jungle and rain forest of the Amazon basin, the plains and swamps of Mato Grosso and Goiás, and the deserts of the arid northeast. The whole area has only 20,000 miles of road

[1] *Geografia e Educação, Serviço Grafico do Instituto de Geografia e Estatistica* (Rio de Janeiro, 1942), pp. 124–129.

(mostly unimproved dirt), 1,200 miles of railroad, and slightly more than 3,400 motor vehicles.[1] The total value of its production in 1938,

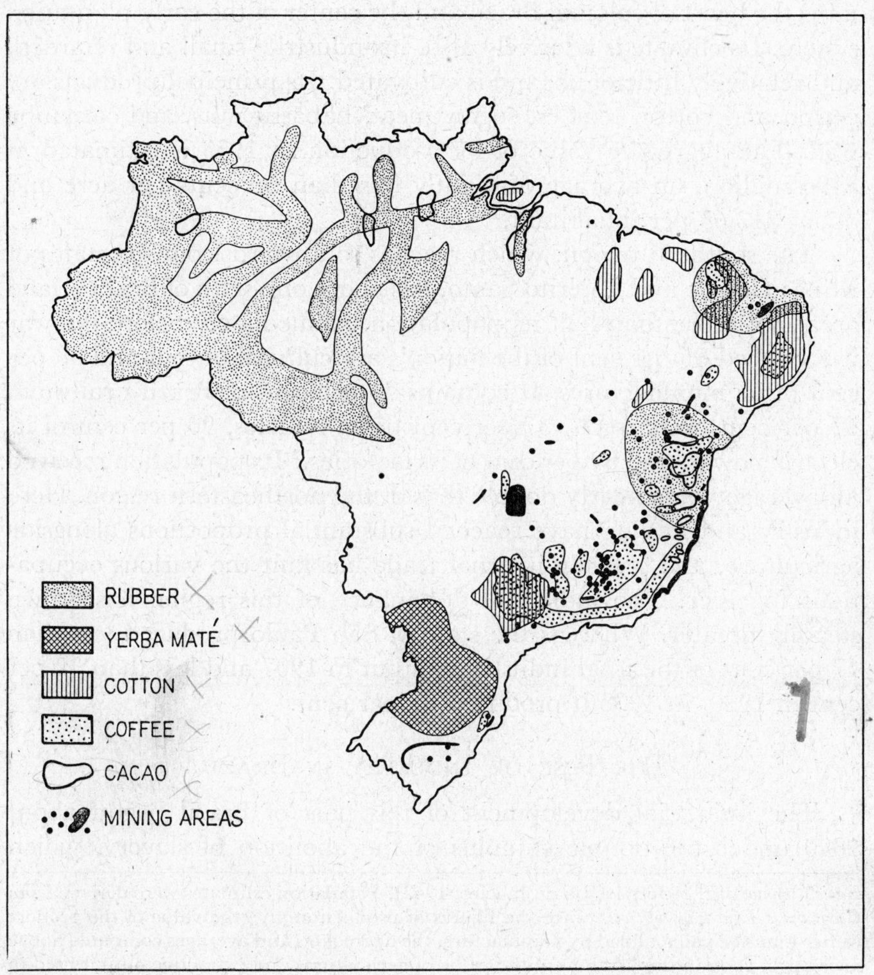

CHART 9.—Brazil. Land use. (*Coordinator of Inter-American Affairs.*)

at a very rough estimate, was slightly more than $38 million, an average of less than 3 cents per acre and only $13.86 per inhabitant.[2]

[1] *Ânuario Estatístico do Brasil* (January, 1940).

[2] For this and other estimates of total incomes and of income per acre and per capita in the regions of Brazil, estimates of industrial production have been taken from Ministério das relaçôes Exteriores, *Brasil*, 1940–41, p. 306 [English translation: *Brazil* 1940–41, *An Economic, Social and Geographic Survey* (Rio de Janeiro, 1941)]; estimates for agriculture and the vegetable extraction industries have been compiled from *Ânuario*, *op. cit.*, and Serviço de Estatistica da Produçao do Ministerio da Agricultura, *Production of the Principal Brazilian*

The northern coastal region, which includes the states from Maranhão on the north coast around to Baía on the east coast, contains the heart of colonial Brazil and the center of the early plantation system. Its climate is relatively arid, its industries small and retarded, and relatively little of its land is cultivated. Its principal products are cotton and cotton textiles, sugar, meat, babassu nuts, and carnaúba wax. The aggregate value of its production in 1938 is estimated at $196 million, an average of slightly less than 52 cents per acre and about $12.63 per inhabitant.[1]

The southern region, which reaches southward from the states of Minas Geraes and Espirito Santo, has about one-sixth of Brazil's land area, but more than half its population. Immediately before the war it produced 85 per cent of the nation's agricultural output and 88 per cent of its manufactures. It contains 74 per cent of Brazil's railways, 67 per cent of its roads, 87 per cent of its vehicles, 90 per cent of its electric power, and 89 per cent of its factories.[2] Its population received an average wage nearly double that of the northeastern region. Here industry and mining have reached substantial proportions alongside agriculture, and a lively internal trade has knit the various occupations together. The industrial dominance of this region has grown steadily greater. Whereas the state of São Paulo produced less than 17 per cent of the total industrial output in 1907 and less than 32 per cent in 1920, in 1938 it produced 43 per cent.

The Rise of Industry in Brazil

The industrial development of this part of Brazil began about 1890 under the double stimulus of the abolition of slavery, which

Basic Commodities, 1936–41 (Rio de Janeiro, 1942). Population estimates were derived from *Geografia e Educação*, *op. cit.* Since the figures of production give the value of the product rather than the value added by manufacture, the aggregates and averages computed above necessarily contain duplications of the value of agricultural and extractive output used in manufacture. This means that the total value of production and the average per acre and per capita must be even less than is here indicated. All dollar figures both in these estimates and elsewhere have been converted from Brazilian currency at the tourist rate of 20 cruzeiros (formerly called *milreis*). This rate is very near the current "free market" rate of about 19.5 cruzeiros to the dollar, a rate which goes back to 1939. In 1938, according to the official report of the Bank of Brazil for 1941, there was no free market rate and the controlled rate was 17.6 (as compared with the present controlled rate of 16.6). It is believed that the roughness of the estimates here involved does not justify the effort to apply an exact exchange rate.

[1] See Charts 9 and 10, for use of land in Brazil.

[2] Percentages, except for manufacturing, are computed from tables in *Ânuario*, *op. cit.* The percentage for manufactures is derived from *Brasil*, 1940–41, *op. cit.*, p. 306.

made possible the development of an internal market, and the prosperity which was derived from the export trade in coffee.

The First World War was a strong stimulant to industrialization. During the war the number of tons of merchandise imported[1] fell

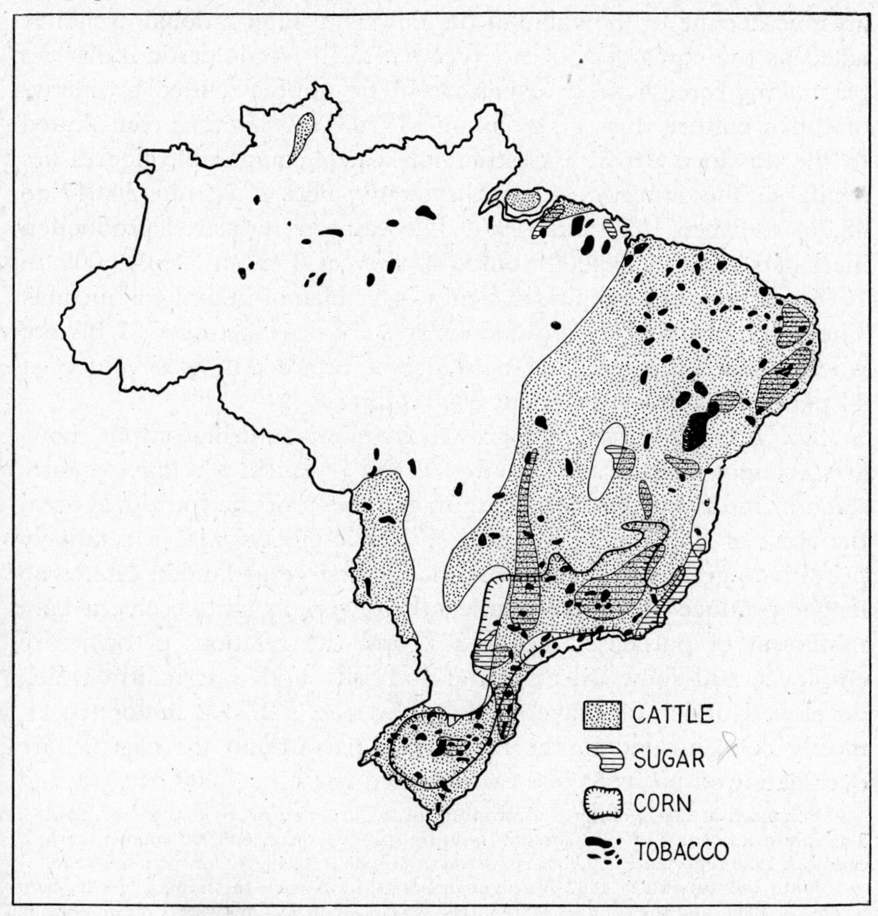

CHART 10.—Brazil. Land use—some important agricultural products. (*Coordinator of Inter-American Affairs.*)

by more than 50 per cent, partly because the productive energy of the warring countries had been diverted to war purposes and partly because of the maritime blockade. Brazilian industry expanded rapidly to serve the domestic market thus presented to it. The value of the nation's industrial production in 1914 has been estimated at about 957,000 contos of reis; by 1918 it had increased to about

[1] *Ânuario, op. cit.*, p. 1359.

2,371,000 contos.[1] In 12 industries for which statistics are available the number of industrial establishments increased from 13,335 to 31,883 during this 4-year period.[2]

Between the two wars the industrial upswing continued. A progressive decline in the value of the milreis in international exchange acted as the equivalent of a protective tariff for domestic industries by making foreign goods expensive.[3] The unprecedented prosperity of coffee culture during the decade 1920–1930 likewise contributed to the advance. In 21 industries for which comparable figures are available the number of establishments increased from 36,017 to 48,769 between 1920 and 1937.[4] The value of industrial production increased from 3,200,000 contos of reis in 1920 to 20,013,000 in 1938,[5] thereby outstripping agriculture as a factor in national income. The value of industrial production in 1938 was just over $1 billion, whereas the corresponding agricultural production was valued at 44 per cent as much, or about $440 million.[6]

The impressive speed of growth in manufacturing output, however, cannot obscure the fact that Brazil is still in a relatively early stage of industrial development. In the heart of the industrial area, the state of São Paulo, industry still rubs elbows with a relatively primitive agricultural society. Although the great landed estates no longer produce all they consume, their workers still receive a bare minimum of purchased necessities, and the relations of owner to employee still show traces of the authority and paternalism which developed under the slave system. The state's 27,000 motor trucks, mostly concentrated in the industrial area around the capital, are overshadowed by its 56,000 two-wheeled carts, its 4,000 oxcarts, and

[1] Simonson in "A Evolução Industrial do Brasil," quoted in *Ânuario*, *op. cit.*, p. 1318. The industrial census of 1907 showed industrial production as 669,000 contos; the next census in 1920 reported 3,200,000. Simonson's estimate is 2,949,000 for the latter year.

Until the autumn of 1942 Brazilian monetary units were the milreis, worth about 5 cents in 1942, and the conto (1,000 milreis), worth about $50 in 1942. A recent revision of the monetary system has changed the milreis to the cruzeiro and has abolished the conto as a unit of reckoning. Figures in the text are given in Brazilian currency wherever historical comparisons are involved, because of the varying exchange rates and the discrepancies between internal and external monetary values; but it should be remembered that there has been a relatively continuous depreciation of the currency for about a century.

[2] *Ânuario*, *op. cit.*, p. 1319.

[3] *Ibid.* p. 1354.

[4] *Ibid.*, pp. 1319–1320.

[5] *Brasil*, 1940–41, *op. cit.*, p. 312.

[6] Vegetable extractive industries were relatively unimportant, valued at only $17,-300,000.

its 5,000 carts pushed by human power.[1] Only 2,540 of the state's 32,128 miles of road are paved or graveled.[2] In one of the principal factories of São Paulo the employees have had, on the average, only 1 year of schooling. In the whole southern area the total annual value of production is still only about $3.34 per acre and $51.26 per inhabitant.

The recent industrial development has taken place primarily in light industries engaged in simple conversion of agricultural raw materials. There is as yet relatively little manufacture of iron and steel, of metal products, of heavy chemicals, of the more complicated industrial apparatus, or even of the more complicated consumers' goods. The foremost manufacturing industries in Brazil are food manufacture and the textile industry, with production valued at $345 million and $231 million, respectively, in 1938. These two industries accounted for nearly 58 per cent of the total value of manufactures in that year. The aggregate value of the products of the next four industries—apparel, chemicals and pharmaceuticals, wood products, and metal manufactures—was about $247 million, or almost 25 per cent more of the national industrial output.[3] No other industry produced as much as $20 million.

Moreover, the typical industrial enterprise is still a small individual proprietorship. At the beginning of 1943 about 2,000 corporate concerns existed in Brazil, and many of those which were corporate in form were actually family enterprises with stock closely held and management personally undertaken by the principal owner. The largest corporation listed for trading upon the Rio de Janeiro Stock Exchange, a railroad, is capitalized at $22,500,000; the second, a dock company, at $18,000,000; and the third, a steel company, at $7,500,000. No other company is capitalized at more than $5,000,000. The listed concerns with less than $5,000,000 capitalization are as follows:[4]

Capitalization	Number
$1,000,000–$5,000,000	20
500,000– 1,000,000	26
100,000– 500,000	130
Less than $100,000	184

[1] *Ânuario, op. cit.*, pp. 278–280.
[2] *Ibid.*, p. 274.
[3] Figures taken or computed from *Brasil*, 1940–41, *op. cit.*, pp. 306–307.
[4] *Ânuario de Valores da Bolsa do Rio de Janeiro* 1938–39, pp. 771–818; *Relatório da Camera Sindical dos Correctores da Bolsa de Fundos Públicos do Rio de Janeiro*, 1941, pp. 210–239.

Except for corporations, figures as to size are available only for the state of São Paulo, which produces about 43 per cent of the nation's industrial output. A 1938 census covering 8,000 establishments there showed that only 29 per cent employed more than 12 workers. This percentage was divided as follows:

Size of Work Force	Per Cent of Total Number of Establishments
12–50	16.5
50–100	4.9
100–500	5.7
500–1,000	0.9
Over 1,000	1.1

Problems Created by the Present War

The economic impact of the present war has centered upon the two outstanding features of the country's prewar economic system. Because of the dependence of the several regions upon foreign and coastal trade, the interruption of trade channels has caused substantial distress. Simultaneously, enforced reliance upon domestic production has fostered a domestic manufacturing boom similar to that of the First World War.

The war has affected Brazil through diversion of foreign industries to war production, diversion of ocean shipping, and blockade of the sea lanes. The first condition has greatly reduced the opportunity to buy many products abroad, particularly metals, machinery, chemicals, and electrical equipment. The other two conditions have reduced the total volume of imports and exports and have diverted to the United Nations and to Brazil's South and Central American neighbors such foreign trade as still continues.

Until March, 1942, these interferences with Brazil's foreign and coastwise trade were felt only moderately. The physical volume of both imports and exports was about 15 per cent lower in 1941 than in 1939. However, largely because of rising prices, the value of exports had risen by nearly 20 per cent and that of imports by nearly 11 per cent. Apart from changes in the volume of shipment of particular commodities required for war, the principal effect of the war during this period was to substitute exchanges with the United States for those with continental Europe. The value of imports from Germany fell from 19 per cent of the total to 2 per cent; that of exports to

Germany from 12 to 1 per cent. Imports from the whole of Europe, which had been 46 per cent of the total, fell to 13 per cent, chiefly from the British Isles; and exports to Europe declined from 46 to 17 per cent. Whereas imports from the United States had been 34 per cent in 1939 and exports to the United States 36 per cent, the corresponding percentages for 1941 were 60 and 57 per cent.[1]

During the first 4 months of 1942, the physical volume of exports declined another 10 per cent, while the volume of imports actually rose by 3 per cent. The aggregate values of both exports and imports rose by 37 and 15 per cent, respectively.[2] However, during the latter part of the year the shipping shortage became much more serious. Brazil was allotted 100,000 tons of imports a month from the United States; and requirements of coal alone were budgeted at 70 per cent of this figure. In the first 9 months of 1942 the actual tonnages of imports and exports for trade with all countries were, respectively, 36 and 39 per cent lower than for the corresponding period of 1939.

The Objectives of Wartime Economic Policy

While showing many similarities to wartime controls in the United States, Brazil's wartime economic policy has had a different emphasis. In a country such as the United States, which could bountifully supply itself with goods were it not for war production, war has stressed the need for diversion of facilities to military uses. In Brazil, where industrial activity is still young and limited and prosperity has traditionally been based upon foreign trade, the most severe restrictions have been imposed from outside, by the obstacles to commerce, rather than from within; and both the war effort and the maintenance of civilian supplies have demanded rapid development rather than diversion of domestic industry. Hence the promotional element in wartime controls has been more conspicuous than in the United States, and there has been less friction among economic groups in getting the program started. There has also been more reason to rescue groups which have lost their normal markets, because in most cases the products and skills of these groups lie in agricultural fields not readily converted to war purposes.

[1] Serviço de Estatística Económica e Financeira do Ministerio da Fazenda, *Comercio Exterior do Brasil, Janeiro a Dezembro*, 1939–41, pp. 4, 5, 8, 9, 13–15.

[2] *Ibid. Resumo Mensal, Janeiro a Abril*, 1941–1942, pp. 4, 9.

The controls arising directly out of the war emergency are aimed at four types of problem.

1. The sudden cutting off of many important markets clogged Brazilian ports, created surpluses of certain export products, brought about or threatened a collapse of prices in the markets still open, and confronted producers with immanent ruin. Such difficulties brought forth efforts to restrict the supply for export, to prevent surpluses from being dumped upon the available markets, and to place a floor under prices. To various degrees, policies of this kind were followed in connection with cocoa, pine wood, oranges, and bananas; and the long-established control over coffee was modified for a similar purpose. Export quotas were established, coupled in the case of cocoa with quotas for purchase by exporters,[1] in the case of pine wood with quotas for mill production,[2] and in the case of bananas with quotas for destruction of domestic supplies.[3] Minimum prices were fixed for export sales. In the case of cocoa there were minimum prices for purchases by exporters as well; but the control over orange exports was accompanied by a sharp decline of domestic prices due to the domestic sale of the unexported surplus. For each product the emergency agencies of control were soon replaced or supplemented by bodies evidently intended to be permanent, which were given broad powers to regulate prices, quantities exported, and domestic supplies.

The cocoa program was assisted in 1942, at the height of the submarine blockade, by an agreement under which the United States government guaranteed the purchase at satisfactory prices of more than half the year's crop. A similar agreement in the same year obligated the United States to buy stipulated quantities of Brazil nuts.

2. The curtailment of international trade also created a scarcity of products customarily imported from abroad. This was particularly true of machinery, metals, and durable consumers' goods. The situation became acute in 1942 during the intensive submarine blockade. Coal imports fell from more than 1,000,000 metric tons in 1941 to less than 600,000 in 1942. Imports of gasoline, fuel oil, and Diesel oil fell from about 883,000 metric tons to 634,000 in the same period.

[1] Resolutions 2 and 8 of the Commission for Defense of the National Economy, dated June 14, 1940, and May 3, 1941. Samples of correspondence supplied by the Baía Cocoa Institute.

[2] Orders 56, 60, and 64 of the commission, dated Feb. 1 and 8 and Mar. 19, 1940. Resolution 1 of the same commission, June 14, 1940.

[3] Decree-laws 3568 and 3621 of Aug. 29 and Sept. 17, 1941; Decree 8327, Dec. 3, 1941.

Shortage of fuel threatened the nation with industrial paralysis. Since 1937 a Federal law has required that consumers make use of at least 20 per cent of domestic coal.[1] However, at the outbreak of the war most of Brazil's industry and a considerable part of Brazil's

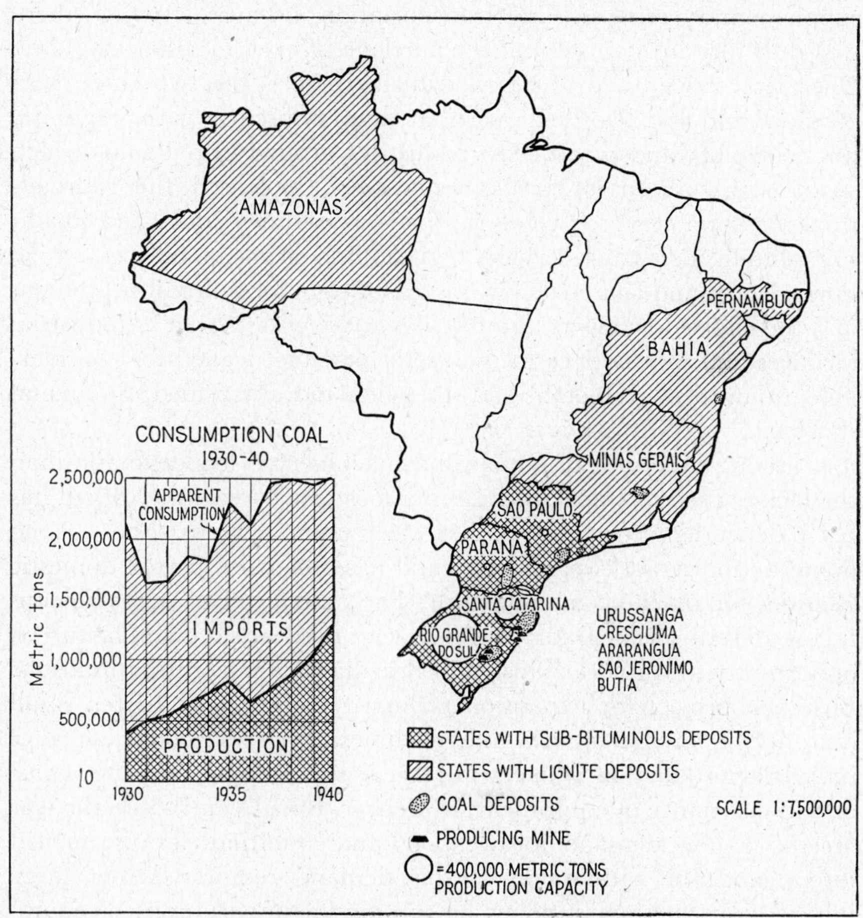

CHART 11.—Brazil. Coal location, production, consumption, imports, and capacity (1930–1940). (*Coordinator of Inter-American Affairs.*)

railroads were primarily dependent upon foreign fuel. All Brazil's automobiles used a carburant in which domestic alcohol was mixed with foreign gasoline. With foreign supplies drastically reduced, such users turned to low-quality domestic coal from Rio Grande do Sul

[1] Decree-laws 1828, July 21, 1937; 2267, Oct. 3, 1940. Before 1937 the use of 10 per cent was required by Decree-law 20089, June 9, 1931.

and Santa Catharina, to firewood, to charcoal, to increased proportions of alcohol in mixture with gasoline, and to such exotic fuels as coffee beans and babassu nuts.[1] The unprecedented haulage required to supply the nation's needs with bulky fuel such as wood created a supplementary crisis in land transportation, because of which there was difficulty in maintaining the carriage of even ordinary supplies. The Central Railroad of Brazil, which connects the two chief cities of São Paulo and Rio de Janeiro, at times refused to carry anything but foodstuffs and wood. The industries around São Paulo, which customarily use motor trucks extensively, increased the railroad-transportation crises by using railroads where they could and sought to maintain their truck services by installing gazogene devices, which burn alcohol and charcoal. The increased need for railroad equipment and the efforts to convert automobiles and trucks as well as industrial furnaces and locomotives to the use of new fuels called for considerable quantities of metal, and this demand intensified the metal shortage.

Although the lack of metals and machinery is less dramatic than the lack of fuel, its impact has been almost as far-reaching. Brazil has been dependent for most of her steel upon imports. She has no domestic sources of copper or tin and has only very limited domestic facilities for machine manufacture. The cutting off of miscellaneous imports of all sorts created a consumers' need and a manufacturers' opportunity for rapid expansion of Brazilian manufacturing industry. But each project for expansion ordinarily requires at least a small quantity of foreign metals and machines. Even the continuance of industrial production is likely to require such supplies for the repair and maintenance of equipment. Moreover, Brazil's entry into the war created a new demand for weapons and munitions for the armed forces, and the satisfaction of this demand required either large importations of such supplies or substantial importations of equipment and metals to make them in Brazil. Thus both military and civilian needs were focused upon the metals.

The controls set up to deal with such problems were intended to increase scarce supplies, to ration their use, and to prevent runaway price movements. Where possible, substitution of domestic products for those formerly imported was required. Prewar requirements that

[1] See Chart 11 for location of coal production and imports of coal.

alcohol be mixed with petroleum[1] and domestic coal with foreign coal[2] were intensified and new rules were made for the use of substitutes instead of tin plate and for the use of caroa, a native fiber, in place of jute.[3] Private motorcars were wholly deprived of gasoline and alcohol; and, in 1942, trucks and taxis were allowed not more than 70 per cent of their 1941 consumption.[1] Conversion of motorcars to the use of producer gas from charcoal was encouraged.[4] Nonessential civilian consumption of petroleum products in 1942 was about 46 per cent below the previous year.[1] In 1941, export of Santa Catharina coal was forbidden, and in 1942 the government undertook to ration 75 per cent of the nation's coal production in order to ensure supplies for transportation and public-utility services.[3] Priority schedules for the purchase and sale of metallic raw materials were developed.[5] For such imports as tin plate and petroleum, efforts were made to establish maximum prices. Importation of various chemicals, metals, and metal products was licensed in order to ration the use of these commodities.

3. The sudden large demands for certain war materials also created special problems. In some cases controls were instituted to make sure that supplies should be available for domestic consumption instead of being drained away to other countries. This was true for cotton yarn, cottonseed oil, meat, and alcohol. In other cases the efforts of foreign governments, particularly the United States, to encourage enlargement of the available supply and its use for war purposes resulted in the establishment of governmental monopolies or close governmental supervision and in public efforts to set prices high to encourage an increase of output. Rubber, particularly, became the focus of far-reaching arrangements to establish new communities of rubber gatherers in the upper Amazon, to limit domestic use of rubber in order to restrict the production and export of nonessential manufactures, and to sell the exportable surplus of crude

[1] *Código de Minas e Legislação Referente a Petroleo, Gases Naturais, Rochas Betuminosas e Perobetuminosas* (Rio de Janeiro 1940); Decree-law 3236, May 7, 1941.

[2] Decree-laws 20089, June 9, 1931; 1828, July 31, 1937; 2667, Oct. 3, 1940; 7511, July 8, 1941; 3605, Sept. 10, 1941; 3837, Nov. 18, 1941; 3986, Dec. 30, 1941; 4613, Aug. 23, 1942.

[3] Decree-law 1950 of Dec. 30, 1939; Resolutions 4 and 5 of the Commission for Defense of the National Economy; Order 285 by the same commission.

[4] Decree-laws 1125, Feb. 28, 1938; 2526, Aug. 23, 1940; 4251, July 24, 1942; 4499, July 20, 1942.

[5] Decree-law 4499, July 20, 1942.

rubber to the United States.[1] The United States also arranged to buy the exportable surplus of babassu nuts and oil, burlap, castor beans and oil, cotton linters and hull fiber, ipecac, and rotenone; and by agreement with the United States, minimum purchase prices were announced to encourage the production for export of rubber, quartz crystals, bauxite, beryl ore, chromite, ferronickel, industrial diamonds, carbonadoes, manganese ore, mica, titanium, and zirconium.

4. A counterpart of the difficulties in trade has been an inflationary price movement which has intensified the problem of livelihood for the working population. Since Brazil's exports of war supplies, plus the emergency purchases of its former export crops, have brought a larger revenue than can be spent for the available imports, Brazil has accumulated unusually large dollar balances in New York and sterling balances in London. Under exchange control these balances are held by the Bank of Brazil, which pays for them with domestic currency. The consequence of such payments, plus issues to finance the government deficit, was an increase in 3 years of 73 per cent in the amount of paper money in circulation in Brazil.[2] This money, distributed throughout the population through the productive processes of those who produce for export, became available to buy a quantity of goods which could not be increased by imports but had actually decreased wherever it depended upon sea-borne trade. Such increases in domestic manufacture as were possible in spite of the shortage of metals and fuels afforded only a minor offset to the inflationary tendencies inherent in this situation. In consequence, by the beginning of 1942 the cost of living had evidently risen to levels 25 to 35 per cent higher than before the war. As this rise became apparent, it was accentuated by the usual tendency to buy in anticipation of one's needs on a rising market; and, so far as imported commodities were concerned, the tendency was strengthened by the knowledge that when current supplies of some commodities were exhausted replacements could no longer be had.

The rise in the cost of living evoked various efforts to protect the consumer against price increases upon necessities of life. Such efforts were devoted first to rents and the principal foodstuffs (especially

[1] Decree-law 5044, Dec. 4, 1942.
Decree-law 4221, Apr. 1, 1942.

[2] Notes in circulation in October, 1939, were not quite 5,000,000,000 milreis (cruzeiros); in October, 1942, the corresponding figure was 8,644,000,000.

meat), and coal. Later they were broadened to cover all important commodities.

The Coordination of Wartime Controls

Many of the controls instituted early in the war were set up case by case and were exercised by special agencies for particular industries. As the area of control broadened, there was increased attention to the need to deal with particular problems in relation to one another. Hence a series of agencies was established with successively broader authority to coordinate existing and future controls.

THE COMMISSION FOR SUPPLY

The first such agency was the Commission for Supply, created in September, 1939, for the purpose of regulating production and commerce in foods, raw materials, drugs, medicines, construction materials, fuel, lubricants, and other articles of prime necessity. This commission consisted of representatives of various governmental departments appointed by the President. It was empowered to fix maximum prices, to make inventories of stocks, to purchase commodities at home and abroad, to distribute these commodities at cost prices, and to requisition necessities and provide for their distribution. Its first action, in October, 1939, was to fix the wholesale and retail prices of more than 200 food items.[1] In practice, its activity is said to have been confined to the Federal District. After the organization of a new Commission for Defense of the National Economy, with functions of broader scope, the Commission for Supply became relatively inactive and was abolished by law in July, 1940.[2]

This first national effort to check an increase in the cost of living was supplemented in the autumn of 1939 and subsequently by various state and local activities directed toward the same end. The state of São Paulo, for example, authorized[3] its municipalities to prevent price increases and speculation in necessities by any necessary steps including requisitions, control of the movement of goods, and price fixing. A state commission was set up to superintend such activities, and infractions of the controls were made punishable by fines of

[1] The commission was created by Decree-law 1607, Sept. 16, 1939. The list of food prices fixed in October is set forth in Hungria, Nelson, *Dos Crimes Contra a Economia Popular*, Rio de Janeiro, 1939, pp. 235–243.

[2] Decree-law 2449, July 25, 1940.

[3] State Decree 10498, Sept. 19, 1939.

$10 to $2,500. In the capital of the state, price increases were forbidden except when based upon costs, a rent ceiling was set, efforts were made to produce a low-priced bread, and salt was informally rationed. Price control commissions were likewise established in Porto Alegre, in the Federal District[1] and in Pará.[2] In some cases the work of these bodies has supplemented Federal controls designed to keep down particular prices; in other instances, while the commissions were trying to keep retail prices down, other control agencies were trying to increase the returns to producers.

The Commission for Defense of the National Economy

The Commission for Defense of the National Economy was established by law 2 weeks after the Commission of Supply.[3] The law creating it asserted that the disturbances of the war were causing the free functioning of market mechanisms to disappear in nearly all countries. A three-man commission appointed by the President was authorized to coordinate the work of Federal, state, and municipal boards created to regulate production and supply within the country, and to set up general directives and norms which, after the President's approval, would be carried out by the appropriate governmental authority. The field of policy for the commission's consideration was defined as follows: making inventories of stocks of merchandise, encouraging exportation of the merchandise more easily salable abroad, facilitating direct agreements with foreign governments concerning exchange of commodities, reviewing the export and import trade in order to afford a regular supply of necessities for consumption and for essential industries, revising the existing restrictions upon the production and exportation of raw materials and foodstuffs, and deliberating upon matters of ocean and land shipping, including their respective freight rates. In July, 1942, the commission was given the power to control the prices and distribution of metals required by the nation's industry.

The commission functioned actively until July, 1942, and issued about 100 decisions which had the force of legal orders. It exercised detailed control over the production, prices, and exportation of pine

[1] The latter was set up on Sept. 12, 1941, by the authority of the Commission for Defense of the National Economy. See Order 203 by that commission and Resolution 17 by the mayor of Rio de Janeiro, Dec. 26, 1941.
[2] State Decree 4155.
[3] Decree-law 1641, Sept. 29, 1939.

wood; fixed maximum prices upon tin plate and made rules as to the use of substitutes for it; inventoried the stocks of metallic materials; restricted exports of bananas, oranges, lard, vegetable oils, and silk and cotton textiles; restricted the exportation of used textile machinery; required the use of a proportion of domestic textile fibers in various textile products; assigned to certain state governors control over the manufacture and sale of rosewood essence; regulated the transportation and prices of foodstuffs; established norms for the marketing of cocoa; fixed export prices of tobacco and prices paid to planters by dealers, and required that the Spanish tobacco monopoly make all its purchases from the Tobacco Institute.

CONTROL OVER CONSTRUCTION MATERIALS

During 1942 special efforts were made to check the rising prices of construction materials. A commission to control these prices was planned in May and established in September. The tariff upon imported cement was suspended in August for a 90-day period, and the suspension was subsequently renewed for 90 days more.[1] The Federal Purchasing Department was authorized to requisition material which might be required for the maintenance of public-utility services and to compensate the owners at prices which did not allow more than 20 per cent profit.[2]

CONTROL OVER EXPORTS AND IMPORTS

As difficulties in foreign trade multiplied because of the war, a Department of Exports and Imports was established by law in the Bank of Brazil.[3] It was authorized not only to extend credit but also to buy and sell goods as agent or for its own account, to help the government buy, and to help make international agreements. Subsequently it has acquired the functions of granting licenses for export and of making recommendations on behalf of Brazil as to the allocation of the shipping space available for imports. Since Brazil's economy still depends primarily upon foreign trade, the authority over exports and imports has involved unusually wide powers in guiding the adjustment of the nation to the war. By limiting export licenses for various commodities to the surplus above domestic needs, the bank

[1] *News Bulletin of the American Brazilian Association*, New York City, Dec. 12–18, 1942. Decree-laws 4588, Aug. 15, 1942; 4598, date not available.

[2] Correio da Manhã, Aug. 21, 1942.

[3] Decree-law 3293, May 21, 1941.

established a flexible control comparable to the formal controls set up by the government over a few products. By determining the relative emphasis which Brazil is to place upon shipping space for various types of imports and for imports destined to different customers, it has achieved in practice considerable authority as to the allocation of imported supplies.

In the summer of 1943 a system for allocation of imported products was established by the Coordinator of Economic Mobilization in collaboration with this department of the bank.

THE COORDINATOR OF ECONOMIC MOBILIZATION

About a month after Brazil entered the war, a decree abolished the Commission for Defense of the National Economy and provided for a Coordinator of Economic Mobilization responsible directly to the President[1] and with authority over nearly all phases of economic life. The statute provided that all economic resources, including human labor, are mobilized in the service of Brazil. To this end the Coordinator was authorized to regulate all industry, including mining and agriculture, in order to enable it to produce with maximum efficiency; to control imports and exports of raw materials and semimanufactured goods; to coordinate transportation; to ration fuel and energy; to determine the utilization of labor; to investigate costs, prices, and profits and establish maximum and minimum prices and wages; to determine conditions of sale; to license producers and dealers; to restrict the amount of merchandise and services sold for public consumption; to govern the operation of public administrations and private enterprises; to take over the management of private enterprises; to requisition merchandise or services; and to provide for the purchase, loan, or rental of materials and equipment needed for operation of expansion. As evidence that these powers were not intended to be narrowly interpreted, the Coordinator was likewise empowered to perform all necessary and appropriate acts for safeguarding the interests of the public and enhancing the return from economic resources and to propose any additional measures appropriate to the defense of the nation's economy.

In January, 1943, the Coordinator's powers to issue rules governing the activities of the public administrations and private enterprises, to provide for material and equipment for industry, and to requisition

[1] Decree-law 4750, Sept. 28, 1942.

were made subject to prior approval by the President of the republic. However, he was given an additional specific duty to provide for the supply of commodities to the civilian population, with specific authority to fix minimum prices upon necessities at levels which would enable producers to recover their cost of production, to provide for the establishment of sales depots in order to ensure the observance of maximum prices, and to adopt measures to facilitate transport and minimize spoilage.[1]

The Coordinator's chief preoccupations at the outset of his work, as indicated by his official acts,[2] apparently were to relieve the nation's fuel shortage and to provide for an adequate supply of necessary consumable goods (particularly food staples) at reasonable prices. One of his first acts was to take control of the importation, processing, storage, distribution, and prices of liquid fuels. In the Federal District and São Paulo he created commissions to ration liquid-fuel supplies, to requisition stocks, to give technical aid in the adoption of substitutes, and to propose a schedule of priorities applicable to consumption. He sought to enlarge the supply of alcohol by authorizing the Institute for Sugar and Alcohol to requisition brandy held by middlemen and likewise the wooden containers in which to ship it and by permitting the production of alcohol, regardless of quotas, by any industrial enterprise for its own use and by any other consumer for his own use as a carburant, provided, in the latter case, that the alcohol was made from oranges. He increased the quotas of motor fuel allowed to the Federal District and the states of Rio de Janeiro, Minas Geraes, and Espirito Santo. He set up a commission to increase coal production in Santa Catharina and a commission to ration and fix the prices of solid fuels in São Paulo. He appointed a delegate to control the production and distribution of peat in and near the Federal District.

In addition to appointing a technical service to consider means of increasing and improving the nation's food supply, he set up a commission to create a standard type of better and cheaper bread, enlarged quotas for sugar production in the southern states, authorized the construction of new sugar mills in the states of the north coast, the far south, and the interior, to which shipment of sugar had become

[1] Decree-law 5176, Jan. 7, 1943.

[2] The discussion which follows is based upon a file of the orders issued by the Coordinator prior to mid-February, 1943.

difficult, and rationed sugar in Rio de Janeiro. To enlarge the meat supply, he temporarily prohibited the slaughter or processing of beef in central Brazil for export, fixed prices of cattle on the hoof in an effort to persuade stockmen not to withhold animals from the market, fixed prices at slaughterhouses throughout Brazil to keep down the cost of living, and established requirements as to minimum stocks and daily quotas for slaughterhouses in the Federal District in an effort to regularize supplies. However, he likewise found it advisable to recognize the requests of certain food producers for protection. He created an agency to regulate the starch industry, its purpose being to find uses for supplies of manioc and to fix production quotas for both planters and producers. He established a new tax on maté, to be used to promote the development of cooperatives among producers and to finance growers through such cooperatives; and he set up an agency empowered to create such cooperatives.

The Coordinator has also frozen the rents of business buildings; required manufacturers to print maximum prices on the wrappers of pharmaceuticals; issued new regulations for the marketing of quartz crystals, formerly controlled by other agencies; provided for control of prices of lead ores and for efforts to expand lead production; required consumers to turn in old containers made of strategic materials in buying goods packaged in new ones; created an agency to promote increased use of Brazilian textile fibers, with power to fix quotas of use by manufacturers, to enforce conformity to official prices, and to control the trade in used sacks; and set up a service to mobilize labor for the rubber areas of the Amazon and to provide assistance to the workers transferred there and to their families.

PROMOTION OF INDUSTRIAL DEVELOPMENT

Two agencies set up by the Coordinator appeared to be of exceptional importance. The first, established in November, 1942, is the industrial-production section, authorized to guide and promote industrial production, to establish priorities for fuel, electric power, raw materials, transportation facilities, and labor, and to simplify and standardize products. This section is conceived primarily as an agency to enlarge Brazil's industrial output and to help solve the various technical problems involved, but its authority to ration makes it likewise the central agency for coping with industrial problems which are due to unavoidable shortages. However, the most crucial of the present shortages, those in fuel, are dealt with by the Coordinator through agencies already existing rather than through this section.

CONTROL OVER PRICES

The second key agency was that established for control of prices. The Coordinator's first order dealt with the price of meat, and various other price problems have been involved in special orders. On Nov. 30, 1942, he established a price section with general authority to study prices, costs, and profits and to develop norms for price controls designed to avoid inflation. The section was instructed to consider both general freezing of prices and orders applicable to particular prices; both direct controls and controls operating through such indirect means as limitations of profits, rationing, and sale of governmentally held stocks of goods when prices rose. On Jan. 8, 1943, the Coordinator chose to freeze the prices of all commodities and of transportation at the levels prevailing on Dec. 1, 1942, with provision for such later readjustments as might be needed. The order likewise provided that minimum wages prescribed by law should be increased by 25 per cent in the capitals of states, in the Federal District, and in the territory of Acre, and by 30 per cent elsewhere. In December, 1943, the prices of commodities for export were specifically excluded from the general program of price freezing.

The instruments of price control originally established were a Federal Price Commission in the Federal District and local price commissions in every municipality.[1] The federal agency was to control prices in the Federal District, to serve as an appellate body, and to coordinate the prices established by the local commissions with a view to developing a proposal for a nation-wide system of maximum prices. The local commissions were to determine prevailing prices on Dec. 1, to hear charges of violation of the law, and to recommend necessary price adjustments to the Coordinator.

As originally planned, the Federal Price Commission and the municipal commissions both contained equal numbers of representatives of sellers and consumers. Soon state price commissions were established to control the municipal bodies and were given member-

[1] A municipality is an administrative area roughly comparable to a county in the United States.

ship or advisory representation on the Federal Price Commission. At the same time various government departments were given representation on the Federal Price Commission, and provision was made for advisory subcommittees of that body containing persons technically informed about various commodities, representatives of institutes and boards which have authority over particular industries, and spokesmen for various interest groups.

An early step in the application of the general price order was the establishment of sales depots through which the Coordinator offered necessities to the public at the official maximum prices. By the end of January, 1943, three such depots had been opened in the Federal District. In August, 1943, the central agency for the control of prices was abolished at the recommendation of the official in charge, and a selective program of decentralized price fixing for particular commodities was substituted. The changes in form of organization apparently expressed an increase in the emphasis placed upon indirect limitation of price increases through efforts to increase production, improve transportation, and ration commodities.

Tendencies Likely to Outlast the War

Although the duration and course of the war must necessarily influence the postwar economic development of Brazil, certain tendencies and problems are already apparent. They are due partly to the nature of the wartime adjustment and partly to the underlying character of the Brazilian economy.

Most obvious is the tendency toward an increasing industrial organization, particularly in the south. The tempo of industrial development has been accelerating for half a century. Brazil's resources and geography are better suited to an economy of light metals, electric power, and transportation by automobile and airplane than they are to the age of steel, coal, and railroads which is passing. The determination to take full advantage of industrial possibilities is general among the nation's leaders. It is probable, however, that the immediate result of the peace will be the collapse of some industrial establishments which have flourished during the war. Rising prices, avid demand for goods, and lack of foreign competition have promoted expansion even by concerns with costs so high that they cannot maintain themselves when imports are once more available. The severity of foreign competition will depend largely upon the commercial and financial policies of governments. It will be intensified if industrial countries subsidize their exports and diminished if the government of Brazil maintains high protective tariffs. It will increase if there should be a rise in the exchange value of Brazilian currency and decline if the exchange rate falls. There is little likelihood, however, that industrial production will recede to the prewar level or that it will fail soon to resume its upward tendency.

Continued use of the government as an agency to promote industrial development is also probable. The tradition of governmental assistance for trading groups, which is characteristic of a country which has been dependent upon export markets, has evolved into a practice of active governmental support for the establishment of industrial enterprises. The nation's largest steel plant, now under construction, has been promoted and financed by the Federal government. Such policies appear to have the support of all important economic groups.

Whether or not the quasi-public control of prices and production will continue after the war is still problematical. In 1938 the government adopted a statute which specifically prohibited many forms of price fixing and restriction of output. Such a policy in the industrial field has been appropriate to a setting in which efforts to diminish the market supply have usually benefited foreign concerns at the expense of small domestic rivals and domestic consumers. Until the present war, the recognized restrictive controls upon marketing in Brazil were limited to a few industries: (1) those producing a few major agricultural commodities upon the profitable sale of which the country's welfare was heavily dependent *viz.*, coffee, sugar and alcohol, salt, maté, and rice; (2) the petroleum industry, in which an endeavor was made to supervise closely the activities of foreign oil companies; (3) the coal and cereals industries, in which the government undertook to force the use of a minimum amount of the domestic rather than the imported product. Nevertheless, some of the controls established to meet war conditions have already been reorganized in forms apparently intended to be permanent, and substantial portions of the authority to administer such controls have been granted to private-interest groups which may be expected to urge continuance of the system. It is significant, however, that the wartime controls which appear to have acquired a permanent character govern agricultural products which are sold largely in export markets.

Obstacles to Industrial Development

The speed with which Brazil's industry will develop after the war must depend largely upon the degree of success achieved in coping with existing obstacles.

The most obvious difficulty is the lack of transportation. So long as there is no continuous transportation along the coast, industrial life must spread outward from the seaports, each port area being relatively independent of the others; and parts of the coastal area not well equipped with harbors are likely to remain undeveloped. So long as there is lack of transportation inland, there can be no substantial industrial or agricultural development of the interior; and without such development there can be no economic basis for the extension of the means of transport. Escape from this dilemma appears to require either a long-range plan of public investment, or a sudden rush of settlers like those who pursued gold to California, or the creation of means of transport less expensive and more flexible than a system of railroads and highways.

A second difficulty is lack of fuel. Domestic coal is of poor quality and is available principally from distant Rio Grande do Sul and Santa Catharina, from which it must be shipped by water to the industrial area. Somewhat better coal deposits, in very thin veins, are now beginning to be developed in Paraná. However, the primary sources of coal have been foreign. Similarly, Brazil has been entirely dependent upon foreign sources for gasoline, fuel oil, and petroleum lubricants; and recent discoveries of petroleum in Baía have not as yet removed this dependence. Even in ordinary times wood furnishes the power for about 30 per cent of Brazil's locomotive mileage.[1] Before the war motorcars were operating in Brazil on mixtures which contained about 12 or 13 per cent of alcohol in São Paulo and the Federal District and as much as 98 per cent of alcohol in Alagoas.[2]

A third difficulty is the lack of capital, both foreign and domestic. In the past, Brazil's largest industrial enterprises have been financed from abroad, but there are difficulties in the continuance of such a system. Foreign investors hesitate to place money in Brazil because of the long history of depreciation of the currency and because of the more recent systems of exchange control which have been used not

[1] Computed from *Ânuario, op. cit.*, p. 257, figures for 1937 and 1938.

[2] Serviço de Estatística Economica e Financeira do Ministerio da Fazenda, *Statistical Tables*, 1932–1939 (Rio de Janeiro, 1941), pp. 143–144.

only to impose special taxes upon the payment of dividends abroad but likewise, at times, to withhold exchange desired for such purposes. Foreign investment in public-utility enterprises is precluded by the fact that the Brazilian government adheres to the policy of basing the rate of return upon the investment in domestic currency, a standard which, because of the persistent decline in the exchange value of the milreis, provides an extremely low return upon foreign funds invested.

Foreign investment is also limited by various legal restrictions designed to avoid foreign control of resources which are economically or politically strategic and to enlarge the opportunities to native Brazilians. Foreigners may not

1. Establish corporations without specific governmental authorization.

2. Exploit mines or water power, either individually or through corporations.

3. Be owners, shareholders, directors, or editors of enterprises which publish newspapers or magazines.

4. Establish public-utility enterprises unless a majority of the officials are Brazilian and all executive authority is in Brazilian hands.

5. Establish deposit banks or insurance companies unless all shares are held by Brazilians.

6. Build or own ships of Brazilian registry, or act as pilots in ports, rivers, or lakes, or engage in the business of transporting merchandise by water between points in Brazil.

7. Engage as individuals in industry or commerce within 150 kilometers of a national land boundary, or establish an industrial or commercial company there unless Brazilians by birth are a majority of its members and exercise all its executive authority.

8. Operate any transportation or communication enterprise within the same zone.

9. Acquire land within 30 kilometers of a national land boundary or live within that zone without authorization.

10. Own agricultural land without either having established permanent residence as a farmer or worked in agriculture in Brazil for at least 1 year.

11. Engage in any liberal profession, except in cases in which reciprocal rights to do so have been established by international treaty; or obtain recognition in Brazil for professional degrees received abroad.

12. Be auctioneers or brokers.
13. Fish in Brazilian waters.
14. Constitute more than one-third of the employees, or of any class of employees, or receive more than one-third of the pay roll, of any industrial, commercial, or public-utility enterprise (except in extractive industries other than mineral industries and in rural industries engaged in processing local agricultural products), unless the government finds that there is a shortage of suitable Brazilian labor.

The need for foreign capital would be less acute if there were better means of raising domestic capital. The Brazilian with money to invest turns usually to land, urban real estate, or government bonds. Until the revision of laws concerning corporations and security exchanges in 1939, the purchase of stock in a corporation was looked upon with distrust as a form of investment; and even today, though the interest in industrial securities has been growing rapidly, the previous tradition is still strong. Most new enterprises are launched by men who themselves possess the necessary money or who can obtain it from their immediate friends and acquaintances. To a limited extent, the banks and the notaries public act as advisors to small business interests as to where investment funds can be found or placed. In larger operations, security brokers approved by Federal or state governments float new issues upon the organized exchanges of Rio de Janeiro, São Paulo, and Porto Alegre and, to a very limited extent, upon a few smaller exchanges. However, a substantial interest in industrial issues has developed among customers of the exchanges only since 1939, and there are not yet any systematic arrangements among the brokers for the joint handling of large issues in one locality or for mobilizing the brokers of various cities in a joint effort. It is still substantially true that no part of the country can readily develop its enterprises except with local capital and that the assets of people who individually have not much to invest are scarcely placed in industry at all. Though the expansion of various companies under the stimulus of war has enhanced the growth of interest in industrial investments, real estate and government bonds are still the dominant outlets for savings.

The lack of a private market for investments is only slightly offset by the use of public funds. At the end of 1941 the Bank of Brazil had among its assets about $118 million in industrial, agricultural, and trade loans; and since such loans may run for as long as 5 years and may thereafter be renewed, they may supply some investment funds as well as working capital. Also important in amount are the funds of the Federal pension system, which collects 6 per cent on the annual pay roll of Brazilian employees—a total of nearly $28 million in 1939—and which holds total investments of about $81 million. Investment of these funds is determined by the government; at present they are devoted primarily to industrial housing.[1]

A fourth difficulty involved in the expansion of Brazilian industry is the lack of an adequate labor supply. Brazil has no class of unemployed industrial workers. Any considerable expansion of its industries must either draw people from nonindustrial occupations or attract immigrants from outside the country.

In so far as resources, capital, transportation, and technical skill can be mobilized to establish industrial enterprises in the north, a considerable supply of labor can be made available by transfer from the relatively unproductive occupations in which many people of the north coast are now trying to earn a living. To a limited extent the need for labor is now being met, at the cost of an increased unbalance in the distribution of Brazil's population and resources, by migration from these states to the southern industrial areas. However, Brazil's industries probably will continue to need immigrants as they did from 1920 to 1940, a period in which nearly 700,000 foreigners entered São Paulo State.[2] At present, Brazil practically prohibits immigration by industrial workers.[3] Presumably this policy was adopted in order to cope with the serious political problems which arose because of the compact settlement of Germans and Japanese in various parts of the nation.

The problem of labor supply is one of skill as well as one of numbers. Several factors apparently limit the present skill of Brazilian labor. First is the lack of the educational training and trade apprenticeship necessary for the more difficult mechanical occupations, for foremen, and for accountants, engineers, and other technical specialists. The scarcity of skilled foremen is probably responsible, in part,

[1] *Brasil*, 1940–41, *op. cit.*, p. 73.

[2] *Ânuario*, *op. cit.*, p. 1307.

[3] Decree-law 3175, Apr. 7, 1941, grants permanent admission only to citizens of Portugal and the United States; husbands, wives, and parents of persons born in Brazil; agricultural workers and farmers; specially qualified technicians; eminent persons; and persons who deposit the equivalent of $20,000 in foreign money in the Bank of Brazil. In 1941 fewer than 10,000 persons were granted permanent admission, according to the Ministry of Labor.

for the fact that the individual operations in a Brazilian plant are often better than the aggregate result. The lack of engineers appears to be responsible for the fact that many plants have not the designs which would make them independent of imported equipment. The lack of accountants is reflected in the absence of systems of cost records to facilitate the control of plant operations and is likewise responsible for an underestimate of the wastes involved in excessive diversification and in partial idleness of factories.

These problems can be dealt with in part by the purchase of designs abroad and by the importation of foreign experts. Their permanent solution, however, requires a considerable enlargement of the scope of technical education and the vigorous development of new plans for trade schools for the ablest employees. A program has been launched for training workers in trade schools.

An important influence reducing the productivity of Brazilian labor is the low wage scale and the consequent low standard of living. The legal minimum wage in São Paulo City is as high as any in Brazil, but it is only 240 milreis, or approximately $12 per month.[1] The average wage of skilled workers in São Paulo appears to be $31 to $32 per month, and that of master workmen about $50 per month. Although when translated into dollars these figures are misleading in their failure to allow for differences in Brazilian and American price levels, studies of the cost of living indicate that food and shelter alone require more than 75 per cent of the income of the workers in São Paulo City.[2] Even in São Paulo the wage level appears to be much nearer the minimum for subsistence than in the United States.

The low wage rates also provide an incentive to a continued low productivity, both because labor is so cheap that there is not much incentive to economize it and because with cheap labor it does not pay to adopt machine processes. For some time to come, devices by which the purchasing power of industrial wages can be raised are likely to pay for themselves in the greater efficiency of the work force and the greater care with which that work force is used by the management.

A further problem faced by Brazil's industry is the improvement of plant organization. Brazilian industrial managers are skillful in borrowing and improving mechanical techniques. They are less skill-

[1] The minimum has since been raised by 25 per cent—Editor.
[2] *Ânuario*, *op. cit.*, pp. 535–536.

ful in arranging their factories to avoid unnecessary handling of products, useless delays, and the clogging of machine production by avoidable hand processes somewhere in the production line. Furthermore, they have been induced by the relative smallness of their markets to expand by making new products rather than by increasing the volume and the standardization of old products; and since this tendency has been carried too far, its consequences have been an undue diversification of the larger industrial plants and a wasteful effort by many to make their own raw materials and perform their own tooling operations on a scale too small for efficiency. Within such plants there is need for better dovetailing of processes. Throughout the industrial area there is need for greater plant specialization, accompanied by greater readiness to purchase materials and machines from, and sell partly finished products to, other industrial establishments.

Still another problem concerns the price policy of Brazilian industry. Brazil's succession of bonanza crops for export has left a tradition of high rates of profit in both agriculture and industry, and the tradition has been strengthened by the high interest rates obtainable in a country which is short of capital funds. Federal government bonds in Brazil pay 5 to 8 per cent on their face value; savings deposits draw 4 to 6 per cent; real-estate mortgages usually yield 9 to 10 per cent; the interest rate on bank loans is 7 to 12 per cent. For venture capital to expect higher rates of return is natural, and apparently the conventional idea of a reasonable manufacturing profit is at least 18 per cent and may run as high as 30 per cent. So long as output consisted of export commodities and a limited array of goods for the upper income groups, the policies of high prices could be made to work. However, these policies have necessarily limited the diffusion of prosperity among the Brazilian people and delayed the development of the domestic mass market which is the indispensable basis of a modern industrial system. Further industrial advance would be facilitated if profits were based upon large volume and quick turnover rather than upon large margins.

The present Brazilian tax system also tends to restrict the domestic market by pushing prices too high. The chief sources of tax revenue for the Federal government are import duties and the consumption tax, each of which produces about 36.5 per cent of the total Federal tax revenue. In 1938 the states derived 38.8 per cent of their income from sales taxes and 15.4 per cent from taxes on trade across state lines.[1] Taken together, these four taxes amounted to about $181 million in 1938, or slightly more than 9 per cent of the probable combined value of the output of industrial, agricultural, and vegetable extractive industries in that year.[2] The Federal income tax, on the other hand, produced only 11.4 per cent of the total Federal revenues from taxation. The development of a larger domestic market would be aided by changes in the tax system designed to reduce the importance of taxes which directly raise the prices of commodities.

It is impossible to predict the speed and effectiveness with which Brazil will meet the obstacles listed above. Highways are being rapidly extended, and plans are afoot to preserve and extend the beginnings of air cargo service and to make inland rivers more navigable after the war. The petroleum field in Baía is being tested, and a transportation line is being pushed westward to tap Bolivian oil supplies. Investment of domestic capital in industrial enterprises has begun, though on a limited scale. Both the Federal government and some of the states have fostered programs to improve public health, nutrition, and housing, the success of which should soon be apparent in the productivity of labor. Limited beginnings have been made in the development of technical education, both at the professional level and in the form of shop training for foremen and skilled workmen. The government has imposed an excess-profits tax[3] and is endeavoring to enlarge receipts from income taxes and to reduce the relative place of consumption taxes in the national revenue. With resources peculiarly well adapted to the newer and more rapidly expanding industries and with the difficult beginnings of an industrial order already behind her, Brazil may well be upon the verge of an economic development comparable in rapidity and variety to that of the United States after 1880.[4]

[1] However, provision has been made in the Federal Constitution for the eventual elimination of state taxes on exports.

[2] *Ânuario*, *op. cit.*, pp. 1268–1270, and *Brasil*, 1940–41, *op. cit.*, pp. 101, 306–307.

[3] This tax is to be waived upon profits invested in equipment certificates which are to be used after the war for importation of foreign capital goods.

[4] For a brief discussion of other developments in 1943, see Ch. VI.

Chapter XII

Chile

by P. T. ELLSWORTH

GENERAL CHARACTERISTICS

If one imagined the state of Texas stretched out into a ribbon of land approximately 100 miles in width, about as long as the United States is broad, he would have a fair idea of the shape of Chile. If he then conceived it as divided into three zones of nearly equal length, the northernmost a torrid, barren desert, the central zone closely resembling our Pacific Coast, and the southern zone a replica of the coastal area of British Columbia and southern Alaska, he would have a reasonably accurate knowledge of its topography and climate. To complete the picture, it would be necessary merely to regard this strip of land as the sea-washed shelf of an unbroken chain of towering mountains.

Almost all of Chile's fertile land, industry, and population are located in the central third of the country. The northern desert supports only 11 per cent of the total population of about 5 millions, while the extreme south, a region of heavy forests and almost continuous rain, accounts for but 2 per cent. The country's mountainous character—in addition to the wall of the Andes, there is a coastal range which drops into the sea where the forest regions begin—severely limits its agricultural possibilities, only 7.5 per cent of the total area consisting of arable land.[1]

In spite of the limitations imposed by topography and climate, Chile contains rich resources. In the barren desert are located the two principal foundations of its export trade—the great natural nitrate deposits, and the bulk of its large copper reserves. The forests of the south comprise an as yet scarcely tapped resource of varied

[1] The reader should consult Chart 12.

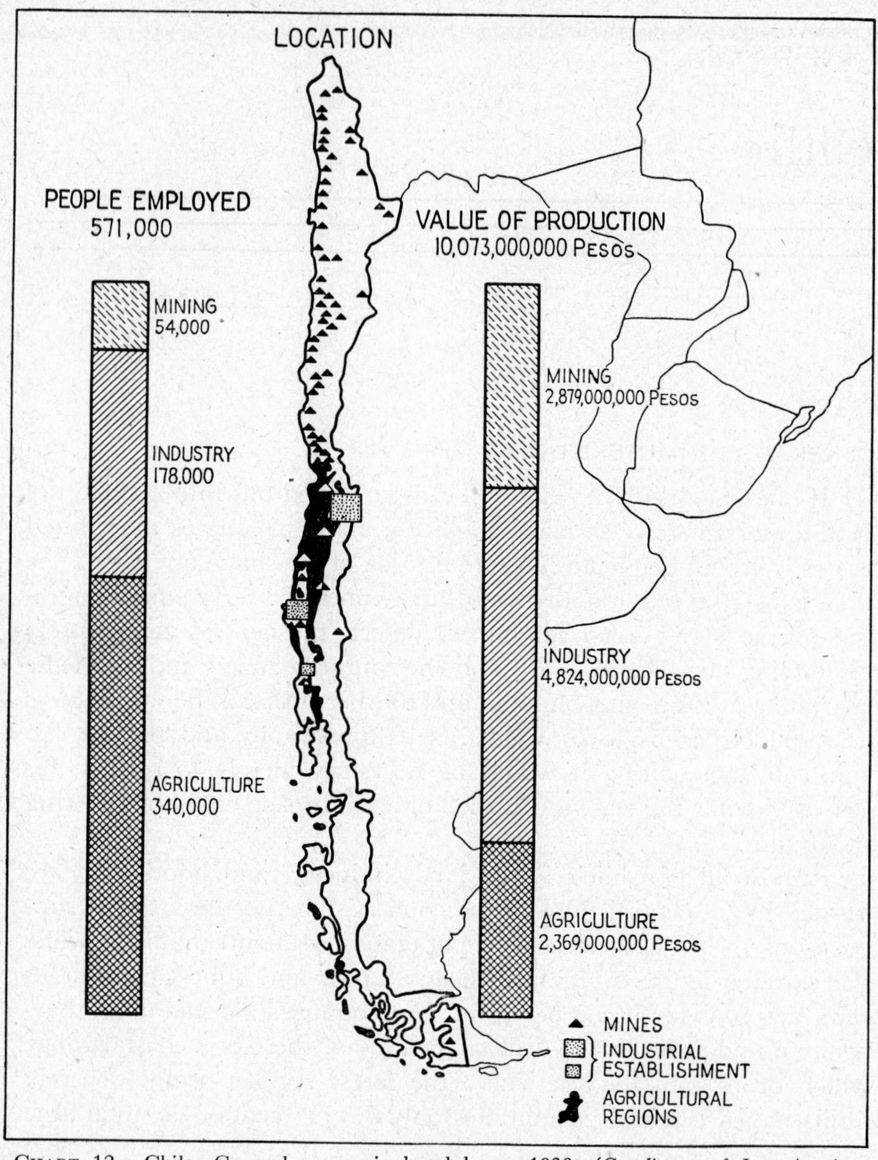

CHART 12.—Chile. General economic breakdown, 1938. (*Coordinator of Inter-American Affairs.*)

types of timber, while the central valley contains some of the richest farming land in the world.

As might be expected of a country with such a small population, located at the periphery of the world's trading routes, and until recently ruled by a landowning plutocracy, Chile's economic structure is dominated by the extractive industries. Of her total working population in 1930, 46 per cent were employed in agriculture, mining, and fishing, 36 per cent in industry and commerce, and the remaining 18 per cent in transportation, government, and other pursuits. While, during the thirties, industry and commerce made substantial progress, it is doubtful if the proportion of workers in these employments yet exceeds that in agriculture, mining, and fishing.[1]

One of the outstanding characteristics of Chile's economy has been its instability. This is the direct consequence of the heavy dependence of the nation upon exports (some 25 to 30 per cent of its income is exported), which consist predominantly of two products, copper and nitrates. These have in recent years comprised 75 per cent of the value of total exports. Both are subject to variable demand; in addition, nitrates have had to meet increasingly severe competition from synthetic substitutes, while discoveries of new copper supplies have worsened market conditions for that metal.

Another striking feature is the poverty of the average Chilean citizen. The per capita income in 1941 approximated $100, as compared with $700 in the United States.[2] This low income appears to be the outcome of a combination of circumstances: the low productivity of agriculture (a result of the traditional inefficient methods of the hacienda), the lack of training in or aptitude for modern industrial techniques on the part of labor, the small size of the national market, and the lack of capital—except in the large American copper mines and nitrate plants—necessary for the most efficient production. Chart 13, which follows, reveals the importance of foreign capital in nitrate, copper, transportation, and public utilities and the large contributions made by the United States. These factors alone would suffice to explain the low productivity and the low income of the Chilean worker. But, with a low income, the mass of the population

[1] The data for 1930 are taken from the census of that year. Although returns from the 1940 census have been compiled, the results have not as yet been published. Estimates for 1938 are given on Chart 12. *Industry* accounts for about *one-third* of the employed and almost *one-half* of the value of product.

[2] Per capita income in the United States is $1200 in 1944.—EDITOR.

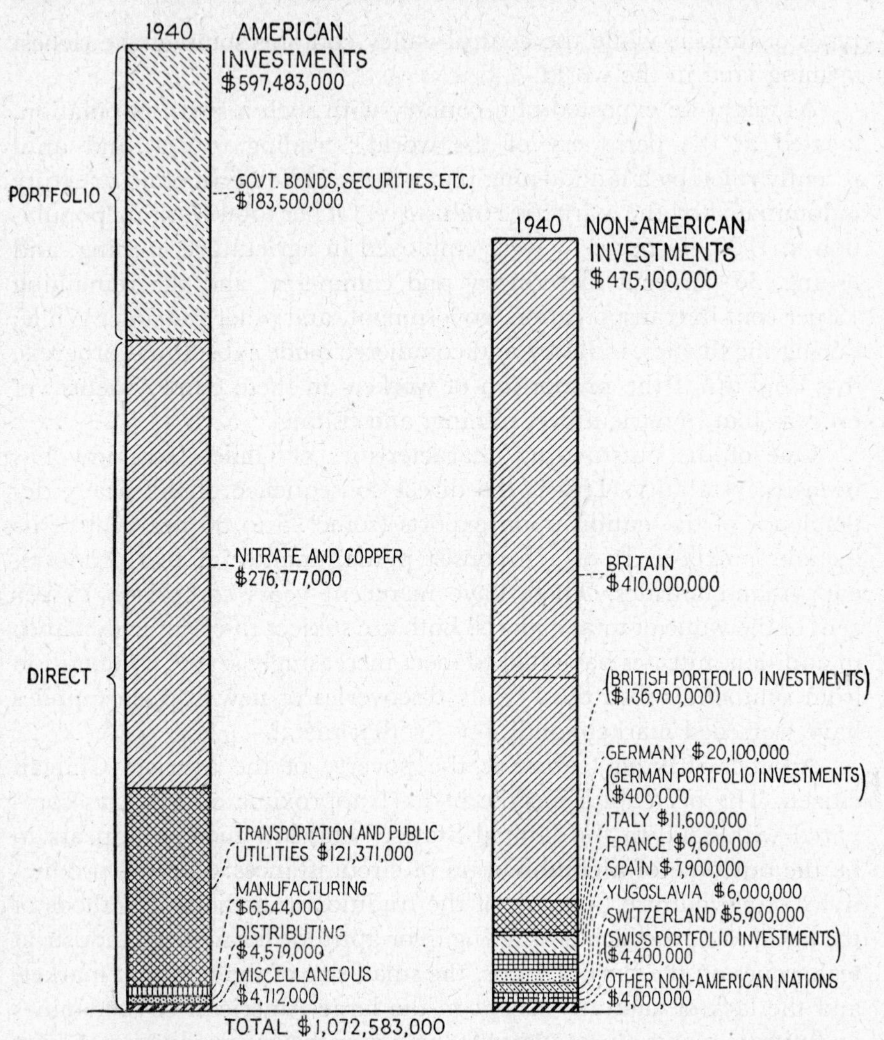

CHART 13.—Chile. Foreign investments, 1940. (*Coordinator of Inter-American Affairs.*)

cannot afford decent housing or an adequate diet; this, in turn, is reflected in unsanitary conditions, a high incidence of disease, excessive alcoholism, and a low degree of energy. Thus a perfect vicious circle has been established.

ASPECTS OF PRODUCTION

1. AGRICULTURE. The most striking characteristic of Chile's agriculture is the large size of the typical production unit, together

with its low average efficiency. The large *hacienda*, or *fundo*, predominates over the small or medium-sized farm. According to a census taken in 1936, 626 holdings of 5,000 hectares or over, representing 0.3 per cent of the estates, accounted for 52.4 per cent of the reported acreage; 2,806 estates of 1,000 hectares (about 2,500 acres) or over, comprising 1.4 per cent of all estates, embraced 68 per cent of the land. In some parts of the arable Central Valley, the concentration of ownership is even greater.

This concentration of landholding is a heritage of the past. A companion inheritance is the inefficient method of cultivation characteristic of most *fundos*. An excessive proportion of arable land is allowed to lie fallow or is given over to grazing, while traditional practices and equipment, such as threshing grain by driving horses over it and employing the oxcart and the ox-drawn plow, are still widely prevalent.

Except for tropical products,[1] Chile produces most of the basic foods consumed domestically. There is, however, a chronic deficit equal to about 10 per cent of the consumption of wheat and cattle, which has to be imported from Argentina. The leading food crops are wheat, potatoes, oats, barley, corn, grapes, beans, peas, lentils, and rice. A considerable proportion of the last four are exported, as well as a fair volume of miscellaneous foodstuffs, such as orchard fruits, melons, and garlic. The sheep industry flourishes in southern Chile predominantly for the export of such commodities as wool, sheepskins, and frozen mutton. Chilean vineyards are the basis of heavy local wine consumption and a small surplus for export. Since the outbreak of the war, the foreign agricultural market has shrunk, but improved prices have generally compensated for reduced sales.

It can fairly be urged that in both grains and cattle Chile does not make the most effective use of her resources. Although the arable land is computed as only 7.5 per cent of the total area of the country, only 22.8 per cent of the arable (*i.e.*, 1,200,000 hectares) was cultivated in 1940. This amount, while somewhat more extensive than in the twenties, has remained fairly constant since 1937, more than 60 per cent of it being planted to wheat. Government efforts to spur wheat production by fixing a floor for wheat prices have called forth relatively slight response. It is believed that expansion of the cultivated area has nearly reached a limit, unless more serious efforts are made to break

[1] Sugar, beverages, (coffee, tea, mate), various fruits and vegetables, and edible oils.

up the *fundo* system of landholding. Stimuli applied to particular crops seem chiefly to effect a transfer of activity within a constant area. Improvement of techniques to bring Chilean agriculture closer to the level of Argentina seems necessary to ensure self-maintenance in the cereal field.

The same statement must be made as to the cattle industry. Here the difficulty is not basically one of meat production, despite a proportionately high meat consumption. While Chile regularly imports cattle on the hoof, dried and frozen mutton is exported. Dairying is highly inadequate to the food needs of the population, though suited to Chile's climate. The country produces only 10 per cent as much milk as Sweden and 15 per cent as much as California, areas comparable in terrain and population. One important difference is that approximately 8.8 square kilometers is required in Chile to pasture a cow under present practices. The Corporación de Fomento has included development of milk, meat, and eggs on its agricultural agenda. It is hoped that it will realize that the problem is not one of finance or price manipulation only, but also one which calls for changes in agricultural organization.

Chile's potentially rich fisheries have been but poorly developed. Measures aimed to provide more adequate fishing fleets and improved storage and distribution facilities, as part of a planned development program,[1] are now in the course of being executed and should help toward balancing the meat deficiency in the country's diet, as well as adding to the volume of exports.

2. MANUFACTURING. Manufacturing had attained only a modest development with the onset of the depression of the 1930's. During the first 3 or 4 years of this decade, the serious economic difficulties which confronted the country prevented appreciable expansion; but, in the 12 years which followed, exchange depreciation, exchange control, the unavailability of imports, increased protection, and direct governmental assistance combined to promote a rapid growth of industry. The index of industrial production, which covers only lines of manufacture that existed in the base years (1927–1929), attained a level of approximately 170 in 1941 and 1942. Moreover, many new industries made their appearance. Prominent among these are radio assembly, the manufacture of electric-light bulbs, plywood, pharmaceuticals, and certain types of chemicals.

[1] See below, discussion of the Corporación de Fomento, pp. 309–310.

By 1940, Chile was largely self-sufficient with respect to the production of a wide range of light consumers' goods, though dependent upon imports for 80 per cent of her iron and steel and for almost all her heavy manufactures.[1]

Although before 1939 the chief cause of the growth of manufacturing industries in Chile was various forms of protection, since that year an increasingly active role has been played by a government development agency, the Corporación de Fomento. By the legislation establishing this institution, it was charged, among other duties, with that of drafting "a general plan for the promotion of national production for the purpose of increasing the standard of living of the people by utilizing the natural resources of the country and lowering production costs, and for the purpose of improving the international balance of payments. . . . "[2]

Plans applicable to a wide range of industries, with particular stress upon electric-power development, were drawn up during 1939. Loans totaling $17 million were contracted with the United States Export-Import Bank for purchases of equipment, while additional funds were made available from domestic sources. These were to be used to finance industrial development, either in the form of loans, direct grants-in-aid, or the purchase of stocks and bonds of various enterprises or to a very limited extent by direct investment in productive activity. At the end of 1941, a total of 428 million pesos had been advanced in one or another of these forms, to a wide range of enterprises of (perhaps excessively) varied types. A year later, this total had more than doubled, amounting on Dec. 31, 1942, to 885 million pesos.

It is too early to tell how significant the activities of the Corporación de Fomento will be for the future of Chilean industry. A key point in its program, the development of electric power, has been seriously retarded by the difficulties of obtaining essential supplies and equipment during wartime. Wisely guided, its activities could do much to foster the growth of industries which could flourish without artificial support. If, however, the corporation follows the insistent advice of those who clamor for self-sufficiency, as there seems some

[1] Plans in the course of execution at the present time call for the completion by the end of 1944 of a steel mill at Concepción to produce the bulk of the country's steel requirements, some 100,000 tons, using coal from local deposits and electricity from one of the main plants being developed by the Corporación de Fomento.

[2] From Article 25 of Law 6640.

danger of its doing, the result will be the creation or the enlargement of many enterprises which can continue in existence only with the protection of the state.

3. MINING. The greatest single industry in Chile is the mining and smelting of copper. In the years just before the war, copper accounted for 45 to 50 per cent of the value of Chile's exports; in 1942, under the stress of wartime demands, this figure had risen to 66 per cent. In 1941, the industry produced approximately 8 per cent of the national income. Employment in the mines and smelters totals some 23,000. Of these workers, one-third are employed in the numerous small mines which account for but 3 per cent of total output; the remaining two-thirds work in the three great American-owned mines, which produce 97 per cent of the ore mined.

Chile's copper is predominantly low cost, some 75 per cent of the output being produced at a cost of approximately 5.5 cents per pound, as compared with a world average of 7.3 cents (exclusive of taxes, 1942). Nonetheless, the industry after the war will face stiff competition from relatively new low-cost producers in the Belgian Congo, Northern Rhodesia, and Canada. Other factors which will determine its postwar position are the degree to which copper is displaced by substitutes such as aluminum and magnesium, the strength of deferred demands, the amount of scrap copper available, the pace of reconstruction in Europe, the tariff policy of the United States,[1] and the general level of employment in the leading industrial nations. With a reasonable combination of these factors, the outlook for Chile's copper industry should be good, though it can hardly be expected to continue to produce at the high wartime levels.

The nitrate industry is second only in importance to copper. Before the war, some 20 to 25 per cent of the value of Chilean exports consisted of sodium nitrate and its companion product, iodine. Approximately 30,000 persons have been directly employed in the industry in recent years. It accounted in 1941 for about 4 per cent of the national income.

Ever since the last war, the competition of the rising synthetic nitrate industry has constituted a growing threat to the survival of Chilean producers. A reorganization of the Chilean industry in 1933 led to the establishment of a government-controlled sales monopoly,

[1] Copper imported into the United States is subject to an import tax. This tax of 4 cents per pound has been temporarily shelved during the war.

the Chilean Nitrate and Iodine Sales Corporation. The policy of this organization has been to price the natural product to sell in competition with the synthetic, regardless of the claims of bondholders. Pursuit of this policy, together with the recovery of world trade after 1933, permitted the maintenance of an average output in the period 1935–1939 only 23 per cent below the record production of the years 1925–1929. In the war years, a severe slump has been avoided because the United States, hitherto the purchaser of some 40 per cent of natural sodium nitrate, increased its purchases to two-thirds the Chilean output. This, together with larger sales to other Latin American countries, compensated for the great decline in sales to Europe and Egypt, Chile's other chief export markets for this mineral.

The outlook for the future of the industry is decidedly unfavorable. With the rise in synthetic production, the excess of potential supply over demand at remunerative prices is constantly being augmented. Even before the war, world capacity in the production of nitrogen products was more than 5 million tons, while peak consumption (attained in 1929) never exceeded 2 million tons. Since 1939, synthetic output has been greatly increased, especially in the United States. Even were the government-owned plants scrapped after the war, expansion in private industry has been sufficient to meet all the domestic, industrial, and fertilizer requirements for nitrates, although a continuing preference of American farmers for the natural product may enable it to retain some of its former market in this country. Wartime destruction in Germany as high as 40 per cent of capacity would still leave Europe able to meet its basic requirements.

Thus the prospects of the postwar market indicate a sharp decline in the demand for the Chilean product. Although Chile can produce at a lower cost f.o.b. portside than, for example, United States producers, shipping charges are approximately one-third the landed costs in the North American market and in similar proportion elsewhere; it would require a revolution in transport to bring down the delivered cost appreciably. Therefore, the outlook in this industry is for a substantial contraction in output. Certainly the older Shanks process, which has furnished some 35 per cent of output in the recent past, is doomed to extinction. Whatever volume of nitrates the country does export will come from two or three large plants using the more modern Guggenheim process.

FOREIGN TRADE

As might be expected of a country in which agriculture and mining are the leading productive activities, Chile's imports consist predominantly of finished and semifinished manufactures (82 per cent in 1939). Imports in general have been well maintained during the war. During 1942, as compared with 1938, they were 12 per cent greater in volume, 25 per cent larger in value. Imports of some particular lines, however, fell off to very low figures, owing to wartime shortages and to lack of shipping facilities. A particularly great decline occurred in iron and steel, machinery, automobiles, tires, and railway equipment. Petroleum imports, on the other hand, rose sharply, because of the need for this product as a fuel in the great copper mines and in industry, while industrial raw materials also experienced a substantial increase.

Exports declined sharply in tonnage, being down 41 per cent in 1942 in comparison with 1938, but they rose 27 per cent in value. The fall in the volume figures is mainly attributable to the cessation of iron ore shipments resulting from submarine sinkings of ore vessels, although the quantity of nitrates and of agricultural products exported has also experienced a decline. Part of the increase in the value of exports may be explained in terms of rising prices, part in terms of the shift from the relatively low-value iron ore to the relatively high-value copper.

The war brought drastic changes in the distribution of Chile's trade by countries. In 1939, the bulk of her exports went to Europe, (50.7 per cent); her imports also came in large part from that continent (43.4 per cent). The British blockade and the submarine warfare combined to bring these figures down sharply; by 1942 they were 6.3 and 12.3 per cent, respectively.

Simultaneously, trade with the United States and with other Latin American countries expanded by leaps and bounds. The United States, which in 1938 took 19 per cent of Chile's exports, in 1942 absorbed 69 per cent. This country, which provided 28 per cent of Chilean imports in the last prewar year, continued to provide 26 per cent in 1942. Both sides of Chile's trade with Latin American nations expanded: imports rose from 13 to 40 per cent of the total, while exports to these sister republics increased from 4 to 14 per cent.

A concise picture of Chilean trade is given in Charts 14 and 15; the large rise in the value of exports and the increased importance of inter-American trade are especially to be noted.

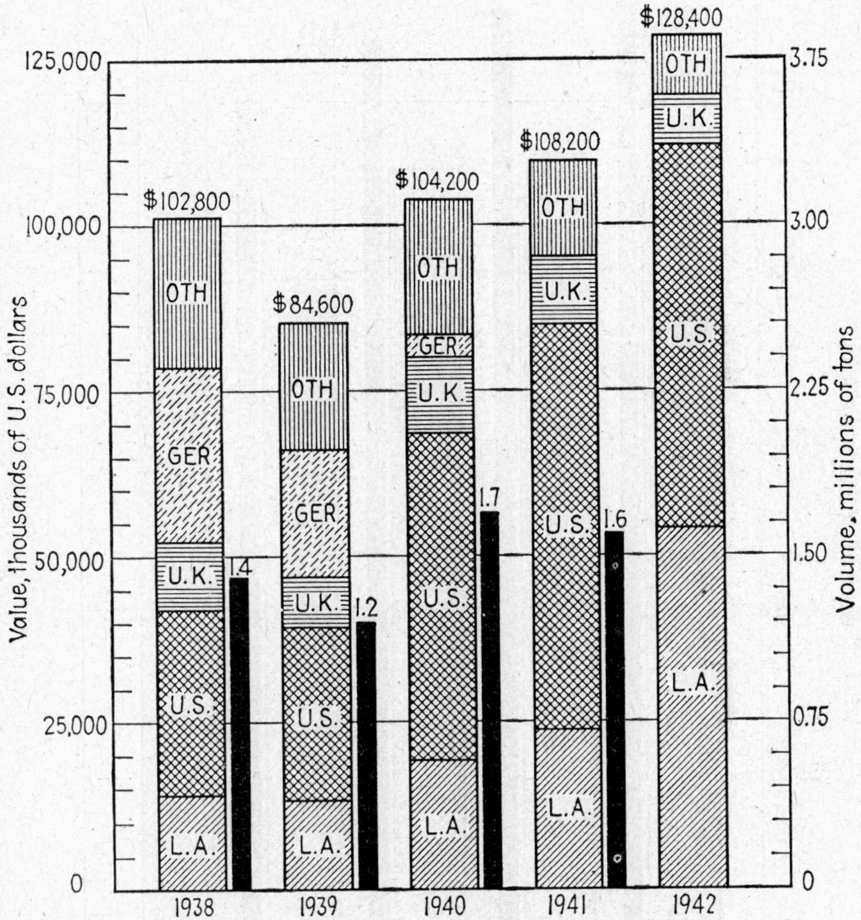

CHART 14.—Chile. Exports by countries of destination, 1938–1942. (*Coordinator of Inter-American Affairs.*)

Since the late 1920's, Chile has increasingly followed a policy of high protection, to a point where import duties in this Latin American republic now approximate or even exceed the level attained in our own Smoot-Hawley Tariff of 1930. Along with other protective devices, such as import quotas and the manipulation of exchange controls, and together with a considerable measure of exchange de-

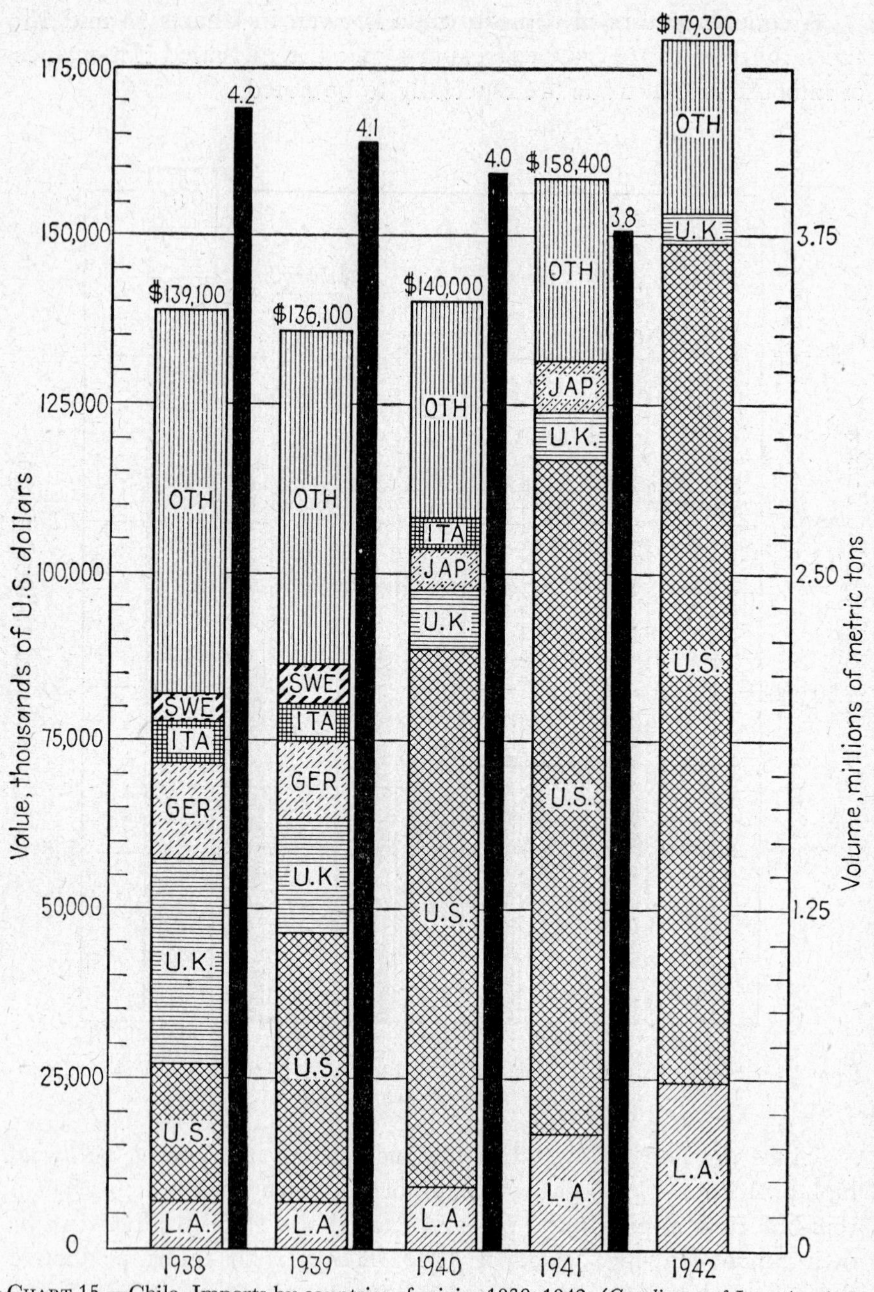

CHART 15.—Chile. Imports by countries of origin, 1938–1942. (*Coordinator of Inter-American Affairs.*)

preciation in the period 1932–1938, high import duties have made possible a considerable portion of the industrial expansion noted above. It is principally manufacturing industries that have been stimulated by these protective measures; the results are visible not alone in the increase in the number of manufacturing establishments, the value of their output, and the volume of industrial employment,[1] but also in the extremely high prices of most manufactured articles in Chile.

Another important aspect of the country's foreign trade policy has been its adherence, since 1931, to a rigorous and complicated system of exchange control. First introduced in a relatively loose and simple form as a means of conserving its dwindling gold reserves, maintaining the external value of the peso, and ensuring the acquisition of essential imports, it has since been elaborated into a complex system which centralizes all Chile's international transactions (with a few minor exceptions) under the authority of a single official board.

One of the characteristics of Chile's exchange control is its use of multiple rates. Five distinct rates of exchange apply to the currencies of countries which have maintained relative freedom in foreign exchange transactions, while still other rates have been set for the currencies of countries following a controlled trade policy. Taking the United States as the leading illustration of a free exchange country, the original "official" rate of 19.37 pesos per dollar (now the "special" rate) applied to the cost of production quota of minerals exports—that portion of the value of these products that remained in Chile, such as wages and taxes—and to a small, arbitrary portion of the value of other exports. In other words, copper exporters may exchange dollars for pesos required to meet domestic costs at 19.37 pesos per dollar. Sales of foreign exchange acquired at this low rate were made only to cover government expenditures abroad.

The "export-draft" rate of 25 pesos per dollar originally applied to most exports and imports, but inflationary developments in Chile after 1939 forced a gradual shift of all but a very narrow range of exports to a higher rate. Since this depleted the supply of exchange available at this rate, a parallel shift of imports to the higher rate was

[1] No reliable data are available to support this statement with quantitative evidence. Such as can be obtained are far from comparable. An economic census now in the process of being compiled, however, should provide a great deal of badly needed information on this and similar points.

likewise made necessary. This process is, of course, tantamount to deliberate exchange depreciation following in the wake of internal currency depreciation.

The present "normal" rate of 31 pesos per dollar, at which most commercial transactions are now carried out, formerly was a special rate ("d.p.," or *disponibilidades propias*), deriving its supply of exchange from exports of gold and of a limited but constantly growing number of commodities. Exchange thus acquired was used to meet a demand arising from nontrading transactions (remittances of interest, dividends, personal expenses, etc.), luxury imports, and, gradually, a growing volume of ordinary imports. Eventually, as most normal exports and imports were transferred to this exchange rate from the export-draft rate, it became the officially recognized normal rate.

The present d.p. rate, which applies to the nontrading transactions in private funds, is a free rate, with exchange bought and sold in competition with the recognized but extralegal black market. In this market, finally, there is the "curb" rate, at which are carried out transactions in private funds not authorized at the d.p. rate.

Though of relatively minor importance since the outbreak of war, compensation or clearing agreements were entered into by Chile with most European countries. These provide for the clearing of foreign exchange transactions through a clearing office in each country, at arbitrarily established rates of exchange. Originating as a means of liquidating credits frozen in Chile at the time exchange control was introduced (in 1931), these compensation agreements ordinarily fixed two rates of exchange, one for frozen credits and for certain types of Chilean exports (usually nitrates) used to liquidate these credits, another for ordinary new business. In addition to these compensation agreements, looser barter arrangements have been established with a number of countries, involving a process of individual clearing of the accounts of private importers and exporters.

PRICE MOVEMENTS

Since the outbreak of war in September, 1939, scarcely a country has escaped some degree of inflation. Chile, far from being an exception, has been in the van in this respect. Of all the nations of the Western Hemisphere, Chile had experienced, up to the end of 1942, the most marked rise of prices. The following table compares wholesale prices and the cost of living in Chile and in the United States during this period.[1]

PRICE CHANGES IN CHILE AND IN THE UNITED STATES, 1939–1942

Date	Wholesale prices		Cost of living	
	Chile	United States	Chile	United States
August, 1939	100	100	100	100
December, 1942	191	135	183	120

SOURCES: United States: Bureau of Labor Statistics indices. Chile: Official indices, published in *Estadística Chilena*. (Both indices are converted, for the sake of ready comparison, to an August, 1939, base.)

It cannot be denied that the inflationary forces operating in the major belligerent nations tended to spread to countries not directly involved in the war or that numerous shortages of goods induced by the disruption of transport have tended to force prices upward. Even making allowance for such influences as these,[2] nonetheless in Chile the principal immediate cause of the sharp rise in all types of prices since 1939 has been the expansion of the money supply. As compared with January, 1929, the total means of payment[3] by November, 1942, had increased 93 per cent, or to approximately the same degree as wholesale prices.

For this development, the central bank was in the first instance responsible. Total loans of this institution expanded up to June, 1942, by an absolutely greater amount than the loans of either the commercial banks or the National Savings Bank.[4] During the following 6 months, central-bank loans receded moderately, while those of the other banks continued to increase. Moreover, by its own loan expansion, the central bank has facilitated increased lending by the other banks. Without the rediscounts provided by the central institution (at an unchanging rediscount rate of 4½ per cent), reserves of the commercial banks and savings bank would have been inadequate to support the volume of loans actually made. Indirectly, too, these reserves have been increased by the transfer to these banks of central-bank funds advanced to other borrowers.

[1] Later figures will be found in Ch. VI.—EDITOR.

[2] See below, pp. 318–320.

[3] This includes currency in free circulation, sight deposits of the commercial banks, and short-term deposits of the National Savings Bank.

[4] Increase in loans, January, 1939, to June, 1942: central bank, 966 million pesos; commercial banks, 928 million pesos; National Savings Bank, 647 million pesos.

For the growth in that category of central-bank loans which has expanded most rapidly, *i.e.*, loans to the development institutes, the government is mainly responsible, since its "authorization" to the bank to make these loans in effect amounted to compulsion. Moreover, the government has itself been a heavy borrower, principally from the commercial banks. During 1940 and 1941 alone the Treasury deficit totaled nearly 600 million pesos, with no unusual heavy expenditures to justify it, and with unemployment at a very low level. Nonetheless, some share of the responsibility for the inflationary expansion of the means of payment must remain with the central bank, since it pursued a completely passive policy with regard to its rediscount rate and looked complacently upon the growth of its own commercial loans. Its loans to the public, which exclude those made to development institutes, increased between 1939 and 1942 at an annual average rate of 16 per cent.

Although the primary cause of rapidly rising prices in Chile during this period was the large expansion of the money supply, nonetheless some of this result may be attributed to nonmonetary causes. The index of prices of imported products rose 91 per cent between December, 1938, and December, 1941.[1] This figure, however, distorts the effect of causes external to the country, for these prices represent, not the landed cost of imports, but prices of such commodities after they have entered the Chilean market. Thus they reflect in considerable part the quasi-monopolistic position of many importers, a position enhanced both by the wartime scarcity of goods and by the restrictive effects of high tariffs and exchange control. An index of the unit value of imports (index of total value of imports divided by the index of quantity of imports) rose by only 12 per cent between 1938 and 1941 (annual averages). The monthly values of this index vary too spasmodically to attach much significance to their variations, which rules out comparison of the December figures. The general impression of a relatively small increase in the landed cost of imports as compared with the rise in the prices of these goods after entry into the Chilean market is, however, borne out by the index of unit value of United States exports (which comprised from one-third to over half Chile's imports during the 3 years in question). This index rose only 29 per cent between December, 1938, and December, 1941. While there

[1] This brief analysis of nonmonetary factors stops with 1941, since in 1942, as will be seen later in the text, new forces made their appearance.

was relatively little increase in transport charges during this period, the Chilean cost of imports was affected by the transfer of a large number of imports from the export-draft exchange rate (25 pesos per dollar) to the then d.p. rate (31 pesos per dollar). As much as 12 per cent should perhaps be added on this account[1] to the increased cost of imports, or 42 per cent in all if a round 30 per cent is allowed for higher landed costs. But imports comprise only some 25 per cent of national income, while the country's money supply is used in purchasing the *entire* income. Therefore higher costs for imports would justify a credit expansion of only one-fourth of 42 per cent, or 11 per cent. To this must be added an increase of credits of approximately 12 per cent to take care of the absorption of labor which became available, or a total of 23 per cent.[2] This is only about half the 45 per cent expansion in normal loans to the public which actually occurred in the interval 1938–1941 and little more than one-fourth the total credit expansion of this period.

The principal effect of the sharp rise in prices between 1939 and 1942 has been to impose forced saving on the Chilean public. This was primarily the consequence of financing industrial development by means of credit expansion. Although Chile's industrialization has thereby progressed more rapidly than would otherwise have been the case, one may legitimately raise the question: Would it not have been better, in a country where the standard of living is so low, for this progress to have been more gradual, and perhaps therewith of a sounder character?

After the summer of 1942, a new element was introduced into the inflationary picture in Chile. Heavy purchases of strategic materials by the United States gave the country a steadily increasing supply of dollars. These dollars, on becoming available to Chilean exporters, were sold to the banks for pesos, thus augmenting the domestic money supply. The demand for dollars to pay for imports, on the other hand, was severely restricted by wartime shortages of goods and materials in the States and by inadequate Shipping facilities. Instead of being extinguished in repurchasing dollars to acquire a larger volume of imports, the newly created pesos remained in circulation, while at the

[1] Each import transferred to the higher rate increased in cost 24 per cent. Perhaps half of total imports were thus affected between 1938 and 1941.

[2] For an explanation of this factor, as well as a fuller account of many of the topics touched upon in this chapter, see my book, *Chile: An Economy in Transition* (The Macmillan Company, New York).

same time Chile's dollar balances increased rapidly. Thus the central bank during the latter half of 1942 issued 238 million pesos to buy gold and foreign exchange, 538 million pesos in the first 4 months of 1943. Commercial-bank deposits also rose, in early 1943, approximately twice as rapidly as loans and investments. This new element has been profoundly disturbing; so far, the only effective remedy—increased saving by the public, the government, or both,—has not been tried.[1]

PRICE CONTROL

While Chile possesses a sort of OPA in the form of a General Commissariat of Subsistence and Prices, this agency has never been very effective. Until relatively recently, it had no budget, subsisting solely on fines imposed on offenders. Moreover, its policy has been to allow controlled prices to reflect increases in costs. Since these are bound to continue to rise so long as no fundamental attack is made on the basic problem of expanding credit and rising incomes, it is idle to expect this agency to bring about effective price control. Close supervision of the importer's margin, however, might bring good results in a limited field.

[1] *Cf.* Chapters VI and VII for further treatment of these issues.—EDITOR.

Chapter XIII

Colombia: with Particular Reference to Price Control

by BEN W. LEWIS *and* HENRY BEITSCHER

THE story of price control in the republic of Colombia is a case study in the operation of emergency economic regulations in a freedom-loving democracy.[1]

Colombia, occupying the northwest corner of South America, covers the southern approaches to the Panama Canal. In addition to the multitude of considerations which have prompted intense interest in wartime Latin America generally, as well as those growing out of special qualities of the Colombian economy and its array of resources, the proximity of Colombia to the Canal Zone has made, and will continue to make, Colombian attitudes and activities a matter of primary concern to the people of the United States.

Topographically, the principal features of Colombia are the three great mountain ranges in the west, running from north to south and ranging as high as 18,000 feet, the Sierra Nevada de Santa Marta in the northeast, the high plateau of Bogotá, and the region east of the eastern cordillera. The last, scantily populated, embraces the watersheds of the Orinoco and Amazon rivers and comprises almost two-thirds of Colombia's 439,828 square miles. Between the western ranges flows the thousand-mile-long Magdalena River, emptying into the Caribbean Sea. The Magdalena, with its tributaries, has served for centuries as the principal transportation artery of the coun-

[1] The statements and expressions of opinion contained in this chapter are those solely of the authors in their personal capacities and are not to be taken in any sense as official statements or expressions of the Foreign Economic Administration or the Office of Price Administration.

try. The greater part of the Colombian population lives in the valleys surrounded by the western ranges. Railroads and highways are exceedingly difficult to construct and maintain in Colombia because of the mountainous character of the country. In recent years, until the outbreak of the war made virtually impossible the importation of necessary machinery and supplies, Colombia was moving rapidly to improve the quality of its transportation system, and in the field of air transport it had come to occupy a preeminent position. Nonetheless, commercial transportation facilities generally are still inadequate and uncertain, and an appreciable part of the economic life of Colombia is carried on today in semi-isolated communities.

Colombia enjoys a wide range of changeless seasons. The mountainous terrain, lying in a tropical latitude, converts the altitude into a weather determinant. With the altitude varying from sea level to 16,000 and 18,000 feet, all kinds of climatic conditions are found. The time required to make the journey from the coast or from the Magdalena to the high tableland of Bogotá marks the difference, the year round, between the hottest of tropical summers and the damp coolness of an early northern spring.

Colombia abounds in natural resources, many of which are still untapped, and all of which are still available for more intensive and more effective cultivation and exploitation. The principal agricultural crops are coffee, corn, bananas, sugar, cacao, tobacco, rice, and indigo. Of these, coffee is by all odds the major crop and the chief export. Cattle raising is one of Colombia's principal industries, and the extensive Colombian forests offer a wide variety of woods, wood products, and medicinal plants. The most important of Colombia's mineral resources are petroleum, gold, and platinum; and a host of other minerals, including lead, copper, mercury, manganese, iron, quartz, and mica, are also present. Colombia is the major world source of emeralds. Coal reserves are extensive; but, as in the case of most of the country's minerals, commercial development on a large scale has not yet taken place.

Of the 4,500,000 economically active people in Colombia (the total population is around 9,500,000), over 3,000,000 are engaged in agriculture and cattle raising. Other forms of primary production account for less than 100,000 active participants, the transforming industries engage the services of slightly more than 500,000, and the service industries include an additional 400,000. The bulk of Colombia's population lives in rural areas; only four cities—Bogotá, Medellín, Barranquilla, and Cali having a population in excess of 100,000. Bogotá, the capital and the country's political center, has a population of some 350,000; Medellín, the largest industrial center, around 175,-000; and Barranquilla, the chief peacetime port, around 150,000.

Living conditions for the greater part of the population are far from good. The prewar earnings of considerably over half the employed population were barely above the subsistence level. Colombian authorities are quite ready to admit that "the situation of our *clases populares* should constitute for public opinion both a source of shame and alarm."[1] The building census of 1938 showed that 81 per cent of the buildings in Colombia lacked electric light, water, and sewage facilities. Only one-half of 1 per cent of the population filed income-tax returns for 1939, and of these 71 per cent paid on earnings of 2,000 pesos or less (1 peso is approximately equal to 57 cents).

Prewar manufacturing in Colombia was restricted almost exclusively to consumers' goods, processed in many cases from raw materials imported from foreign sources. The principal industries were devoted to the production of textiles, beer, sugar, cement, tobacco products, grain products, chemicals and pharmaceuticals, vegetable fats and oils, glassware, chocolate, and footwear. While Colombia has been reasonably self-sufficient in staples, domestic manufacturing of the products enumerated has not overcome dependence upon importation of similar commodities. As a matter of fact, imports have been increasing even though the domestic production of most of the listed articles has also increased.

Exports from Colombia have exceeded the value of Colombian imports for every year from 1933 until the present time, with the exception of 1939, when importation in anticipation of war shortages was extremely heavy. However, the great excess of foreign exchange, which is at the root of Colombia's wartime inflationary problem, has been a significant feature of the Colombian foreign trade position only in very recent years.

The immediate prewar economy of Colombia was marked by a general upward trend in most lines of production. A very large proportion of the country's income flowed from the production for export of coffee, petroleum, and gold, with coffee accounting in 1938

[1] The Colombian Minister of Finance, in *El Economista* (Mexico City), Dec. 1, 1943, p. 26.

for 61.5 per cent of the total value of exports, excluding gold. The principal obstacles to economic stability were constituted by the heavy reliance on foreign trade and the low wage scales which prevented the bulk of the population from purchasing more than the minimum necessities of life.

Colombia's wartime economic difficulties are to be traced largely to the increase in the unbalance of trade resulting from shipping shortages and export restrictions in Europe and the United States. Colombia's exports, although dependent more on coffee now than ever before, have been greater in dollar volume than in any prewar year with the exception of 1938. Coffee accounted for 75 per cent of the country's total export values in 1942 and 86 per cent for the first 7 months of 1943; and, owing to the Inter-American Coffee Agreement and vigorous action by the Colombian government, the prices paid for Colombia's coffee have been at very remunerative levels. Imports, on the other hand, have fallen greatly. Imports from continental Europe have disappeared almost completely, United Kingdom shipments have been greatly reduced, and those from the United States (now, as historically, Colombia's principal supplier) have been sharply lessened. In 1942 the United States reduced its exports in the amount of 65 million pesos—exactly the reduction in Colombia's total import trade. Imports from other South American countries increased by only 10 million pesos. There has been an increase in the trade of a specialized character with certain other Latin American countries, but in the main their industries are not equipped to produce the range of manufactured products which Colombians require. The excess of exports in 1940 was 20 million pesos; in 1941, 16 million pesos; and, in 1942, 87 million pesos. At the same time, gold and foreign exchange of the central bank rose from 39 million pesos in 1941 to 153 million pesos in 1943, and the deposits of commercial banks rose from 132 million pesos in 1940 to 217 million pesos in 1943. In the same period, investments and loans of commercial banks rose from 158 million pesos to 202 million pesos.

The volume of goods from outside the country has been very substantially curtailed, and domestic production has been in no position to fill the gap. As has been indicated, Colombia is just starting its industrial career, and for the most part its small manufacture is still in an early stage. Industry in Colombia cannot engage in expansion without the importation of foreign machinery and materials, and these are even more difficult than consumers' goods to obtain in wartime. While it is true that increased emphasis upon agricultural production has stimulated additional output, it must be remembered that transportation difficulties intervene to prevent nation-wide benefits from any such movement, and, in addition, agricultural production as well as manufacturing requires imported machinery for significant expansion. The picture, then, since the outbreak of the war has been one of increasing shortages of goods and progressively increasing surpluses of dollar exchange and circulating media.

The effect upon the domestic price level of too much purchasing power and too few goods has been augmented by additional factors: the forced resort to higher cost sources of supply to take the place of lower cost sources no longer available; price increases in the countries of origin of imported goods and materials; increases in ocean freight rates and war-risk insurance charges; distortion of normal channels of import trade, and consequent utilization of new and less favorable distributive channels and agencies; diversion of import shipments from Caribbean ports to Pacific ports, resulting in longer shipments and the utilization of ill-adapted facilities; and the bogging down of internal transportation due to diversion of shipments, shortages of railroad and highway building materials and equipment, and dearth of vehicles and tires.

While the general increase in prices, and particularly in those prices bearing directly on the cost of living, had not been great up to the beginning of 1943, the elements making for inflation were clearly recognized and understood by governmental authorities, and prices of particular items had in some cases risen so sharply as to excite the public generally. Government action was clearly indicated.

Before dealing in detail with the government's program, however, it will be worth while to consider the Colombian political situation. Colombia is politically conscious in an extreme degree, and its people actively enjoy the utmost in freedom of discussion on public affairs—both in personal participation and in the press. Public issues are laid open and analyzed in Colombia's high-grade newspapers with confident frankness and intelligent penetration. Although discussions of personal matters are far from absent, the plane of discussion is uniformly on rather a high level.

The national government of Colombia since 1886 has been unitary republican in form, with legislative, executive, and judicial branches, as in the United States. Suffrage is limited to males twenty-one years of age and older, engaged in some lawful occupation. The president is elected by direct vote for a 4-year term and is ineligible to succeed himself. His cabinet is composed of the nine heads of the executive departments. Senators are elected for 4 years by the department legislatures, and deputies are elected for 2 years directly by districts. Supreme Court justices are elected for 5 years.

Since August, 1930, when Enrique Olaya Herrera assumed the presidency, the Liberal Party has held the reins of administration. The outstanding figure in recent Colombian political life has been Alfonso Lopez Pumarejo, who played a large part in Olaya Herrera's election and who succeeded to the presidency in 1934. During his administration, Lopez instituted an aggressively liberal domestic and foreign program. Measures were passed abolishing poll taxes and literacy tests for voting and making primary education free and compulsory in state schools and removing education from church control. Income taxes were instituted, and heavier taxes were imposed upon foreign corporations and larger domestic firms. A mild agrarian reform program was begun, and legislation favorable to workers and to labor organizations was carried through. On the foreign front, domestic recognition was accorded to Soviet Russia and was denied to Italy's seizure of Ethiopia.

From 1938 to 1942 the presidency was held by the more conservative Liberal, Eduardo Santos, and the election of 1942 resulted in a victory for former President Lopez over a more moderate Liberal candidate. Although the Conservative Party has fought vigorously to regain control of the government, recent issues have reflected cleavages between the moderate and the more advanced wings of the Liberal Party as fully as battles between the Liberals and the formal Conservatives. An outsider would have reason to believe that, if the Liberal Party in Colombia could compose its own internal differences, it would have no great difficulty in remaining in power for some time to come. By the beginning of 1943 President Lopez and his wing of the Liberal Party seemed to be unshakably in command. The full extent to which the actual political facts were belied by surface appearances was not disclosed—and then with serious implications for price control—for several months.

In this situation and against this background, the law of Mar. 2, 1943,[1] was passed, authorizing the President to establish wartime price control. It was determined to make quick use of the new grant of power. In preparation for the promulgation of a price control decree, the Minister of Finance, Dr. Alfonso Araujo, appointed an informal committee drawn from a number of government agencies, to prepare a preliminary draft; and through the Colombian Embassy in Washington invited advice from the government of the United States. Two members of the United States Office of Price Administration[2] arrived in Bogotá early in April and remained for a period of 6 weeks. The advisers from the United States worked directly with the Minister of Finance, conferring at first with the Minister's informal committee, and during the later weeks with the President's Commission of National Economic Defense—constituted by outstanding representatives of industry and government under the chairmanship of the President.

The Price Control Mission found an economic situation in which, because of the restrictions on imports coupled with a full flow of purchasing power resulting from huge exports of coffee, a measure of inflation was virtually inevitable. The basic forces could be dealt with only by measures so devised as to divert purchasing power and to prevent it from operating with full force upon the level of prices. Direct price control, at best, could be no more than a partial weapon—it could serve partially to stem the tide of rising prices until more fundamental remedies could be applied, and it could be useful in striking down extraordinary price increases in particular speculative situations. There was reason to believe that direct price con-

[1] Law 7 of 1943 (Mar. 2, 1943) declared that articles of prime necessity, such as foodstuffs, drugs, and merchandise for common consumption among the common people, should not be subject to undue speculation and required that the government take the steps necessary to fix and maintain maximum and minimum sale prices in the different markets throughout the country. The government was authorized, as part of the same program, to import goods on its own account or under contract, to control house rents, to establish or subsidize cooperative societies for the production, distribution, or consumption of foodstuffs, and to suspend or modify exchange-control regulations. The President was required to establish a Commission of National Economic Defense to study and recommend measures which might be adopted to (1) direct industry, agriculture, and cattle raising toward greater productivity; (2) regulate the importation and exportation of raw materials and manufactured and semimanufactured goods, for the purpose of stimulating economic development; (3) coordinate and improve transportation; and (4) prepare financial measures necessary for the execution of the foregoing.

[2] Ben W. Lewis, co-author of this chapter, and James R. Nelson, co-author of Ch. X on Bolivia.

trols, if carefully drawn and effectively aimed, could be of real help.

New controls are always questionable when freedom-loving people are involved. There had been full public discussion, however, and prominent newspapers had for some time been clamoring for vigorous action. The government itself did not expect price controls alone to achieve miracles; it was fully prepared to adopt other more basic measures and to place price control in its proper role. It was true that Colombia had no long tradition in this area and no skilled body of public servants into whose hands the task of controlling prices could be given. On the other hand, considerable statistical data necessary to a price control program were available, the country had some months' experience in controlling the prices of tires and nails, and an efficient control of imports had been built up over a period of several years. The administration seemed firmly entrenched, and the political atmosphere was encouraging. On the balance, the chances of successful price control appeared good.

In presenting its recommendations, the mission acted on the assumption that price control was certain to be adopted and that the concern of the mission related solely to the character of the program. It was also taken for granted that price control was only one of the measures which the government would employ to combat inflation. In a series of memoranda, the mission stressed the desirability of setting up price control measures carefully adapted to Colombian conditions and directed to the particular inflationary evils which price control could reasonably be expected to reach. An analysis of proposed types of programs was made, and distinctions drawn and related to Colombian conditions, between price freezes, formula prices (costs and markups), and specific or flat pricing. The government was urged not to put itself in the position of appearing to promise more than it could accomplish—to move ahead vigorously, but not overconfidently. In the selection of commodities for specific pricing, it was pointed out that attention should be given to those goods which were important in the cost of living, whose prices gave evidence of serious increase, and whose characteristics made them amenable to control. It was suggested that certain imported commodities important in the life of the community (*e.g.*, drugs and farm tools) might well be chosen for first action by the price authorities. The value of simple regulations, local determination of local prices at the earliest possible date, and the securing of public understanding and active cooperation both from business and consumers was stressed in the mission's statements.

The issues which received primary attention from the Commission of National Economic Defense bore largely on matters of organization —whether the price control function should be exercised by an independent agency or by a branch to be established as part of an existing old-line agency; and whether the powers of price control should be vested in a single person or in a board. It is interesting to note that representatives of existing agencies were determined that the price control function should not be attached to their offices—there was a thoroughly understandable unwillingness to jeopardize the happy existence of an established agency by harnessing to it a control venture involving such a high degree of political risk. The issue as between a price controller and a price control board was fortunately resolved by providing for a single officer with final responsibility and a board whose advice he was required to seek on major policy issues. On one other matter which occasioned some debate, it was decided that the power to control food prices should be vested in the Office of Price Supervision, but that assurances should be given that control of prices to be charged by farmers was not contemplated.

The price control decree (No. 928 of 1943), issued May 11, 1943, established the Office of Price Supervision and made the following articles of "prime necessity" subject to such price control resolutions as the office might issue: foodstuffs, clothing, footwear, construction materials, drugs and health articles, fuel, laborers' tools, machinery and parts, seeds and other agricultural goods, schoolbooks and school supplies, and rentals of urban premises and dwellings. The Price Supervisor was to be appointed by the President, as were the four members of the Advisory Board, who were to represent manufacturers, import merchants, agriculture, and labor. The office was provided with its own judge, with necessary assistants, to act in cases involving enforcement and protests, and to facilitate the procurement from business firms of necessary reports and records. In addition to the usual powers of administration, the Price Supervisor was granted the authority to issue such resolutions as in his judgment might be necessary, establishing maximum and minimum prices, preventing hoarding, establishing rationing systems, providing for the buying and selling of goods, issuing and revoking sales licenses, preventing the issuance of import and export licenses, determining the continuance or expansion of output of any goods or articles, and making exemptions and adjustments in particular cases, and to take appropriate steps for the proper execution of the resolutions issued under the decree.

The promulgation of the decree excited vigorous public debate. Opposition and questions came to a surprising degree from sources which until the moment of issuance had been insisting that price control was an absolute necessity. Much of the opposition arose from the misconception that the generous powers granted to the office were to be employed immediately and without regard to the need for control in specific instances or to the capacity of the office to operate effectively. Public uncertainty and incipient public hostility were reflected in the difficulty which the President encountered in securing a person to fill the position of Price Supervisor. Men of sufficient stature and experience to carry the position successfully were well acquainted with reports of the plight of Leon Henderson in the United States, and they had no desire to thrust themselves into what promised to be a completely thankless task. It must be remembered that, although Colombia had broken off relations with the Axis Powers, no open declaration of hostilities had at that time been made, and a prospective supervisor could not plan on conducting his control operations in the relatively favorable atmosphere of wartime patriotism. The Advisory Board was quickly named, and after a prolonged delay (and reputedly after two other nominees had indicated their unwillingness to serve) the President prevailed upon Dr. Alberto Arango Tavera, an experienced industrialist, to assume the post of Price Supervisor. Alfonso Castillo Gomez, who had worked both with the Minister's Committee and the Price Mission, was transferred from the Superintendency of Imports to act as secretary.

Details of the organization of the Colombian Office of Price Supervision have never been available in the United States, and little more of the structure of the office as established is known here than that the organization was built along commodity lines, that delegation of authority to local representatives to deal with local situations (with appropriate safeguards to protect basic policy) was made, and that a specialized public relations and information unit was set up.

The most gratifying reliance of the new office upon the recommendations of the Price Mission is represented by its now well-established policy of securing accurate and usable inventory, cost, selling-price, and distribution data before taking control action. The first resolution issued by the new office provided that all firms engaged in the production and processing of any goods and those engaged in distribution and sale of all articles subject to price control must register data relating to capital investment and the average monthly movement of goods in 1942 (specifying the names and all distinguishing features of the goods, units of measure, and wholesale and retail selling price in January, 1941, and on June 15, 1943) and that all industrial establishments must declare stocks on hand of finished goods and raw materials. Mayors in areas producing potatoes, wheat, barley, corn, rice, beans, and panela were required to submit prices paid to producers for these articles between June 15 and July 10 and to specify "normal" prices in that period.

Similarly, later resolutions issued by the office requesting inventory, cost, and price information have indicated a grasp of the problems with which the office was faced and a determination to proceed on an informed and businesslike basis. Information of this kind was called for on July 24 with reference to wheat, rice, cocoa, oats, spices, condensed and powdered milk, yeast, and canned vegetables and on July 27 on enumerated drugs (drugstores and laboratories). On July 24, information was requested relative to rentals charged during the months of January and July for the years 1941–1943 for residential and tenement houses in all cities of more than 7,000 inhabitants.

The pressure of generally rising prices forced the office soon to abandon any intention it may originally have had to restrict its activities to a small group of named commodities. On July 16, 1943, a general price freeze was instituted, fixing the prices prevailing on June 15, 1943, as the maximum lawful retail and wholesale selling prices for clothing, textiles, construction materials, drugs, pharmaceuticals, heating materials, laborers' tools, agricultural machinery and parts, agricultural implements, school texts and supplies, and imported foods. It is notable that foods of domestic origin, on which the great mass of the Colombian population depends, were not included and that footwear, fuel, and agricultural seeds were also omitted. There is strong reason to believe, also, that many prices had been materially advanced by June 15, in anticipation of the freeze.

As soon as possible after the imposition of the general freeze, the office turned its attention to specific prices, and in successive orders important items in which inflationary tendencies were present and which were susceptible of control were made the subject of specific maximum price resolutions. On Oct. 5, 1943, specific factory, wholesale, and retail prices were named for nails, and on Oct. 6, wholesale and retail prices for foreign and domestic tools; also, on Oct. 6, specific *minimum* prices for wheat and maximum prices for flour were set, as part of a program to prevent a temporary wheat surplus from unduly depressing the price of wheat and to encourage general wheat production; on Oct. 7, prices at all levels of distribution were set for construction materials in different cities, with provision for geographic differentials; on Oct. 16 and subsequent dates, specific retail prices were named for drugs classified by producers; on Nov. 6, imported ladies' stockings were subjected to specific prices; on Nov. 22, retail prices, differentiated geographically, were set for batteries; on Dec. 17 and thereafter, specific prices applicable only to the city of Bogotá were fixed for coal, processed milks, and at wholesale and retail for beef; on Feb. 17, 1944, specific prices (involving substantial reductions) for the sale of vegetable lard at all levels in Bogotá were coupled with a priority system; and on Mar. 3, 1944, country-wide specific wholesale and retail prices were named for sugar. It is significant that the office has limited its control of foods to a few items, and for the most part to a single city.

A rent freeze, based on levels prevailing in July, 1942, and applicable to dwelling places charging monthly rents under 200 pesos in cities with a population of more than 10,000, was ordered into effect on Oct. 29, 1943, affording a promise of substantial relief to the average Colombian tenant.

Colombia's attack on inflation has proceeded on other fronts in addition to that of direct price control. Price control of imported goods, which has enlisted major attention from the Office of Price Supervision, was supplemented by direct governmental imports. The Caja de Crédito Agrario has imported barbed wire, solder, screws, tin plate, and other critical items from the United States and has distributed many of these staples to agriculturists and cattle raisers at cost. The Caja de Crédito Agrario has also acted as distributing agent for tires imported from Brazil, and consideration has been given recently to a proposal to make it exclusive importer of other essential and critically short items. There is much reason from Colombian experience to believe that the presence on the market of increased supplies is a much more important factor in checking price increases than any direct price control measures which can be put into effect.

In a further attempt to protect the standard of living, the government has promoted the development of municipal markets and has extended substantial financial assistance to the growing consumer cooperative movement. Late in 1943, President Lopez authorized a loan of 100,000 pesos to the Bogotá Consumer Cooperative for the expansion of its stores up to a total of 50. The Municipal Council of Bogotá and the department of Cundinamarca subscribed an additional 70,000 pesos. The limited capital and small radius of operation of consumer cooperatives have prevented them, however, from exercising any considerable effect upon the general level of prices. It is worth comment that government support of consumer cooperatives in Colombia has found favor among many business interests strongly opposed to government price control.

The most significant single measure undertaken by the Colombian government for the control of inflation was the decree of June 10, 1943 (as supplemented July 3, 1943), providing for the boldest and most thoroughgoing governmental siphoning of excess purchasing power ever attempted by any American republic. Under the terms of the decree, business houses were required to invest 20 per cent of their net profits after tax deductions and 50 per cent of their depreciation (originally 100 per cent) and regular reserves after deduction of portions required for investment in public debts in government non-negotiable certificates of deposit bearing 4 per cent interest annually and convertible after 2 years into gold, United States dollars, or domestic currency at the option of the investor. Importers were required to invest 5 or 10 per cent (depending upon named conditions) of the value of their imports. Banks were ordered to increase their cash reserves by 100 per cent, investing the increase in certificates of deposit bearing 3 per cent interest. It was estimated that this measure would absorb in 2 years the excess inflow of 100 million pesos resulting from Colombia's favorable balance of payments. By the end of July 1943, 13 million pesos of certificates of deposit had been sold. As a complement to the measure, Colombia's central bank adopted a policy of decreasing its loans to the public, instead of pyramiding them on its greatly increased reserves.

The "siphoning" decree is intimately related to price control in Colombia both because it constitutes a companion device to remove the upward pressure on prices and because it came shortly to be the focal point for a widespread and effective attack upon the government's campaign against inflation. It is the lesson of experience that price control can operate with conspicuous success only if it receives substantial public support and enlists widespread public cooperation. In a democratic environment where the public is indifferent or actively in opposition, direct price control can produce nothing better than partial and discriminatory effects. The establishment of the Office of Price Supervision in Colombia and the publication of its many resolutions have, as was to be expected, aroused a measure of opposition. It seems altogether likely, however, that, if national political unity had been more nearly present, the unrest resulting from direct price control operations could have been held to a minimum and the program could have gained steadily in support and accomplishment.

Colombia was far from being united politically in the fall and winter of 1943–1944. The dissension within the Liberal Party and the always present opposition of the Conservative group joined in this period to form an attack upon the government's entire program. There is no point in attempting here to detail the events or to appraise the many political and economic issues which were brought to the fore and which resulted in major changes within the Liberal Party and in the make-up of the President's official family. It will suffice for this account to note simply that furious and effective pressure was exerted by business firms and chambers of commerce to effect a modification of the "siphoning" decree. Weakened by other attacks, the government was forced first to suspend the obligation of importers to purchase certificates of deposit and to eliminate the increase which it had ordered earlier in the legal reserves of banks. Finally, in December, 1943, the government cut to 10 per cent the amount of net business profit after tax deductions required to be invested in deposit certificates.

The over-all political situation and the opposition directed against the government's major anti-inflation measure could scarcely have failed to leave their mark upon the government's direct price control activity. It is a matter of record that to date the Office of Price Supervision has not retreated either in program or policy, but there is much evidence to indicate that events of the past few months have not contributed either to the ease or to the effectiveness of its operations. The first appointee to the office of Price Supervisor assumed his position in June, 1943. He resigned in September to become Minister of War. In the interim his position was filled by an acting supervisor, who received a full appointment on Oct. 4, 1943. On Oct. 13, the original supervisor was reappointed; but, because of his inability to serve, the office continued under an acting supervisor until the appointment of Alvaro Diaz S., formerly Minister of Posts and Telegraphs, in January, 1944. The reaction of particular groups to certain of the resolutions issued by the Office of Price Supervision has been bitter, and information with reference to the actual course of prices since May, 1943, while sketchy, indicates that cooperation and compliance with the price control regulations in general have not been wholehearted, precise, or complete.

The price situation in Colombia is not good—nor yet too alarming. Since 1939, the general wholesale price index for Bogotá has risen by 25 per cent, and the greatest part of the upward movement has occurred despite the application of price control measures during 1943. The cost-of-living index for a worker's family in Bogotá has gone up by 29 per cent since 1939—exceeding the rise in the wholesale price index for the same period. Like the course of wholesale prices, the upward acceleration in the cost of living was most marked in 1943. From January, 1943, to November, 1943, the rise in the cost of living totaled 19 per cent, as compared with 16 per cent in the same period in 1942 and a rise of 1 per cent in the corresponding period of 1941.[1] A 4 per cent rise in the cost of living occurred during the month of October, 1943. These figures, of course, relate only to Bogotá and represent only officially recognized average price increases. There are many indications that the prices of individual items have risen to much higher levels and that the price situation in Colombia outside of Bogotá is certainly no less serious than in the capital city. The government has not set producer ceilings on foods, and the Office of Price Supervision is able at present to present only a weakened front in the face of forces making for dangerous speculation and further increases. The situation is not too dissimilar to that which confronted the government in lesser degree in early 1943, with the major difference that in 1944 the government has already employed its heaviest weapons and appears now to be on the defensive.

Despite the picture which has just been drawn it is far too early and too speculative to conclude that price control in Colombia has

[1] Both in 1940 and 1941 the cost of living in Bogotá was substantially below the level for 1939.

not achieved a very substantial measure of success. As a matter of fact, the record of price control in Colombia is still not clear, nor are its prospects certain. Prices have risen more sharply and on a wider front since the institution of the Office of Price Supervision than before the control effort was begun. On the other hand, the underlying cumulative forces making for inflation on a devastating scale have been operating throughout the period with increasing pressure, and there can be little doubt that, without the imposition of control, prices would have risen far beyond their present level. The price situation in Colombia today is much better than that prevailing in most Latin American countries, and there is no reason as yet to believe that inflationary forces are—or will get—seriously out of hand.

Structurally considered, price control in Colombia has proceeded since its inception on a sound, realistic basis. Operations have gone forward no more rapidly than events have required, and only after careful analysis, planning, and study of relevant facts. The price control measures have been well directed and, to an outsider, reflect a high degree of economic "sophistication" on the part of the officials responsible for their form, content, and timing. The problem of food prices has not been handled with conspicuous vigor and success, but it must be borne in mind that even in the United States, with its years of experience, its tremendous facilities, and under what should have been most auspicious conditions, food pricing still constitutes the most difficult problem of control. Incidentally, the pressure of agricultural interests for increased food prices, familiar in the United States, is augmented in Colombia by objective advocacy of higher prices as a measure for stimulation of long-run agricultural development.

Price control in Colombia must bear a slight share of responsibility for the deterioration in the political situation (as, indeed, it must in the United States); but it should not be saddled with more. In the main, price control has been a victim of and has suffered from a political situation which has impaired its effectiveness both directly and through the virtual destruction of its principal ally—the "siphoning" decree. It is a fair guess that history, taking full account of the circumstances in Colombia, will accord very substantial credit to the institution and operation of the Office of Price Supervision for the maintenance, in a critical period and against tremendous odds, of a bending but still unbroken advance line of defense against the ravages of wartime inflation.

Chapter XIV

Cuba: Sugar and Currency

by HENRY C. WALLICH

CUBA, in recent years, has been "exposed to authors" in the field of the social sciences as much as, if not more than, any country in Latin America. Our peculiarly close relations with the island, arising from our preferential tariff agreement and, until 1934, from the Platt Amendment, have aroused the interest of economists, the concern of political scientists, and not infrequently the ire of reformers of varying persuasions. Valuable information on Cuba has also been contributed by students of international sugar problems and by various United States technical missions which have visited the island. In view of this wealth of material,[1] it seems justifiable to forego a discussion of general aspects in this chapter and to concentrate on two subjects which seem to me to be of particular interest: the problems of the sugar industry, and the monetary situation.

[1] For general discussions of Cuban economic and social problems, see Foreign Policy Association, Inc. Commission for the Study of Cuban Affairs, *Problems of the New Cuba* (New York, 1935); Leland H. Jenks, *Our Cuban Colony* (New York, 1928); Carleton Beals, *The Crime of Cuba* (Philadelphia, 1933); and Juan Alienes, *The National Economy of Cuba* (Directorio Oficial, Camara de Comercio de la República de Cuba, Havana, 1942). For studies of the sugar industry and of agriculture in general, see Ramiro Guerra y Sanchez, *La Industria Azucarera de Cuba* (Havana, 1940); and P. G. Minneman, *The Agriculture of Cuba* (U.S. Department of Agriculture, Washington, D. C., 1942). The Cuban tax system is discussed in E. R. A. Seligman and Carl Shoup, *Informe sobre el Sistema Tributario de Cuba* (Havana, 1932); and Roswell Magill and Carl Shoup, *The Cuban Fiscal System* (New York, 1939); also, J. M. Perez Cubillas, *Legislación Fiscal Cubana* (Havana, 1936). For monetary problems, see J. M. Perez Cubillas and Felipe Pazos y Roque, *El Problema Monetario de Cuba* (Havana, 1940); Felipe Pazos y Roque, *La Banca* (Havana, 1941); and "Report to the Cuban Government of the American Technical Mission to Cuba," *Federal Reserve Bulletin*, August, 1942, pp. 774–801.

The topic of sugar is in itself so broad that it touches upon practically every phase of Cuban economic life. Although it is tobacco that has made Cuba famous the world over, it is sugar that has made her rich—and at times poor. In 1938, for example, sugar contributed 30 per cent of the national product,[1] while tobacco, the second

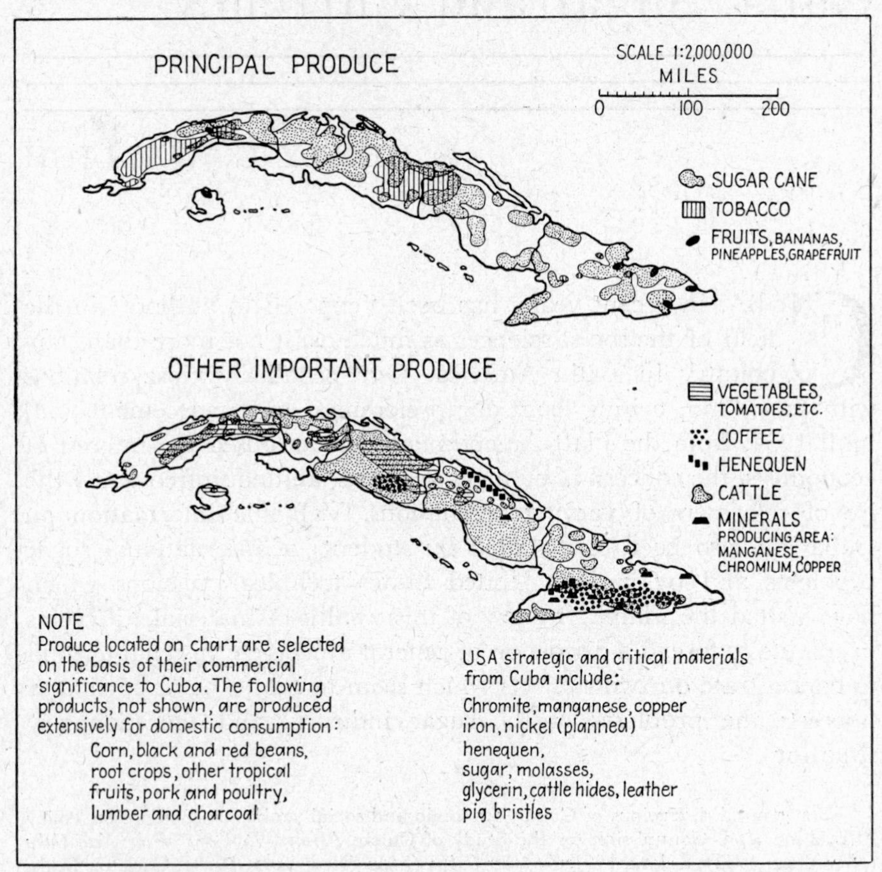

CHART 16.—Cuba. Land use—nonurban areas. (*Coordinator of Inter-American Affairs.*)

largest product, accounted for only 10 per cent; throughout the period of the thirties, sugar on an average made up 70 to 80 per cent of total exports. Cuba thus enjoys the dubious distinction of being one of the purest one-crop countries in the Western Hemisphere; the problems which are characteristic of most Latin American countries appear in Cuba in their most extreme form.

[1] Alienes, *op. cit.* pp. 85–86.

The accompanying Charts 16 and 17 illustrate the importance of sugar to the Cuban economy, the geographical distribution of output, the countries of destination, and the ownership of mills.

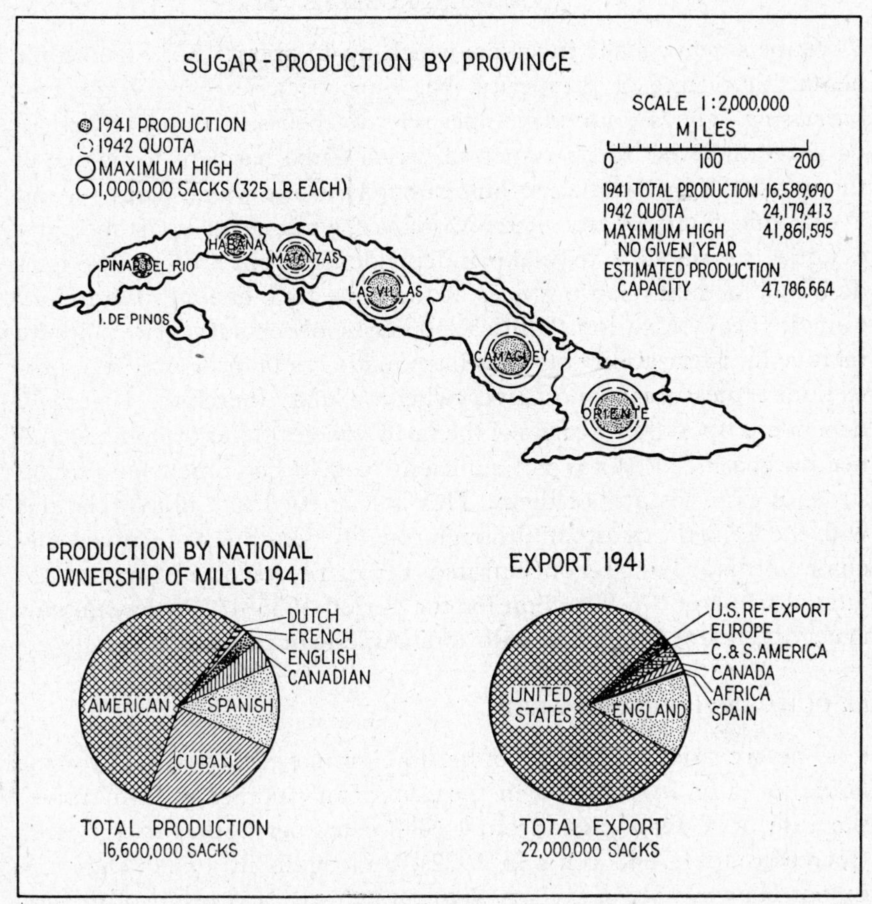

CHART 17.—Cuba. Sugar production, ownership, and export, 1941. (*Coordinator of Inter-American Affairs.*)

The monetary question, while less vital than matters concerning sugar, deserves attention because of the unusual character of Cuban monetary developments. From a pure dollar currency, Cuba in recent years has moved toward a dual currency system, but so far she continues to be the only major country in Latin America which is practically without any of the ordinary instruments of monetary policy. The fact that a proposal for a central bank at present is under discussion in the legislature lends particular interest to a study of this phase of Cuban affairs.

I. Sugar Problems

Cuba's heavy stake in sugar, which up to about 1927 secured for her a fair degree of prosperity, has since become increasingly embarrassing. The Cubans sometimes refer to their situation as a case of national diabetes. The product, of which Cuba happens to be one of the most efficient producers, unfortunately is one which can be—and is—produced almost anywhere. Moreover, while sugar is a sufficiently essential commodity to make independence from overseas sources desirable for many nations, it is at the same time enough of a luxury to invite heavy taxation. Political pressures for self-sufficiency and the relative indispensability of sugar have made it a favorite object of protectionist measures almost everywhere. Cuba, therefore, is largely dependent upon the vagaries of the tariff policies of her customers, and her purchasing power is not sufficient to give her much bargaining strength vis-à-vis any of them. This is true even of Cuba's relations with the United States; for although roughly two-thirds of Cuba's purchases ordinarily are concentrated there, representing an average annual value of $72.9 million for the period 1935–1939, this amount is negligible in comparison with total American income.

a. Cuba's American Market

The precarious character of her foreign markets was first brought home to Cuba in 1921, when the American emergency tariff raised the rate on Cuban sugar from 1.0048 cents per pound to 1.6 cents (increased to 1.7648 cents in 1922), and again in 1930, when the Smoot-Hawley rate of 2 cents went into effect. As a result of the advantage enjoyed by American domestic and insular producers, Cuba's share in the American sugar market dropped from an average of 51.4 per cent during the period 1922–1931 to 25.4 per cent in 1933. In 1934, after the island had passed through an intense economic crisis, accompanied by revolution and social upheavals, Cuba's share was stabilized at close to 30 per cent under the Jones-Costigan Act, which allocated marketing quotas to American domestic and insular producers, as well as to Cuba. The act also made possible a general increase in sugar prices, by allowing aggregate quotas to be limited in accordance with the needs of the market.[1] Further relief was accorded to Cuba in 1934 by two successive tariff reductions, the second under the 1934 trade agreement, which lowered the duty on sugar to 0.9 cent per pound. Under the second supplementary trade agreement of 1942, finally, the duty was cut to 0.75 cent.

The American quota system has prevented Cuba from losing further ground, but her position before the war continued to be imperiled by recurrent demands of American domestic producers for a larger quota, at the expense of Cuba. Against the considerable political strength of these interests, the island can count on the aid of American sugar refiners on the eastern seaboard, whose income is derived from the refining of imported offshore raw sugar. Apart from this, however, the defense of Cuban sugar rests mainly upon the following arguments: (1) A large part of the Cuban sugar industry is owned by American investors.[2] (2) A reduction in American purchases from Cuba must inevitably lead to a reduction in Cuban purchases from the United States. (3) Next to domestic sugar production, Cuba is the safest source of supply in wartime. (4) Since Cuba is a friendly country, bound to the United States by close historical and political ties, the American government has a moral obligation to prevent, as well as a political interest in preventing, social and political disturbances so close to its doorstep.

b. THE IMPACT OF THE WAR

When the Second World War began in 1939, one of the many erroneous conclusions which were drawn from the experience of the First World War was the belief that Cuba would soon reexperience the prosperity of that earlier period. Sugar prices jumped, and the price of shares of sugar companies responded. These hopes, however, were dashed within a few weeks. The United States quota system was temporarily suspended in order to prevent an undue price rise; thereupon the American market was flooded with supplies, and prices fell back to their previous level. European buyers meanwhile,

[1] The artificial restriction of supplies has made the sugar price in the United States completely independent of prices in the world market. The latter is likewise regulated by a quota system, under the International Sugar Agreement of 1937. Cuba's output thus is sold in three separate quota-determined markets: the American market, the world market, and the Cuban home market.

[2] In 1939, about 56 per cent of total sugar output was produced in American-owned mills.

instead of spending their foreign exchange resources on sugar, preferred to reserve them for arms purchases. Thus for Cuba the year 1940 passed in gloomy depression.

In 1941, however, matters began to improve. A growing demand for sugar in the United States, accompanied by the increasing inability of Philippine and Hawaiian producers to ship their quotas, enabled Cuba to dispose of her entire 1941 crop, plus a substantial carry-over, at rising prices. The average Cuban price, which in January, 1941, had been quoted at 1.30 cents per pound, rose to 2.54 cents 1 year later, and in the American market sugar was quoted at 3.80 cents in August, 1941, before the OPACS set a ceiling price of 3.50 cents. In view of the threatening shortage, the American government contracted for 95 per cent of Cuba's 1942 crop, which later was fixed at 4,400,000 short tons, at a price equivalent to 2.65 cents per pound of sugar.[1] The consummation of this deal promised a higher degree of prosperity than Cuba had known in more than a decade. Apprehensions began to be voiced that farmers might neglect their vegetables and other crops and might overextend cane plantings, and that the laboriously fostered diversification program would thus go by the board. For a time, however, the fear of excessive prosperity remained unfounded, for the sugar picture soon changed once more. Enemy submarines, which decimated our merchant shipping in the Caribbean, also destroyed expectations of a continuance of the Cuban sugar boom. Of the large 1942 crop, 1,770,000 tons had to remain in Cuban warehouses, American sugar consumption was rationed, and for 1943 the American government contracted for no more than 3,000,000 tons of sugar.[2] The price remained unchanged at 2.65 cents per pound, in spite of a substantial rise in costs, and was made even less attractive by various incidental changes in the contract. Cuba relapsed into gloom.

The depression which seemed in prospect at the end of 1942 did not, however, materialize. The only substantial slump which occurred was that in the spirits of the business community, whereas indices of

[1] Part of the total was to be delivered in the form of high-test molasses, at 2.50 cents per pound of sugar content.

[2] The reduced amount of the purchase was due, not to any feeling that the sugar was not wanted, but to the fact that the War Shipping Administration could not guarantee shipping space for more than 125,000 tons monthly. Since Cuban carrying capacity was only about 3,750,000 tons, a purchase even of 3,000,000 tons, in conjunction with a carry-over of 1,770,000 tons, was likely to create a serious warehouse situation, inasmuch as practically all the 1943 crop would be made by May 1.

retail sales, bank clearings, and wage payments continued upward after a brief interruption. Credit for averting a depression was due to a variety of factors, among them several measures taken jointly by the Cuban and American governments. Among other things, provision was made for the planting of substantial amounts of corn, beans, and peanuts. Rice production also was increased. Irrigation, road building, and other public works were undertaken with the aid of an Export-Import Bank credit which had been authorized but not disbursed in January, 1941. The exploitation of Cuba's nickel and other mineral resources was pushed aggressively. Facilities for distilling molasses into alcohol were established by numerous sugar mills, and the activities of the American naval base also added to Cuba's income.

Meanwhile, the submarines were being driven out of the Caribbean, the general shipping situation improved, and Cuban sugar began to move more freely. (Both the expansion of exports and the improved position of the United States are evident in the accompanying chart.) This opened the way for a much larger crop to be produced in 1944. The desirability of such a crop became increasingly evident in the light of rising military and lend-lease requirements[1] (particularly since production in the United States had fallen far short of expectations) and because of the potential need for sugar to feed liberated areas. In December, 1943, therefore, the American government contracted for a minimum of 4 million tons of sugar, as well as for any exportable excess that Cuba might be able to produce. The price continued at 2.65 cents per pound, in spite of the bitter protests of producers. Disagreement persisted for a while concerning the sale of blackstrap (a by-product of sugar), which the American government wanted to acquire for munitions purposes, while the Cubans hoped to sell it to us in the more profitable form of distilled spirits. The conflict between gunpowder and gin eventually was decided in favor of the former; with the sale of these molasses, total proceeds from the 1943 sugar crop will have been well in excess of $300 million.

The prosperity which this crop is likely to bring to Cuba will be very substantial, although probably not so great as that which prevailed during the last war, when the American government paid up to 5.50 cents per pound for the island's sugar crops. All classes of Cubans are likely to participate in this prosperity, since the Sugar

[1] A sugar equivalent of approximately 1 million tons was required for alcohol for explosives and synthetic rubber.

Coordination Law of 1937 aims to secure an equitable share in the benefits of a high sugar price for all productive factors. The law makes the price which the mills pay to planters for their cane directly proportionate to the price of sugar. Such purchased cane accounts for approximately 85 per cent of the total milled. The wages paid by planters to their fieldworkers likewise are proportionate to the price of sugar. This price also governs the pay of millworkers, although not

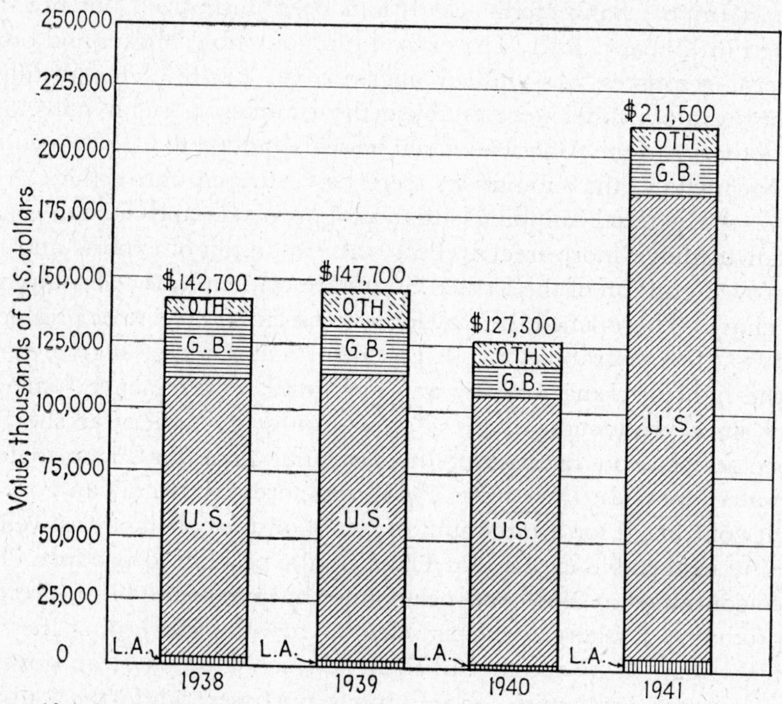

CHART 18.—Cuba. Exports by countries of destination, 1938–1942. (*Coordinator of Inter-American Affairs.*)

in direct proportion. A special wage increase of 59 per cent, however, was granted to millworkers in December, 1942, by government decree.

c. SUGAR AFTER THE WAR

The immediate postwar outlook for Cuban sugar appears to be fairly good, since Far Eastern production will be unavailable temporarily and may remain so for a considerable time if the mills have been dismantled by the Japanese, as present reports indicate. The destruction of part of the European beet production will also favor

Cuban sugar; this destruction so far seems to have centered in eastern Europe, whereas central and western European production appears to have been fairly well maintained until now.

The long-run outlook for Cuban sugar, however, although obscure, is not too bright. In the world market, where before the war Cuba had a basic quota of 940,000 tons, Cuba's best customer has been Great Britain, taking approximately two-thirds of Cuba's total world-market sales. During most of the thirties, however, Cuba was losing ground to British beet sugar growers and to producers in the dominions and colonies. One must expect that after the war Great Britain will further reduce her purchases from Cuba, not only because of the pressure of these rival interests, but primarily because of her difficult exchange position. The impoverished countries of the continent, some of which purchased a certain amount of Cuban sugar directly and another part indirectly, after it had been refined in Great Britain, likewise cannot be regarded as promising customers. There is a possibility, no doubt, that an increase in Far Eastern demands, particularly from China, may make up for a shrinkage in the European part of the world market. While Java and, under certain circumstances, the Philippines would be the primary beneficiaries of any demand developing in their neighborhood, Cuba would benefit from the reduced competition of these rival suppliers. It is interesting to speculate on the demand that might develop if the Chinese should begin to take sugar with their tea, but it is quite likely that any increase in Chinese demand will in good part be satisfied from internal sources. The fertile Canton delta is almost ideally suited to a further development of the so far not very extensive Chinese sugar industry (400,000 tons in 1941). There is also the prospect that Formosa, where, in spite of high costs, as much as 1,650,000 tons were produced in 1938, will fall to China after the war. The danger finally that India, the world's largest sugar producer, might force her way into the export market will continue to hang over the heads of all producers. Cuba's world-market prospects, therefore, are not encouraging in the long run, even on the assumption that the International Sugar Agreement is continued in some form. Without the agreement the outlook is distinctly poor.

Although a shrinkage of the world market would be a grave blow to Cuba, the American market is of course by far the more important one, and it is there that the future of Cuban sugar will in the main be decided. The chief question is that of the continuance of the quota system and of our relatively liberal tariff policy. Since the quota system had worked satisfactorily in many respects before the war, the assumption is justified that it will eventually be put into effect again.[1] Within its framework, the chief variables affecting Cuba's position will be the domestic beet sugar quota, the Philippine quota, and the amount that may be allocated to other foreign countries.[2]

It is believed in some quarters that the force of the beet producers' protectionistic arguments has been considerably weakened by the disappointing wartime showing of our domestic beet sugar output.[3] One of the main points upon which these interests used to rest their case was the need to ensure a domestic sugar supply in wartime; but when the issue was put to the test, the industry failed to meet the challenge. This poor showing was due partly to the government's failure to define its sugar program in time for spring sowings and partly to the lure of higher returns from competitive crops and to the almost inevitable wartime labor shortage. Recent technological developments, on the other hand, may enable the beet industry to introduce more highly mechanized processes,[4] thereby allowing it to reduce its costs and to widen its potential marketing area. These conflicting factors are likely to intensify the pressure for changes in the beet quota in one direction or the other.

The position of Philippine sugar after the war, when the islands are slated to become fully independent, will depend largely upon the tariff and quota treatment to be accorded to our former possessions. Since the application of the full duty of 1.87½ cents per pound, or even that of 0.93¾ cent established under the trade agreement with Peru, might shut out Philippine sugar from the American market, unless and until a substantial price rise occurred, the Philippine product, if it is to be admitted at all, would probably have to be given a considerable degree of tariff preference. The higher the Philippine quota is set, the greater will be the tariff preference required to enable this relatively inefficient producer to fill it.

[1] It was suspended in April, 1942, to permit entry to all available sugar.

[2] There seems to be no particular reason to anticipate changes in the Puerto Rican and the Hawaiian quotas. Changes in the domestic cane quota probably would not affect other producers very greatly.

[3] Output for the crop year 1943–1944 fell to 996,000 tons, compared with an average of 1,773,000 during the crop years 1938–1939 and 1939–1940.

[4] Elimination of the need for thinning the young plants, through an improved segmentation of seeds, is extremely important in this respect.

It is not unthinkable that after the war a number of Latin American countries will obtain wider access to the American sugar market, since it may become necessary to compensate them for the cessation of American war purchases. Among these relative newcomers might be the Dominican Republic, Peru, Brazil, Haiti, Mexico, and Ecuador, all of whom are actual or potential exporters of sugar, although only the first two have a substantial exportable surplus. These countries probably would enjoy the relatively advantageous tariff rate of 0.93¾ cent per pound (compared with 0.75 cent on Cuban sugar) recently granted to Peru and universalized by virtue of the most-favored-nation clause. The threat to Cuba from this source, however, does not seem particularly grave.

d. THE NEED FOR DIVERSIFICATION

The foregoing considerations indicate that Cuba, while one of the most efficient producers, is likely to remain a marginal supplier in both the world and the American market. This peculiar vulnerability to adverse foreign legislation has figured importantly in a controversy current in Cuba regarding the basic merits of the sugar industry. In contrast to the common view that sugar production represents the most efficient utilization of the island's resources, it has been argued than the sugar industry is undesirable for Cuba, that it has always lived on special favors at the expense of other potential activities, and that Cuba would be altogether better off without it.[1] This contention, insofar as it is predicated merely upon the relative efficiency of different uses of Cuban resources, appears to take rather too rosy a view of the alternatives open to the island. It is very unlikely that Cuban land and labor could be more efficiently employed than in the sugar industry, where their productivity is enhanced by enormous amounts of foreign capital. When the prospects of the industry are regarded in relation to the tariff policy of the United States and other countries, however, serious doubts arise as to the possibility of translating productive efficiency into equivalent monetary income. For this reason, Cuba may be well advised to look about for other means of livelihood.

[1] *Cf.* Herminio Portell Vilá, "La Industria Azucarera y su Futuro," *Revista Bimestre Cubana,* September, 1942, pp. 161–179, and the same author's introduction to Fernando Ortiz, *Contrapunteo del Azucar y Tobaco* (Havana, 1940). For the opposite view, *cf.* Ramiro Guerra, *La Industria Azucarera de Cuba* (Havana, 1940), Ch. I, and Antonio Barro y Segura, *La Verdad sobre el Azúcar en Cuba* (Havana, 1943).

This does not imply, as has been suggested by one of the critics of the industry, that it might advantageously be abandoned altogether unless it can be placed on an entirely new basis.[1] Apart from the enormous difficulties of transition, Cuba's natural superiority in sugar suggests that full advantage should be taken of it to the extent that market conditions permit. The uncertainties surrounding the latter, however, do make it desirable to devote a decreasing proportion of the island's resources to sugar.

The need for diversification has received practical recognition since 1927, when a sharply protective tariff was launched as a counterpoise to the sugar restriction program initiated at that time.[2] Agricultural diversification in Cuba is favored by the fact that the island, unlike other Caribbean areas, does not suffer from overpopulation. Agricultural land is plentiful, and the introduction of new crops does not require the withdrawal of land from sugar cane. A shortage of labor in the sugar industry likewise ought not to result from a diversification program, unless very large sugar crops are in prospect. Temporary spurts in sugar output, therefore, such as have been experienced during the war, need not interfere with other activities.

In addition to agricultural diversification and stimulation of new industries, there is the possibility of diversifying the output of the sugar industry itself. Numerous suggestions in that direction have been made in recent years. One possibility which currently is being exploited on a substantial scale is the production of industrial and beverage alcohol. Cuban cane alcohol not only is proving itself important to our munitions and rubber programs, but as an admixture to gasoline is also helping Cuba to overcome her critical motor-fuel situation. Alcohol as a base of synthetic rubber and as a partial substitute for gasoline has very interesting postwar aspects. The demand from either of these sources is potentially enormous, but its realization in the short run depends largely upon American rubber policy and ultimately upon the trend in world oil reserves. Various other uses for industrial alcohol have somewhat more concrete prospects; in the postwar period, however, Cuban cane alcohol is likely to encounter stiff competition from alcohol made from different raw materials.

[1] Portell Vilá, *op. cit.*

[2] Strenuous efforts have been made ever since to increase Cuba's agricultural self-sufficiency and to encourage the growth of local industries. More success has been achieved in the agricultural field than in the industrial, so that shortly before the war the only foodstuffs imported on a major scale were wheat flour, rice, and lard.

Another interesting possibility is the conversion of surplus bagasse (leftovers from crushed cane) into cellulose for paper pulp, rayon, and for filler in certain types of plastics. The process is technically feasible, but so far not commercially profitable. Less ambitious projects might include the extraction of cane wax from the "mud" ejected in the process of sugar making; the bacterial fermentation of molasses to produce the higher alcohols; the increased manufacture of better grade liquor and of candy; and the use of molasses for cattle feed. The possibility of utilizing the seasonal excess capacity of the mills for the dehydration of fruit or to supply power for regional electrification has also been suggested. Off-season operation of the mills, however, would require the use of imported and hence expensive fuels, since the bagasse which is used to run the mills during the crop season usually is little more than sufficient for the needs of that period.

A broadening of the range of products along these or other lines might create a wholly new outlook for the sugar industry and would considerably reduce Cuba's dependence on foreign purchases of her sugar. The realization of the various proposals seems to be in good part a matter of scientific research, a field in which the industry, partly for lack of funds, has been backward. To remedy this deficiency the Sugar Research Foundation was established in 1943 to explore new uses of sugar and its by-products and to conduct investigations into the nutritional value of sugar.[1]

II. The Money Question

The large volume of dollar reserves which American sugar purchases have bestowed upon Cuba provides an opportunity for a much needed reorganization of the Cuban currency system. Cuba's monetary troubles, which will form the topic of this section, entered into an acute stage in 1939, when the peso depreciated by as much as 18 per cent. The origin of these troubles, however, dates back to 1932, when the first break was made in the system established in 1914.

a. THE OLD MONETARY SYSTEM

Under the monetary law of 1914, the American dollar and the Cuban gold peso, both having the same gold content, were unlimited legal tender. The 24 million gold pesos which were coined, however,

[1] The foundation is backed by a group of producers representing over 90 per cent, by volume, of the American, Cuban, Puerto Rican, and Hawaiian sugar industry.

soon disappeared from public circulation, and Cuba's currency until 1932 was in effect the dollar, supplemented by a small amount of Cuban silver currency. This system was obviously a very solid one, and at the same time highly elastic. The latter characteristic it owed partly to the rapidity with which swings in the balance of payments caused dollars to flow into and out of the country, and more particularly to the readiness of the branches of foreign banks to bring in funds from their head offices whenever the local supply was insufficient.[1] The use of the dollar was of course expensive, since for Cuba it was not a fiduciary medium, but the equivalent of a pure gold currency, obtained by surrendering an equivalent amount of resources. It may be doubted, however, that Cuba could have reduced this cost materially by replacing the dollar with a fiduciary Cuban currency. The psychological repercussions of such a change probably would have caused a large outflow of funds, which would have prevented the Cuban government from calling in the entire dollar circulation for exchange against Cuban currency.

The main significance of the dollar system was that it deprived Cuba of an independent monetary and exchange policy. In many respects the automatic character of the system may have been salutary, but there were at least two occasions on which the power to conduct an independent monetary policy would have been desirable. The first was the crash of 1920, when an issuance of domestic currency, coupled perhaps with some degree of depreciation, might have saved part of the Cuban banking system and might have prevented the wholesale passage of foreclosed properties into foreign hands. The second occasion for independent monetary action arose in 1932 and 1933. Although depreciation would hardly have enabled Cuba to increase her exports very much, it might have improved her bargaining position in the schemes for international sugar control in which she participated and would have reduced bankruptcies. Largely because relief was not forthcoming from the monetary side, the Cuban government in 1933 had to yield to demands for a moratorium on domestic mortgages. The renewal of this moratorium in 1934 and 1940 has caused substantial losses to banks and other lenders and has greatly hindered the development of a capital market.

[1] After the highly developed Cuban banking system had been wiped out by the sugar crash of 1920, about 80 per cent of the banking business was being done by the branches of large American and Canadian banks. From 1923 to 1938, Cuba also was served by Federal reserve agencies.

It may be argued, however, that an independent policy might easily have been carried to extremes and that its results might have been worse than the rigidity which it was to correct. Under most circumstances, moreover, and certainly under those prevailing immediately before the war, a policy of stability vis-à-vis the dollar is desirable for Cuba, since sugar exports cannot expand beyond quota limits and since a substantial increase in domestic production cannot be expected from depreciation.

b. THE SILVER ISSUES

The first breach in the dollar system was made in 1932, when President Machado, trying desperately to raise funds for the maintenance of Cuba's foreign-debt service, hit upon the expedient of issuing subsidiary silver coin, which yielded a seigniorage profit of about 75 per cent.[1] The first coinage amounted to only 3.6 millions, equal to the unissued balance of the 12 millions of silver coin authorized by the 1914 legislation. Since the legal-tender power of the coins remained limited to 8 per cent, however, and since the bulky material was inconvenient and expensive to handle in large amounts, a discount on silver currency developed which in September, 1932, reached 5 per cent. The government eased the situation by accepting silver up to 35 per cent of tax payments and by using army trucks to haul the payments which banks made to their branches. Early in 1933 these measures had reduced the discount sufficiently to make possible a second issue, amounting to 6 million pesos.

A third issue, in the spring of 1934, was preceded by measures which appeared to herald a bold new policy aimed at the creation of an independent monetary system and an ultimate break with the dollar. In a sweeping decree,[2] the government made silver pesos full legal tender for the discharge of old as well as new obligations contracted in dollars or Cuban gold pesos. This measure exposed holders of such obligations to losses from the actual and potential depreciation of the silver peso, and in retaliation the banks allegedly threatened to export all dollars from Cuba. The government first backed down and repealed the legal-tender clause insofar as it referred to old contracts, then struck back by imposing a mild form of foreign exchange con-

[1] The Cuban silver peso is of the same weight and fineness as the United States silver dollar.

[2] Decree-law 244, May 23, 1934, *Gaceta Oficial.*

trol. This proved a stimulus rather than a restraint upon capital flight, since dollars could easily be carried out in travelers' pockets, and the control was lifted after a few weeks. The clause making the silver peso legal tender for new dollar obligations also was repealed, since it resulted in an extreme restriction of dollar loans, while the volume of pesos was not yet sufficient to permit all bank loans to be made in silver. Nothing thus remained of the 1934 reform but the legal-tender status of silver for all contracts in such currency.

Early in 1935, the government began to issue silver certificates, backed 100 per cent by silver pesos in the Treasury, thereby doing away with the inconvenience of using the heavy coins. From then on until early 1938, by which time a total of 69.5 millions of silver currency had been created, the discount rarely exceeded 2 per cent and usually amounted to less than a fraction of 1 per cent.

The forces which produced this stability in spite of the rising tide of issues are not hard to discern. In retail transactions, as well as in tax and wage payments, no distinction was made between dollars and pesos, and the two currencies therefore had identical purchasing power. It was only in the sphere of foreign trade and other large-scale transactions that the peso was at a discount from the dollar, because of the greater confidence enjoyed by the latter, and its international acceptability. A substantial discount tended, in accordance with Gresham's law, to drive out the dollar from the retail sphere, which we may call the internal market, into the other—external—market. But as long as the volume of peso currency and deposits remained insufficient to take care of the circulatory needs of the internal market, and dollars were thus required to make up the deficiency, any tendency to withhold dollars from circulation increased the demand for pesos, which in turn would narrow the discount enough to enable dollars to stay in circulation.

c. DEPRECIATION OF THE PESO

Most people in Cuba, and certainly the government, knew that this relatively satisfactory state of affairs was bound to come to an end once the volume of pesos began to exceed the needs of the internal market. This occurred after the middle of 1938, when the government, on the basis of a rather optimistic appraisal of the market, started to circulate another issue designed to bring the total currency to 89.5 millions. The venture happened to coincide with a pronounced contraction in business, and the combined effect of an increased supply and a reduced demand for currency drove the peso to a discount which by the end of June, 1939, had passed 5 per cent. At that moment the government, sorely in need of cash, took the ill-advised step of announcing a new issue of 15 millions. The peso broke sharply, and on July 5 a discount as high as 18 per cent was quoted. Thereupon, the government, to its great credit, decided to forego further seigniorage profits and to cancel the proposed issue, causing the discount to shrink to approximately 10 per cent. Around this level it fluctuated until the end of 1940.

With the disappearance of the dollar from the internal market, Gresham's law ceased to be operative and the peso began to act much like any free paper currency. One important difference must be noted, however. Whereas ordinarily the value of a free currency is determined directly by the balance of payments,[1] the value of the peso was determined in the first instance by the requirements of the internal market for means of payments, *i.e.*, by the level of business and prices. This, of course, is predominantly influenced by the balance of payments, which thus becomes an indirect determinant of the peso rate. It is at least thinkable, however, if not probable, that at times the deflationary effect of a passive balance of payments might be more than offset by an increase in domestic investment, which would cause business to expand and the peso to rise.[2]

The government did not stand by idly while its currency depreciated. Even while it was still aggravating the situation by increasing the volume of circulation, it took a series of measures to check the drop in the peso. Lacking exchange resources for pegging the currency, however, as well as proper instruments of monetary control, it confined its measures to a series of awkward improvisations. The first of these was a decree issued in July, 1938, requiring the banks to accord equal treatment to dollar and peso deposits. This was followed by a Treasury order instructing the banks to carry in pesos 75 per cent of their legal reserve of 25 per cent, and by the withdrawal of government funds from the banks and their subsequent deposit with the Treasury. Both measures aimed to induce the banks to

[1] It is understood, of course, that the balance of payments is not the ultimate determinant of the exchange rate but merely the focal point at which basic factors, such as incomes and prices, become effective.

[2] The foreign exchange required to sustain the passive balance of payments would come out of the dollar holdings existing in the external market.

purchase pesos. In April, 1939, a stabilization fund was created, which, however, could not operate very effectively, since it could put into the market no more dollars than it had previously taken out. Finally, the legal-tender power of the peso was once more extended so as to cover certain existing and future dollar obligations.[1]

In so far as these measures had any effect, it was only that of mitigating the depreciation of the peso; they did not succeed in reducing the discount below the average level of 10 per cent which prevailed during the latter half of 1939 and throughout 1940.

With the improvement in the business situation, however, which took place in 1941, the discount began to diminish, and by the end of the year parity had been reestablished. It was to be expected that the rise of the peso would be checked at that point, for any demand for additional means of payment could henceforth be met by the entry of dollars into circulation. Dollars indeed returned into circulation in large volume, but the peso nevertheless went to a small premium, which at its height, on Feb. 5, 1942, reached 1.125 per cent.[2] After substantial amounts of dollar currency[3] had been imported, however, this premium gradually abated; after the end of the crop season it disappeared completely, although it recurred during certain months of 1943.

[1] For a detailed discussion of these measures, *cf.* Perez Cubillas and Pazos y Roque, *op. cit.*

[2] The explanation of this phenomenon, which occasioned a good deal of discussion, appears to have been twofold. In the first place, the premium which appeared was essentially not one upon the peso over the dollar, although that was the expression which it found in the exchange market, but a premium upon notes of small denominations. The local supply of such notes was insufficient for the pay-roll needs arising out of the large 1942 sugar crop. The sugar mills and others requiring such notes therefore had the choice of importing dollar bills through the banks, reimbursing them for their expenses, or of bidding for the available supply of small peso notes. The latter was cheaper up to the point where a premium upon pesos had appeared equal to the cost of importing small dollar notes. It cannot be said with certainty whether or not the peso premium ever went beyond the banks' charges for importing currency, since bank practices as regards shipments and charges to customers were not uniform and since transport expenses were not identical for all denominations. It seems probable, however, that for a while at least the premium did exceed bank charges, since at its peak it amounted to 1.125 per cent, while maximum shipping costs on $1 bills at that time appear to have been only 0.75 per cent. It must be assumed, therefore, that a second set of factors contributed to the strength of the peso. These must be sought in a certain resistance to the reintroduction of the dollar resulting from changes in customs and contracts, and perhaps also in a lack of confidence in the American unit motivated by the inauspicious start of the war.

[3] During the first 6 months of 1942, over $70 million was shipped to Cuba, part of this amount by the United States Treasury, in connection with the purchase of the Cuban sugar crop.

d. CREATION OF A GOLD RESERVE

Meanwhile the government undertook to increase the supply of pesos by issuing additional silver certificates. Unlike earlier issues, the new ones were in no way ascribable to the profit motive. They were made against a reserve of 98 per cent in dollars or gold and yielded only an insignificant seigniorage. The underlying idea was to take advantage of Cuba's large active balance of payments for the creation of a monetary reserve, which later could be turned over to the proposed central bank, studies for which were in progress.[1] The certificates, however, continued to be convertible only into silver, and no provisions were made for their withdrawal against gold or dollars, if the peso should weaken.

From May, 1942, when the gold purchase program started, to the end of 1943, a total of 51 million pesos was issued against gold or dollars. This amount, however, represented only a minor part of Cuba's total dollar inflow during the period. Although complete data are not available, it appears that from January, 1942, to the end of 1943 approximately $182 million was shipped to Cuba, $137 of this after the initiation of the gold purchase program.

Whereas currency imports in 1942 were due largely to the need for circulating medium, a substantial part of the 1943 influx was motivated by a monthly tax of 0.15 per cent on Cuban investments abroad, which the government imposed in order to curb what it regarded as an unwarranted export of capital from Cuba. Whatever the merits of such a tax in normal times, at present it not only causes unnecessary shipping and insurance costs, but also contributes very distinctly toward inflation. Many wealthy Cubans who ordinarily would prefer to leave part of their funds in the United States are now transferring them to Cuba, where they can do little more with their money than to bid up one another's property, the volume of new physical investment being limited by shortages of materials. As long as the Treasury does not intend to capitalize upon this inflow by absorbing all dollars into its monetary reserve, Cuba probably would be better off if the funds were allowed to remain in the United States.

[1] On the basis of recommendations made by an American mission, a bill for the creation of a central bank was introduced in the Cuban Congress on June 30, 1942. *Cf.* "Report to the Cuban Government of the American Technical Mission to Cuba," *Federal Reserve Bulletin*, August, 1942, pp. 774–801. The acquisition of gold was facilitated by a stabilization agreement entered into with the United States Treasury in July, 1942.

The total volume of dollars in Cuba, at the end of 1943, exclusive of those absorbed by the Treasury against newly issued pesos, was estimated at $174.3 million, of which $900,000 formed part of the Treasury's cash holdings, $94.2 million were held by the banks, and $79.2 million were estimated to be in circulation.[1]

e. THE POSITION OF THE BANKS

A few words must be said regarding the exchange and credit policy of the banks, for the former in the past has significantly influenced the value of the peso, while the latter is of importance in evaluating the need for a central bank. With the appearance of the peso discount, the banks were faced with the problem of having to operate in two currencies. They met it by setting up separate dollar and silver accounts, and by adopting a general policy of balancing assets and liabilities in each currency, so as to avoid taking speculative positions.[2] As long as the discount remained small, however, at least a few of the banks deviated seasonally from a policy of exact balance, taking a long position in silver during the dead season, when the discount was relatively high, and a short one during the crop period, when it was lowest. Small exchange profits were realized from these operations, which at the same time helped to stabilize the market. After 1938, when depreciation became more serious, the banks as a group endeavored to maintain an exact balance at all times, in view of the uncertainty surrounding the future of the peso. The data available do not support the contention, sometimes heard in Cuba, that the banks were partly responsible for the drop in the peso in 1939.

With respect to the credit policy of the banks, it is frequently being claimed that the volume of credit is insufficient, that some sectors of the economy are being neglected, and that certain rates are excessively high.[3] The banks counter with the statement that they are extending as much accommodation as is warranted from a credit standpoint. Both claims appear to be justified. The critics of the banks may point to the fact that of total loans of 68.1 million dollars and pesos outstanding at the end of 1942, the sugar industry and commercial interests accounted for 29 millions and 28.2 millions, respectively, while agricultural loans, other than to cane growers, were no

[1] Ministerio de Hacienda, *Distribución de la Moneda*, Dec. 31, 1943.

[2] In their exchange operations, the banks treat the dollar as the "home currency" and the silver peso like any other foreign currency.

[3] *Cf.* Felipe Pazos, "La Banca," *Revista Bimestre Cubana*, October, 1941.

more than 800,000 pesos. Growers of crops other than cane, therefore, usually must obtain their credit from wholesale merchants and country storekeepers, frequently under ruinous conditions.[1] It is also true that, on certain types of loans, rates of 8 per cent or more are being charged. The banks, on the other hand, may point to the fact that past experience, in the political as well as in the economic sphere, has demonstrated only too clearly the need for a cautious policy. Mortgage loans, for example, have proved unsafe in view of successive moratoria, the last of which will not be fully wound up until 1970. Certain types of loan contracts are not so easily enforcible under Cuban law as in the United States. Crop loans to small farmers are not feasible, because, among other things, they require a great deal of supervision and, for loans to other than sugar growers, also involve considerable crop risks which the banks can hardly be expected to assume. Inadequate marketing conditions for numerous products are an obstacle to loans on crops already harvested. For sound loans, on the other hand, there is intense competition among the banks, and the rates charged to good commercial borrowers are not much higher than in the United States.

From these factors one can hardly fail to conclude that there is a gap between the volume of credit which the banks can extend without excessive risk to themselves and the amount which would be desirable for an unhampered development of the Cuban economy. To bridge it, new methods and probably new institutions are required.

f. REVIEW AND OUTLOOK

Although numerous plans for the reorganization of the monetary and credit system of Cuba have been officially discussed, such measures as have been taken, with the exception of the abortive attempts at reform in 1934, have been largely of a hand-to-mouth character. This is particularly true of the silver policy, which, while conceived as a means of raising revenue, has actually resulted in the creation of a new monetary system.

The obvious defects of the dual currency system have frequently been made the basis of a general criticism of the silver policy. The dual system is inconvenient for business and has the effect of reducing the elasticity of the monetary system, thereby at times giving rise to

[1] *Ibid.*

credit shortages.[1] The silver policy probably has also stimulated the tendency of wealthy Cubans to export their savings. It has led, moreover, to the accumulation of large stocks of silver by the government, which do nothing to strengthen the currency and also constitute a rather unpromising speculation. On balance, however, the silver policy probably has done more good than harm, since it represented practically the only means of deficit spending and money creation open to Cuba during the depression and allowed a mobilization of the island's dollar reserves.[2] No doubt a full-scale monetary reform, with the immediate elimination of the dollar from circulation, would have been more effective in some ways, but it would have required the conversion of all contractual relationships and might have been profoundly unsettling. The piecemeal procedure of repeated peso issues allowed a smoother transition. Without the issuance of silver, moreover, irregularities in the service of the external debt might have been much greater.

The gold purchase policy initiated in 1942, unlike the silver policy, was part of a fairly definite plan. It was intended as an interim measure, pending the establishment of a central bank, for which plans were being drawn. The interim, however, is threatening to become permanent, and as a permanent arrangement the gold policy in its present form is no solution. It is true that at present the state of affairs is more satisfactory than at any time since the start of the silver policy. While the current situation resembles that of the middle thirties in that dollars and pesos are circulating side by side, the two currencies are now at par with each other, and until recently there even was a small premium upon the peso.[3] The apparent stability of the peso, however, should not blind the Cuban authorities to the uncertainties of the underlying situation. The amount of peso currency outstanding at the end of 1943 was 141.8 millions, as compared with 89.5 millions in 1939. At that earlier period the circulation nevertheless was in excess of business needs, as indicated by the then prevailing discount of about 10 per cent. Unless Cuba's path in the future should be one

[1] Particularly after the passage of the law permitting the discharge of certain dollar obligations in pesos, which made the banks unwilling to give dollar loans to customers whom they suspected of willingness to avail themselves of this privilege.

[2] Owing to its inability at that time to borrow either at home or abroad, the Cuban government's only way of obtaining credit was to fall behind on the payment of bills and salaries. This source of credit was exploited fairly liberally.

[3] Owing to the peso premium, the dollar until recently was more often seen in circulation than the peso.

without any pitfalls, the demand for circulating medium must be expected to contract once more, although for a while it may continue to expand. In a depression, the dollar may once more become the preferred medium, and a small peso discount would then reappear. If the contraction should be severe enough to allow monetary requirements to be covered exclusively with pesos, the dollar probably would go out of circulation, and the peso would then tend to depreciate sharply, as it did in 1939. So far, the government does not appear to have provided the technical means to use its gold holdings for stabilizing the peso, although it would not be difficult to create the necessary machinery.[1]

A minimum program for monetary reform should therefore comprise the following measures: (1) Machinery should be created to utilize the gold reserve for stabilizing the peso, in anticipation of the time when this may become necessary. (2) The gold purchase program should be expanded so as to absorb a maximum of dollars, since reserves held by the Treasury can be made more effective for stabilization purposes than dollars in circulation are likely to be.[2] By doing so the government would also avoid the recurrence of the peso premium and would be working toward the gradual elimination of the dollar from the monetary system. (3) To increase effective reserves, the silver legislation should be changed to permit the sale of existing silver holdings at relatively favorable wartime prices. (4) If the inflow of funds should prove too inflationary, as it easily may, it should be pared down by eliminating the tax upon investments abroad.

These measures are modest, but they would go far toward providing an independent currency for Cuba. A broader question is whether monetary reform should be implemented by a reorganization of the credit system, *i.e.*, whether in addition to or in place of a stabilization fund Cuba should have a full-fledged central bank. Cuban sentiment, outside banking circles, seems to be in favor of a central bank, the slow progress of the present project and the failure of all earlier ones notwithstanding. On economic grounds there is much to

[1] Because of the 2 per cent seigniorage taken on the recent issues, the government would have the choice of stabilizing the peso at a discount of that magnitude or of stabilizing at par and renouncing the possibility of retiring the full amount of these issues, unless the difference were to be made up out of budgetary resources.

[2] This could easily be accomplished by increasing the percentage of dollar proceeds which sugar exporters are required to turn over to the Stabilization Fund against pesos.

be said for such an institution. If the use of the dollar should become further restricted, by law or custom, the elasticity of the monetary system will be much less than at present, because the foreign banks will probably be hesitant to bring in dollars and convert them into pesos. A lender of last resort would therefore be of value. The fact, furthermore, that certain sectors of the economy, as well as the government itself, are not and perhaps cannot be adequately financed by the existing banking system calls for the creation of other credit agencies, which for part of their funds would have to rely upon a central bank.

Against these advantages must be weighed the danger that the central bank may be mismanaged and that it may become the source of monetary disorders. The Cuban business community appears to feel very strongly that the pending central-bank project courts this danger by giving control of the institution preponderantly to the government. A minor problem lies in the fact that the bank may find it difficult to obtain a sufficient volume of earning assets, which might tempt it into unsound operations. The relative ineffectiveness of monetary policy in countries with Cuba's economic structure,[1] finally, while perhaps not by itself an argument against a central bank, does lend additional weight to other adverse considerations.

Whether or not the ultimate decision is made in favor of a central bank, it is important to take advantage of present conditions to reshape Cuba's monetary structure. Cuba cannot expect to find a more favorable opportunity than now, when the peso is at par and exchange reserves are large. It would be unfortunate if this opportunity were lost.

[1] *Cf.* Ch. IV on Central Banking and Monetary Management.

Chapter XV

Haiti

by DON D. HUMPHREY

HAITI is the most densely populated nation in the Western Hemisphere, with double the population of the Dominican Republic, which occupies almost two-thirds of the same island. The 10,700 square miles of mountainous terrain support an estimated population of over 3 millions. The total area, which is a little larger than Vermont, has a population about nine times as great.

The disproportion between population and resources is the more severe because of the lack of capital. Haiti is an agricultural economy literally without a plow. Consequently, the peasants live at the Malthusian level.

In the colonial period, Haiti was France's richest holding in this hemisphere. French is still the official language, but the peasants speak a patois or Creole. Following the revolution at the close of the eighteenth century, which established Haiti as the second independent republic in the New World, the plantation system tended to disappear, and the soil now is exploited primarily by small individual landholders.

Large-scale agricultural investment, which is almost entirely American, played only a minor role in the nation before the Second World War. The investment in sugar is estimated at $8 to $10 million and in bananas at $1.5 to $2 million. Plantation Dauphin, which was the principal producer of sisal, covered 12,000 to 15,000 acres before the war. Coffee, which is Haiti's leading export crop, grows wild or half wild and is harvested by the peasants, as are also cotton and cocoa.

The Effect of the War

The immediate effect of the Second World War was the interruption of shipping. The result was that prices soared for some imports, such as cement and flour, but the arrival of a single boat was often sufficient to break the market. Trade was also dislocated by the diversion of boats to Port-au-Prince from the other coastal cities. Internal transport was not organized to handle the traffic load thrown on it. The absence of bridges and the mercurial rise and fall of Haitian rivers produced shortages outside the capital, which, if short-lived, were nonetheless acute. Transport was further limited by the rationing of gasoline and tires. But rationing did not, of course, affect the two principal methods of transportation, which are, first, the head loads of produce carried by the peasants, mainly women and children and, second, the little donkeys, which stoutly resist giving the right of way to automobiles. While the dislocation of transportation loomed large to the importers and to the small urban population, the effect of the war upon Haitian agriculture was more fundamental to the nation.

The search of the United States for sources of rubber in this hemisphere led to large-scale rubber planting in Haiti, where rubber had not previously been grown commercially. Sisal, which furnishes the cordage industry a substitute for Manila fiber, had been grown successfully during the decade preceding the war. The acreage was greatly expanded. The rubber and sisal planting represented an agricultural investment program of a magnitude hitherto unknown in the little republic. This, together with the improvement in the coffee market, created considerable apprehension lest the nation be plunged into a radical inflation.

The equivalent of the war economy in Haiti was the diversion of resources from food production for local use to export crops. In these terms, Haiti undertook a large war program and experienced some of the problems characteristic of a war economy. In addition to a radical change in the character of production, there was a substantial increase in economic activity. The shift from self-employment to hired employment resulted in an exceptionally large increase in the money income of the mass of workers. The great increase in employment of an investment character was accompanied by an actual cut in the volume of imports. The resulting developments, if they can be called "inflationary problems," are of a somewhat different nature from those which are typical of industrial nations.

Shada

The Société Haïtiano-Américaine de Développement Agricole (Shada) is a government corporation jointly controlled by the American and Haitian governments for the purpose of developing Haitian agricultural resources. Its general funds are provided by the Export-Import Bank and guaranteed by the Haitian government.

Under contract from the Rubber Development Corporation, Shada undertook a war program—principally for the production of rubber—involving almost one-twentieth the nation's arable land area.

Growing along the fences and roadside in the Gonaïves region is a graceful vine, cryptostegia, with many whips which yield a sap similar in appearance to that of milkweed. The sap of these cryptostegia vines yields pure latex—the highest quality rubber. A research station was set up at Gonaïves in August, 1942, two days after the Rubber Reserve Corporation authorized Shada to extend its rubber research, and there are now several hundred acres of cryptostegia adjacent to the research station. About half the workers on Shada's Cap-Haïtien pay roll in September, 1943, were clearing and cultivating 11,000 acres devoted to cryptostegia. More than three-fourths the 16,000 acres at Bayeux are planted in cryptostegia. But the largest and most advanced cryptostegia planting is southwest in the Cayes region, where seven farms cover more than 20,000 acres. The insect pest, maroca, made it necessary to abandon cryptostegia culture in the Artibonite Valley.

Since the commercial production of rubber from cryptostegia had not been tried previously, it was necessary for Shada to pioneer the development of methods of culture and harvest. Approximately one-half the Cayes acreage was seed planted beginning in February, 1943. In May, the seed plantings were discontinued in favor of nursery-grown stumps. Eleven months later, in November, 1943, the early plantings of cryptostegia were harvested by tapping the whips of the vine. Harvesting rubber of any type has always been a tedious process. Cryptostegia harvesting appears to be especially costly. It remains to be seen whether or not some ingenious method of harvesting can be developed that will make it economical to produce rubber from cryptostegia. The great advantage of cryptostegia lies, of course, in the shorter growing period. The more familiar hevea tree requires a growing period three or four times as long.

TABLE 1.—SHADA'S CRYPTOSTEGIA PROGRAM*
(Thousands of acres)

	Land acquired	Land cleared	Field planting	Nursery planting
Cap-Haïtien	23.5	10.6	2.3	0.4
Bayeux	25.7	16.2	7.7	0.3
Cayes	23.3	21.9	11.7	0.4
Grand'Anse	25.2	10.1	2.0	0.4
St.-Marc	8.6	3.7	1.8	0.4
Gonaïves	0.5	0.5	0.5	
Total	106.9	63.0	26.1	1.8

* Aug. 31, 1943.

It is not expected that the government will continue to furnish capital to produce cryptostegia after the war. If production is continued, it will probably be, not under the plantation system, but by individual peasant proprietors.

The rubber tree was introduced into Haiti in 1903, and 700 hevea and 5,000 castilla trees are now being tapped by Shada. Thirty-two hundred additional acres of hevea were planted at Bayeux as part of a longer term program.

Shada has also taken over the harvesting of sisal acreage in the region of Cap-Haïtien and, in addition, planted substantial new acreage. American capital, which had already developed a highly successful sisal plantation, has almost doubled operations during the war.

The Bayeux Division, west of Cap-Haïtien, includes a variety of minor products: citronella, teak, balsa wood, mahogany, tung oil, and derris root. Another of Shada's longer term projects is the management of 150,000 acres of forest land owned by the Haitian government.

INFLATION

Before the war, the total hired employment of agricultural workers varied seasonally between 10,000 and 15,000. The principal employers were the Standard Fruit and Steamship Company, the Haitian-American Sugar Company, the Plantation Dauphin, and the Haitian

Agricultural Corporation. The Shada program, which employed 15,000 workers in late 1942, called for an expansion to approximately 100,000 by the end of 1943.[1] Minimum wages were established at 30 cents per day, which was substantially above the prewar level.

To many observers, the magnitude of Shada's expenditures appeared to be inflationary. While large in money terms, the total effect of Shada's program seems more moderate in terms of the nation's economic potential. While it is difficult to find a satisfactory standard for comparison, if the value of home production is included at local market prices, the prewar national income of Haiti is estimated roughly between $60 million and $70 million. Shada's 1943 budget of $12 million represents not more than one-fifth the prewar national income, in contrast to a large industrial nation, such as the United States, where war expenditures in 1943 greatly exceeded the prewar national income. Such comparisons, of course, have only a limited usefulness. A poor agricultural economy cannot divert so large a fraction of its resources to war as can a rich industrial nation.

The hiring of peasants has produced some improvement in their material well-being. Particularly in the south at the Cayes region, where the cryptostegia program is most advanced, there was an observable improvement in the peasant housing, and the textile inventories of the dealers had moved to the backs of the peasantry.

The rapid expansion in employment produced a notable increase in outstanding currency. In fact, Shada was forced to import United States currency to meet its pay roll.[2] The urgent need for additional currency resulted from the fact that labor was shifting from self-employment to hired employment. As of late 1943, none of this money was flowing back to the Haitian banks. It will be interesting to observe whether or not the United States' money is ever returned. It would not be surprising if it were hoarded as long as the physical conditions of the currency will permit, which, by Haitian standards, is a long time. Since the war program involved a shift from home consumption to monetary exchange and since the tendency to hoard is apparently quite high, money in circulation should not be relied upon as an index, for it yields an exaggerated measure of the effect of Haiti's war program upon the real economic life of the nation.

[1] The actual program fell considerably short of this goal. Employment on the cryptostegia program in July, 1943, totaled 64,400.

[2] The gourde is the Haitian monetary unit.

Food prices increased from 35 to more than 100 per cent between 1941 and 1943. This was probably desirable in that it encouraged food production and provided a means of distributing the Shada pay roll broadly throughout the community. In the Cap-Haïtien area in the north, food prices in 1943 were up more than 100 per cent, but this was in part due to an unusually long dry season. Also, private employers as well as Shada were expanding acreage in this area, and food supplies were relatively short compared with the Cayes region in the south. Striking regional differences in prices were observable. Internal markets, which were never well organized, and transportation, which was never good, did not improve during 1942 and 1943. Acute shortages, however, were local and temporary.

It seemed out of the question to think of attempting direct price control for domestic produce. In the first place, local markets are in large part unorganized. The bargaining process plays a dominant role. One explanation of higher food prices advanced by a Haitian was that foreigners had spoiled the market because they would not take time enough to bargain with the peasants.[1] In the second place, price control of local products did not seem desirable—even if it were feasible. It was natural, however, with the rest of the world concerned about inflation, that there would appear some apprehension as prices rose. But Haiti represents the type of economy that is well suited to resist the more critical dangers of a radical inflation. Compared with a highly industrialized nation, the dangers of inflation are small in an agricultural economy which is characterized by small independent owners of land. Since most families produce the bulk of their own foodstuffs, the consequences of rising food prices are less serious than in the case of many other Caribbean islands which are dependent upon imports. Haiti is largely self-sufficient in respect to food, although at a meager subsistence level. Among the more critical dangers of inflation are the danger of the liquidation of a class, such as occurred in Europe following the First World War, the danger of impairing production by the speculative withholding of goods, and the danger of general social and economic disorganization resulting from violent instability —in short, the danger of revolution. The elite and middle class in Haiti are quite small, probably less than 5 per cent of the population, and their assets are often held in real estate rather than money and

[1] The author found that his laundress wished to make a new bargain, not only for each week's laundry, but for each separate piece of linen every week.

credit instruments. Since Shada wages are relatively attractive, a substantial increase in prices from prewar levels is probably desirable and a radical increase in prices would not be so disastrous as in highly organized industrial countries.

The conclusion that the dangers of a radical inflation in Haiti's war program are relatively slight does not mean that there are no serious or difficult problems. The shortage of food supplies is more pronounced in many other islands of the Caribbean, and higher prices attract an abnormal volume of exports from Haiti. This is particularly true of rice, which is a staple in the peasants' diet. The government undertook to license exports of food in order to control this situation, but the price of rice doubled. At the same time that rice was being exported, complaints were common that food supplies were short because of the shift of acreage to cryptostegia and sisal. Food supplies doubtless have been reduced in local areas, but resources are adequate to increase food production sufficiently to offset the loss resulting from the planting of war crops. Shada adopted a helpful policy by leaving substantial garden space around the homes of the peasant workers in the areas under Shada's cultivation and by granting its workers time off at gardening season.

The increase in the acreage of export crops is probably a necessary step if there is to be economic progress in Haiti. At the same time, it is recognized that such a shift will make the peasants more dependent upon the uncertainties of foreign markets. The shift to hired employment and the production of export crops is requisite to any improvement in living standards even though it subjects the economy to the instability of international markets. Their independence of the market is the basic fact which frees the Haitian peasants from inflation or deflation but which, at the same time, keeps them in poverty.

The investment of the United States in Haiti's war program[1] has involved a budgetary outlay but no outlay of goods. We have exported money, but we have not exported goods or services beyond those of a small number of Americans who help manage Shada. In spite of the payment of funds to Haiti, the balance of trade is, in fact, favorable to us during the war.

This points to a significant proposition. Suppose the investment in cryptostegia does not pay out. What will be the *cost* to the United States? The real labor cost, of course, is borne by the Haitian peasants,

[1] The contract between the Rubber Development Corporation and Shada.

who work harder than before. The investment has involved no diversion of labor and production on our part. Our loss will be whatever transfer problem is created by the impairment of the capital of the Rubber Development Corporation.

TABLE 2—HAITIAN FOREIGN TRADE, 1937–1943
(Millions of dollars)

Fiscal years	Imports	Exports
1937–1938	7.6	6.9
1938–1939	8.2	7.3
1939–1940	7.9	5.4
1940–1941	7.4	6.7
1941–1942	8.5	8.6
1942–1943 (9 months)	7.2	8.3

The basic problem arising out of the rapid development of Haiti's war program is the problem of labor supply. While the peasants work more and receive far more money wages than before, the opportunities for spending are even more narrowly limited than usual. From time to time, it has proved difficult to obtain a full labor force despite the huge potential supply. Unquestionably there are many thousands of peasants who do not seek hired employment and others who leave hired employment when they could improve their position in money terms by working for wages. Perhaps no explanation is needed beyond the fact that the Haitian peasant has different values from the industrial worker, although this is not the whole story.

Problems of labor management are responsible, in part, for labor shortages. The local field foreman sometimes fails to pay off all his workers, who naturally quit. The peasant, it will be remembered, speaks neither English nor French and does not know to whom to appeal. In order to overcome these difficulties and to increase productivity, a system of piecework was inaugurated for groups of 20 workers under a straw boss. But it proved difficult to estimate, for example, the proper price for clearing 10 acres. A handsome price when the soil was damp turned to be unbearably low after a dry spell.

It is quite impossible to determine how much of the unwillingness to work is the result of the peasant's values or of his physical disability, chronic malaria, for example, and how much is due to

1. Specific problems of labor management.
2. The limited supply of imports.

3. The price of local foods.
4. The alleged tendency to work less when wages are high.

To the extent that the short labor market results from the excess of money over goods, in a sense, it may be regarded as an "inflationary problem." We do not forget that absenteeism has been a familiar complaint in industrial nations though it is not usually regarded as an aspect of inflation as, perhaps, it should be.

Local employers and "ancient Haitians" are unanimous in an opposite opinion. It is their confirmed view that the peasants take time off merely because they now have more than a subsistence wage. This familiar notion that workers have fixed wants and, consequently, that higher wages reduce the labor supply is an ancient dogma that has harassed many agricultural workers before they became capitalistic-minded. It is noted that, while every employer is certain that higher wages reduce the willingness to work, in no case does he subscribe to the view that higher food prices would increase the labor supply.

Price Control in Haiti

In prewar years about one-third of total imports were textiles. Wheat flour is the leading imported food. Cured fish, edible fats and oils, soap, and gasoline almost complete the list of important consumers' goods. Most of the peasants do without many of these items, but every peasant must from time to time buy a little cotton cloth, which is by far the most important import.

The importers are the leading merchants of the nation. In prewar years competition was exceedingly keen and margins extremely low. The advent of the war offered, of course, an opportunity for speculation and profiteering, particularly since prices paid by importers were largely controlled in the United States. In view of the powerful position of the importers it seemed desirable to attempt to control the price of the leading imported commodities. Beginning in January, 1942, Haiti adopted a policy of establishing maximum margins on the basic necessities which were imported. The specific goods on which such margins were established included coarse cotton fabrics, wheat flour, yeast, cooking oil, lard, fish, spices, soap, kerosene, pharmaceutical products, newsprint, and schoolbooks. The maximum price was determined by adding a fixed margin to the cost of landed goods. The margin established for importers appears to be quite liberal.

The same method was employed to determine the maximum retail price. A few large retail establishments in Haiti usually import directly, but the great bulk of retailers are very small proprietor shops. The retail margins are less than the importer's margins and seem extremely tight. Competitive practices generally extend beyond price competition and result in short weights and measure. Textile stores, for example, employ two or even three yardsticks, and merchants, from smallest to largest, feel it necessary to use varying weights and measures.

It is too early to attempt any evaluation of the decree of Feb. 10, 1944, which froze rents at the levels prevailing 3 months prior to that date.

The control of commodity prices is limited to margin control on imports of basic necessities and works as well as can be expected with a staff of five or six. Even on this limited scale it presents a number of familiar problems, for example, the question of determining fair margins when the volume is drastically cut by war controls. Should all the importers be kept in business with a reduced volume? In fact, it was found that importers who suffered from impaired volume of imports were often able to enter the export field. A second fundamental policy question familiar to price control officials concerns the frequency of recalculation of ceiling prices. Should a new price be established on each new lot, and should old stocks be adjusted to the new price? The principal problem, however, is in the field of enforcement. Here, one discovers quaint new names for all the old deceptions.

In summary, Haiti has had a boom as a result of the war. Capital has flowed in, and important rubber and sisal programs have been launched. A monetary inflation of substantial proportions is being experienced. Yet monetary expansion *in part* reflects merely the increased importance of the money economy; and, as a consequence of the price inflation, the gains resulting from new demands have been diffused more widely.

As a result of United States export controls which prevent Haitians from increasing imports in response to the inflow of capital, the real cost of the investment in export crops has been borne by the Haitians —at least for the war period.

Since this essay was written, Shada has abandoned the entire cryptostegia program. With this sudden cancellation of war contracts, Haiti faces "reconversion pains." The Haitians are likely to feel that they could have spent the money more advantageously, and that their economy has been seriously dislocated and then abandoned to the forces of deflation. For the same reason that inflation was less disasterous than in a highly industrialized nation, the deflation will, similarly, be less critical. The shift from hired employment back to self-employment will be a relatively easy one. Nevertheless, the monetary deflation will impede real productive activity and hamper the nation's economic progress. Whether or not the war stimulus will afford lasting benefits depends upon the postwar policies pursued in both nations. If we succeed in maintaining levels of income and a structure of production that offers a more favorable export market, then Haiti's war shift to export crops will not have been wasted effort.[1]

[1] Recent trade figures, now available, make clear the important contribution of Haitian exports to our war effort. There has been a large volume of exports to the United States and a substantial excess of exports over imports.

HAITI: TRADE WITH THE UNITED STATES, 1942–1944
(Millions of dollars)

Calendar years	Imports from United States	Exports to United States
1942	5.2	6.1
1943	7.4	8.0
1944 (6 months)	4.8	6.6

Chapter XVI

Mexico: with Special Reference to Its International Economic Relations

by NORMAN T. NESS

I. INTRODUCTION

Mexico, with an area of 758,258 square miles and a population in 1940 of 19,753,552, ranks third among the Latin American countries in point of size and second in terms of population. As in the case of the other countries of Latin America, its economy is primarily devoted to agriculture. Its mines, which contribute so preponderantly to the export trade, are reported to have given employment to but 80,000 people in 1939; and although the industry undoubtedly has been led by wartime demands to enlarge its personnel, mining still forms a relatively minor field of employment. Manufacturing occupies a larger proportion of the working population; and "service," if interpreted broadly enough to include merchandising, is also more important. For some details see Chart 19.

The agriculture which primarily engages the nation's energy is largely self-sufficing. This characteristic lies at the base of a *dualism* which marks Mexico's (as it does much of Latin America's) economy. Informed Mexicans estimate that 70 to 80 per cent of the population lives largely or wholly outside the commercial framework typified by the cities. The boundary between the economies cannot, of course, be sharply drawn, but that fact does not lessen its significance. It is, for example, to the relatively restricted sphere of markets and monetary incomes that the "Latin American economics" expounded elsewhere

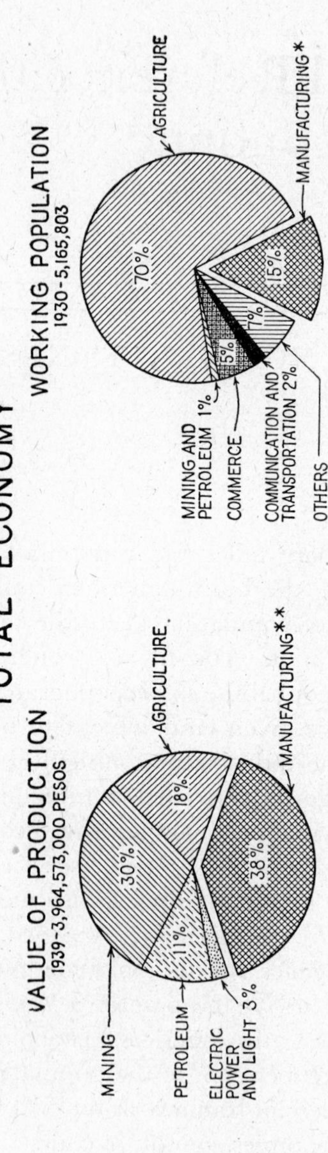

MANUFACTURING

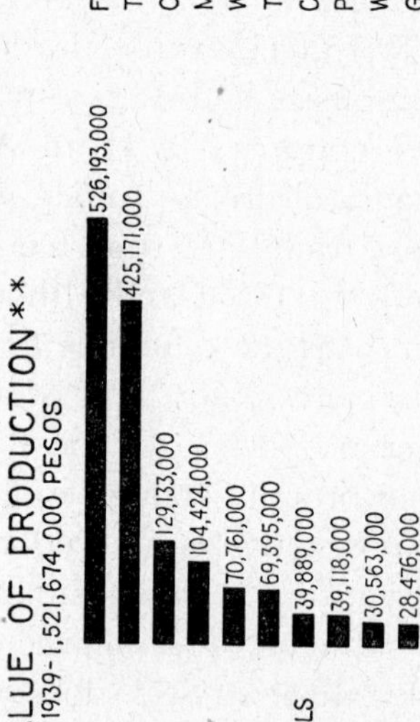

* BASED ON INFORMATION FOR ALL MANUFACTURING ESTABLISHMENTS

** BASED ON INFORMATION FOR MANUFACTURING ESTABLISHMENTS WITH ANNUAL OUTPUT OF MORE THAN 10,000 PESOS

WHILE THESE ESTABLISHMENTS COMPRISE ALMOST THE ENTIRE VALUE OF PRODUCTION ESTABLISHMENTS WITH ANNUAL OUTPUT OF LESS THAN 10,000 PESOS ACCOUNT FOR A LARGE PROPORTION OF THE WORKERS EMPLOYED IN INDUSTRY

CHART 19.—Mexico. Total economy—prewar. (*Coordinator of Inter-American Affairs.*)

in this volume has its primary application.[1] Exports create *money* incomes, and the international trade multiplier relates exports to the sphere of wages and salaries.

It has been estimated that Mexico's national income was 7 billion pesos ($1.4 billion) in 1942 and 8 billion pesos ($1.6 billion) in 1943.[2] Comparison of these income estimates with total export values—945.9 million pesos ($194.9 million) in 1942 and 1,127.5 million pesos ($232.5 million) in 1943—fails adequately to reveal the role of export trade. Actually, such a comparison is in part spurious, for exports are properly related only to the commercial economy, and their ratio to the income of that restricted sphere is substantially greater than the one-eighth which has prevailed between total exports and total income. The same observation is, of course, to be made of the role of public expenditures, which happen, in Mexico, to be not greatly different in magnitude from total exports and which, like those exports, count significantly as income determinants.[3] Prices, foreign exchange, etc., are likewise primarily relevant to the commercial economy. The course of events in Mexico in recent years is significant not only because of the importance of the country but also because of the demonstration it affords of the role of exports in Latin American economy.

II. FOREIGN TRADE

The official statistics of Mexico's exports, contained in Table 1, are misleading. Prior to 1941 mineral exports were valued c.i.f., and the change in that year to the f.o.b. basis means that the data of 1940 and before are not comparable with those for 1941 and subsequent years. An examination of the volume of exports clearly suggests, however, that, had a single method of valuation been used during the period covered by the table, the value data would have shown a steady year-to-year increase. The decline in the value of metal exports, to which alone the change of valuation methods in 1941 applied, fully accounted for the decline in total exports in that year. Quantities increased substantially in most cases. Exports of zinc concentrates, for example, increased from 150,000 metric tons in 1940

[1] See, for example, Ch. V on fiscal policy, by Henry C. Wallich.

[2] Banco Nacional, *Review of the Economic Situation of Mexico*, Jan. 31, 1943, Dec. 31, 1943.

[3] It may be observed that in Mexico, as in any other country which relies substantially upon export duties for public revenues, the use of gross figures for exports and public revenues involves some duplication.

to 225,000 tons in 1941, but the reported value declined from 69 million pesos to 29 million pesos.

TABLE 1.—TOTAL EXPORTS AND IMPORTS AND BALANCE OF TRADE OF MEXICO, 1938–1943
(In millions)

	In national currency			Conversion rate	In U.S. dollars		
	Exports	Imports	Balance		Exports	Imports	Balance
1938	P/832.7	P/493.8	+338.9	0.2212	$184.2	$109.2	+75.0
1939	904.8	627.4	+277.4	0.1930	174.6	121.1	+53.5
1940	959.8	668.8	+291.0	0.1852	177.7	123.9	+53.8
1941	730.0	914.4	−184.4	0.2060	150.4	188.4	−38.0
1942	945.9	752.4	+193.5	0.2066	194.9	155.0	+39.9
1943	1,127.5	910.0	+217.5	0.2060	232.5	187.6	+44.8

There is, in addition to the distortion imparted by the change of valuation methods, an irregularity in Mexican export statistics which has its origin in the fact that the country is an important primary producer of the monetary metals. It is, presumably, for this reason that the Bank of Mexico differentiates between exports of merchandise and of the monetary metals. Gold and silver, in Mexico, are industrial products, but (and particularly is this true of the former) they tend

TABLE 2.—MEXICAN EXPORTS, 1939–1943, CLASSIFIED IN TERMS OF POSITION IN THE BALANCE OF PAYMENTS
(In millions of pesos)

	Merchandise controlled by			Monetary metals			Total exports
	Mexican capital	Foreign capital	Total	Gold	Silver	Total	
1939	278.8	275.6	554.4	172.7	177.7	350.4	904.8
1940	280.2	304.7	584.9	216.2	158.8	375.0	959.9
1941	334.7	169.0	503.7	86.0	130.3	216.3	720.0
1942	433.5	236.6	670.1	153.7	122.2	275.9	946.0
1943	790.1	281.3	1,071.4	16.9	39.2	56.1	1,127.5

to move in response to the rest of the balance of payments. If credits generally exceed debits—as when, for some reason, the world demand for Mexico's products is great—gold is systematically retained at home by the Bank of Mexico; and in the same circumstances the consequent increase in the circulating medium enlarges the demand for silver coin, and silver may also be withheld from export. As exports of merchandise increase, therefore, their rise may fail of full showing in the statistics of total exports. The force of these influences is reflected in the data of Table 2.

The clearest instance of the operation of the principle is afforded by the events of 1943, when a sharp increase of merchandise exports, particularly in the products of Mexican-owned firms, was accompanied by an abrupt diminution in the exports of the monetary metals. In 1941, on the other hand, when total exports and merchandise seemed to decline appreciably, the outflow of monetary metals *fell* with them. It was in that year that the new system of valuation was introduced; but while the change of method applied to silver and gold as well as to the baser metals,[1] quantities of monetary metal exports, especially of gold, declined appreciably. Production both of gold and of silver fell in 1941 from 1940 levels, but not enough to account for the decrease of exports. On the face of things, accordingly, the combination of events lends support to the proposition earlier advanced, *viz.*, that Mexican exports, despite the official record, have grown steadily over the 6-year period 1938–1943. Inasmuch, however, as it is impossible to demonstrate statistically what became of the retained metals, the case is inconclusive and may largely reflect a statistical irregularity, *e.g.*, a year-end lag in reporting.

Meantime, the character of Mexico's exports has been undergoing change. The commodity-by-commodity distribution of exports is not now available, and the classification by groups or categories contained in Table 3 must suffice for analysis.

Vegetable products have in recent years superseded the common metals in first place; but if the several classes of minerals are aggregated, they constitute two-thirds the country's total exports. Vegetable products have characteristically consisted of perishables destined for seasonal markets in the United States, but lately a prominent place has been taken by oilseeds and vegetable fibers. It is notable, however, that Mexico's exports of textiles have lately increased out of proportion. Staple foods have formed no appreciable part of the whole, and Mexico at the moment is as a matter of fact importing corn and wheat.

[1] This is at least true of the exports of unrefined gold and of all silver. The change would, of course, have no appreciable effect upon the exports of refined gold.

TABLE 3.—MEXICAN EXPORTS BY GROUPS, 1939–1942
(In millions of pesos)

	1939	1940	1941	1942	Per cent of total 1939	Per cent of total 1942
Animal products	41.5	38.6	48.8	72.9	4.6	7.7
Vegetable products	135.4	125.9	168.8	199.3	14.9	21.1
Mineral products*	113.8	124.3	60.1	78.5	12.5	8.3
Yarns, textiles, and their manufactures	3.5	7.4	13.5	68.4	0.4	7.2
Foodstuffs, beverages, tobaccos, and chemicals	6.1	6.9	14.7	26.0	0.7	2.7
Common metals and their manufactures	235.9	235.4	154.9	191.5	26.0	20.2
Gold in bars	127.5	126.8	28.4	126.4	14.1	13.4
Silver in bars	136.6	121.3	106.2	105.8	15.1	11.2
Fuel and derivatives	82.6	89.4	70.4	35.1	9.1	3.7

* Distinguished from other minerals classes by reason of crude state of ores, etc., here included.

The United States has long been a more important market for Mexico's exports than all the rest of the world taken together, but

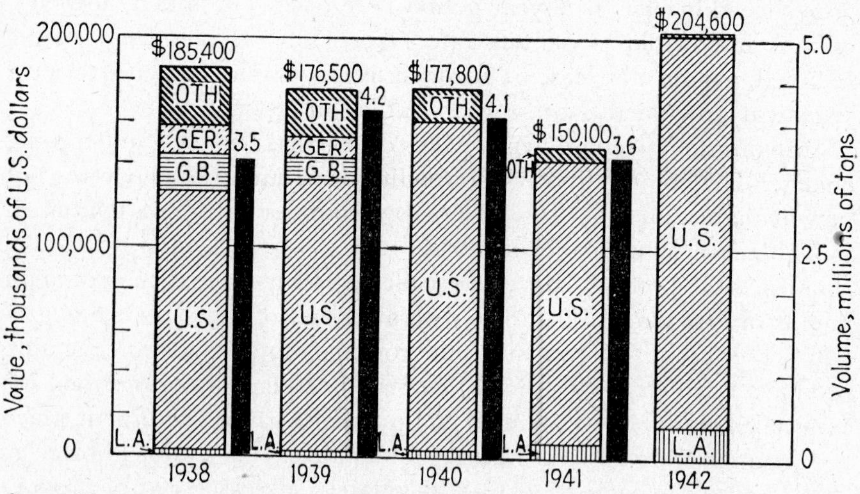

CHART 20.—Mexico. Exports by countries of destination, 1938–1942. (*Coordinator of Inter-American Affairs.*)

lately the position of dominance has given way to one approaching exclusion. It took 67.4 per cent of Mexico's exports in 1938 and 91.3 per cent in 1942. Strikingly, almost all the rest of the country's exports went to the remainder of Latin America: 3.6 per cent to Central America; 2.8 per cent to the Caribbean republics (chiefly Cuba); and 2.0 per cent to South America. In large part these latter shares consisted of manufactures, including the textiles whose expansion has previously been called to attention. Two charts here give the general outlines of trade and reveal the increased significance of trade with the United States (Charts 20, 21).[1]

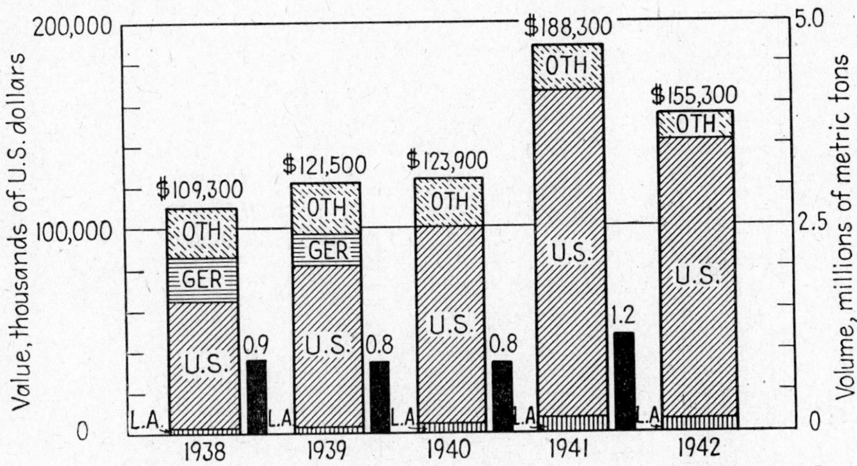

CHART 21.—Mexico. Imports by countries of origin, 1938–1942. (*Coordinator of Inter-American Affairs.*)

III. FOREIGN EXCHANGE AND PRICES

The currency unit of Mexico, the peso, has a long-period history of depreciation, but it has lately been stable in value and has even appreciated. From 27.7 cents in February, 1938, it declined irregularly to 16.7 in May, 1940, after which it recovered by October of that year to the 20.7-cent level it has maintained ever since. Mexico is one of the seven countries of Latin America which has not employed exchange control.

The Bank of Mexico holds substantially all the country's gold and foreign exchange resources. The bank, which is the country's sole issuing agency and the holder of by far the greater part of the commercial banks' reserves, is required by law to keep a 25 per cent reserve against its liabilities. All its excess reserves are by law segre-

[1] Reservations concerning trade figures should be kept in mind, however. The relative importance of United States direct investments tends to increase this trade (Chart 22).

gated in "Authorized Investments," the account in which the bank records also its holdings of Treasury obligations, shares, etc. Inasmuch as the content of this account is never revealed to the public in any detail it is impossible to derive from published statements the amount of gold and foreign exchange held by the bank.

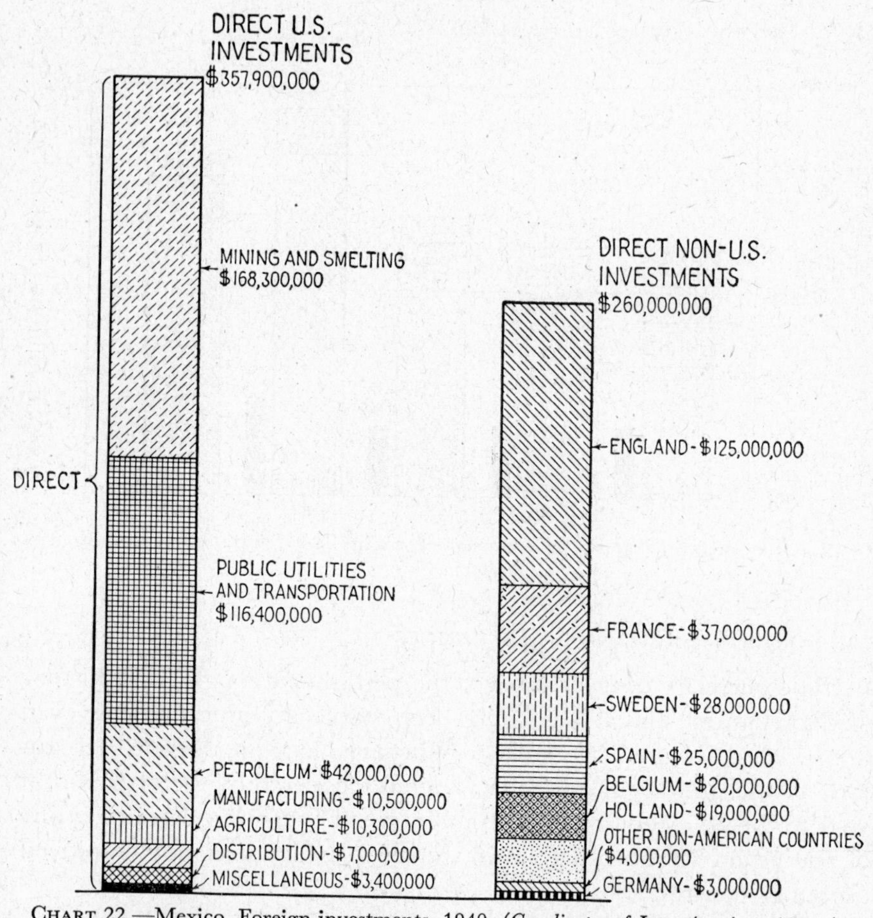

CHART 22.—Mexico. Foreign investments, 1940. (*Coordinator of Inter-American Affairs.*)

Such holdings, however, have increased substantially in recent years, and especially in the first half of 1943. President Avila Camacho, in his address to the newly convened Congress in September, 1943, reported that "from April of 1942 to June of this year such resources [of gold and exchange] have increased one hundred and sixty million dollars." The interval between February and May is said by the Bank of Mexico in its annual report for 1943 to have been especially productive of additions to the stock of gold and exchange. Some notion of the course of accumulation can be derived from the following published record of the bank's gold holdings.[1] Values are in millions of United States dollars.

Dec. 31, 1938	29
Dec. 31, 1939	32
Dec. 31, 1940	47
Dec. 31, 1941	47
Dec. 31, 1942	39
Dec. 31, 1943	203

In the absence of any indication of the size of the bank's foreign exchange resources it is impossible to do more than summarize broadly, as follows: In the years 1939–1941 Mexico's gold and exchange resources did little more than maintain a modest level, whereas in 1943 (and in 1942 if President Avila Camacho's statement be interpreted to mean that the period of growth began in April of that year) such resources mounted rapidly.

This summary is supported by the statistics of money and credit for the period. As is indicated in Table 4, the circulating medium in Mexico has risen steadily over the years under consideration.

TABLE 4.—MONEY IN CIRCULATION AND DEPOSITS IN MEXICO, 1938–1943
(In millions of pesos)

End of period	Coin	Currency	Bank deposits	Total	Money in banks	Net circulation
1938	273.4	296.5	250.4	820.2	52.3	767.9
1939	278.2	373.0	316.6	967.8	48.4	919.4
1940	330.7	420.7	443.2	1,194.6	88.1	1,106.5
1941	308.3	563.1	510.5	1,381.9	67.0	1,314.9
1942	347.6	753.2	801.3	1,902.1	72.5	1,829.6
June, 1943	395.2	915.2	1,157.2	2,467.6	138.5	2,329.1
December, 1943	446.8	1,170.8	1,313.9	2,931.5	128.3	2,803.2

Broadly, this growth can have had its origin in either or both external or internal phenomena. The former must, of course, be reflected in changes in the net foreign assets (gold and foreign exchange) of money-creating institutions, *viz.*, the Bank of Mexico and the commercial banks, whereas the latter involve net *domestic* assets.

[1] *Federal Reserve Bulletin*, February, 1944, p. 200.

The coin circulation constitutes a somewhat special case, for it is the liability neither of the Bank of Mexico nor of the commercial banks. It is here treated not only as the money *created* but as *money creating* as well, and the following analysis relates only to notes and deposits.

As previously noted, the gold and foreign exchange resources of the Bank of Mexico are contained in two accounts—Metallic Reserve and Authorized Investments—in the second of which are also included the bank's holdings of government securities. The mixture of these two quite dissimilar elements in Authorized Investments renders analysis difficult but, for restricted periods, not impossible. The President of Mexico has, for example, made it known that between April, 1942, and June, 1943, the bank's gold and exchange resources grew by $160 million, equivalent to 776 million pesos. In the same period the two above-named gold and exchange accounts together rose from 755.9 million pesos to 1,488.5 million pesos—an increase of 732.6 million pesos. The bank's portfolio of governments (the remaining constituent of authorized investments) would therefore appear to have fallen by some 43.4 million pesos. If, now, there be excluded from consideration the two previously cited accounts—Metallic Reserve and Authorized Investments—and the bank's note and deposit liabilities (which enter in the money supply) as well, its remaining net assets showed virtually no change at all, *viz.*, a decrease of 6.5 million pesos.

The episode has a general significance in that it portrays the Bank of Mexico as an institution whose greatest influence is wielded via gold and exchange resources, on the one hand, and issues of government paper, on the other. The increase of its note and deposit liabilities from 823.3 million pesos to 1,549.4 million pesos was brought about by a growth of its gold and exchange resources of 776.0 million pesos, partly offset by decreases of 43.4 million pesos and 6.5 million pesos in government securities and other assets, respectively.

The foreign assets of deposit banks, meantime, were declining by 10.8 million pesos, while their other *net* assets (again excluding deposits[1]) increased by 260.4 million pesos, owing to a 261.6-million-peso rise in their loans and investments.

[1] More accurately, "deposits less reserve accounts at the Bank of Mexico." The procedure here employed has the effect of counting as money *all* deposits at the central bank plus member-bank deposits less reserve accounts. The procedure is justified by convenience of exposition and by the fact that the summation in the next paragraph of data for the two classes of institution yields exactly the same results as would the more conventional procedure of counting as money *all* member-bank deposits plus central-bank deposits minus reserve accounts.

The growth, apart from the coin supply, of 974.7 million pesos in Mexico's circulating medium in the period April, 1942, to June, 1943, is, accordingly, accounted for as follows. Values are in millions of pesos.

Increased gold and exchange*	765.2
Increase (net) of banks' other assets	209.5
Total	974.7

* Including, of course, gold produced and retained at home. Given, however, the previously noted connection between gold retention and the state of the balance of payments, no great error is involved in using this figure as an index of "external" forces.

Clearly the period was one in which the increase of the money supply (and with it, the increase of economic activity in which the growth of the circulation had its origin) was dominated by external forces. Inasmuch, indeed, as some among the loans extended by the deposit banks must have been directed to the increase of Mexico's export facilities, the growth of the money supply is even more largely associated with external forces than is indicated by the foregoing summary table.

The significant fact is not the increase of the circulating medium but rather the enlargement of productive activity and of income in which the new money had its origin. Except, indeed, for accuracy of factual description there would be little occasion to emphasize the preponderance of external influence in the course of events. The volume of money and the level of productive activity and incomes could as effectively have been raised by a program which was wholly internal. For example, had the government of Mexico engaged to purchase and to stock-pile the mineral and other products which have been demanded by the wartime industries of the United States, and had it undertaken to finance such purchases with funds borrowed from the Bank of Mexico, the substantive result would have been almost exactly the same. Had the terms of purchase been the same, the volume of money would have grown in the same amount, and employment would have been given to as many workers at as high rates of pay. The one element of difference appears at a point not yet dealt with except in passing.

An increase of incomes, especially within such a country as Mexico, may be expected to induce an increase of imports. The fact, as reference to Table 1 will make clear, is that imports, at least in value terms, did increase, and they would undoubtedly have grown even more had there been unrestrained access to the productive resources of such supplying nations as the United States and Great Britain. If, therefore, Mexico had undertaken a purely internal program of expansion, it would have met with difficulty in financing imports. The Bank of Mexico's holdings of foreign exchange and gold were apparently modest at the beginning of the period in which American demands for mineral products, etc., began to expand, and the accumulation of gold and foreign exchange resources during 1942 and 1943 as a consequence of sales abroad has provided it the wherewithal to meet the demands for import financing. Except for this one function, these resources have identically the same position which government obligations would have occupied among the assets of the Bank of Mexico had the government of that country embarked upon a purchase program of its own. The significant fact, as emphasized previously, has been the increase of productive activity.

One of the consequences of the increase of income has been a marked rise in the level of prices. In Table 5 there appear the price relatives for wholesale prices and for the cost of living in the Federal District. In the column next to each of these series there is placed, for purposes of comparison, the ratios of the Mexican indices to comparable ones in the United States.

TABLE 5.—INDICES OF WHOLESALE PRICES AND COST OF LIVING IN MEXICO*

	Cost of living		Wholesale prices	
	Mexico (1929 = 100)	Ratio to United States index	Mexico (1929 = 100)	Ratio to United States index
1939 (annual av.)	155.4	100.0	127.0	100.0
1940	157.2	96.1	128.2	95.0
1941	163.9	106.7	135.8	101.0
1942	188.6	110.6	148.3	97.4
December, 1943	272.5	149.8	200.8	126.7

* Comparisons are made with the U.S. Department of Labor and Bureau of Labor Statistics indices. The designation of 1929 as 100.0 does not necessarily imply that exchanges in that year were "normal" or "equilibrated" but is intended merely to facilitate comparison. Rough allowance is made for changes in the peso-dollar rate by weighting the United States indices by an index (1929 = 100) of average peso rates on the dollar.

In each case these two facts stand out: Prices have risen abruptly in Mexico, and that rise has been more rapid than in the United States. Each fact carries with it a separate set of problems. The rise of prices within Mexico has, first of all, all the unfortunate consequences ordinarily associated with a rise in the cost of living. Inasmuch as the most marked increases have, as a matter of fact, occurred in the fields of foodstuffs and clothing, the impact has been especially severe upon people in moderate circumstances; as a consequence, there have arisen widespread demands for advances in wages and salaries, and some steps have been taken in that direction. Second, the rise in prices has nourished speculative instincts, with the result that there has been some withholding of goods in anticipation of further price rises, and prices as a consequence have risen even more.

The disproportionate rise in Mexico's prices also involves a somewhat different set of problems. There is involved the possibility that the war's end will find the Mexican economy confronted with a situation in which, goods once again being freely available from abroad, demands will be turned toward foreign suppliers by the attraction of relatively lower prices. There is involved, in short, the possibility of a disequilibrium in international price levels—a disequilibrium the more troublesome because it appears to threaten the quick exhaustion of the presently large gold and foreign exchange resources, which, with some exercise of foresight, Mexico could presumably turn to better employment than the indiscriminate purchase of large quantities of consumers' goods. It may, of course, prove to be the case that Mexican prices will drop when once the present export demand diminishes, and it may be that United States prices will rise when wartime controls are released. Either development would remove some of the prevailing disequilibrium, but neither may be taken for granted.

The rise in the price level is not the consequence of any absolute shortage of goods. Indices of physical production are inadequately developed in Mexico, but it would appear from those which are available that the volume of production has been increased not only in enterprises catering to the export trade but in agriculture and in manufacturing as well. Nor have the imports whose increase was recorded in Table 1 grown only in terms of value. The volume of imports has, on the whole, risen in the period under review. Physical aggregates of all imports have, of course, substantially little meaning, but the restrictions upon production and export in the United States have tended particularly to exclude from Mexico's imports such durable goods as automobiles, office machinery, and industrial equipment. The volume of imports destined for consumption has, in short, apparently been fairly well maintained.

The inference from all this would seem to be that the rise in prices within Mexico is, in substantial part, the consequence simply of a marked increase in productive activity and national income. It is, indeed, not amiss to venture the judgment that had imports been freely available prices would nonetheless have risen substantially. This is not to deny that freedom of importation would have had the effect of moderating somewhat the price rise. In the first place, there would have been a more considerable supply of goods available, and, second, the "leakage" from the income stream involved in purchases outside the country would have reduced the demand for goods at home. To presume otherwise would be to suppose that money incomes denied an outlet in the purchase of foreign goods are invariably sterilized by their owners. Such "sterilization" has undoubtedly occurred in some measure. Expenditure of capital funds of business await the reopening of foreign sources of tools and equipment, as do some private funds awaiting an inflow of consumers' durable goods. Given the low-liquidity preferences which seem to be characteristic of Latin American economies, however, a considerable part of such balances may safely be assumed to have "splashed" over into the domestic market. The situation is akin to that which would prevail were Mexico (or a similarly situated country) to embark upon a domestic purchase program only to find that its inability to finance enlarged imports forced it to institute restrictions upon foreign purchases.

It is, in this connection, significant that after the middle of 1943 the volume of imports into Mexico from the United States was considerably increased. In the latter half of the year, as a matter of fact, exports and imports were almost equal. A comparison of exports and imports by quarters, such as appears in Table 6, indicates that the

TABLE 6.—MEXICO: EXPORTS AND IMPORTS, 1942–1943
(In millions of pesos)

Quarter	Exports		Imports	
	1942	1943	1942	1943
First	314.1	293.9	218.9	176.4
Second	207.4	320.9	190.5	245.7
Third	216.0	246.7	167.8	231.3
Fourth	254.0	266.0	175.8	256.6
Totals	991.5	1,127.5	753.0	910.0

export balance for the entire year 1943 had, in fact, been accumulated by the end of the first half of that year.

This shift, moreover, was the consequence, not simply of a diminution of exports, but of a substantial growth of Mexican imports as well. The pressure upon prices was insofar eased somewhat.

The case, then, seems to be this: Mexico, having passed through a series of years in which it has been impossible to secure the full range of goods it has desired, will have accumulated substantial backlogs of demand; more perhaps than any other Latin American country, it will during the war have defined new programs for publicly directed economic expansion and development; and there may exist a discrepancy in national price levels whose effect will be to divert even more purchasing power to foreign markets than would be directed there by the influences just named. The end of the war, or an initial postwar period necessary for reconversion, will again witness relatively free inflows of supplies. At that time there will undoubtedly develop very substantial inroads upon the foreign exchange resources which the country has by now accumulated and to which it will presumably add by the end of hostilities. Mexico may, accordingly, have to wrestle with the problem of husbanding its resources if it is best to serve its national purposes.

Mexican authorities are not unmindful of the problem. In the annual report of the Bank of Mexico for the calendar year 1943, there is this passage:

> There exists in the country a deferred demand for machinery, tools, repair parts, raw materials, etc., along with a great, latent purchasing power. When the present restrictions upon exports are reduced in the United States, the indiscriminate import of goods may very well increase, with the danger that articles of luxury or those which compete with national industry . . . will rise to exaggerated levels, perhaps greatly exceeding that of production goods. This possibility would justify the application of measures to select imports with the end not only of maintaining the development of the industrial processes but of preserving a satisfactory situation with respect to employment in the country. Above all is this true if it is realized that our experience indicates that in the descending phase of the economic cycle mineral exports decline rapidly, the reinvestment of profits is reduced, and demand for exchange to provide the service of capital and for other capital movements is increased.

The bank authorities indicate in no way that a choice among the possible measures of control has yet been made. The Mexican government and the banking authorities, however, have taken steps to moderate, during the war, the growth of the forces which, according to the previous analysis, promise to bear adversely upon the postwar situation.

The effort has, first of all, been made to enlarge as much as possible the supply of goods available in the markets of the country. Thus it has been sought to increase domestic production by according special privileges to the granting of credit for "productive" employments, including agriculture. In this field, for example, the government has undertaken to guarantee loans. The Mexican-American Commission for Economic Cooperation, constituted as one result of the meeting, in the spring of 1943, of Presidents Avila Camacho and Roosevelt, surveyed Mexico's most pressing needs and established a joint committee charged with the duty of expediting, insofar as was consistent with wartime demands, the supply of productive facilities and materials to Mexico from the United States.

The Mexicans have adopted a number of counterinflationary devices. It has been the viewpoint of the government that direct measures of price control hold no great promise for success in that country; and although some such measures have been put into effect, chief reliance has been placed upon indirect controls. The Bank of Mexico, for example, has set in operation a number of measures calculated either to restrain or actually to reduce the volume of purchasing power in existence. Reserve requirements for deposit banks have been increased until they now stand, for the institutions in the Federal District, at 45 per cent. The bank has engaged in the sale of gold coins and gold ingots to the public, and with the cooperation of the deposit banks and the Nacional Financiera has sought to sell some of the government's securities contained in its authorized-investments portfolio directly to the public. It has, moreover, taken advantage of the widespread demand for silver coins to supply freely the peso pieces and "tostones" (50 centavos) which, quite apart from their use in exchange, constitute the hoarding medium of the more poorly circumstanced sectors of the population.

The government, for its part, has sought to reduce its contribution to the income flow. In his address to the Congress in September of 1943, President Avila Camacho reported that between January and August the government had realized a surplus of revenues over disbursements adequate to permit it to pay the Bank of Mexico 157 million pesos in retirement of interest and principal of outstanding obligations. The budget of the government for 1943 anticipates revenues at the all-time record level of 1,100 million pesos and directs these funds to the discharge of a reduced ordinary budget and the financing of the extraordinary budget for public works (ordinarily covered by borrowing) and to 200 million pesos worth of debt retirement. To secure this high level of revenues the government has increased income taxes. In his year-end message President Avila Camacho announced the government's intention to establish restrictions upon exports; to import prime necessities and, if necessary, to subsidize their sale; and, finally, to make ceiling prices effective. The merger, within the Finance Department, of all price control agencies has only recently been announced. In late 1943 the government proposed to sell 200 million pesos worth of bonds, the proceeds of which it proposed to employ in the acquisition of securities abroad. This issue met, however, with an unfavorable market, and nothing much has come of it.

Mexico is, then, aware of the long-run as well as of the short-run implications of the inflation it is at present experiencing. The measures it has thus far adopted cannot be said to have been successful in moderating the inflationary process, and it may be anticipated that the years 1944–1945 will witness greater efforts to that end, as well, perhaps, as an undertaking to settle upon measures to be adopted when the war's end threatens the depletion of the bank's present ample exchange resources.

Chapter XVII

Paraguay: with Particular Reference to Price Control

by GEORGE R. TAYLOR

I. The Economic Background

BEFORE dealing directly with the problem of inflation control in Paraguay, brief attention may well be paid to the general economic pattern as it exists today. This can be done most effectively perhaps by pausing briefly to examine three statements that are sometimes made concerning this country, *viz.*, that in all South America it is the poorest country, that it is the one most exclusively agricultural, and, finally, that it is least affected by the war.

1. THE POVERTY OF THE COUNTRY

Those who assert that Paraguay is the poorest country of South America do not give a bill of particulars, but their meaning is fairly clear. They are asserting that the average standard of living is lowest or that per capita productivity is the lowest for any country on the continent. In the absence of any reliable figures on these points either for Paraguay or for most of the other small Latin American countries, this generalization is not easily proved or disproved. Yet students and travelers are so generally agreed upon the poverty of the country that it can hardly be disputed. Without raising the question as to whether some Latin American country may not indeed be poorer, let us examine briefly why Paraguay is such a very poor country in the economic sense.

First, two usual causes of national poverty are not important. It is true the country is small, but it is not densely populated. Although

Paraguay has an area of only about 162,000 square miles (approximately the size of California), its population is not crowded, for the total number is about 1 million persons, or almost 7 to the square mile. With the possible exception of Bolivia this is the smallest density of population in any South American country. In the second place, the extreme poverty can hardly be ascribed to lack of natural resources; for while important mineral deposits are almost completely lacking, the agricultural resources both for farming and for grazing are very considerable either in an absolute sense or relative to the population.

Why then is the country so poor? This is a question worthy of very thorough examination, but only brief note can be taken here of the six most important factors.

1. Of fundamental importance is the remoteness of Paraguay from the markets of the world and the difficulties of transportation both within and without the country. Landlocked, in the center of the continent, and shut off by the Andes from egress to the west, Paraguay has only one route to the markets of the world, down the tributaries of the River Plate. Fine as these waterways are and navigable by huge river steamers, it must be emphasized that the distances are great (Asunción is about 1,000 miles by river from Buenos Aires) and transshipment is ordinarily necessary at Montevideo or Buenos Aires. Moreover, river freight rates are high, the cost of shipment from Paraguay to Buenos Aires being generally greater than from Buenos Aires to world markets.

The disadvantage of these transportation costs is especially great because Paraguayan exports are similar to and must compete with those of Brazil, Uruguay, and Argentina, countries which are nearer to market and whose internal systems of transportation are much superior to Paraguay's. Except for the hard-surfaced road recently built with American capital, which goes from Asunción to Villarrica, the international railroad which goes from Asunción south and east to the border, and the rivers, Paraguay has no effective means of bringing domestic products to local shipping points. In fact, the difficulty of local transportation is one of the important causes for the predominance of cattle raising, for the steers can take themselves to market.

2. The prevalence of diseases and almost complete lack of modern sanitation are doubtless both a cause and a result of the great poverty. Hookworm is almost universally prevalent in the rural areas. Al-

though malaria, venereal diseases, and various tropical complaints are not uncommon, probably the most serious in retarding the productivity of the country are the debilitating effects of hookworm.

The almost universal custom, especially in the rural areas, of going barefoot and the failure to observe the simplest of sanitary arrangements make progress against disease very difficult. The towns and cities, even the capital, Asunción, which has around 100,000 in population, have neither sewer systems nor a central water supply. Modern hospitals are now being erected for the first time. This is being done with United States capital and under our direction. A few well-trained physicians are available in the larger cities, but the great majority of the poorer people in the cities and practically all in rural areas live and die without ever being attended by a trained physician.

3. Although some progress has been made toward the adoption of modern methods of agricultural production and improved stockbreeding, for the most part modern methods of scientific agriculture are not in use. In fact, methods are generally most primitive. The economy is based on oxen, and farm implements are extremely crude, wooden plows still being used to a considerable extent.

The government is taking strenuous measures to improve agricultural methods and is working very closely with an agricultural mission which has been sent from the United States for this purpose. Improvement in the breed of cattle and the quality of seed planted, the development of experimental and model farms, the training of the Army in simple agricultural methods—all this which is now being attempted should help. But until these improvements affect large numbers of the people, their productivity will remain low and their poverty great.

4. In no small degree at least, the wealth of a country is dependent upon its educational system and the skill and competence of its technical, professional, and political leaders. The system of popular education in Paraguay is one of the most backward in Latin America. Add to this the fact that her ablest and best educated citizens are constantly drained away to other countries. Just as the most ambitious farm boys in this country go to the cities to get their education and usually do not return to the farm, so many of the ablest Paraguayans go to Montevideo, Buenos Aires, or, less often, to Europe or the United States for their technical or professional education. The greater oppor-

tunities in these countries lead many of them to settle permanently outside their native land.

To the above must be added the effect of political instability within Paraguay. This has been especially serious in that it has led to the exiling from the country of a very appreciable number of the ablest intellectual, technical, and professional leaders.

5. Another factor which is both cause and effect of the poverty of the country is the lack of capital. Foreign capital has not been greatly attracted to Paraguay for a number of reasons. Outside of utilities and to some extent stock raising, there has been little to attract it. Moreover, political instability and a record of defaults on foreign loans have been discouraging factors. Recently, however, both Brazil and the United States have advanced considerable sums to the Paraguayan government for the purpose of road building and general economic development.

The very poverty of the country has made difficult the domestic accumulation of capital. Moreover, the institutions of the country have not been favorable to saving. Lotteries to an extent even greater than in most other Latin American nations have taken the place of savings institutions. A few savings banks or so-called *banks of capitalization* do exist. Here one may entrust capital sums for safekeeping. The history of these institutions is not such as to promote great confidence. Moreover, they are partly merely gambling institutions, for the depositors receive, not regular interest on their money, but only the right to participate to the extent of the interest due them in periodic lottery drawings.

6. No single country of the Western Hemisphere has been so impoverished and devastated by wars as has been the republic of Paraguay. The War of the Triple Alliance (1865–1870), in which Paraguay fought Brazil, Uruguay, and Argentina, was one of the most sanguinary and terrible in history. With the country overrun by foreign troops, Paraguayans fought on not only until the country was completely devastated but until there were almost none left to fight. By 1930 the blighting effects of this war were still evident, but a major recovery had been made. Then came the Chaco War. The destruction of wealth and the loss of manpower, although by no means equal to that of the earlier catastrophe, were still very serious indeed. Paraguay won recognition to its claims to the Gran Chaco, but for this it ex-

changed its small accumulation of wealth, added seriously to the national debt, and contributed the lives of thousands of its citizens.

When the effect of these disastrous wars is considered in connection with the other disadvantages outlined above, one is not greatly surprised to be told that this is sometimes regarded as the poorest country in this hemisphere. In fact, he is likely to be amazed at the rugged vitality of these people, who, despite all these disadvantages, are in these war years making some real strides toward the improvement of agricultural methods, the development of a highway system, and a general amelioration of living conditions.

2. AN AGRICULTURAL ECONOMY

No country in Latin America is more exclusively agricultural than is Paraguay. Mining and fishing are of negligible importance, and only a very small beginning has been made in manufacturing. Outside of the handicraft production of such goods as shoes and furniture and such neighborhood industries as milling and tanning, practically all manufacturing is limited to the processing of a few farm and forest products. Two large meat-packing companies and a small one process the beef which constitutes the most valuable export. Quebracho extract, a product made from the quebracho tree and used chiefly in the tanning of leather, is the chief industry built on forest products, although sawmills and woodworking plants do turn out much lumber. Three cotton textile mills use domestically produced cotton to supply a part of local needs for coarse cotton cloth.

But these manufactures, as well as others of minor significance, are subsidiary to and of much less importance than cattle raising and farming, which provide the chief occupations of the people. Like the adjoining sections of Argentina, Paraguay is a great cattle-raising country, and the owners of the great *estancias* are among the few really well-to-do people. In recent years more than 350,000 beef cattle have been slaughtered annually. Something more than one-half of this is consumed within the country; for Paraguayans are great meat eaters, and beef is an important part of the diet of even the poorest people.

Typically the people are small farmers producing most of the food for their own needs. Tropical and semitropical fruits flourish with little or no care; garden truck, the chief of which are manioc, corn, and native grasses provide food for man and beast; and a small production of some cash crop furnishes the income for necessary store purchases and taxes. The principal sale crops are sugar cane, cotton, tobacco, yerba maté, oil of petitgrain, rice, manioc, and peanuts. All these are produced chiefly for use within the country with the exception of cotton, most of which is marketed abroad.

3. THE EFFECT OF THE WAR

The government of Paraguay severed relations with Germany, Italy, and Japan in January, 1942, but has taken no active part in the war. Although Paraguay has not escaped the reverberations of the Second World War, yet she has been less directly affected than most Latin American countries. Paraguay has no shipping. Devoid of metals, oil, or significant war materials, she has no products which are of first importance to the war effort. Her four chief exports are canned beef, hides and skins, quebracho extract, and cotton. The demand for the first two of these has been favorably affected by the war, but exports of neither quebracho extract nor cotton have been significantly affected.

Moreover, Paraguay is so largely self-sufficing that the shortage of shipping space and the resultant curtailment of imports have affected the economy less seriously than would have been the case in a more specialized economy. Manufactured goods have been scarce, but essential supplies have been provided for through United States export control. Absolutely essential gasoline has been provided, but the new paved road from Asunción to Villarrica is used less for automobiles than as a pedestrian promenade. Some foods such as sugar have been a little short, but scarcities have not been serious.

Nevertheless, the effects of the war have been appreciable. A period of relatively good times, rising prices and wages, and full employment has resulted. In some part this is the result of better prices for cattle, but of major importance probably are the loans by the United States and Brazil and the public works programs which have resulted from them. Moreover, foreign countries, especially the United States, have greatly increased their representation in Asunción. Sanitary, military, and agricultural commissions have brought to this relatively poor city unwanted purchasing power and an unusual demand for many types of goods and services. Finally, the government itself has appreciably expanded its military program. All these indirect results of the war have had a seriously inflationary tendency and have given rise to governmental attempts to avoid a rising price level.

II. The System of Price Control

1. historical development

A survey of price control in Paraguay properly begins with the decree of Apr. 18, 1936, which established authority under which the prices of all the necessities of life could be controlled.[1] Specifically designated as subject to price control were not only practically all foods of common consumption but also such items as ordinary clothing, rent of houses, petroleum products, firewood and charcoal, agricultural and road-building machinery, freight rates, and charges for electricity. Administration of these powers was delegated to the Junta Reguladora de Precios, provision for the establishment of which was set forth in the decree. This new agency was made directly responsible to the Ministry of Agriculture.

As provided for in this decree, a price control agency was promptly organized, and during the remainder of 1936 it proceeded to set prices on certain food items. However, from the end of that year until the early autumn of 1938 the organization appears to have been inactive. But in September, 1939, came a new burst of activity. Orders were issued designed to hold down prices on a large number of items, including staple foods, textiles, and clothing. This revival of price-fixing action apparently resulted from the appearance of inflationary tendencies in Paraguay and the general belief that the outbreak of war in Europe would cause serious price increases.

As an outgrowth of this new attention to rising prices and also because of political changes in the Paraguayan government, a new general price control law was issued on Nov. 23, 1939.[2] Although the Decree-law of April, 1936, has never been repealed and therefore may be regarded, at least theoretically, as still in effect, the law of 1939 is actually the fundamental document upon which price control in Paraguay has operated since that date.

This new law was substantially similar to the earlier one. Responsibility for administration remained in the hands of the Ministry of

[1] Decree-law 787.
[2] Law 282.

Agriculture, which had in the meantime become the Ministry of Agriculture, Commerce, and Industry. The chief provisions of this law follow:

1. The price control authority may itself determine which products shall be controlled as to price.

2. Broad power is given to control the supplies of goods. (This was subsequently extended and made more specific, especially in Decree 11394, which placed extensive rationing responsibilities on this office.)

3. Quality as well as price may be controlled.

4. The price control agency is authorized to make necessary inspections, and merchants are required to make available on request certain of their records. Merchants are also required prominently to display their ceiling prices.

5. Heavy penalties may be imposed by the price control authority for infractions of its regulations, but appeal to the courts is provided.

As in most countries remote from the actual conflict, the immediate inflationary effects of the European war were less pronounced in Paraguay than had been anticipated. Apparently as a result of this situation, only nominal attention was given to price control during 1940. However, by the beginning of the following year, inflationary forces were very much in evidence, and since January, 1941, a continuous effort has been made to combat inflation. An attempt was made to freeze the prices of many important commercial products at the January, 1941, levels; but, this proving generally unworkable as time went on, various modifications were made in price control procedure, and considerable price advances were authorized from time to time.

The present price control authority is the direct successor of the Junta Reguladora de Precios of 1936, although there have been protracted periods of inactivity and many changes in personnel. The Ministry of Agriculture, Industry, and Commerce retained the direction of the price control agency up to August, 1943. At that time a separate Ministry of Commerce and Industry was created, and price control was made one of its functions. At the present time the office in which price control is handled has about 12 employees. However, price is only one of many responsibilities, for a great deal of work must also be performed in connection with rationing, including the control and allocation of imported goods, and export control.

Although the decrees of 1936 and 1939 appear to centralize all price control activities in the one authority, actually other agencies have considerable price-fixing functions. Under Decree 11541, May 31, 1937, the Ministry of Agriculture was empowered to set minimum prices on agricultural products. The first action under this decree was the setting of minimum prices for sugar, on July 9, 1941. In the following month similar action was taken for nine other products, the most important of which were cotton, rice, sweet potatoes, corn, peanuts, and alfalfa. This program has been continued and the number of commodities covered somewhat increased. The actual prices are set by the Ministry of Agriculture, but administration of the scheme is delegated to the Banco de Agrícola. Public-utility rates are set by the Ministry of Interior and Justice, and prices of drugs and medicines by the Ministry of Public Health. The special arrangements for control of the price of meat are discussed on pages 403 to 404.

The Paraguayan price control office has used two methods of preventing price advances: (1) For some commodities, prices have been set in absolute terms, *i.e.*, in a specified number of centimos per unit. This procedure will hereafter be referred to as *flat pricing*. (2) For certain other commodities, prices at wholesale and retail are determined by permitting sellers to add designated percentages to costs. Prices determined in this way will be referred to as *formula prices*.

2. CONTROL BY THE USE OF FLAT PRICES

The present period of active price control in Paraguay began on Jan. 25, 1941, with the publication of a list of flat prices which set maxima for both retail and wholesale transactions. The list included prices for 31 cost-of-living items. Although most were foods, as, for example, sugar, rice, and bread, other items such as kerosene and charcoal were included. The prices designated were approximately those prevailing in the market at the time.

Since then the list has been revised and modified from time to time. Also, special resolutions have been issued whenever it was deemed necessary to raise individual prices. Thus Resolution 144, July 6, 1943, increased the price of potatoes from 16 pesos per kilo to 30 pesos and onions from 20 pesos per kilo to 30 pesos, corresponding increases being permitted for retail sales. The most recent issue of this flat-price list appeared in Resolution 124, Jan. 13, 1943. The extent to which these flat prices have been raised is discussed in Section III.

In addition to the flat prices just described, the price control authority has also published lists of prices for hardware and textile items. Resolution 8, June 23, 1941, set prices for 12 hardware items, and this list was reissued in expanded form on three different occasions, the last being Mar. 27, 1942. One similar list, which set prices on about 50 textile items, was issued on Feb. 27, 1942.[1] Both the hardware and the textile lists represent an attempt to prevent merchants from profiteering from increased prices on goods already in stock and to hold down the prices of standard items commonly bought by consumers having small incomes. It is very important to note, however, for the documents themselves are none too clear on this point, that the prices set forth in these lists for hardware and textiles apply only to goods imported before February, 1941. Goods brought into the country since that time are priced under the formula method described below.

On what basis has the price control authority made upward adjustments in its published maximum prices? The determining considerations have varied somewhat for different commodities. Where the Ministry of Agriculture has established minimum prices to producers for certain important national farm products, the price control authority has used these minimum prices as the basis upon which it determines prices at wholesale and retail.

For items other than those for which minimum prices are set by the Ministry of Agriculture, the policy is to hold the flat prices as long as possible. But when producers or importers can bring strong representations showing that their costs have advanced, a new maximum price is set, based upon costs plus what is adjudged a customary and reasonable margin of profit. Determination of the cost of imported staples is arrived at on the basis of customs declarations and evidence submitted by the wholesalers as to their costs of doing business. In those cases where the product is produced domestically and is also imported in significant quantities, the price set for importing wholesalers is used as the basis for determining the price of the Paraguayan product.

For those commodities which are not imported in appreciable amounts and on which the Ministry of Agriculture has not placed

[1] Resolution 29.

minimum prices, the basis for fixing the prices is the cost of production as roughly estimated by the price control authority. This estimate is made largely on the basis of complaints by producers and, of course, general familiarity of the price control agency with the situation. Detailed cost studies are not made, nor would they be possible with the small staff available.

3. CONTROL BY THE USE OF FORMULA PRICES

In addition to the flat-pricing procedure just described, the price control authority also has a system of margin control, or formula prices, which applies to imports not covered by flat prices. Decree-law 5019, Feb. 10, 1941,[1] froze the prices of all imported goods at the prices prevailing on Jan. 31, 1941, and directed the price control agency to proceed with dispatch to the determination of maximum prices on all goods imported. In performing this task they were directed to take into account the cost of the imported merchandise, the accommodations necessary for carrying on the business, fair returns to middlemen, and the exchange rates fixed by the Bank of the Republic.

Under the broad powers of this decree, the price control authority required each merchant to continue to sell those goods which he had on hand on Jan. 31, 1941, at the prices then prevailing. Whenever merchants have imported goods since that time, they have been required to submit papers showing all costs of imports, including duties assessed and transportation and exchange charges paid. On the basis of these records and the representations of the merchants as to their costs and their necessary and customary rates of profit, the price control authority has designated the legal maximum price which may be charged by each merchant on each item on every shipment received.

It should be noted that the prices thus fixed are of necessity rather arbitrary, for no detailed rules have been laid down by which an importer can make his own price determination. The actual price permitted depends upon the judgment of the price control officers as to the validity of the cost data presented and their estimate of the direct and indirect costs of doing business and the correct margins of profit. Thorough examination of each separate case is obviously impossible. The result has been that the merchants' own determina-

[1] See Appendix D of the regulations.

tions are generally accepted. However, the price control office has gradually developed certain general notions as to justifiable margins, and where these are exceeded, prices are reduced.

4. PRICE CONTROL OUTSIDE OF ASUNCION

As Asunción contains perhaps one-tenth the total population of Paraguay and is the commercial center of the republic, the primary effort has been devoted to regulating prices in this city. In theory, the price regulations described above apply equally to Asunción and the rest of the country. The price control authority has taken the position that prices outside Asunción should differ from those prescribed within the city only by the amount of necessary transportation costs.

Actually, the price control measures have had little effect in the country. In Decree 9649, Nov. 11, 1941, the government, recognizing that rising prices outside Asunción were a serious problem, provided for the creating of local committees for the purpose of making price control legislation more effective there.[1] This decree instructed each locality to establish a price control commission composed as follows:

1. The *intendente* or the president either of the municipal council or of the administrative economic board. This official was to act as president of the commission.
2. The local justice of the peace.
3. The chief of police.
4. A merchant selected by the local chamber of commerce.
5. A reputable citizen designated by representative people of the community.

As set forth in the decree, the functions of the price control commission are: (1) to fix local prices as directed by the price control authority in Asunción; (2) to report violations of price regulations; (3) to enforce all price control regulations.

To date, this experiment has not been very successful. Some localities have not completed the organization of their commissions. Others, though set up, exist merely as honorary bodies. A few are active and have had some success in discouraging speculation and in retarding price advances. Three main causes may be pointed out as contributing to the limited effectiveness of the plan:

[1] See Appendix F of the regulations.

1. People in the outlying regions have shown practically no interest in price control.

2. The price control authority has lacked the personnel to give this part of its work vigorous attention.

3. The committees are typically composed in large part of persons whose financial interests are primarily in trade and merchandizing and who can hardly be expected to take vigorous action to halt price advances.

5. MEAT PRICES

The war very early caused an increase in the demand for Paraguayan beef, with the result that the packing houses tended to divert an increasing proportion of the supply to export purposes. The domestic market was threatened with a reduction of supplies and with mounting prices which most people clearly could not afford to pay. Faced with this situation, the government has taken measures for the purpose of securing adequate beef supplies for domestic consumption at moderate prices. Decree-law 10831, Jan. 30, 1942, as extended and modified by later decrees,[1] provides an ingenious system for this purpose. As now in effect the plan sets the following prices on cattle:

Weight, Kilos	Price, Centimos per Kilo
Steers under 340	12
Steers over 340	12.50
Cows under 300	10
Cows over 300	10.50

It provides further that producers must sell at least 60 per cent of their cattle for domestic consumption. Thus no rancher is permitted to sell more than 40 per cent of his cattle to the packing plants. The law further requires that the packers must pay, in addition to the legal price stated above, 7 centimos per kilo on all cattle purchased. One-half of this, or 3½ centimos per kilo, they pay directly to the seller of the cattle; the other half must be paid to the Banco Agricola del Paraguay for the account of the Comisión de Compensación. The commission uses these funds to operate the system and to pay a premium on the cattle purchased for domestic consumption.

The premium paid on cattle purchased for domestic consumption is appreciably less than the 3½ centimos which is received on all

[1] See especially Decree 14856, Oct. 1, 1942, and Decree 18834, July 5, 1943.

sales to the packing plants. Moreover, complaints have been made to the effect that the government is slow in making its premium payments. Cattlemen have thus had considerable incentive to make the largest sales possible to the packing plants and have shown a disposition not only to oppose the law but to circumvent it whenever possible. Complaints of considerable violation of the regulation have been made. At the present time the government is giving careful attention to improving its procedures and tightening the enforcement of its regulations.

If the advantages contemplated by the plan were to be fully realized by the public, it was apparent that all buying for domestic consumption must be carefully controlled and that fair maximum prices must be set on meat at wholesale and retail. The law, therefore, now requires that all cattle destined for domestic consumption must be sold to the municipalities or to independent slaughterers who operate under close municipal supervision. Responsibility for administration of this part of the plan rests in each municipality with the Junta de Faenamiento. These juntas are responsible both to the municipal governments and to the Ministry of Agriculture.

The municipality or cooperating private slaughterer sells the beef carcasses to retail venders at the following prices:

Class	Price, Centimos per Kilo
1	17
2	16
3	15

The increase in price over that paid the producers covers the costs of handling, slaughtering, and administration.

Enforcement of these maximum retail prices for meat has proved difficult in the spring months, when ranchers are less inclined to market cattle than at other seasons of the year. The Junta de Faenamiento in Asunción made considerable efforts to secure compliance in the spring of 1943. Articles appeared in the local newspapers calling attention to the legal prices, and publicity was given to action taken against violators. Moreover, the government took measures to force producers to market their cattle for domestic consumption more evenly over each 12 months period.

III. Recent Movement of Prices

Despite the efforts to achieve price control which have been described above, Paraguay has continued to be troubled with major changes in the general level of prices. An examination of the nature and extent of these price movements is essential to an understanding of the present and postwar problems of price control.

1. Price movements, 1930–1938

Brief attention may first be given to the movement of prices from 1930 to 1938. At the beginning of this period, Paraguay experienced along with the rest of the world the price deflation characteristic of the great depression. But the reversal of price tendencies in 1933 was much more pronounced here than elsewhere owing to the Chaco War. The price advance beginning in that year moved rapidly into a major inflation.

Table 1.—Annual Index of Prices and Index of Exchange Rate for Argentine Pesos, 1930–1938 *
(1929 = 100)

Year	Price index	Index of exchange rate with Argentine pesos
1930	100	100
1931	83	100
1932	67	101
1933	73	137
1934	118	254
1935	167	398
1936	235	384
1937	304	400
1938	402	380

* Price index published by the Ministry of Economics; foreign exchange index computed by the Bank of the Republic.

Our only record of this price cycle is the annual price index published by the Ministry of Economics and prepared by the Bank of the Republic.[1] This index is shown in Table 1 along with an index of the rate of exchange with Argentine pesos. Although these two indices do not show close harmony in year-by-year movements, both confirm

[1] Information is not available as to the items used in this index or the method of its construction.

the conclusion that by 1938 the purchasing power of the Paraguayan peso had fallen to about one-fourth its 1930 level.

2. PRICE MOVEMENTS, 1938–1943

From 1938 to the present we have available the indices computed by the Statistical Division of the Bank of the Republic on the basis of data collected by the Department of Statistics. These are shown in Table 2. Index *A* is a relative of aggregates based on retail prices of 24 food products of major importance in the diet of moderate and low-income families. Index *B* is a relative of aggregates which includes the 24 food products of Index *A* and adds to them retail prices of 10

TABLE 2.—PRICE INDICES FROM REPORTS OF THE BANK OF THE REPUBLIC, 1938–1943
(1938 = 100)

Date	*A* 24 food items	*B* 10 nonfood necessities plus items in Column *A*	*C* 10 items of indirect consumption	*D* General index
1938	100	100	100	100
1939	106	107	113	110
1940	108	110	124	117
1941	125	126	133	129
January, 1942	133	133	139	136
February, 1942	138	138	139	138
March, 1942	139	139	141	140
April, 1942	139	139	141	140
May, 1942	138	141	153	147
June, 1942	139	141	159	150
July, 1942	140	142	159	150
August, 1942	135	142	159	150
September, 1942	135	142	159	150
October, 1942	132	139	160	149
November, 1942	138	145	166	155
December, 1942	139	147	166	156
January, 1943	146	151	196	172
February, 1943	149	153	196	173
March, 1943	162	161	201	180
April, 1943	163	162	206	183
May, 1943	162	162	208	183
June, 1943	166	167	217	190
July, 1943	154	157	234	191
August, 1943	152	156	247	196

nonfood items of general and direct consumption. As data on rents are not available, Index *C* is designed to serve as the best substitute. It is composed of the prices of 10 items of construction and building materials such as cement, timber, wire, and nails. Index *C* is not based on an aggregate of prices but is derived from a geometrical mean of the prices of the 10 items included. Index *D* is a combination of Index *B* (which includes Index *A*) and Index *C* and is secured by taking the unweighted geometrical mean of these two indices.

Like all index numbers, those shown in Table 2 have limitations which must be carefully noted in order that conclusions based on them may be properly tempered. The following points should be kept in mind:

1. The annual indices are based on December prices and are not an average of prices for the 12 months.

2. The weighting of the individual items in each index depends on the unit of measure selected and the price. While there is every reason to believe that this weighting has been carefully and intelligently done, it should be borne in mind that it is an estimate and is not based on any statistical investigation of family expenditures in Paraguay.

3. It must be assumed that the indices at least slightly understate the full amount of price increases. Even though they may take some account of black-market prices, official government statistics rarely show the full effect of such transactions.

4. The prices are based on Asunción retail quotations and may not correctly reflect conditions in the country.

5. The selection of items is designed to reflect changes in cost of living for lower income groups, although a few items such as coffee and potatoes which would not ordinarily be consumed in appreciable amount by this group are included. Study of individual prices leads to the conclusion that the selection of items and the weighting are such as slightly to overstate the rise in the cost of living for families in the lowest income groups. On the other hand, the index slightly understates the price increase for those in moderate circumstances. Finally, these indices very appreciably minimize the degree to which living costs have advanced for the highest income receivers.

6. As Index *B* is a combination of food and nonfood items, it does not give a separate picture of the price behavior of the nonfood items of direct consumption. In order to provide this, I have simply made an

index of the aggregate prices of these 10 items from data kept by the Statistical Division of the Bank of the Republic. This index appears as Index *E* in Table 3.

TABLE 3.—INDICES OF PRICES OF NONFOOD ITEMS AND OF THE COST OF LIVING, 1938–1943*
(1938 = 100)

Date	*E* Index of prices of 10 nonfood items of general consumption	*F* Adjusted cost-of-living index†
December, 1938	100	100
December, 1939	108	108
December, 1940	116	113
December, 1941	128	128
January, 1942	133	135
February, 1942	138	138
March, 1942	138	139
April, 1942	138	139
May, 1942	145	144
June, 1942	145	145
July, 1942	145	146
August, 1942	155	146
September, 1942	155	146
October, 1942	151	144
November, 1942	156	150
December, 1942	161	152
January, 1943	...	162
February, 1943	...	164
March, 1943	...	171
April, 1943	...	173
May, 1943	...	173
June, 1943	...	179
July, 1943	...	176
August, 1943	...	179

* Computed from records of the Bank of the Republic.

† The figures for 1943 are correct as given in this table. The draftsman, in drawing the chart on retail prices for the cost of living in Paraguay, unfortunately skipped a block 160–180 "adjusted" (see Chart 23).

7. The method used to construct Index *D*, the general cost-of-living index, results in approximately[1] the following weighting:

Index *B*: Food	30	
Nonfood items of direct consumption	20	50
Index *C*: Items of indirect consumption		50
Total		100

[1] "Approximately" because the use of aggregates causes the exact weight to vary somewhat from month to month.

As this appears to give too much importance to the items in Index *C*, I have used the same data to construct an adjusted cost-of-living index, which appears as Index *F* in Table 3. I have taken the weighted arithmetic mean of Indices *B* and *C*, using the following weights: Index *B*, 75; Index *C*, 25.

A study of the indices, especially Indices *A*, *E*, *C*, and *F*, which are shown in Tables 2 and 3, gives a fairly reliable picture of cost-of-living trends since 1938. Prices have moved upward with generally increasing momentum. By December, 1941, the cost of living was 28 per cent above the same month in 1938, and by August, 1943, the

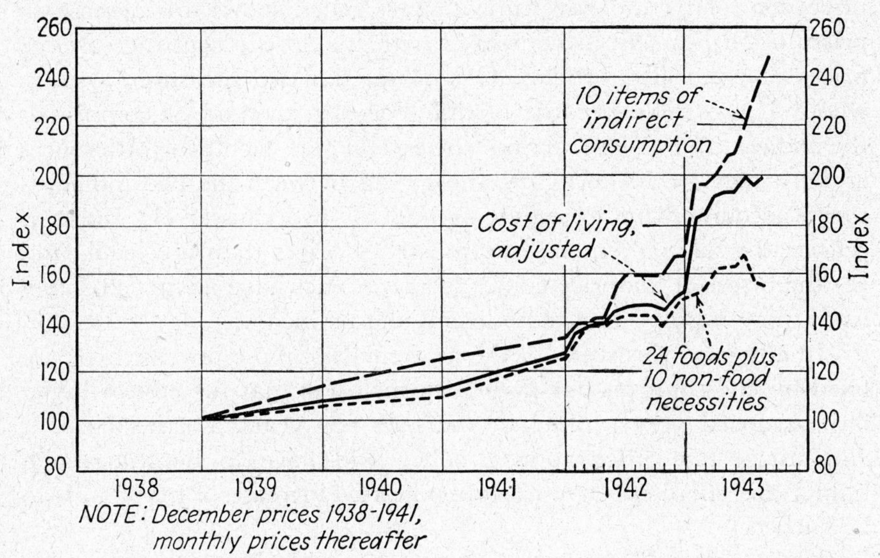

CHART 23.—Paraguay. Cost of living, 1938–1943 (1938 = 100). (*Bank of the Republic of Paraguay.*)

index stood at 179. Although prices for articles of indirect consumption (Index *C*) have advanced most sharply, having reached 247 in August, 1943, the other prices also have registered major increases. Thus in August of that year food prices were 52 per cent and prices for nonfood items of direct consumption 61 per cent above 1938 (see Chart 23).

In order to supplement this picture, we may observe the movement of the prices of articles of the first necessity as fixed by the government. The first such list was published in September, 1939, and contained 29 items. Of these, 20 were found to be comparable with items published in the list of January, 1941. Similarly, it was found that 23 of the items quoted in 1941 were comparable with those published in January, 1943, as corrected to take account of any increases made to Nov. 8, 1943. By means of a chain relative based on the simple arithmetic average of the relatives for each list, the advance in legal prices over those of September, 1939, was found to be 16 per cent in January, 1941, and to have reached 40 per cent by November, 1943.

The items included in these lists of legal prices are most closely comparable with those included in Index *B* as shown in Table 2. About three-fifths the items included in Index *B* are subject to flat-price control by the government. This index shows an increase in prices of 56 per cent as compared with the 40 per cent increase for prices of controlled articles. Of course, the two measures are not wholly comparable because of differences in method of computing the indices and in the period covered. These technical differences aside, it may be assumed that the spread between the two indices is to be accounted for by either or both of two causes: (1) Index *B* reflects the sale of commodities at higher prices than are legal, and (2) the prices of nonprice-controlled necessities have advanced somewhat more rapidly than those legally determined.

In any case, this study of the movement of those prices which are fixed by law confirms our previous conclusion that the cost of living has advanced very rapidly in the past few years. Furthermore, it emphasizes that price control policy will have to become much tighter and more effective in stopping price increases if inflation is to be curbed.

3. COMPARISON WITH URUGUAY AND ARGENTINA

Finally, the Paraguayan price situation may be advantageously compared with that of Argentina (the country with which commercial ties are closest) and with Uruguay (the country most similar in general economic position). Table 4 shows cost-of-living indices for these two countries. The comparison indicates that, although both Uruguay and Argentina have experienced increased living costs, the advance has been much greater for Paraguay, especially since 1940. To some extent the wide difference may be due to differences in method of index-number construction.[1] Both the Argentine and Uruguayan

[1] Some questions have been raised as to whether or not the Argentine index reflects the full increase of living costs during 1943.

TABLE 4.—PRICE INDICES FOR ARGENTINA AND URUGUAY CONVERTED TO BASE 1938 = 100*

Date	Food cost-of-living index		General cost-of-living index	
	Uruguay	Argentina	Uruguay	Argentina
1938	100	100	100	100
1939	106	101	106	102
1940	112	103	110	104
1941	111	106	110	107
1942	115	116	113	113
January, 1943	117	118	115	116
February, 1943	119	117	116	115
March, 1943	124	127	119	122
April, 1943	124	122	119	120
May, 1943	121	122	118	120
June, 1943	121	117	117	117
July, 1943	121	112	117	
August, 1943	121	113	117	
September, 1943	129	115	121	

* From official reports.

indices are based on studies of actual expenditures by low-income-receiving families. It is possible that the general cost-of-living index

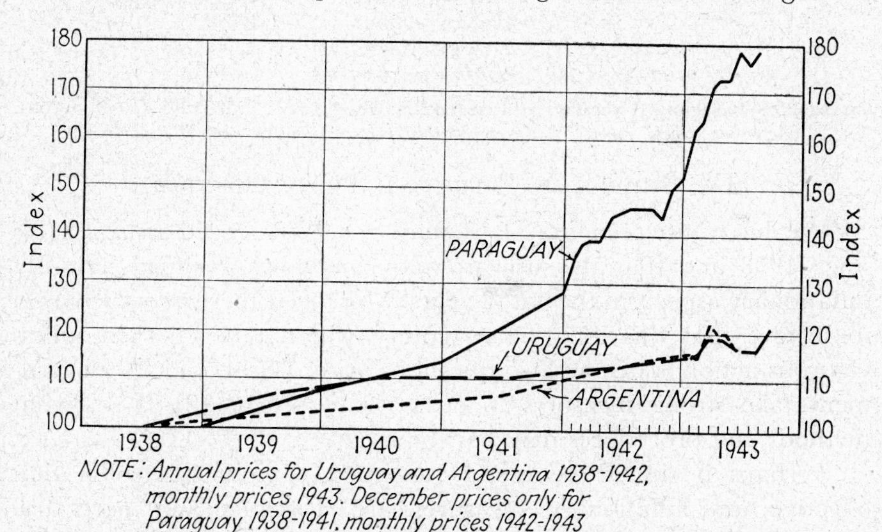

CHART 24.—Paraguay, Uruguay, and Argentina. Cost of living, 1938–1943 (1938 = 100). (*Paraguay: official reports, Uruguay: official reports; Argentina: official reports.*)

for Paraguay reflects the cost of imports slightly more than do the indices of the other countries (see Chart 24).

The indices of the food cost of living are most closely comparable, for the items included for all three countries are substantially similar. Although the contrast between price increases in Paraguay and the other two countries is least striking in this case, it is still very marked. Thus food costs of living have increased in Paraguay nearly twice as rapidly as in Uruguay and more than three times as fast as in Argentina (see Chart 25).

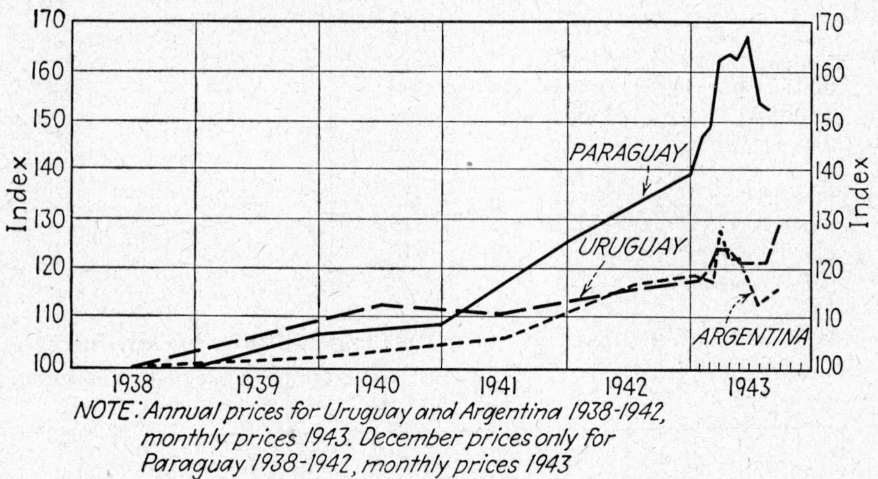

CHART 25.—Paraguay, Uruguay, and Argentina. Food prices 1938–1943 (1938 = 100). (*Argentina: official reports; Uruguay: official reports; Paraguay: bank of Republic.*)

IV. NEED FOR EFFECTIVE PRICE CONTROL

We have just seen that Paraguay has experienced rising prices since 1938 and that this upward movement has assumed seriously inflationary aspects in the past 2 years. Moreover, there is every reason to believe that this inflationary course will not be checked unless vigorous action is taken. Two questions arise: (1) Should the government take strong measures to curb rising prices? (2) If so, what methods and procedures may best be used?

Perhaps it should be merely assumed without discussion that effective anti-inflationary measures are desirable and necessary. However, I believe that at least brief analysis is worth while in order that the full need for price control may be correctly appraised. Such appraisal is not always so easy as it appears. Not only does the extent of damage done by inflation vary with the conditions under which it takes place, but under special circumstances favorable results may be sufficiently substantial to warrant their being carefully weighed against the unfavorable aspects.

1. THE EFFECT OF RISING PRICES IN OTHER COUNTRIES

The argument has been made that inflation is inevitable because of the movement of world prices, that Paraguay has no choice, for, with increasing import costs, prices must advance. Certainly, if prices do rise in those countries with which Paraguay has substantial trade, the problem of stabilizing prices is made more difficult. But it may be noted in the first place that, as the cost of living has advanced more rapidly in Paraguay than in the United States, Argentina, or Uruguay, Paraguay seems to be more of a leader than a follower in this procession. All three of these countries are making strenuous efforts to control prices. The United States has now (1943–1944) perfected its export price control to a point where there should be little trouble from that source. As a matter of fact, some actual decrease in the landed cost of imports should result from the lowered cost of ocean shipping, especially the reduction in insurance rates.

In the second place it is quite possible for this country, as long as it is not on the gold standard or does not have its currency tied to that of any outside nation, to divorce its domestic price movements to a very considerable extent from those of other countries. Already Paraguay has done this in the case of meat, as pointed out above. By one means or another, the government always has in its power the ability to seize the fortuitous gains which result from rising prices abroad and to use these funds either to reduce the cost of imports to its inhabitants or to subsidize the consumption of domestic goods.

2. FOREIGN CREDITS AS A SOURCE OF INFLATION

Only brief attention need be given to the argument that the present inflation is not bad or dangerous because its basis is sound. Thus the belief may be expressed that a major reason for rising prices is the extensive credits which have been granted to the Paraguayan government by the United States and Brazil. Of course, if these credits immediately took the form of imports, they might even have a deflationary influence. But actually they have to a considerable extent remained as credits abroad and have been used by the government as the basis for internal expenditures. This type of inflation is no doubt safer than the free issue of fiat money, for it does have a definitely fixed upper limit. But a rapidly rising price level is inflation no matter what its basis. Even gold itself, as we well know, may be the basis of disastrous inflationary movements. The consideration, therefore, that the present inflation may be based in considerable part on valid foreign credits does not in the least mitigate its harmful results or make it desirable.[1]

3. THE RELATIVE UNIMPORTANCE OF MONETARY TRANSACTIONS IN LARGE PORTIONS OF PARAGUAYAN ECONOMY

Some may hold that, while the further inflation of Paraguayan prices is not especially to be desired, still it will do relatively little damage because of the nature of the country's economic structure. The point may be emphasized that the nonmonetary character of much of its agricultural production and the small degree of industrialization will save Paraguay from those stresses and strains, those maladjustments and injustices which are so characteristic a result of appreciable price inflation in highly industrialized countries.

This reasoning has some validity. At least considerable numbers of workers in the agricultural areas are not greatly affected by price movements. Many cultivate small holdings from which they get almost their whole living. Others are agricultural workers who receive compensation for their toil in goods and services and are without the need for money payments or even money calculations. Insofar as this is the situation a part of the population is more or less insulated from the worst effects of rapidly rising prices. Moreover, when deflation comes, these people can count on something to eat and drink, for farms, unlike factories, do not ordinarily shut down when depression comes.

Yet farming in general can by no means escape the inflationary evils. Those workers on farms and ranches who are paid in money, or in kind based upon money values, must already have found their standard of living falling as money wages have failed to keep pace with rising food and other costs. Landlords and ranchers, though gaining temporarily from this situation, are confronted with rising costs for those things they must buy, such as oxen, horses, construction materials, and equipment of many kinds. Nevertheless, landowning farmers may be relatively prosperous for the time being. Already

[1] In Ch. I a case has been presented for a moderate rate of inflation. In Paraguay, however, the rate of monetary expansion has been altogether too rapid to merit support as a moderate inflationary episode.—EDITOR.

farm-land prices are reported to have increased considerably. Herein lies the real danger for the future, especially to the extent that agriculturists are purchasing land, stock, or equipment on credit. When prices fall, as sooner or later they always do, the usual inflationary disasters can hardly be avoided.

It may also be pointed out that factory workers and, in fact, wage-workers of all kinds in Paraguay often produce part of their own food by means of small gardens or the keeping of pigs or poultry. To the extent that this is true they do have a modicum of protection from lowered real wages when prices are rising and from unemployment when they fall. But the best that can be said is that they are not quite so badly off as are the workers who are completely dependent upon money wages.

Furthermore, even though relatively large numbers of persons in Paraguay are not living on fixed money incomes, still the number who are so living must be appreciable. Those living on savings, annuities, pensions, or fixed incomes of any kind already find their incomes will buy them less than two-thirds of what it would in 1938. The same is true for salaried workers, schoolteachers, and government workers of all kinds.

Thus, while Paraguay may not in some respects suffer as acutely as many more completely industrial countries from extended price inflation, still the penalties and disadvantages are sufficiently serious to make it desirable to avoid them as far as possible.

4. THE POSITIVE ARGUMENT FOR RISING PRICES

One final defense of inflation must now be considered. This defense rests on the peculiar position of Paraguay at the present time, admits the dangers and disadvantages of inflation, but holds that these are more than offset by substantial long-run gains. Briefly stated in its most logical form, the following argument can be made: Paraguay has tremendous potentialities for increased production, but their realization is dependent upon putting through far-reaching and expensive programs relating to new industries, health and sanitation, popular education, agricultural rehabilitation, and road building. Without this program little increase in Paraguayan production can be expected; with it national production may be tremendously enlarged.

Of course, if the outlays for these purposes resulted in immediately augmenting production, they would not necessarily be inflationary. But, although some immediate improvement may be realized, significant dividends cannot be expected for some years at least. Furthermore, if these funds are used for military or other unproductive purposes, the whole argument is obviously invalid.

It may be held that the government should use taxation and not inflation to finance needed improvements. Certainly taxation is preferable insofar as it is possible under present circumstances. But this is a council of perfection which governments rarely achieve. The program is so costly that it would place an impossible burden on present tax administration. Moreover, the new taxes which would have to be imposed would cause very difficult problems of internal economic adjustment and might well alienate popular support for the government's program.

The fact is that inflation by means of the expansion of government credit is merely a drastic and dangerously easy means of taxation. It gives the government command over goods and services by taking purchasing power away from the public through a reduction in the value of money. Despite its dangers and disadvantages governments have not hesitated to use this procedure when the need has been believed sufficiently great. As a method of raising funds for a government, inflation is in general disrepute because weak governments have used it as a substitute for necessary taxes and as an easy way to secure control over funds without the public being aware of exactly what is happening. Nevertheless, no great war of the past has been fought without this device of taxation through monetary depreciation, and it may be used for the more positive purpose of making possible large-scale programs of economic development. Thus Russia in the first stages of her tremendous economic reconstruction made use of inflation as one of the devices to transfer purchasing power from the public to the government.

The foregoing argument for inflation is one concerning which the Paraguayan government must make its own decision. This decision, whatever it be, should be a deliberate one; further, if a policy of rising prices is approved, the need for wise price control is in no way decreased. Inflation is a powerful and often unpredictable medicine. It may greatly harm the patient, even kill him, or it may be habit-forming and destructive of sound commercial morality. The danger is very great that inflation will benefit favored groups in the economy or give speculators profits at the expense of honest producers. There is great danger that inflation once begun will break away into an uncontrolled orgy of rising prices which may destroy all hope of achieving those worthy objectives for which it is designed. Therefore, no nation can safely take the risk of a major inflation without the most careful planning and the establishment of a strong, well-financed, and properly staffed price control agency.

V. Some Requisites for Effective Price Control

1. techniques of price control

As we have seen, Paraguay has already made some progress in developing an effective price control technique. The system of flat pricing which is already in use should be expanded to cover an increased number of items. Where formula prices are unavoidable, they should be reexamined and tightened. This should be done wherever possible with the aim of preventing the pyramiding of costs. Moreover, the extremely indefinite formula now used should be replaced by exact procedures which are made known to the public.

The price control office must be equipped to do some substantial work in accounting and statistical and economic analysis. Indices of prices, production, and wages are badly needed not only to permit appraisal of measures in effect but also to assist the price control office in planning for the future.

2. administration of price control

Real price control cannot be very successful until the office is adequately staffed and administration generally improved. Effective control simply cannot be bought for the absurdly small sums now appropriated for this purpose. The present staff must be greatly increased, and persons with business experience or economic training should be appointed.

In order to make price control effective outside Asunción, the present volunteer system will have to be abandoned and a strong field organization established, with paid personnel and with field offices located in each region of the country.

Enforcement of price control regulations depends to a very great extent upon public understanding and support. Practically nothing had been done by the Paraguayan government either to explain regulations or to convince people of their necessity. Recently, however, the government has shown some appreciation of the need for publicity. Of course, such an educational campaign will have to be reinforced by impartial and vigorous prosecution of violators of the regulations. The existing legal sanctions are more than adequate, but again effectiveness will depend upon good administration and the provision of an adequate and well-trained staff.

3. FISCAL POLICY

Like too many other countries Paraguay has attempted to achieve price control by fiat and without reinforcing it by supplementary measures which are in the long run requisite to success. This is especially true in the field of fiscal policy, for a permanently unbalanced budget makes price control extremely difficult or even impossible.

As far as can be judged from published information, the Paraguayan budget has not been balanced in the past few years. Although some economies have been effected by the present government, expenditures have appreciably expanded, especially for military purposes. Governmental revenue comes largely from imposts on foreign trade and from excise taxes. Duties on imports were raised in 1943, making even more difficult the attempt to stabilize the prices of imported goods. A tax on merchants' profits was imposed in the same year.[1] Present indications are that it will produce very little revenue. The citizens of Paraguay are really very lightly taxed. If national expenditures are continued at the present rate, it seems clear that the government can expect little success in its attempts at either balancing the budget or effecting price control unless an effective system of direct taxes is promptly introduced.

4. CONCLUSION

Paraguay is a poor country beset with many problems. These will surely not be entirely solved in the war years or, indeed, immediately after the war is over. Nevertheless, recent developments give some promise for the future. The need for improved transportation, for hospitals and sanitary measures, for better governmental administration, and for inflation control is being increasingly recognized by the government and by the people. Brazil and the United States are giving

[1] Decree-law N 18190, Apr. 27, 1943.

real assistance both through sending commissions to Paraguay and by furnishing needed capital.

Given a stable government and peace with her neighbors, Paraguay may well in the postwar years make real progress toward overcoming present handicaps and greatly improving her economic position.

Chapter XVIII

Venezuela[1]

by E. G. BENNION

LYING north of Brazil and east of Colombia, the republic of Venezuela extends northward from the equator to about 13° north latitude and stretches for 1,000 miles east and west along the northern coast of South America. Venezuela is shaped somewhat like the state of Texas, minus its panhandle, but covers an area (352,170 square miles) about one-third again as large as Texas. The surface of Venezuela may be divided into four physiographic provinces (see the accompanying relief map): (1) the Maracaibo basin, the V-shaped area surrounding (and including) Lake Maracaibo, which occupies the triangle between the Sierra de Perija, extending northward along the Colombian-Venezuelan boundary, and the Sierra de Mérida, which branches off from the Sierra de Perija at a point south of Lake Maracaibo and extends northeastward to the Caribbean Coast; (2) the Venezuelan highlands, formed by the Sierra de Mérida, just described, and its extension eastward along the Caribbean Coast to the eastern extremity of the Paria peninsula; (3) the Orinoco llanos, the wide, low-lying alluvial plain on both sides of the magnificent Orinoco River, which drains the surface of all eastern Venezuela and flows into the Gulf of Paria between Venezuela and Trinidad; (4) the Guiana highlands, the mountainous region, largely unexplored, which lies to the south of the Orinoco llanos and constitutes about one-half the total area of Venezuela.

[1] This paper could not have been written in the time allowed without the cooperation accorded me by the Economics, the Treasurer's, and the Producing departments of the Standard Oil Company (New Jersey). The responsibility for any interpretations or opinions expressed rests, of course, solely with me.

TOPOGRAPHICAL MAP
OF VENEZUELA

More completely than that of most countries, the present-day economy of Venezuela is conditioned by a quirk of nature. For more than 3,000 miles, from Cape Horn northward to central Colombia, the great series of ranges we know as the Andes maintains a linear pattern along the western margin of the continent of South America, each range trending roughly northward parallel to its fellows. But in Colombia a lofty prong, or spur, departs abruptly from this established pattern and thrusts off northeastward. Within a few hundred miles this range, in turn, splits to form the Sierra de Perija and the Sierra de Mérida, already described. Except for this conspicuous departure from the established trend of the Andes, the Venezuelan highlands and the Maracaibo basin would never have been formed and the featureless Orinoco llanos would have persisted unbroken to merge into the coastal plain along the Caribbean Coast. Since most of Venezuela's petroleum—Venezuela is the third largest petroleum producer in the world—has come from the Maracaibo basin, and as the overwhelming bulk of her important agricultural products comes from the Venezuelan highlands, it is clear that Venezuela's present economic order could scarcely have attained so high a level had it not been for the curious episode in geologic history which, long ago, turned the Andes from their well-established path and girded them off, almost at right angles, into Venezuela.

The population of Venezuela—some 3,840,000 according to the preliminary figures of the 1941 census—appears to be distributed among the four geographical areas roughly as follows: (1) the Maracaibo basin, slightly more than 10 per cent; (2) the Venezuelan highlands, a little less than two-thirds; (3) the Guiana highlands, less than 5 per cent; (4) the Orinoco llanos, close to 20 per cent. The fact that more than two-thirds of the populace can neither read nor write serves only to complicate the already difficult problems of development which confront the Venezuelan people.

Although other industries are indicated on the accompanying industries and raw-materials map, none of these is of real significance as compared with those of petroleum, gold, coffee, cocoa, and livestock.[1] Recognizing this, a cursory examination of the map goes far toward explaining the geographical distribution of the population.

[1] A possible future exception to this is iron ore, important deposits of which are believed to exist in the northeastern part of the Guiana highlands between San Felix and El Callao. Cement is a second possible exception; for Venezuela has, in abundance, both the raw materials with which to work and—of equal importance—cheap fuel.

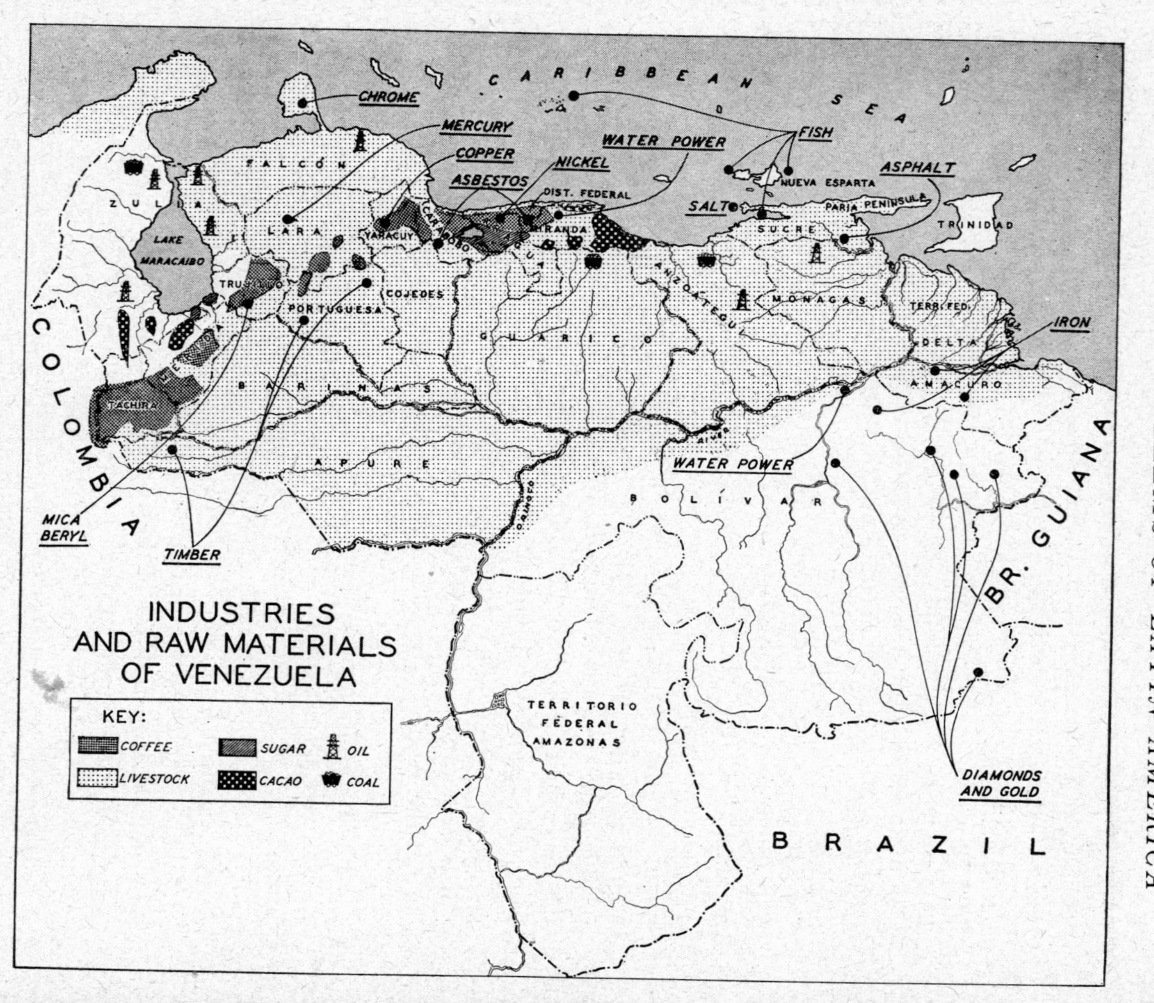

CARIBBEAN SEA
CHROME
MERCURY
COPPER
ASBESTOS
NICKEL
WATER POWER
FISH
SALT
ASPHALT
IRON
DIAMONDS AND GOLD
WATER POWER
TIMBER
MICA BERYL
TRINIDAD
BR. GUIANA
BRAZIL
COLOMBIA
ZULIA
LAKE MARACAIBO
FALCON
LARA
YARACUY
PORTUGUESA
COJEDES
TACHIRA
BARINAS
APURE
GUARICO
ANZOATEGUI
MIRANDA
DIST. FEDERAL
NUEVA ESPARTA
PARIA PENINSULA
SUCRE
MONAGAS
TERR. FED.
DELTA
AMACURO
BOLIVAR
TERRITORIO FEDERAL AMAZONAS
INDUSTRIES AND RAW MATERIALS OF VENEZUELA
KEY:
COFFEE
LIVESTOCK
SUGAR
CACAO
OIL
COAL

With Venezuela the world's third largest producer of petroleum, and with the bulk of Venezuela's petroleum coming from the Maracaibo region, it is not surprising to find over 10 per cent of the population centered in this relatively small area. No more surprising is it to find nearly two-thirds the populace of this predominantly agricultural country in the Venezuelan highlands, which embrace the Federal District, the principal coffee-growing country, and the rich Valencia basin, where much of the lean livestock raised in the Orinoco llanos is fattened. That the extensive Orinoco llanos should contain less than 20 per cent of the population is, at first glance, striking. Considerable expanses of this area, however, are subject to alternate inundation during the rainy season and drought, much of it is not otherwise suitable for cattle ranges, and ticks and nuche flies abound; for these reasons, among others, the country is less hospitable to livestock raising than one might otherwise expect.

Predominantly agricultural though Venezuela is, her important agricultural output is confined to a relatively small group of tropical products; in the field of manufactures, no more than a handful of industries exists. The lack of manufacturing industries is due to a number of factors: to insufficient domestic raw materials; where domestic raw materials do exist, to the doubtful quality of some of these materials (hides are a fairly good example of this); and to an effective demand inadequate to justify the capital expenditures requisite to economical manufacture, for probably not much over one-third the population can be regarded as constituting the Venezuelan market for manufactured goods. It is, therefore, not particularly surprising[1] to learn that Venezuela ranked sixth in 1938 among all Latin American countries as an importer and that, of these six countries, she ranked second in per capita imports.[2]

[1] Venezuela's importance in Latin America as an importer cannot, however, be fully understood unless it is recognized that she is essentially an agricultural nation only in the sense that agriculture is the most important domestically owned industry. At present, at least, petroleum is the dominant factor in the Venezuelan industrial picture. The petroleum companies, although almost entirely foreign-owned, are by far the most important source of demand for bolivars (see petroleum drafts in the balance of payments, Table 1) with which to meet Venezuelan expenditures such as taxes, royalties, and wages and salaries. Without this important credit item in the Venezuelan balance of payments, Venezuela's imports could clearly not loom so large.

[2] This chapter being primarily concerned with the economic problems of Venezuela in the present and immediate future, only the superficial industrial background requisite to a better grasp of these problems has been attempted in the preceding introductory remarks. For a more complete understanding of the above aspects of the Venezuelan economy, the reader is referred to such works as Preston E. James, *Latin America* (Lothrop,

Exchange Rates

Because of the importance of international trade to Venezuela, an analysis of her economy ought to begin with her international trade. Foreign-owned industry plays such an important role in the development of Venezuelan resources, however, that an initial consideration merely of Venezuela's exports and imports would postpone undesirably an adequate understanding of the functioning of her economy. To grasp the significance of the distinction between foreign-owned and domestically owned industry, it is therefore desirable to follow the more difficult route of first considering the balance of payments (Table 1). For reasons that will become obvious, this, in turn, requires some knowledge of the various rates of exchange between the dollar and the bolivar.[1]

During the 2-year period prior to August of 1934, the bolivar appreciated steadily from some 7.75 bolivars to the dollar in August of 1932 to 3.05 bolivars to the dollar in August of 1934. Complete liquidation of the externally held national debt in the fiscal year 1930–1931, with the subsequent decline in demand for foreign exchange from this source (a demand which had existed, without interruption, for 15 years) and a rise in petroleum drafts, contributed substantially to this strength in the bolivar. The devaluation of the dollar accentuated the strength in the bolivar.

The abrupt increase in the value of the bolivar meant that it cost more, in dollars, to secure bolivars; and this, in turn, meant that Venezuelan exporters had to lower the bolivar prices of their commodities, if they wished to continue to sell as much as before. This constituted a real hardship to the agricultural interests of Venezuela, and the government decreed on July 25, 1934, a direct subsidy to cocoa- and coffeegrowers.[2] At the same time, fixed and multiple exchange rates were introduced. The exchange rate was pegged at 3.90 bolivars to the dollar for cocoa and coffee producers. The same

---

Lee & Shepard Company, New York, 1942); Fred A. Carlson, *Geography of Latin America* (Prentice-Hall, Inc., New York, 1943); publications of the Venezuelan government such as *Anuario Estadístico de Venezuela*, *Guía Comercial de Venezuela*, *Estadística Mercantil y Maritima*, the *Memorias* of the various departments, and *Libro Amarillo;* and other sources noted throughout this essay.

[1] This section is intended to cover only some of the more important aspects of exchange rates as determined by agreements between the Venezuelan government and the petroleum companies, by decrees, and by the banking system.

[2] *Gaceta Oficial*, July 25, 1934.

rate was set for two-thirds of the petroleum companies' dollars, which were to be sold to the banks; and the remaining one-third of the petroleum dollars was to be sold to the government at the theoretical gold import point of about 3.03 bolivars to the dollar. Controls were, however, insufficiently strong to make it possible for the banks to absorb more than about 2 per cent of the petroleum dollars during the remainder of 1934, the balance being sold to the government at the gold import point.

A series of measures in the field of exchange control followed in an effort to stabilize the rate of exchange at a level corresponding to its normal equilibrium rate and to alleviate the hardship imposed upon agriculture by the stubborn tendency of the bolivar to rise. These measures culminated, however, in a decree of July 23, 1941, which authorized the operations of a controlled and a free market.[1] The newly created Central Bank of Venezuela, which began operations in 1940, took over the functions of the National Exchange Control Office and was to manage the controlled market, supplying dollars to the commercial banks at 3.335 bolivars to the dollar; the rate to the public was set at 3.35. A return to multiple exchange rates also took place, the sale of certain dollars through the central bank at fixed rates being made obligatory: petroleum dollars were assigned a rate of 3.09; export premiums were abolished; cocoa was assigned a rate of 4.60; coffee and cattle, a rate of 4.30. The free market was to be operated by the commercial banks, which were to deal in all other exchange, and a system of import permits was instituted to force the imports of luxuries and semiluxuries into this market. The central bank reserved the right to enter this market for stabilization purposes.

More favorable prices abroad for Venezuelan products made it possible, in May and June of 1942, to abolish the preferential rate for cattle and to reduce the rate for hulled coffee and cocoa to 3.75; the rate for fine coffee remained at 4.30. The improved exchange position also made it possible, on May 18, 1942,[2] virtually to eliminate import permits and to discontinue the controlled market, commercial banks being allowed to sell dollars freely at 3.35. The central bank continued to receive exchange derived from petroleum drafts and from the export of coffee and cocoa and to distribute such exchange required by the banks at the rate of 3.335. Under this decree, still in effect, the

[1] *Gaceta Oficial*, July 23, 1941.
[2] *Ibid.*, May 19, 1942.

TABLE 1.—VENEZUELA: BALANCES OF INTERNATIONAL PAYMENTS, 1935–1942
(In millions of bolivars)

	1935		1936		1937		1938		1939		1940		1941		1942	
	Debit	Credit	Debit	Credit	Debit	Credit	Debit	Credit	Debit	Credit	Debit	Credit	Debit	Credit	Debit	Credit
1. Merchandise items:																
Total merchandise exports (incl. petroleum at real value)[1]		336.0		483.1		611.6		565.0		515.0		479.9		695.0		461.8
Total merchandise imports[1]	158.6		206.7		300.6		310.0		326.2		311.1		287.8		215.7	
Net merchandise balance		177.4		276.4		311.0		255.0		188.8		168.8		407.2		246.1
2. Service items—est.																
Freight and insurance	8.5		14.0		17.6		17.6		24.4		30.7		32.8		38.9	
Other charges	14.9		17.4		18.3		17.5		17.8		16.7		15.9		13.4	
Net service balance	23.4		31.4		35.9		35.1		42.2		47.4		48.7		52.3	
3. Foreign-owned industries items:																
Petroleum exports (real value)[1]	275.0		404.0		531.0		506.0		457.0		428.0		634.0		387.0	
Foreign producers' unminted gold exports—est. (see text)	10.0		10.3		10.7		11.2		12.3		11.2		13.1		10.4	
Petroleum drafts[2]		135.9		161.3[5]		176.4[5]		228.3		249.2		213.0		247.9		208.1
Gold drafts—est. (see text)		5.0		5.2		5.3		5.6		6.2		5.6		6.6		4.8
Imports of petroleum companies[1]		52.5		54.4		94.2		104.4		81.9		72.1		60.2		52.6
Imports of gold companies[3]		1.5		0.7		1.2		1.1		0.8		0.7		0.6		0.4
Net foreign-owned industries balance	90.1		192.7		264.6		177.8		131.2		147.8		331.8		131.5	
Net balance, Categories 1, 2, 3 above		63.9		52.3		10.5		42.1		15.4	26.4			26.7		62.3
4. Gold and silver movements:																
Exports		1.4		5.2		20.8										
Imports	66.6[4]		4.9		4.0		0.9		0.2							
Change in earmarked gold at Federal Reserve Bank, New York															88.8[9]	
Net gold and silver movements	65.2			0.3		16.8	0.9		0.2						88.8	
5. Capital movements:																
Change in central-bank deposits abroad[6]											7.9		36.1			15.3

TABLE 1.—VENEZUELA: BALANCES OF INTERNATIONAL PAYMENTS, 1935–1942.—(*Continued*)

	1935		1936		1937		1938		1939		1940		1941		1942	
	Debit	Credit	Debit	Credit	Debit	Credit	Debit	Credit	Debit	Credit	Debit	Credit	Debit	Credit	Debit	Credit
Change in Venezuelan commercial banks' deposits abroad[7]		10.8		2.5	15.7		8.3			22.2	21.3			21.0	4.5	
Change in known United States loans outstanding to Venezuela[8]						0.2	0.1		0.1			0.4		0.7		12.5
Unrecorded capital movements (and errors)	9.5		55.1		11.8		32.8		37.3			55.2	12.3			3.2
Net capital movements		1.3	52.6		27.3		41.2		15.2			26.4	26.7			26.5
Net balance, Categories 4 and 5	63.9		52.3		10.5		42.1		15.4			26.4	26.7		62.3	

[1] 1935–1942 from annual issues of the *Estadística Mercantil y Maritima*, published by the Ministerio de Fomento, except real value of petroleum exports, which came from the *Anuario Estadístico de Venezuela*, 1942, p. 552.

[2] Treasurer's Department, Standard Oil Company (New Jersey).

[3] 1935–1938 from Juan Compo, "Las Balanzas de pagos venezolanas de 1935 a 1939," *Boletin de la Cámara de comercio de Caracas*, May, 1940, pp. 7659–7671; 1939–1941 estimated; 1942 from Luis A. Cardenas, "Balance de pagos de Venezuela en 1942," *Revista de hacienda*, September, 1943, p. 2.

[4] Import of coin by the national government.

[5] Includes deposits to the credit of the Venezuelan government in New York, in the amount of $3,630,413 in 1936 and $2,430,000 in 1937.

[6] *Boletin del Banco central de Venezuela*, July, 1943, p. 12. See text foı adjustment.

[7] *Boletin de la Cámara de comercio de Caracas*, pp. 6390–6391, 6638–6639, 6868–6869, 7132–7133, 7362–7363, 7596–7597, 7972–7973, 8322–8323, 8764–8765.

[8] From confidential sources.

[9] Annual report, 1942, of the *Banco central de Venezuela*, p. XXXIII. See text for adjustment.

central bank does not sell exchange directly to the public but is prepared to intervene in order to maintain the rates now fixed by it.

Balance of Payments

Equipped with a knowledge of the course and nature of the various bolivar-dollar exchange rates over the past decade, we may turn to a consideration of Venezuela's balance of payments. A balance of international payments is simply a statement of known transactions between a particular country and the rest of the world. It is a statement, on the one hand, of transactions which entitle the particular country to payments from the rest of the world and, on the other hand, of transactions which entitle the rest of the world to payments from the particular country. The former type of transactions is, therefore, logically listed as a credit (exports of goods, services, gold, and credit instruments are examples of this); and the latter type is listed as a debit (imports of the same items are illustrative of this). Barring the possibility of charity, the statement must balance, if all transactions are known; for what a country imports must be paid for either by an export of goods, services, and gold or by credit extended to it. As all transactions are, in practice, never known, a balance is achieved through an appropriate debit (or credit) to some residual account—in our case, the Unrecorded Capital Movements account.

It should be understood that capital movements have precisely the opposite effect upon the balance of payments from that of movements of goods, services, and precious metals. An export of goods, services, or precious metals entitles a country to receive something therefor; hence, these exports are credit items. An export of capital (an exodus of liquid funds) from a country is the equivalent of an import of credit instruments (of an influx of securities, for example), and the country which parts with these credit instruments is being paid for them by the capital export; hence, capital exports are debit items. Credit instruments which may be imported are varied in form; but, for our purposes, it is sufficient simply to distinguish between long-term and short-term capital movements. Illustrative of long-term credit instruments are securities: the country *importing* these securities is said to have *exported* long-term capital. Illustrative of short-term credit instruments are demand deposits acquired in banks outside of a country: the country acquiring these deposits abroad (which are, of course, liabilities of the banks abroad to citizens of the country concerned) is said to have exported short-term capital.

Confusion should be avoided between capital movements and payments upon capital invested in a country. An exporter might sell his commodity abroad and acquire, for example, a deposit in some foreign bank. This transaction would mean, in the balance of payments, a credit to the merchandise items account and a debit to the short-term capital movements account. If, on the other hand, the exporter used his proceeds to pay dividends to foreign stockholders, this transaction would mean a credit to the merchandise items account and a debit to service items—for the service items account embraces, among other things, payments *upon* capital invested between countries.

CONSTRUCTION

A balance of payments is, at best, somewhat difficult to understand. Our Venezuelan balance of payments, being heavily weighted with items growing out of the fact that foreign-owned industries are such an important factor in the development of Venezuela's resources, is even more complex. If, however, the effort requisite to an understanding of the logic behind the particular setup of this balance of payments is made, a sounder grasp of the Venezuelan economy can be achieved. The concluding portion (that dealing with Adjustments) of this section is also quite technical; but that portion can be omitted by the reader without seriously detracting from his understanding of the Venezuelan economy.

It is rarely possible to say what particular debits offset what particular credits, although the credit item arising from exports by domestic companies must be offset, in the balance of payments, by an equal debit. And, in the case of credits arising from exports by domestic companies, we seldom know more than that, *from the viewpoint of the country as a whole*, those credits were paid for by imports of merchandise, by the acceptance of credit instruments (by the export of capital), by an import of precious metals, or by foreign countries' rendering services. It is not, however, customary *for the individual domestic companies* to accept payment for their exports in gold, in merchandise imports, or in foreign services. Rather, if they are paid in foreign currency, they sell this foreign currency to their banks in Venezuela for domestic currency; and the banks, in turn, sell this foreign currency to someone indebted to that foreign country for (say) imports. With the proceeds from their exports the domestic companies then pay their various expenses and dividends (mostly) to people living in the exporting country.

The exports of foreign-owned companies likewise create, in the balance of payments, a credit in the merchandise items category; and this credit must also be offset by an equal debit. Unlike domestic companies, however, the foreign-owned companies cannot return to the exporting country all the proceeds from their exports; for the foreign-owned companies must pay expenses incurred outside the exporting country and (if possible) show a profit, which belongs to the foreign investors whose capital investments in the exporting country contributed toward the development of that country's resources. Our major problem is, therefore, to determine what part of the proceeds, arising from the exports of the foreign-owned companies, returns to the exporting country and what part remains abroad. This is the purpose of the Foreign-owned Industries Items account in our balance of payments.

By including the exports and imports of the foreign-owned companies in total merchandise exports and imports, we ascertain the credit balance of the Merchandise Items category accruing to Venezuela as a result of her foreign trade in merchandise. To determine the proceeds from the exports of foreign-owned companies, we make a contra debit in the foreign-owned industries category for the full value of petroleum exports (as the petroleum companies are almost wholly foreign-owned) and for that part of the value of unminted gold exports estimated to belong to foreign-owned companies.[1]

That part of the proceeds returning to Venezuela is divided into two general items: (1) drafts (in foreign currencies) of the foreign-owned companies sold to Venezuela in exchange for bolivars with which to meet Venezuelan expenditures such as taxes, royalties, and wages and salaries; (2) imports of the foreign-owned companies. Accordingly, we enter as credit items the drafts of the petroleum and foreign-owned gold companies;[2] and we make a contra credit for the full value of the imports of the same companies. The difference between our debit and credit items under our Foreign-owned Industries

[1] This latter is an estimate based on the assumption that foreign-owned companies are responsible for the same proportion of unminted gold exports as they are for production.

[2] This, too, is an estimate based on the assumption that one-half the value amount exported by foreign-owned gold companies returns to Venezuela. The authority for this estimate is R. E. Tello in the *Revista de Hacienda*, Vol. III, No. 5.

Items category yields us a debit balance which represents that part of the proceeds of the exports of foreign-owned companies not returning to Venezuela.

It should be understood that the debit balance of this category tells us only what portion of foreign-owned companies' exports did not return to Venezuela; it does *not* tell us how that portion is distributed among payments on foreign capital invested in Venezuela, payments to defray expenses incurred outside Venezuela, and capital exports. It seems, however, a safe assumption that a large part of this debit balance is, in fact, payments on foreign capital in the period under review; but even a close approximation to the correct amount of such payments is not possible.[1] Moreover, fluctuations in this debit balance do not necessarily signify fluctuations in payments on foreign capital in the same direction.

The service item debit of Other Service Charges includes estimated Venezuelan payments for fire and life insurance, interest and dividends, tourists' expenditures, transit charges, commercial commissions, and government services. The service item of freight and insurance is likewise an estimate in which an attempt has been made to take into account changes in freight and insurance rates over the major trade routes, as well as changes in the origin of Venezuelan imports (and therefore in the sea routes traversed) under the impact of war. In the area of service item estimates, some danger of error unquestionably exists; but such error as may have arisen from this source ought not to be of much relative importance.

The data on capital movements into and out of Venezuela are fragmentary. The only available figures known to the author are those of changes in the deposits abroad of the Central Bank of Venezuela, changes in known United States loans to Venezuela, and changes in the net deposits abroad of the Venezuelan banks. Unrecorded capital movements include, therefore, in addition to any net errors arising from estimates, adjustments, and omissions, such net movements as those occasioned by transactions in securities, changes in Venezuelans' deposits with banks abroad, and possible loans made

[1] This is true, not only because foreign-owned imports and drafts are not the sole expenses incurred and because capital exports may be involved, but also because in some years some (indeterminate) part of foreign-owned imports and drafts should doubtless be classified as capital imports. Moreover, the value of petroleum exports is the "real" value as computed by the Ministerio de Fomento; and this value may or may not be an exactly accurate representation of the value of these exports to the petroleum companies.

by agencies of the United States (and of other countries) to Venezuela, information on which is not readily available.

It will be noticed that the net balance of categories 1, 2, and 3 combined is precisely offset by the net balance of categories 4 and 5 combined. It will readily be recognized that this must necessarily be so when it is realized that credit items are items which entitle a country to payments from others, whilst debit items are those which entitle others to payments from a country. Thus, if a country has a greater credit than a debit in the sum of the first three categories (if, in other words, it exports more in goods and services than it imports), it must have an exactly offsetting debit in the sum of the last two categories (*i.e.*, it must have been paid for that excess with precious metals, or it must have lent others the means with which to acquire the excess from it).

INTERPRETATION

In 1935, it will be observed, the credit balance arising out of the first three categories was liquidated through Venezuela's debtors exporting gold to Venezuela in an amount almost exactly equal to the credit balance. Actually, what happened was that the government purchased gold abroad[1] in the amount of about 60 million bolivars. Conceivably this figure was translated into bolivars at the 3.06 par of exchange rate, in which event the bolivar figure for gold and silver imports is understated (for our purposes) by approximately 15 million bolivars—for our other figures are (presumably) at a rate closely approximating the banks' selling rate of 3.93. If the gold has been translated into bolivars at the 3.06 rate, our unrecorded capital movements (which is simply the residual item which forces a balance) is overstated by about 15 million bolivars and should show a small unrecorded capital import instead of an unrecorded capital export of 12.9 million bolivars.

In 1936 the substantial credit balance of the first three categories is almost entirely offset by a very large unrecorded export of capital. A part of this might be accounted for by the probably erroneous assumption that the declared value of all imports and exports is at the 3.93 selling rate of the banks, whereas the free market rate averaged 4.17[2] during 1936; but the fraction thus accounted for would be

[1] League of Nations, *Balances of Payments*, 1937, p. 211.

[2] *Inter-American Statistical Yearbook*, exchange rates section.

small. It is not improbable that the biggest portion of the unrecorded capital export is to be explained by the death of President Gomez in December of 1935, which may have given rise to temporary political and economic uncertainties and a consequent brief but substantial flight of capital; this, of course, appears as a debit, since it is the equivalent of an import by Venezuelans of credit instruments such as securities or deposits abroad.

The years 1937–1939 are all years of substantial capital export, with the unrecorded capital exports looming quite large in the last 2 years. A possible explanation for this may be speculation in the future course of the exchange rate. The official market rate had risen[1] from 3.93 in 1936 to 3.19 in 1939, and the free market rate had increased from an average of 4.17 in 1936 to 3.21 in 1939.[2] This was a substantial appreciation in the bolivar, and it is possible that a considerable amount of foreign exchange, acquired in the course of trade, was simply left abroad in the hope that the bolivar would later decline in value and the foreign exchange then could be translated into a greater amount of bolivars. If this was the case, the hope was, as a matter of fact, justified, since the bolivar subsequently fell somewha[t] in the free market.

In 1940 both the central bank and the commercial banks expor[t] capital (acquired balances abroad) despite a debit balance in the [first] three categories of the balance of payments. This could have [been] accomplished only by virtue of a substantial unrecorded ca[pital] import as a compensating credit item. Presumably this repres[ents] repatriation of funds and possibly some unrecorded private and investment from abroad.

The credit balance arising from the first three categories is further augmented by a substantial reduction in commerc[ial] deposits abroad. These two credits are almost entirely off[set by a] large increase in central-bank deposits abroad[3] and by an [...] capital export of 12.3 million bolivars.

[1] Lest this be confusing to the lay reader, a movement from 3.93 to 3.1[9 is] a rise in the value of the bolivar; *i.e.*, a dollar costs *less* in terms of bo[livars, a] bolivar is worth more in dollar terms.

[2] *Op. cit.*

[3] It should be noted that the gold (and, presumably, the deposits a[broad) are carried on] the central bank's books at 3.09 bolivars to the dollar rather than at t[he] selling rate of 3.35 used in this balance of payments. For this reason [these] two items appear on the central bank's books as smaller amounts t[han in the balance of] payments. See Adjustments, pp. 436–440.

An outstanding feature of the 1942 balance of payments is a debit of 88.8 million bolivars in the form of earmarked gold purchased by the central bank[1] with dollars acquired during the year and with some of its previously acquired deposits abroad. This debit, in conjunction with the credit balance for the first three categories, yields a debit balance of some 26 million bolivars before capital movements. Capital imports (credit balances) of roughly equal amounts in the forms of a reduction in central-bank balances abroad and of known United States loans, plus an unrecorded capital import of 3.2 million bolivars, made this debit balance before capital movements possible.

Our residual item of unrecorded capital movements indicates an import of capital in that area for 1942. As noted on pages 432 to 434 and 441, however, it is probable that our merchandise credit is too large by perhaps as much as 8 million or 10 million bolivars in 1942. This would have the effect of understating our unrecorded capital movements credit by 8 million or 10 million bolivars. It is possible, therefore, that there was actually an unrecorded capital import of as much as 11 million to 14 million bolivars. This conclusion seems, in fact, to be borne out by the nature of the figures on extraordinary admissions of controlled *Devisen* for 1942;[2] for these figures suggest the possibility of loans to Venezuela from the outside substantially in excess of the known United States loans.

ADJUSTMENTS

Upon recalling what has been said about the various bolivar-dollar exchange rates, it is immediately apparent that there are numerous obstacles to overcome in constructing even an approximately accurate balance of payments. Part of our data is in bolivars (notably, exports, imports, and service items), some of the most important elements of our data (petroleum drafts, for example) are in dollars, and different rates of exchange apply to certain elements. As these obstacles are not much more readily overcome by stating the balance of payments in dollars, the more appropriate course of using bolivars has been followed.

To avoid overstating the bolivar value of some items at the expense of an exactly equal understatement of the bolivar value of other items, it is clearly necessary to translate dollar data into bolivars at the

[1] *Cf.* preceding footnote.

[2] *Cf.* footnotes in the 1942 annual report of the Banco Central de Venezuela, p. XXXIV

bolivar-dollar rate of exchange for which dollars were to be sold *by the banks.* Petroleum drafts, for example, are available in dollar terms, and these were sold to the government, as we have seen, at varying rates which were frequently well below the selling rate of the banks. From the balance-of-payments viewpoint, however, it is not the rate at which the petroleum companies sold dollars that counts—rather, it is the value of these dollars to the purchaser who uses them to buy the goods and services of the United States; and this value is, presumably, the official selling rate of the banks. Hence, petroleum drafts were converted to bolivars at the banks' selling rate, taking account of changes over time in that rate.

The central bank's earmarked gold in the Federal Reserve Bank of New York as of Dec. 31, 1942, was carried at 81.9 million bolivars. According to the 1942 annual report of the Banco Central de Venezuela, $26.5 million were required to purchase this gold.[1] The gold was therefore carried at a bolivar-dollar rate of 3.09. Presumably this means that this gold was valued in bolivars at the same rate at which dollars were acquired from the petroleum companies. The bolivar value of the earmarked gold has been raised in the balance of payments to a figure corresponding to the banks' present selling rate of 3.35. On the assumption that central-bank deposits abroad are also carried at the conversion rate of 3.09, these bolivar figures have been increased in the same manner as the gold bolivar figures. For this reason these two sets of figures do not agree with the figures as stated on the central bank's balance sheets.

A comparison of the 1941 and 1942 figures on coffee and cocoa dollars, bought by the central bank at premium exchange rates, with the declared bolivar value of these exports in the same years seems to make it clear that the declared bolivar value of these exports is too great to represent the dollar value converted into bolivars at the banks' official *nonpremium* selling rate of 3.35. The preferential exchange rates (and, in earlier years, subsidies and export premiums) have, therefore, apparently led to an overstatement—for balance-of-payments purposes—in the declared bolivar value of these exports. No clear-cut consistent method of making an appropriate adjustment for this, on the strength of available information, suggested itself, and the declared bolivar-value data have been retained in the balance of payments. It should be noted, therefore, that, since these figures give us a merchan-

[1] *Ibid.*, p. xxxiii.

TABLE 2.—FOREIGN TRADE BY PRINCIPAL-PRODUCTS CLASSIFICATION
(Excluding coined gold, silver, and nickel. Volume in thousands of metric tons. Value in millions of bolivars)

Exports	Volume									Value								
	1913	1935	1936	1937	1938	1939	1940	1941	1942	1913	1935	1936	1937	1938	1939	1940	1941	1942
Coffee	64.4	53.6	61.6	41.7	35.9	27.4	28.8	44.6	35.6	83.9	30.8	39.7	38.1	25.7	21.3	18.7	23.9	37.3
Cacao	17.9	15.0	16.5	16.3	20.6	15.4	15.3	12.9	12.2	25.2	6.8	11.5	13.9	10.0	9.7	8.5	6.1	9.1
Cattle, cattle and goat hides	13.3	8.0	16.6	16.3	11.9	9.4	6.6	8.5	15.6	12.3	2.7	5.7	6.9	3.2	3.7	2.7	3.7	5.6
Other agricultural and forest products[1]	23.1	10.2	11.8	13.4	8.9	8.2	4.4	7.0	9.8	15.7	1.3	3.3	2.0	1.2	1.6	0.9	6.0	2.4
Gold—unminted	0.7[2]	5.1[2]	4.8[2]	5.1[2]	4.9[2]	5.8[2]	5.3[2]	5.0[2]	3.8[2]	2.0	14.3	14.7	15.3	14.9	17.6	16.8	16.0	13.9
All other, including reexports	85.5[3]	32.6	12.4	12.7	20.1	17.2	12.1	12.2	12.4	10.7	5.1	4.2	4.4	4.0	4.1	4.3	5.3	6.5
Total, excluding petroleum and coined gold and silver	204.2	119.4	118.9	100.4	97.4	77.6	67.2	85.2	85.6	149.8	61.0	79.1	80.6	59.0	58.0	51.9	61.0	74.8
Petroleum and products	81.7[4]	21,475.4	23,320.6	25,970.8	27,498.5	29,593.1	26,738.6	32,705.3	20,486.2	3.0[4]	275.0	404.0	531.0	506.0	457.0	428.0	634.0	387.0
Total merchandise, excluding coined gold and silver	285.9	21,594.8	23,439.5	26,071.2	27,595.9	29,670.7	26,805.8	32,790.5	20,571.8	152.8	336.0	483.1	611.6	565.0	515.0	479.9	695.0	461.8

TABLE 2.—FOREIGN TRADE BY PRINCIPAL-PRODUCTS CLASSIFICATION.—(*Continued*)

Imports	Volume									Value								
	1931	1935[5]	1936[5]	1937[5]	1938	1939	1940	1941	1942	1913	1935[5]	1936[5]	1937[5]	1938	1939	1940	1941	1942
Dutiable and free imports																		
Foodstuffs and beverages		45.8	59.1	72.5	82.5	137.5	101.7	104.4	74.1		16.6	22.4	30.0	34.4	46.5	42.9	41.3	36.4
Textiles		6.8	9.2	13.5	9.2	11.4	12.0	9.2	6.3		25.8	34.1	44.0	31.5	36.3	39.5	37.9	38.6
Animals and their industrial products		0.5	0.4	1.0	1.6	1.4	1.7	1.7	3.5		3.1	4.0	5.5	5.2	5.7	4.8	5.6	5.3
Plants and their industrial products		1.6	2.2	3.2	3.0	4.2	3.9	10.7	6.2		2.2	3.5	4.0	3.8	3.9	4.5	8.0	7.3
Wood and paper		14.5	20.8	37.6	42.3	33.3	26.7	31.3	14.6		4.5	6.4	9.8	10.1	9.8	9.8	11.2	7.4
Mineral products		82.5	120.2	189.5	199.8	236.8	174.0	126.7	88.2		8.6	11.3	16.7	16.4	17.0	17.9	15.9	11.9
Metals		76.7	98.8	183.8	168.0	179.7	163.7	115.9	62.9		32.9	38.4	65.6	63.9	64.2	59.1	48.1	31.7
Machinery and equipment		25.0	34.2	52.3	62.1	63.0	63.5	42.9	21.3		42.4	57.0	88.0	103.3	100.4	93.4	74.7	42.7
Chemicals		12.1	16.1	23.7	22.3	27.2	22.8	27.1	16.5		14.0	18.1	22.9	22.6	25.1	23.6	28.8	21.7
Miscellaneous		2.9	3.8	5.4	6.0	5.9	5.5	5.5	3.5		8.5	11.5	14.1	16.5	15.4	14.7	14.1	11.9
Total	136.4	268.4	364.8	582.5	596.8	700.4	575.5	475.4	297.1	93.4	158.6	206.7	300.6	307.7	324.3	310.3	285.6	214.9
Imports for the national government (*Especies fiscales*, etc.)	[6]	[6]	[6]	[6]	1.4	1.9	1.0	1.8	0.4	[6]	[6]	[6]	[6]	2.3	1.9	0.8	2.2	0.8
Total merchandise imports	136.4	268.4	364.8	582.5	598.2	702.3	576.5	477.2	297.5	93.4	158.6	206.7	300.6	310.0	326.2	311.1	287.8	215.7
Imports of foreign-owned companies											54.0	55.1	95.4	105.5	82.7	72.8	60.8	53.0
Merchandise imports exclusive of imports of foreign-owned companies											104.6	151.6	205.2	204.5	243.5	238.3	227.0	162.7

[1] Including tonka beans, divi-divi, rubber, lumber, sugar, chicle, fruits and vegetables.
[2] Thousands of kilograms.
[3] From the limited data available it was impossible to discover the explanation for the size of this item. Since the comparable figure for values is not unusually large, it seems likely that the total volume of exports in 1913 may have been overstated.
[4] Asphalt only.
[5] Exonerated imports and total imports of the national government have been distributed among the various classifications on the basis of the average percentage distribution of these imports in the 4 years 1938–1941.
[6] Not available.
SOURCE: *Análisis del comercio exterior;* annual issues of *Estadística mercantil y maritima.*

dise credit probably too high throughout (perhaps by as much as 8 million or 10 million bolivars in 1942), the excess necessarily causes an equal overstatement (understatement) of the residual account of unrecorded capital movements on the debit (credit) side; where, in other words, we have an unrecorded capital export (a debit), it is probably overstated; and where we have an unrecorded capital import (a credit), it is probably understated.

Exports and Imports

Much stress is frequently placed upon the question of whether or not a country possesses a "favorable" balance of trade. The preceding analysis should have made it apparent that this question is not the all-important one in the case of Venezuela. A comparison of exports and imports is, however, useful provided that it is accompanied by a proper understanding of the complex functioning of Venezuela's economy in the sphere of international trade.

BY PRINCIPAL-PRODUCTS CLASSIFICATION

Table 2 shows Venezuela's merchandise exports and imports by major-products classifications. As the imports of the foreign-owned industries are important factors in the development of the Venezuelan economy, and frequently in directly improving the welfare of the country, these imports have been included in the major classifications. It should be borne in mind that this results in an overstatement of imports[1] from the viewpoint of the demand for foreign exchange and that the bulk of these imports is in the metals and the machinery and equipment categories. The shifts, from year to year, between the classifications of imports are self-evident, and no comment on these appears to be necessary.

At least two observations should, however, be made with respect to merchandise exports (exclusive of petroleum exports) and merchandise imports (exclusive of imports of foreign-owned industries). It should be noted, first, that Venezuela's principal merchandise exports were no greater in 1936, in terms of physical volume, than they were in 1913 and that, in terms of value, her position was much worse in 1936 than in 1913; that, in spite of the worsened export position,

[1] Because they are frequently made without requiring foreign exchange. The foreign-owned industries, for example, use dollar balances to purchase capital equipment (in the United States) for importation into Venezuela; and these imports have no direct effect upon the relationship between the bolivar and the dollar.

Venezuela's merchandise imports were, in terms both of physical volume and of value, substantially increased from 1913 to 1936. From our previous analysis we know that the explanation for this apparent paradox lies, in no small measure, in the fact that merchandise exports *exclusive of petroleum* (the variable under discussion here) do not include Venezuela's share in the foreign-owned companies' exports of one of her most important natural resources—a share which is roughly approximated in the petroleum drafts which place at Venezuela's disposal large quantities of foreign exchange with which to finance the present deficiency created by merchandise imports (exclusive of imports of foreign-owned industries) in excess of merchandise exports (exclusive of petroleum exports).

It should be observed, second, that Venezuela's merchandise exports and imports have followed a pattern, since the close of 1940, familiar to all Latin American countries. Exports exclusive of petroleum expanded 9.1 million bolivars in 1941, while imports exclusive of those of foreign-owned companies fell by 11.3 million bolivars. These changes, coupled with a rise of 34.9 million bolivars in petroleum drafts in 1941, were the major factors which gave Venezuela, before precious metals and capital movements, a credit balance in 1941 of 26.7 million bolivars as opposed to a debit balance of 26.4 million bolivars in 1940.

The same general picture is found for 1942. Merchandise exports exclusive of petroleum rose in that year by 13.8 million bolivars, while imports exclusive of those of foreign-owned companies declined by 64.3 million bolivars. Thus, despite a decline of 39.8 million bolivars in petroleum drafts, Venezuela's credit balance, before precious metals and capital movements, rose in 1942 to 62.3 million bolivars—an increase over 1941 of 35.6 million bolivars. This phenomenon, occasioned by the unusual conditions of the present war, has confronted Venezuela with a difficult situation, discussed in the section on Monetary Problems below.

BY DESTINATION AND ORIGIN

Table 3 shows value exports (exclusive of petroleum)[1] by destination and total imports by origin. Exports and imports from this view-

[1] Inclusion of petroleum would show over 95 per cent of petroleum exports going to the United States and to Central and South America, the former accounting for only 15 per cent. The high percentage to Central and South America is, in large part, for refining purposes in the West Indies, included under Central and South America.

point have obviously undergone an enormous—but logically to be expected—change. In 1938, Europe took 62 per cent of Venezuela's exports, England being responsible for 17 per cent, and European countries now controlled by the Axis for virtually all the remaining

TABLE 3.—VALUE OF FOREIGN TRADE BY GEOGRAPHICAL AREAS
(Excluding coined gold, silver, and nickel. In millions of bolivars)

	1935	1936	1937	1938	1939	1940	1941	1942
Destination of merchandise exports excluding petroleum:								
North America								
United States	14.31	23.01	19.78	15.74	30.20	40.21	46.83	58.75
All others	0.01	0.01		0.01			0.75	0.18
Total North America	14.32	23.02	19.78	15.75	30.20	40.21	47.58	58.93
Central and South America	7.40	10.82	9.42	5.61	4.80	4.72	10.67	14.40
Europe								
Non-Axis controlled								
England	13.02	14.11	15.59	10.25	1.99	0.84	0.27	0.37
All others	3.55	1.43	0.50	0.11	0.19	0.58	0.86	0.93
Total non-Axis controlled	16.57	15.54	16.09	10.36	2.18	1.42	1.13	1.30
Axis controlled	22.57	29.26	34.91	26.53	20.50	4.05	1.03	
Total Europe	39.14	44.80	51.00	36.89	22.68	5.47	2.16	1.30
Africa	0.11	0.13	0.06	0.06	0.03	0.01	0.01	
Asia and Oceania	0.07	0.28	0.36	0.70	0.29	1.47	0.59	
Grand total	61.04	79.05	80.62	59.01	58.00	51.88	61.01	74.84*
Origin of merchandise imports:								
North America								
United States	79.19	95.37	157.79	175.14	199.57	229.44	226.84	158.44
All others	0.21	0.31	0.19	0.46	3.12	6.51	6.39	4.82
Total North America	79.40	95.68	157.98	175.60	202.69	235.95	233.23	163.26
Central and South America	2.95	3.66	4.95	6.10	7.50	8.81	22.49	31.67
Europe								
Non-Axis controlled								
England	19.16	21.38	28.41	21.87	19.89	23.55	17.18	15.66
All others	4.40	4.19	3.14	3.53	4.89	8.91	5.92	3.87
Total non-Axis controlled	23.56	25.57	31.55	25.40	24.78	32.46	23.10	19.53
Axis controlled	47.49	71.99	94.85	96.03	82.73	21.09	4.05	0.25
Total Europe	71.05	97.56	126.40	121.43	107.51	53.55	27.15	19.78
Africa	0.02	0.05	0.01	0.01	0.03	0.13	0.35	0.05
Asia and Oceania	5.14	9.76	11.27	6.88	8.38	12.70	4.61	0.93
Grand total	158.56	206.71	300.61	310.02	326.16	311.14	287.83	215.69

* This total includes 0.21 million bolivars of exports whose destination is not declared.
SOURCE: Annual issues of *Estadística Mercantil y Maritima.*

45 per cent; the United States took only 27 per cent, and Central and South America, 10 per cent. By the end of 1941, Venezuela's European market had almost disappeared under the influence of war conditions, and 1942 was scarcely an improvement over 1941. Into the breach, however, had stepped the United States and Central and

South America, the two combined areas absorbing, in 1942, a volume of Venezuelan exports substantially in excess of Venezuela's total 1938 exports.

Venezuela received, however, only 39 per cent of her imports from Europe in 1938, England accounting for 7 per cent and Axis-controlled Europe being the source of 31 per cent; the United States was the origin of 56 per cent of Venezuela's 1938 imports. By the end of 1942, imports had shrunk well below their 1938 level; Europe's role had dwindled enormously; and only the United States, Central and South America, and England were able to supply Venezuela with a significant quantity of goods, thus alleviating somewhat the unfortunate situation which the war had forced upon Venezuela.

Monetary Problems

The increasing credit in the Venezuelan balance of payments, since the close of 1940, arising primarily from the excess of merchandise exports (other than petroleum) and petroleum drafts over merchandise imports (other than those of foreign-owned companies), has created a strong tendency for funds to flow into the Venezuelan banking system.[1] This tendency follows, of course, from the fact that these mounting credits constitute sums owing to Venezuelans from foreigners. The effects of this upon the central bank are readily discernible from the figures below:

Table 4.—Selected Assets and Liabilities of the Central Bank
(In millions of bolivars)

Dec. 31	Gold and *Devisen*	Credit outstanding*	Notes in circulation†	Deposits
1940	95.7		110.4	6.8
1941	164.9	4.7	156.4	44.3
1942	233.3	9.3	206.1	65.6
1943	315.8	0.8	272.3	73.9

* Excludes the amount owed by the national banks to the central bank for notes of the former taken over by the latter.

† Includes national-bank notes which are gradually being replaced by notes of the central bank, the latter alone now having the right of issue.

Gold and foreign exchange of the central bank have increased by some 230 per cent during the last 3 years, or by an amount of 220.1 million bolivars. This factor alone accounts almost entirely for the

[1] The banking and price-index figures in this section were taken from various bulletins and annual reports of the central bank.

rise of 229 million bolivars in notes in circulation and deposits combined. The rise in the latter two items is, of course, inflationary in tendency, since it means an increase both in the circulating mediums (in the case of notes in circulation, about 60 per cent of the increase of which has found its way into the hands of the public) and in the base against which the commercial banks can expand credit (in the case of deposits with the central bank).

Although the credit operations of the central bank have not constituted an item of much absolute importance, it should be noted that credit outstanding has declined significantly since 1942. This is deflationary in tendency and indicates that the influx of foreign funds has made it possible for the money market to repay most of its loans at the central bank. The position of the commercial banks was so strong that they had completely liquidated their short-term indebtedness to the central bank by Dec. 31, 1943, the 0.8 million bolivars then outstanding being rediscounts to agriculture, livestock, and commerce and industry.

The effects of this influx of funds have been transmitted to the commercial banking system, as Table 5 shows.

TABLE 5.—SELECTED ASSETS AND LIABILITIES OF THE COMMERCIAL BANKS
(In millions of bolivars)

Dec. 31	Cash and deposits with central bank	Loans and discounts, etc.	Deposits
1940	162.3	172.7	175.0
1941	181.2	177.2	177.2
1942	214.5	163.9	219.5
1943	258.0 (Nov. 30)	231.8	296.3

Thus we find an increase, since 1940, of 95.7 million bolivars in cash and deposits with the central bank. As the commercial banks' loans have increased only 59.1 million bolivars and as deposits have expanded but 121.3 million bolivars (only 25.6 million bolivars more than they would tend to increase under the impact of the 95.7-million-bolivar rise in the commercial banks' cash and deposits with the central bank), the conclusion is suggested that the commercial banks have restrained themselves rather well. Whether owing to conditions imposed upon them by the times (to the inability to find sufficient satisfactory borrowers) or to voluntary action, this certainly appears to be the case up to 1943; but the appearance of restraint is less obvious in 1943. Quite aside from any tendency of the commercial banks to contribute an inflationary impulse by credit creation, however, it is still true that the expansion of deposits arising from an increase in cash and deposits with the central bank inevitably increases the monetary purchasing power of the country.

The end result of these monetary forces has been to increase the annual average circulating media (demand deposits of the public and of the government plus cash in the hands of the public), from 1940 to 1943, by some 43 per cent. During this same period the general price level (annual average) has risen only 31.2 per cent. Obviously, therefore (if the general price-level index is even approximately accurate as a gauge of changes in prices), the velocity of circulation must have fallen, or the volume of transactions must have increased, or both—for, otherwise, the price level would have risen as much as have the circulating media. And, of course, if the volume of transactions has decreased (as we know it probably has), the velocity of circulation must have fallen even more.

To the author's knowledge, no figures for the velocity of circulation in Venezuela exist. By a series of heroic assumptions we can, however, reach a rough approximation of this. Central-bank clearinghouse figures are available since Apr. 15, 1941. By assuming the last 8½ months of 1941 to be representative of that year, we can get the average monthly clearings for each of the last 3 years. By dividing these figures by their respective average monthly demand deposits for each of these same years, we have the monthly rate at which these deposits turned over in each of those 3 years. If we represent the 1941 turnover as 100, the velocity had dropped to 79 in 1943. If the 1940 velocity was identical with that of 1941 and if cash turned over at the same rate as did demand deposits, it follows that the effective circulating media increased from 100, in 1940, to only 113.0, in 1943; that is, 143 (the 1943 index of circulating mediums) $\times$ 79 = 113.0.

As the average price level is simply the amount of money spent divided by the number of things bought, it would follow that the volume of transactions has fallen since 1940 from 100 to 86.1 in 1943; that is, 131.2 (the general price-level index) = 113.0/86.1. If, therefore, our assumptions are approximately correct, the 31.2 per cent increase in prices is traceable, roughly, to a 13.0 per cent increase in the effective circulating media and to a 13.9 per cent decrease in the volume of transactions since 1940. While the volume of transactions is not to be identified with the amount of available goods, this probably gives us a rough approximation to the behavior of the amount of available goods.

It is self-evident that there are, in general, but two ways by which the upward pressure upon prices can be alleviated: by increasing the amount of available goods and by decreasing the effective circulating media. The amount of available goods can, in turn, be increased only by increasing domestic production for domestic consumption and/or by increasing imports. Although some headway has been made in the former direction, it is clear that the peculiar nature of Venezuela's prewar economy does not lend itself readily to an overnight expansion of domestic production for domestic consumption; with her not-very-widely-diversified economy, what she produces in significant quantity is almost invariably produced in an abundance far beyond her own needs—and any increase in output in these areas is of no immediate benefit to her unless she receives increased imports in payment therefor. And war conditions have, at least until recently, made anything other than a decrease in imports quite impossible. Since, as will be apparent from the section on Public Finance, the Venezuelan prewar revenue system is not such that strong income control measures calculated to reduce the effective circulating mediums can be easily adopted, it is to be hoped that war conditions will soon permit some expansion of imports.

Public Finance

Revenues are broken down, in Table 6, into the four major categories of revenue from petroleum and mining companies,[1] direct taxes, indirect taxes, and other internal revenue. Perhaps it should be emphasized that this particular breakdown was chosen only because it served to bring out those features of the revenue system which appeared to the author to be the most germane to the problems

[1] The petroleum-revenue item should not be taken as equivalent to the petroleum companies' contribution to the real income of Venezuela. Rather substantial sums are constantly being expended by the petroleum companies for roads, housing facilities, and similar projects, as well as for wages and salaries. Although these sums are costs to the petroleum companies, and although a large (but indeterminate) proportion of them results in a creation of wealth for Venezuela just as real as if the wealth had been the result of public works expenditures by the government, they do not, of course, appear in a statement of Venezuela's revenue.

TABLE 6.—GOVERNMENT REVENUES AND EXPENDITURES
(In millions of bolivars)

	Calendar years								Budget est. fiscal year
	1935	1936	1937	1938	1939	1940	1941	1942	1943–1944
Revenue									
Revenue from petroleum and mining companies:									
Petroleum, excl. consumption tax on refined products[1]	71.3	77.3	101.9	118.0	114.1	99.6	136.6[7]	84.1	125.3
All other	0.2[5]	0.2[5]	0.3[5]	0.2[5]	0.3	0.3	0.3	0.3	0.3
Total revenue from petroleum and mining companies	71.5	77.5	102.2	118.2	114.4	99.9	136.9	84.4	125.6
Direct taxes:									
Inheritance and legacy taxes	0.3	0.3	1.2	0.9	0.8	1.3	1.7	1.4	1.3
Income taxes (30 per cent of)									3.0
Total direct taxes	0.3	0.3	1.2	0.9	0.8	1.3	1.7	1.4	4.3
Indirect taxes:									
Import duties and other *aduana*[2]	59.5	74.7	113.1	112.1	131.6	121.8	97.8	70.6	71.5
Stamp and sealed paper taxes (75 per cent of)	7.9	10.8	13.9	15.3	16.8	16.4	16.6	16.5	16.4
Cigarette taxes	15.5	20.1	23.4	24.6	27.4	26.6	25.0	26.9	25.0
Liquor taxes	10.9	14.0	16.4	17.7	22.0	21.8	25.6	27.2	27.2
Consumption tax on refined pet. products	4.5[5]	5.0[5]	5.5	6.9	8.4	10.6	19.2	17.9	22.0
Consular fees (other than those paid by petroleum companies)	2.2	2.7	5.5	5.7	5.6	5.5	6.2	4.6	3.8
Total indirect taxes	100.5	127.3	177.8	182.3	211.8	202.7	190.4	163.7	165.9
Other revenue:									
Match and salt monopolies	8.6	6.2	6.0	6.8	7.7	8.0	7.4	8.2	8.4
Stamp and sealed paper taxes (15 per cent of)	1.6	2.2	2.8	3.1	3.4	3.3	3.3	3.3	3.3
Profits of the National Exchange Office					3.1	5.4	1.0	1.8	
Coinage	20.0	4.6	15.9	0.5					
All other	3.9	2.7	6.2	28.5	9.7	9.5	18.6	24.5	9.2
Total other revenue	34.1	15.7	30.9	38.9	23.9	26.2	30.3	37.8	20.9
Total revenue	206.4	220.8	312.1	340.3	350.9	330.1	359.3	287.3	316.7
Expenditures, by Departments									
Administration:									
Treasury	34.2	17.2	24.8	23.0	33.4	29.1	30.0	27.5	27.1
Exterior Relations	5.0	6.8	5.8	6.0	6.0	5.8	5.0	6.2	5.5
War and Marine	34.1	37.9	36.4	39.6	37.4	37.0	35.7	34.6	37.9
Interior Relations—est.[3]	28.2	31.9	36.8	50.0	55.1	56.2	56.0	54.0	43.6
Total administration	101.5	93.8	103.8	118.6	131.9	128.1	126.7	122.3	114.1
Development:									
Interior Relations—est.[3]	12.0	16.3	23.5	29.9	37.2	39.4	38.9	37.3	31.3
Public Works	31.8	73.2	77.1	69.3	79.5	82.5	60.8	54.9	110.6
Development (*Fomento*)	12.9	5.2	6.3	15.5	10.2	9.5	6.1	9.5	7.5
Education	9.5	13.8	19.9	22.7	24.1	24.3	22.0	22.5	23.8
Health and Agriculture[4]	23.0	4.2							
Agriculture		30.6	38.9	47.3	54.9	46.7	44.4	22.7	21.1
Health and Social Assistance		8.4	17.4	18.7	19.6	18.4	16.1	15.7	20.9
Labor and Communications	[6]	11.9	17.9	18.8	20.7	20.3	19.0	18.6	18.6
Total development	89.2	163.6	201.0	222.2	246.2	241.1	207.3	181.2	233.8
Budget alterations									0.6
Total expenditures	190.7	257.4	304.8	340.8	378.1	369.2	334.0	303.5	348.5
Surplus (+) or deficit (−)	+15.7	−36.6	+7.3	−0.5	−27.2	−39.1	+25.3	−16.2	−31.8
Proceeds of loans								4.5	31.8
Treasury balance:									
Jan. 1	83.3	99.0	62.4	69.7	69.2	42.0	2.9	28.1	
Dec. 31	99.0	62.4	69.7	69.2	42.0	2.9	28.1	16.4	
Increase (+) or decrease (−)	+15.7	−36.6	+7.3	−0.5	−27.2	−39.1	+25.2	−11.7	

[1] Includes estimated 6 per cent of total import duties, estimated 99 per cent of total lights and buoys tax. estimated 40 per cent of total other dock and pilotage charges, estimated 10 per cent of total stamp and sealed paper taxes, actual portion of total consular fees paid by the petroleum companies except 1935, 1936, and 1940, which are estimates, and estimated 70 per cent of total income tax in 1943–1944.

[2] Includes estimated 94 per cent of total import duties, estimated 1 per cent of total lights and buoys tax, and estimated 60 per cent of total other dock and pilotage charges.

[3] For 1935–1941, 60 per cent of the *situados* (grants to the states and territories) have been allocated to development expense. The remainder of the department's expenditures are allocated to administration expense.

[4] In the cabinet reorganization of 1936 this department was disbanded and its activities divided between the Departments of Agriculture and Health and Social Assistance.

[5] Estimated.

[6] Included with Development (*Fomento*), above.

[7] Including 30.9 million bolivars in settlement of royalty claims for earlier years.

SOURCE: Annual issues of the *Memoria* and *Cuenta*, Ministerio de Hacienda; *Gaceta Oficial*, June 30, 1943.

discussed in this chapter. For other purposes, different classifications might be vastly superior.

It should also be stated that the allocation of the various forms of revenue to these categories has been beset with difficulties. Six per cent of total import duties has been allocated to revenue from petroleum and mining companies, the remainder being allotted to indirect taxes. This—as well as certain other items indicated in footnotes to Table 6—is an estimate.[1] Moreover, some of this former 6 per cent should probably be included in indirect taxes; for if we mean by indirect taxes those which are borne by the ultimate consumer, some of the petroleum companies' dutiable imports (those sold in company stores, for example) doubtless have the duty passed on to the consumer. But errors arising from such sources as these should be quantitatively unimportant, and our results should, therefore, be substantially accurate.

Strictly speaking, at least some of the items under other revenue should be, for our purposes, allotted to other categories. Coinage profits, for example, to the extent that the increased monetary circulation thus caused occasions a rise in prices, amount to an indirect tax upon consumers; or, again, profits of the National Exchange Office probably would be, for the most part, more properly classified under revenue from the petroleum companies. There being no clues available as to the proper division of such items among the other categories, these items were placed under other revenue. Allowance should be made for this shortcoming by recognizing that our first three categories are somewhat understated.

During the 1935–1942 period some 90 per cent of the government's revenue came from the petroleum and mining companies and from indirect taxes. Of this 90 per cent, petroleum companies contributed about 33 per cent, and indirect taxes were the source of 57 per cent. These are significant observations.

The high proportion of indirect taxes—a not uncommon phenomenon in Latin American countries—suggests a correspondingly low proportion of direct taxes.[2] The lack of a tax structure considerably weighted with direct taxes—particularly, the deficiency in the income-tax area—makes it extremely difficult, if not impossible, for

[1] The figures are, however, factual for the years 1941 and 1942.

[2] But not all Venezuela's taxes are direct or indirect taxes upon Venezuelans. Most revenue from the petroleum companies is, for example, neither a direct nor an indirect tax.

Venezuela effectively to combat her present inflationary problem with an adequate rise of taxation.

Faced with a decline in the available supply of goods—a decline which the country cannot materially remedy—and with an increase in purchasing power, the country's sole remaining remedy is to abstract some of that purchasing power from the current income of income recipients by means of an appropriate fiscal policy, if the upward pressure upon prices is to be alleviated. Specifically, what is required is that the government increase the amount which it abstracts from the country's income—and, then, hold that increment idle until the emergency is past, in order that the increment so abstracted cannot continue to influence prices. This might, of course, be attempted by an increase in consumption taxes. But this would, in itself, raise prices, would probably distribute the additional tax burden in a fashion which most people would agree was inequitable, and would be both costly and difficult to administer.

The most obvious solution to the problem is to institute an increase in income taxes, plus a possible program of borrowing from the current income of income recipients. At best, however, such a program could only alleviate the inflationary problem—it could not possibly solve the problem in Venezuela's case, since, from a practical viewpoint at least, the amount by which income taxes can be increased in a given period of time is a function, among other things, of the income-tax structure which previously existed; and, prior to 1943, Venezuela had no income tax whatsoever.

It will be noted in Table 6 that the government estimated that its maiden income-tax law would yield 10 million bolivars annually, each full fiscal year. This being Venezuela's initial income-tax law, and there being, to the author's knowledge, no available statistics either on national income or on the distribution of that national income, an accurate estimate is exceedingly difficult; this estimate should, therefore, be accepted with some reservation.[1] The author's estimate that 70 per cent of this amount would come from the petroleum companies and 30 per cent from other businesses and individuals must, for the same reasons, be accepted with even more reservation.

The inauguration of an income-tax law was unquestionably desirable; but it might be observed that revenue coming from the

[1] This was written in December of 1943. I understand that this estimate has now (March of 1944) been revised upward to 40 million bolivars.

petroleum companies—whether in the form of income taxes or otherwise—does nothing to alleviate, under the existing circumstances, the inflationary problem. This follows from the fact that the revenue from the petroleum companies is purchasing power received by the government *from outside Venezuela;* it is not purchasing power *transferred* from income recipients *within* Venezuela to the government. An increment to revenue from the petroleum companies is, therefore, an *addition* (unless it is held idle) to the money stream; and this, of course, tends to raise prices.

This last statement should *not*, however, be interpreted as meaning that inflationary tendencies would *necessarily* be any less were the increment to government receipts not raised by an increment to revenue from the petroleum companies. If, for example, government receipts had to increase by some given amount—no matter how that amount was raised—and if that amount were raised by the sale of the government debt to commercial banks, the inflationary tendencies would be just as great as if that amount had been raised by an increment to revenue from the petroleum companies. But an increment to revenue from the petroleum companies is clearly more inflationary in tendency than if that increment is raised from the current income of income recipients who would otherwise have spent that money for Venezuelan goods and services.

Under ordinary circumstances, the fact that an increment to revenue from the petroleum companies is not a transfer of purchasing power from income recipients within Venezuela to the government might be of much less importance than it presently is. For, with international goods freer to move toward Venezuela, an expansion of the Venezuelan money stream would probably be substantially less inflationary in tendency. During the present period of enforced reduction in imports, however, it is clear that an increment to revenue from the petroleum companies does not alleviate the inflationary problem—unless, of course, that increment is held idle by the government. That increment could be held idle, however, only if the government were able to reduce its expenditures and/or to increase the funds flowing to the government from Venezuelan income recipients by further taxation or by borrowing from the current income of these income recipients. A mere glance at the sums involved, in conjunction with recollection of the fact that Venezuela had no income tax prior to 1943, makes it evident that it would be virtually an impossibility (practically speaking) to make a great deal of headway in this direction.

The preceding analysis seems to lead rather decisively to the conclusion that Venezuela's new income-tax law was designed essentially to raise revenue. To an equitable revenue-raising measure there can be no logical objection, since this is one of the primary objectives of any fiscal program. Fiscal policy, however, has other objectives than that of merely raising revenue; and not the least important of these is that of mitigating the unfortunate effects of forces making for undesirable movements in the price level. Impossible though it might be to siphon off a very substantial portion of the excessive purchasing power, it is unfortunate that greater progress could not have been made in this direction in Venezuela's initial income-tax law; for an estimated 3 million bolivars in income taxes from Venezuelans is only 1.6 per cent of the estimated 191.1 million bolivars of revenue to be raised from sources other than petroleum and mining companies.[1]

Our comments on expenditures are brief—although something further will be said about them in the concluding section on Projects Planned. Expenditures have been arbitrarily broken down by departments into the two general categories of administration and development. It will be noted that, since 1935, estimated expenditures of those departments which are essentially administrative have increased only 12.4 per cent, while estimated expenditures of those departments which are essentially developmental have increased 163 per cent.

The most important increases in estimated developmental expenditures have taken place in the Departments of Interior Relations, Public Works, Education, and Health and Social Assistance. As it seems indisputable that the most pressing of Venezuela's long-term problems are in these areas, the government has evidently chosen well the uses to which to put its expanding expenditures.

That expenditures should be expanded, at this particular time, is perhaps less certain. Venezuela's inflationary problem is caused by a rising national income in monetary terms, while the supply of available goods which this money could buy has been decreased. It is clear, from Table 6, that the increase in funds, by which the expanded expenditures are to be financed, will come from sources which cannot

[1] On the basis of the revised estimate of 40 million bolivars in income-tax revenue and of the assumption of 30 per cent of this amount from other than petroleum companies sources, 12 million bolivars, or 6.0 per cent of 200.1 million bolivars raised from other than petroleum companies sources, would be forthcoming from these sources.

fail further to swell monetary national income. Hence, against the social benefits to be derived from the increased expenditures must be set the possible injuries from the further inflation which these expenditures may engender.

Projects Planned

A survey of the Venezuelan economy would be incomplete without a word about Venezuela's economic future. The standard of living of Venezuela can undoubtedly be raised by the simple expedient of better developing her resources. To that end are required, among other things, greater educational facilities, improved sanitation, greater diversification of industry, expansion of some of the already existing industries, better housing, and improved transportation facilities.

The most recent direct contribution of the state toward these objectives, as planned by the government, centers in President Medina's program for public works. Announced on Jan. 31, 1942, the program was to be undertaken during the balance of his presidential term, which expires in 1946. The total cost of the program was estimated to be in the neighborhood of 400 million bolivars and was to be financed 39 per cent from current ordinary government revenue, 39 per cent from internal borrowings, and 22 per cent from the transfer of special reserve funds and from the income of self-liquidating projects included in the plan. Among the uses to which the funds were to be put were: the construction of sanitary-engineering projects, in the amount of more than 150 million bolivars; the repair of 1,700 kilometers of existing roads; the construction of bridges and of 1,470 kilometers of new roads; the building of 19 new airdromes and the enlargement of 39 landing fields; slum clearance; the construction of new hospitals, schools, penitentiaries, municipal markets in Caracas, and a new Federal capitol; the installation of new harbor works and the dredging of the mouth of the Orinoco River, to aid marine and river shipping.[1]

Any estimate of anticipated investment by private enterprise, calculated to serve the above-mentioned objectives, necessarily has doubtful value at the present time. A compilation of known projects either planned or actually in progress, all involving either expansion

[1] From the files of the Standard Oil Company (New Jersey). If the complete information on this exists in any one publication, I have not chanced upon it.

of existing facilities or establishment of new facilities, shows a total of 29 enterprises concerned. The estimated amount of net investment entailed is around 300 million bolivars.[1]

Of the estimated 300 million bolivars of planned expenditures by private enterprise, 245 million bolivars represents domestic capital distributed as follows:

Industry	Amount in Bolivars
Railroad	120,000,000
Housing and building	100,000,000
Cement	13,000,000
Airport and air freight	5,000,000
Fish	2,900,000
Leather tanning	1,100,000
Sugar	1,000,000
All other	2,000,000
Total	245,000,000

The estimated 30 million to 50 million bolivars of foreign capital is distributed among two tire companies, a steel company, a container company, a match company, an air-lines company, and an iron-products company.

The estimated total of private-enterprise and public expenditures calculated to increase the wealth of Venezuela is, then, in the neighborhood of 700 million bolivars. As this is better than a 10 per cent increase in the only estimate of Venezuela's wealth which the author has seen, it is an amount of considerable relative importance.

For such a program to develop successfully, however, a large volume of supplies and materials will have to be imported by Venezuela; and this is obviously true quite irrespective of the proportion of foreign capital invested *in the specific projects concerned.* It is therefore clear that Venezuela must, if this program is to develop, adopt measures calculated either to encourage exports (without inducing a corresponding increase in imports *for consumption*) or to induce an influx of capital (in the balance-of-payments sense—which is more inclusive than is investment in the specific projects concerned), or both; for unless one or both of these things are done, Venezuela will not have the means with which to pay for the supplies and materials needed for such an extensive program of development.

In view of this, it is perhaps fitting to close on the note that the war may, after all, prove to have been, for Venezuela, a blessing in

[1] This information was compiled from a number of public and private sources.

disguise. For the expanded exports and the reduced imports of the war period have forced upon her an export of capital in the form of deposits acquired abroad and an import of gold in the form of large holdings of gold earmarked abroad. She has, therefore, been bequeathed a substantial volume of funds which can be used—provided that the country does not insist upon an excessive increase of imports for consumption uses—to finance the import of a considerable part of the supplies and materials needed for her development program.

APPENDIX

Area and Population of the American Republics

Country	Population		Area	
	Year	Number	Square kilometers	Square miles
Argentina	1942	13,709,238	2,797,100	1,079,965
Bolivia	1942	3,533,900	1,077,544	416,040
Brazil	1942	43,550,000	8,511,189	3,286,170
Chile	1943	5,178,260	741,767	286,396
Colombia	1942	9,523,200	1,139,155	439,828
Costa Rica	1941	672,043	49,827	19,238
Cuba	1938	4,227,597	114,524	44,218
Dominican Republic	1941	1,768,163	50,070	19,332
Ecuador*	1943	3,105,541	323,750	125,000
El Salvador	1942	1,862,980	34,126	13,176
Guatemala	1942	3,410,762	109,724	42,364
Haiti	1940	2,663,000	27,704	10,700
Honduras	1942	1,154,388	153,226	59,161
Mexico	1940	19,653,552	1,963,890	758,258
Nicaragua	1941	1,013,946	150,000	57,915
Panama	1940	631,637	88,498	34,169
Paraguay	1940	1,014,773	438,399	169,266
Peru†	1943	7,395,687	1,249,049	482,258
Uruguay	1939	2,146,545	186,926	72,170
Venezuela	1942	3,996,095	912,050	352,143
Total	....	128,226,390	20,118,527	7,767,767
United States	....	135,603,500	7,827,982	3,022,387

* The area of Ecuador is not accurately known; the figure cited is the estimate used by the government of Ecuador, pending completion of the boundary survey and demarcation.

† The area cited is that used by the government of Peru in 1940 and does not include all the territory which Peru will receive upon completion of the official boundary survey and demarcation.

SOURCE: Coordinator of Inter-American Affairs, Research Division, November, 1943.

Sources[1]

Argentina: (1) PAU, American Nations Series, No. 1, 1941; (2) La Población y el movimiento demográfico, Años 1942 y 1941.

Bolivia: (1) PAU, American Nations Series, No. 2, 1941; (2) Sección Demográfia, Dirección General de Estadística, 1942.

Brazil: (1) Sinopse Preliminar dos Resultados Demograficos, Rio, 1941; (2) PAU from Instituto Brasileiro de Geografia e Estatistica, 1943.

Chile: (1) PAU, American Nations Series, No. 4, 1942; (2) Estadística chilena, Año XVI, No. 3, March, 1943.

[1] (1) Indicates source of areal data; (2) indicates source of population data.

Colombia: (1) Síntesis estadística de Colombia, 1941; (2) El Mes financiero y económico, Año VII, Nos. 70 to 71, March to April, 1943.

Costa Rica: (1) and (2) Informe de la Dirección General de Estadística, Año 1941.

Cuba: (1) and (2) Movimiento de población, 1938, Dirección General de Estadística.

Dominican Republic: (1) Anuario estadístico de la Republica dominicana, Tomo I, 1937; (2) Dirección General de Estadística, 1942.

Ecuador: (1) PAU from Ecuadoran Embassy; (2) Registro Oficial No. 857, July 7, 1943.

El Salvador: (1) Anuario estadístico de 1940, Tomo No. 1, 1941; (2) PAU from Dirección General de Estadística.

Guatemala: (1) Quinto Censo general de población, June, 1942; (2) Diario de America Central, órgano oficial del gobierno, May 29, 1943.

Haiti: (1) Woodring, W. P., *et al.*, "Geology of the Republic of Haiti," Port-au-Prince, 1924; (2) Bulletin de la quinzaine, January, 1941.

Honduras: (1) Resumen del censo general de población, 1942; (2) Movimiento de población, October, 1942.

Mexico: (1) and (2) Sexto Censo general de población de los Estados Unidos Mexicanos, March 6, 1940. Mexico, 1942.

Nicaragua: (1) PAU from Secretary of Nicaraguan Embassy; (2) CIAA microfilm copy of official estimates of Dec. 31, 1941.

Panama: (1) Dirección de censo y estadística, 1940; (2) Estadística panamena, March, 1942.

Paraguay: (1) and (2) Ministerio de Agricultura, Comercio y Industrias del Paraguay, Boletín No. 7, Dec. 1940.

Peru: Revista de hacienda, 2° trimestre de 1941; (2) PAU from Ministerio de Hacienda y Comercio, July, 1943.

Uruguay: (1) and (2) Síntesis estadística, 1940, Publ. CLXI, Año 1940, No. 18, 1940.

Venezuela: (1) Anuario estadístico de Venezuela, 1940; (2) PAU from Ministerio de Fomento, Dirección General de Estadística, 1942.

United States: (1) Sixteenth Census Report on Population, Vol. 1, 1942; (2) Press Release, Series P3, No. 34, Mar. 22, 1943.

Index

K

L

M